**REMAKING THE EARTH,
EXHAUSTING THE PEOPLE**

MICAH S. MUSCOLINO

REMAKING THE EARTH, EXHAUSTING THE PEOPLE

The Burden of Conservation in Modern China

University of Washington Press   Seattle

Remaking the Earth, Exhausting the People was made possible in part by a grant from the Samuel and Althea Stroum Endowed Book Fund.

Additional support for this publication was provided by the Chiang Ching-kuo Foundation for International Scholarly Exchange.

Copyright © 2025 by the University of Washington Press

Acknowledgments for previously published materials appear on pp. ix–x and should be considered an extension of the copyright page.

Design by Mindy Basinger Hill / Maps by Kate Blackmer

This book will be made open access within three years of publication thanks to Path to Open, a program developed to bring about equitable access and impact for the entire scholarly community, including authors, researchers, libraries, and university presses around the world. Learn more at https://about.jstor.org/path-to-open/.

UNIVERSITY OF WASHINGTON PRESS   uwapress.uw.edu

LIBRARY OF CONGRESS CATALOGING-IN-PUBLICATION DATA

Names: Muscolino, Micah S., 1977– author
Title: Remaking the Earth, exhausting the people : the burden of conservation in modern China / Micah S. Muscolino.
Description: Seattle : University of Washington Press, 2025. | Includes bibliographical references and index. Identifiers: LCCN 2024059305 | ISBN 9780295753973 hardcover | ISBN 9780295753980 paperback | ISBN 9780295753997 ebook
Subjects: LCSH: Gansu Sheng (China)—Rural conditions—History—20th century | Gansu Sheng (China)—Environmental conditions—20th century | Environmental policy—China—Gansu Sheng—History—20th century | Agriculture and state—China—Gansu Sheng—History—20th century | Soil conservation—China—Gansu Sheng—History—20th century | Water conservation—China—Gansu Sheng—History—20th century
Classification: LCC HD2100.G36 M87 2025 | DDC 338.10951/45—dc23/eng/20250616
LC record available at https://lccn.loc.gov/2024059305

∞ This paper meets the requirements of ANSI/NISO Z39.48-1992 (Permanence of Paper).

CONTENTS

Acknowledgments *vii*

Introduction *1*

ONE "Tianshui's Three Treasures" / Conservation in Wartime Gansu *19*

TWO "Speak Bitterness to Floods" / Mobilization and Resistance in the Early 1950s *42*

THREE "Getting Organized Is Powerful" / Conservation and Collectivization *74*

FOUR "Dams Have Really Worn Us Out" / Labor, Local Knowledge, and the 1956 Irrigation Campaign *103*

FIVE "Learn from Dengjiabao" / Conservation Militarized and Aestheticized *132*

SIX "Water Has Aroused the Girls' Hearts" / Gender and Conservation *159*

SEVEN "Conservation Was Primary, Farming Was Secondary" / The Great Famine and Its Aftermath *182*

Epilogue *208*

Glossary of Chinese Characters *219*

Notes *225*

Bibliography *269*

Index *297*

ACKNOWLEDGMENTS

In the eight tumultuous years that have passed since I started work on this book, I have accumulated many debts. My ability to conduct research in China between 2017 and 2019 would not have been possible without my affiliations as an honorary professor at Shaanxi Normal University and Lanzhou University. I thank Hou Yongjian and Yang Hongwei for arranging those appointments. Chu Jingzheng and Wang Xingguang also provided crucial contacts and introductions.

I owe the greatest debt by far to the people in Gansu who welcomed me into their homes and spoke with me about their experiences during campaigns to conserve water and soil more than seven decades ago. I have omitted their names to preserve anonymity, except those of individuals whose stories were widely publicized in print, but I would like to convey my utmost respect and appreciation to them all. In California, Qiu Haiming and his wife, Ye Heping, graciously invited me to have lunch and chat about the career of Ye's father, the renowned botanist and conservation expert Ye Peizhong.

From the time I began doing research for this book, I have depended on Gao Guannan and He Mimi for their assistance and encouragement. Zhang Lijie provided expert research assistance, and her command of the eastern Gansu vernacular proved essential when it came to conducting and transcribing interviews with elderly residents. Liu Xiang also helped to navigate the local dialect and transcribed interviews. Lu Chunxian offered additional research assistance. Deciphering the handwritten notebooks analyzed in chapter 7 required help from Sun Lin.

My research in China was funded by a British Academy Mid-Career Fellowship and a research grant from the Chiang Ching-kuo Foundation for International Scholarly Exchange. I thank Aileen Mooney, formerly research development officer at the University of Oxford Faculty of History, for her administrative support in preparing those applications. The Paul G. Pickowicz Endowed Chair in Modern Chinese History at the University of California, San Diego, provided additional financial support.

My colleagues at UC San Diego have strengthened and sustained this work in many ways. I am grateful to Sarah Schneewind for her camaraderie and guidance during the toughest of times. Sarah has read so much of my writing that I have lost track, but I benefited greatly from the comments that she and Barry Naughton provided on an early draft of chapter 4. Denise Demetriou, Karl Gerth, Li Huai, and Paul Pickowicz have also been constant sources of friendship and advice. I thank Robert Edelman, Weijing Lu, and Victor Shih for their feedback on specific portions of the book. UC San Diego's Chinese studies librarian, Xi Chen, somehow made it possible to keep research going during a global pandemic. Sherry Hu and Susan Zau of UC San Diego's 21st Century China Center organized the inaugural lecture for the Pickowicz Endowed Chair, in which I presented this book's central arguments for the first time. I thank Lei Guang, Mark Hanna, Ruixue Jia, Dana Velasco Murillo, and Susan Shirk for the excellent questions they posed at that event.

The book has benefited enormously from the contributions made by the talented coterie of PhD students in UC San Diego's modern Chinese history program. The writing group formed by Thomas Chan, Niall Chithelen, and Ben Kletzer served as a test audience for early drafts of nearly every chapter. I have had many fruitful discussions about environmental history with Peter Braden, who later gave me insightful comments on the introduction. Mingcong Bai, Shumeng Han, Anran Tu, Yixue Yang, and Kiki Zhao provided research assistance and offered feedback on parts of the book; Ian Dubrowsky and Ning Zhang also read and commented on a preliminary version of chapter 2.

I am grateful to Prasenjit Duara, Qitao Guo, Erika Milam, Rebecca Nedostup, Hans van de Ven, Yang Kuisong, and Wen-hsin Yeh for their invitations to present work in progress. I received valuable questions and comments at workshops, conferences, and seminars from John Alekna, Emily Baum, Jeremy Brown, Yu-chi Chang, Janet Chen, Chris Courtney, Robert Culp, Daigengna Duoer, Feng Xiaocai, Minghui Hu, Judd Kinzley, Lien Ling-ling, Ruth Mostern, Rebecca Nedostup, David Pietz, Brian Spivey, Sun Huei-min, Eddy U, Jeffrey Wasserstrom, and Jongsik Christian Yi. Jacob Eyferth and Gail Hershatter shared knowledge via email. Henrietta Harrison, Ian J. Miller, Rana Mitter, Ruth Morgan, Julia Strauss, Verena Winiwarter, and Xia Mingfang also supported the project in various ways.

During my yearslong pursuit of a fellowship that would give me the break from teaching and service duties needed to complete the book, I pestered Elisabeth Köll, Robert Marks, John R. McNeill, David Pietz, Peter Perdue, Kenneth Pomeranz, and Wen-hsin Yeh for more letters of recommendation than I care to admit. Sakura Christmas, Evan Dawley, Denise Demetriou, Robert Edelman, Karl Gerth, Matthew Mosca, and Sarah Schneewind gave helpful feedback and suggestions on my proposals.

Financial support from a 2023–24 Andrew W. Mellon Foundation Fellowship at the Center for Advanced Study in the Behavioral Sciences (CASBS) at Stanford eventually afforded me the luxury of uninterrupted time to finish drafting and revising the manuscript. I would not have been able to accept that fellowship without the administrative support provided at UC San Diego by Jamie Gonzales, Jennifer Hollis, and Leah Tamayo-Brion. Drina Adams, Janzen Alejo, Rebecca Hidayetoglu, and Sally Schroeder handled matters on the CASBS end.

The bucolic setting at CASBS, where I inhabited a study with a panoramic view of the Stanford University campus and San Francisco Bay, was an ideal place to think and write. I thank the interdisciplinary community of CASBS fellows for the stimulating questions they raised when I presented this project at one of the center's weekly seminars. Sammy Barkin, Lucas Bessire, Beth DeSombre, Thung-hung Lin, Rachel St. John, and Louis Warren generously took time away from their own work to read and discuss the book's introduction. My work was also enriched by conversations at CASBS with Jennifer Hollowell, Stefan Link, and Erica Robles-Anderson.

Special thanks are due to Michael Szonyi, who read the entire manuscript and commented on it in detail. Stevan Harrell offered incisive feedback on my first book proposal and an earlier iteration of chapter 6. Other colleagues who read and critiqued individual chapters include Kathryn Edgerton-Tarpley, Matthew Lowenstein, Victor Seow, and Stephen A. Smith. Carol Muscolino evaluated the introduction from the perspective of a general reader. Martha Schulman provided editorial advice on how to decrease the book's length and improve its clarity. Kate Blackmer displayed cartographic skill and attention to detail in drawing the maps.

Segments of chapter 1 previously appeared in "Tianshui's Three Treasures: Water and Soil Conservation in Wartime Northwest China," *Journal of Modern Chinese History* 13, no.1 (September 2019) and "Wartime Water and Soil Conservation in Gansu," in Brett Sheehan and Wen-hsin Yeh, ed., *Living and Working in Wartime China* (Honolulu: University of Hawai'i Press, 2022); chapters 6 and 7 reproduce parts of "'Water Has Aroused the Girls' Hearts': Gendering Water and Soil Conservation in 1950s China," *Past & Present* 255, no. 1 (May 2022).

At the University of Washington Press, Caitlin Tyler-Richardson guided this book to publication with efficiency and patience. Dandi Meng assisted in preparing the images and manuscript files. Joeth Zucco oversaw production and Laura Keeler copyedited the manuscript. Finally, I would like to extend my thanks to the two anonymous reviewers for their excellent suggestions on how to sharpen the book's presentation and increase its accessibility. I have done my best to heed the advice I received from them and others. All errors of fact and interpretation that remain are mine alone.

REMAKING THE EARTH,
EXHAUSTING THE PEOPLE

FIGURE 1. A model for the construction of mountainous areas—Dengjiabao

INTRODUCTION

Many people who grow up in Northwest China's Gansu Province never see ducks unless they move elsewhere. Ducks love water, and arid Gansu does not offer suitable habitats. For that reason, the booklet *A Model for the Construction of Mountainous Areas—Dengjiabao*, published in 1958 by Gansu's Department of Water Conservancy, made a statement when it featured a flock of ducks on its cover (fig. 1).[1] The picture showed that Dengjiabao, an upland village about seven kilometers from the seat of southeastern Gansu's Wushan County, had water. Ponds and ducks were rarities in Gansu during the first decade of the People's Republic of China (PRC, 1949–), but the booklet declared that "water and soil conservation" (*shuitu baochi*) had brought them to the village. Conservation, in this context, meant using the environment and its resources in ways that would guarantee perpetual benefits for humans. The cover illustration further depicted the advantages of conserving water and soil with a drawing of tractors tilling level fields on a terraced hillside and trees growing in the distance. Like the booklet's cover, the colorized photos within signaled that conservation had turned Dengjiabao from a village surrounded by dry and denuded hillsides into a landscape of interconnected terraces, irrigated fields, and lush green trees.[2]

The depiction of mechanized farming was aspirational. Although Dengjiabao did not have any tractors in the late 1950s, level terraces had at least created the conditions for using machinery that could not operate on steep slopes. But the ducks were real. During one of my visits to Dengjiabao, an elderly man told me, "In the place where there's a temple now there was a lily pond where lots of ducks were raised. The ducks came back in the evening. During the day, they went over there to the dam." In a village previously plagued by water scarcity, ducks waddling from one pool of water to another was a remarkable sight. As another man recalled of the water storage reservoir behind the small dam, "Ducks were raised in the reservoir. In the gully. Reeds were planted around it. The ducks were raised in the reeds. Later, no one maintained it and it deteriorated."[3] Today, no traces of the lily pond, the reservoir, or the ducks remain (figs. 2 and 3).

Other conservation projects initiated in the 1950s have left traces on the land as well as local people's memories. Looking north from a dusty

FIGURE 2. Former site of dam and reservoir, May 2018. Photo by the author.

FIGURE 3. Former site of duck pond, May 2018. Photo by the author.

road outside Dengjiabao, one sees row upon row of terraces ascending, cut through in some places by gullies and ravines, like green and brown steps up the hillsides on either side of the Wei River valley below.

This book narrates how, between the 1940s and 1960s, the building of terraces, reservoirs, and other water and soil conservation measures undertaken in Dengjiabao and elsewhere in Gansu, the poorest province in China, remade the biophysical environment. As they changed the land, these efforts to conserve soil and water profoundly affected the lives of people in Gansu's countryside. State-building and revolution in modern China, in addition to transforming people's relationships with one another, profoundly altered human relationships with the natural world. Adding an environmental dimension to "grassroots" histories of modern China, especially during the PRC period, I contend that fully comprehending "processes of change and continuity over time from the perspective of relatively unknown historical actors" requires an attentiveness to their everyday interactions with the environment.[4]

Gansu is part of China's Loess Plateau, a semiarid region covering 640,000 square kilometers located southeast of the Gobi Desert along the middle reaches of the Yellow River. With a landscape composed of loess, a fine sediment formed by the accumulation of windblown dust, the region suffers from the world's highest rates of soil erosion and acute water shortages (map 1). From World War II into the PRC era, state-initiated schemes intended to conserve soil and water resources and maintain their productive capacity remolded the Loess Plateau's terrain. These interventions created some of the most prominent and visible environmental transformations in modern China.

Narrating that environmental history, I trace connections among state authority, landscape transformation on a dramatic scale, and the embodied experiences of rural men and women. In the twentieth century, most of China's populace lived in the countryside and farmed, depending on soil and water for its basic livelihood. By highlighting the burdens that state-led conservation campaigns placed on rural people, this book attends to the power relations that characterized conservation, the uneven distribution of its costs and benefits, and the inequalities that it reinforced.

Due to climate variability and the reach of the East Asian monsoon, Gansu and the rest of the Loess Plateau experience inconsistent annual precipitation. Rainfall varies from an average of six hundred millimeters per year in the southeastern Loess Plateau to less than three hundred millimeters in its northwestern sections. Five times more precipitation can fall in rainy years than in dry ones. Around 78 percent of rainfall occurs between May and October, with heavy storms during summer. There is little rain in the rest of the year. Much of the precipitation comes in downpours, often after prolonged dry periods. When covered by vegetation, loess soils retain moisture well and no runoff occurs even during heavy rainstorms. But without vegetation, the Loess Plateau has the most erodible soil in the world. Rain that falls on bare loess soil loosens its particles, and runoff erodes fine loess material that is no longer protected by the roots of trees and grasses. Fertile topsoil washes away and, over time, new soil stops forming. Rainwater, rather than being retained by soil or vegetation, flows downhill as runoff, resulting in chronic water shortages and drought. The silt-laden runoff from the Loess Plateau creates the heavy loads of silt carried by the Yellow River

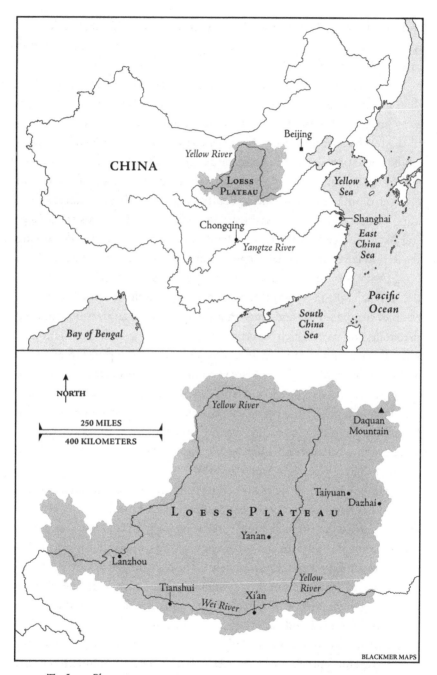

MAP 1. The Loess Plateau

and its tributaries. Deposition of this sediment in the Yellow River's lower reaches accounts for its frequent changes of course and its catastrophic history of flooding.[5]

Humans have long manipulated the Loess Plateau's environment. More than five thousand years ago, farmers on the Loess Plateau began to strip away surface soils more rapidly than the natural forces of erosion. But until the tenth century, as Ruth Mostern has shown, loess soil covered with ample vegetation absorbed rainfall and limited runoff. After that, however, deforestation and destruction of grasslands led to "a phase of severe and rapid erosion."[6] Garrisons and agricultural colonies that the rulers of the Tang Dynasty (618–907) established to defend against rivals from Central Asia impinged on fragile grasslands and forested hillsides, destroying vegetation cover and accelerating erosion. Conflict between the Northern Song Dynasty (960–1127) and its military adversaries on the Loess Plateau, the Xi Xia (1038–1227), wreaked further changes. Soldier-farmers and their families cleared forests and grasslands for agricultural cultivation, building materials, and fuel, which accelerated erosion. Large-scale destruction of natural vegetation and intensified erosion "caused the primordial gentle and flat ground of the Loess Plateau to begin its transformation into the deep-gullied and steep-highland landscape characteristic of the contemporary Loess Plateau."[7] The current landscape, dissected by gullies and hills, has existed for just 1,000 to 1,500 years.[8] Conservation measures intervene in these biophysical processes by targeting the interface between hydrosphere and pedosphere—between water and soil.

It is impossible to say with any certainty when terracing began in Northwest China. The earliest textual references to the Chinese term for terraces (*titian*) date to the 1100s; farmers cultivating inclined land must have built them for longer.[9] Terraces and other engineering works intercept silt-laden runoff, retaining water and soil in fields. The dryland agriculture practiced in Gansu and other parts of the Loess Plateau depends on precipitation, so conserving water provides a buffer against unpredictable rainfall. Preventing soil loss on sloping farmland increases productivity.

Yet even if the terraces that sculpt the hillsides of Gansu look like they have existed for centuries, most are recent. Before the mid-twentieth century, farm households implemented conservation measures on a limited scale.

The terraces that now sculpt nearly every hillside did not yet exist. Things changed after 1949, when the Chinese government's efforts to harness the Yellow River and make it run clear necessitated fighting erosion on the Loess Plateau in the river's middle reaches, where most of its silt originates. By mobilizing the rural populace to conserve water and soil, China's leaders sought to prevent flood disasters in the Yellow River's lower reaches, prolong the life of dam and reservoir megaprojects begun in the 1950s, and increase agricultural productivity by checking erosion and making rain-fed farmland into irrigated fields.[10] Terracing, afforestation, check-dam construction, and other conservation measures carried out on the Loess Plateau between 1949 and 1978 reshaped over 58,240 square kilometers of land, an area almost the size of Denmark or West Virginia.[11] This transformation was realized not with mechanized technology but through intense physical labor: rural people dug channels, moved earth, and tamped down embankments using their muscle power alone.

The impact of these conservation measures extended to the planetary scale. Human action began to accelerate erosion on the Loess Plateau and increase sedimentation in the Yellow River some three thousand years ago; erosion and sedimentation greatly intensified around one thousand years ago. But since the 1950s, the process has reversed. Dam and reservoir megaprojects, along with water and soil conservation in the Loess Plateau region, have dramatically reduced the volume of sediment that the Yellow River transports to the sea. Due to this decrease in sediment flux, subsidence of the Yellow River's delta has outstripped sedimentation. The delta, which previously grew due to the accumulation of waterborne sediment, has started to recede. Similar human-induced changes in sediment delivery to the coastal ocean have occurred in river deltas around the world; some scientists see them as a geophysical marker of the Anthropocene, the recent slice of the Earth's history in which human-induced environmental change has ushered in a new geological epoch.[12] Investigating how these planetary transformations played out in villages, on farms, and within households, I find that conservation schemes undertaken in Gansu after 1949 were inseparable from a system of political and economic relations that marginalized and disadvantaged China's rural populace.

Beginning in the 1950s, the PRC's economic development strategy depended on a form of state accumulation that involved unequal exchanges between the agricultural and industrial sectors. The government purchased agricultural products at depressed prices, kept the price of industrial goods high, and profited from the difference. In this manner, the PRC party-state extracted surpluses from China's large agrarian sector to fund rapid industrialization. Yet this developmental model heavily burdened rural populations.[13] Although Mao Zedong and the Chinese Communist Party (CCP) had pledged to eliminate the "three great differences" between industry and agriculture, city and countryside, and mental and manual labor, China's rural-urban divide worsened between the 1950s and 1970s. Rural people ate less food, earned less money, and enjoyed fewer benefits than their urban counterparts. The PRC's household registration (*hukou*) system tightly controlled migration to keep people designated as peasants in the countryside and prevent them from flocking to cities in search of work and grain.[14] To be a "peasant," as anthropologist Myron Cohen has written, "is to be disadvantaged."[15]

Today, rural communities that labored to conserve water and soil during the Mao era remain far poorer than the residents of China's cities, whose industrial development they facilitated via state accumulation. Carbon dioxide emissions derived from that industrialization, in turn, have contributed directly to anthropogenic climate change that makes life harder for marginalized rural people in Northwest China. In recent decades, air temperature on the Loess Plateau has risen by 0.6 degree C, annual precipitation has decreased, and droughts occur more frequently. The rural poor in ecologically vulnerable areas like Gansu, of course, have fewer resources to cope with climatic changes that exacerbate environmental hazards such as uneven rainfall and unstable soils than their downstream urban counterparts.[16] In China, as elsewhere, it is the economically and socially disadvantaged who disproportionately bear the costs of climate change and environmental destruction.

The history of water and soil conservation in modern China cannot be understood in isolation from these patterns of state accumulation, uneven development, and rural-urban inequality. If the cost of China's industrialization fell mostly on its rural population, the cost of conservation did as well. Emphasizing the importance of connecting environmental sustainability with socioeconomic justice, the chapters that follow demonstrate how the Chinese state imposed the burden of conservation on marginalized rural communities and how these communities navigated those demands.

INTRODUCTION 9

MAP 2. Gansu Province, Tianshui Prefecture, and Wushan County

Water and Soil, State and Society

This story begins about 95 kilometers east of the village of Dengjiabao, near the city of Tianshui, in southeastern Gansu. This urban center, like Wushan County, is currently part of the larger administrative unit known as Tianshui Prefecture (see map 2). During China's Anti-Japanese War of Resistance (1937–45), inspired by transnationally circulating understandings (primarily from the United States) of the causes and consequences of soil erosion, which some have termed "the first global environmental problem," Chiang Kai-shek's Nationalist regime selected tracts of inclined farmland in the hills overlooking Tianshui as the site of China's earliest soil and water conservation programs.[17] Walter C. Lowdermilk, assistant chief of the United States Soil Conservation Service and agricultural adviser to the Chinese Nationalist regime in 1942–43, oversaw the establishment of the Tianshui Water and Soil Conservation Experiment Area. During the 1940s, Chinese conservation specialists aspired to remake human interactions with the environment to efficiently utilize resources and increase productivity in support of wartime mobilization. To realize these goals, conservation had to adapt to local socioecological realities and the priorities of Tianshui's rural populace. The Nationalist regime made only limited headway in that regard.

When the CCP came to power in 1949, it inherited blueprints for reengineering human relations with the environment from the Republican period (1912–49). These plans pertained to water and soil conservation and other sectors. Unlike the Nationalist government, however, the CCP put them into effect.[18] Employing many of the same technical personnel who served the Nationalist regime during World War II, agents of the PRC party-state mobilized the rural populace to build terraces and other conservation infrastructure on a larger scale than its rivals and predecessors could have imagined. PRC leaders expected conservation to limit sedimentation along the Yellow River and thus prolong the life of dam megaprojects downstream. By increasing crop yields in hilly "mountainous areas" where water and soil loss hampered agricultural productivity, conservation would also expand the surplus that the state could extract from the countryside to support China's industrial development. In Gansu, these crops were primarily wheat and maize, followed by potatoes, millet, buckwheat, and other grains.[19]

Beginning in the early 1950s, technical personnel from the Tianshui Water and Soil Conservation Experiment Area and authorities in Wushan County made the village of Dengjiabao into a model in China's battle against erosion (map 3). With guidance from these state agents, Dengjiabao gained nationwide renown over the next decade as an exemplar of water and soil conservation work, frequently appearing in the *People's Daily* and other government publications. In this regard, Dengjiabao's "model experiences" resembled those of other locales that the PRC party-state valorized and promoted to advance its policymaking priorities.[20] Dengjiabao's accomplishments, publicized via firsthand observation visits and state-sponsored publications, demonstrated conservation methods to cadres and villagers

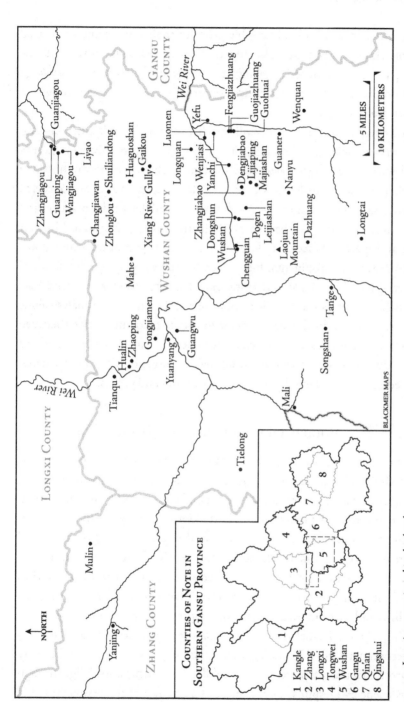

MAP 3. Locations mentioned in this book

from other locales, offered tangible proof of their results, and convinced people elsewhere to undertake similar efforts. Eventually, in 1957–58, the PRC party-state launched a "Dengjiabao campaign" (*Dengjiabao yundong*) to promote the village's experience conserving water and soil throughout Gansu and China as a whole.

In Dengjiabao and the many villages that sought to emulate it, conservation was a complex and contested enterprise. Capturing this history requires a local perspective. Larger scales of analysis tend to obscure, to borrow historian Stephen Mosley's words, "how conflict, difference, and power over access to nature and natural resources—as well as routinized day-to-day practices and consumption behaviors—have shaped human environment relationships over time and space."[21] Since every local environment is part of the wider global environment, environmental history lends itself to "playing with scales."[22] Situating local histories of conservation in relation to planetary, transnational, and national trends—and oscillating between different scales of analysis along the way—this book offers a multitiered investigation of interactions between the forces of nature, state-directed environmental management policies, and the ordinary men and women in China's countryside who dug trenches, moved earth, and planted trees on steep hillsides and gullies.

Mao-Era Environmental History from the Ground Up

The first generation of environmental histories of the Mao era (1949–76) put forth thoroughly condemnatory judgements of the PRC's environmental record. Judith Shapiro, for instance, contended that the polarizing, adversarial stance toward nature that characterized Maoist ideology greatly accelerated the destruction of China's environment after the founding of the PRC.[23] More recent environmental histories, on the other hand, have identified an array of Mao-era policies that promoted sustainable agricultural practices based on local knowledge, advocated tree planting, protected endangered wildlife, and encouraged conservation of scarce resources through waste recycling.[24] Sigrid Schmalzer has shown that the current designation of terraces in certain parts of China as "agricultural heritage" sites builds on Mao-era efforts to document, preserve, and mobilize traditional knowledge through mass science.[25] Despite the contributions made by earlier assessments of the PRC's treatment of the environment after 1949, however, we know precious little about the specific local iterations of the environmental transformations witnessed during the Mao era and their implications for ordinary people's lives. This book expands on previous studies by combining the methodologies and perspectives of environmental and social history to recount what water and soil conservation meant for men and women in rural Gansu and how it changed the ways they lived and worked.

Given the priority that the PRC party-state placed on water and soil conservation and the extent to which it transformed China's landscape, it ranks among the most significant components of the Mao era's environmental legacy. Focusing on the imbrication of social divisions and environmental change at the local scale highlights who gained and who lost when state conservation programs transformed interactions between people and the environment. I ask who had a choice in the decision to conserve what and how, assessing the distribution of the costs and benefits of environmental degradation and conservation.[26] I also examine the contradictions, contestations, and compromises that the PRC party-state's environmental interventions triggered in rural society.

This mode of analysis draws inspiration from the fields of political ecology and environmental justice. Political ecology examines how political and economic relations shape access to and control over resources, as well as the implications of such interactions for environmental health and sustainable livelihoods.[27] Environmental justice scholarship addresses the question of how to ensure that marginalized groups do not suffer disproportionately (as they usually do) from environmental hazards and that efforts to achieve sustainability do not aggravate social inequalities.[28]

PRC leaders clearly recognized the importance of building terraces, planting trees, and enacting other measures to limit water and soil loss. The party-state presented water and soil conservation to rural people as key to alleviating the erosion, drought, resource shortages, and poverty that had plagued them for decades. Official propaganda promised that conservation would bring environmental improvement and future economic prosperity, and this message resonated with many villagers. Some of these promises came true, at least for a time. Until 1956, terracing and other measures that limited water and soil loss in Dengjiabao steadily increased grain yields and villagers' access to food. Planting trees and grasses increased fuel availability, while digging ponds and wells to catch runoff alleviated water shortages and facilitated irrigation. Since the gendered division of labor in rural China defined gathering fuel and water as women's work, greater access to these resources particularly improved the lives of female villagers.

Despite these benefits, however, conservation programs undertaken during the 1950s altered patterns of control over the land and its resources in ways that frequently had negative consequences for rural people. Fundamental tensions existed between the Chinese state's conservation policies—which operated at the scale of the Yellow River basin and furthered the national goal of economic development—and the priorities of the rural populace. Even though conservation initially brought environmental improvements, the full-scale collectivization of agriculture after 1956 meant that these campaigns weighed heavily on villagers. Water and soil conservation required arduous physical labor that endangered the health and well-being of rural people and had lasting effects on their bodies. The heaviest burden fell on women, who had to balance conservation work with collective farming and the domestic labor obligations that ensured social reproduction.[29]

When conservation projects such as building terraces and dams made labor unavailable for farming and handicraft production, they could jeopardize villagers' immediate livelihoods. And because the PRC party-state's grain procurement system siphoned off agricultural surpluses from the countryside at cheap prices to support industrialization, most of the increase in crop yields that resulted from conserving water and soil did not accrue to the rural populace. Per capita grain consumption in Dengjiabao increased from 1952 until 1956 but declined precipitously in the late 1950s. The place of the rural sector in the political economy of Mao-era China dictated that villagers who did the work of remaking the land to conserve water and soil got precious little in return for their effort. For the rural populace, conservation went hand in hand with intensified labor demands, diversion of time and energy away from other forms of production, and heightened exploitation.

The contradiction between the goals of the PRC party-state and the subsistence priorities of rural people was most acute during the Great Leap Forward (1958–61). During this campaign, villagers across China joined communes with tens of thousands of members, built reservoirs, and smelted steel in backyard furnaces. In Dengjiabao, as in other parts of Gansu, the Great Leap involved mass mobilization for afforestation, terracing, and dam construction campaigns. Rural residents—especially women—worked harder and devoted more of their time to conservation projects, leaving farmwork undone. The disruption of agricultural production that resulted from these conservation campaigns, in addition to other Great Leap Forward policies, helped precipitate a subsistence crisis that from 1958 to 1960 resulted in over 49,000 famine-related deaths in Wushan County and 185,000 in Tianshui Prefecture. In China as a whole, casualties related to the Great Leap Forward famine reached 15–40 million.[30]

Per capita grain consumption in Wushan, Tianshui, and the rest of China recovered to prefamine levels in the early 1960s, but stagnated due to state extraction until the 1980s, when collectivized agriculture had come to an end.[31] To be sure, limiting rural consumption brought improvements in other aspects of rural life. Agricultural collectives mobilized members' labor and resources to invest in irrigation, roads, electricity generation, and other rural infrastructure. Public health initiatives improved life expectancy and rural education levels increased. But because most of the increased grain output that resulted from these improvements was directed to the urban-industrial sector, rural people did not see gains in per capita consumption at a level commensurate with their intensified labor.[32]

Not all rural people accepted these demands. From the beginning, county officials, grassroots cadres, and other villagers engaged in a persistent push and pull over conservation. The rows of terraces conceal a legacy not only of exploitation, but of resistance, negotiation, and accommodation.[33] State agents, ordinary people, and nature played active parts in this history. Local archives contain abundant evidence of rural people's ambivalence and outright opposition to conservation work, as well as detailed accounts of how local cadres and other state agents responded. Schmalzer has observed that narratives of resistance to the introduction of new agricultural technologies found in Mao-era sources follow a familiar arc: "A new technology was introduced, people resisted, they were presented with various forms of persuasion, and in the end they accepted the new technology."[34] These accounts served political purposes and must be read carefully. However, as Schmalzer underscores, "there is every reason to believe that the conflicts described in the narratives reflected real tensions at the local level."[35] Previous studies of the Mao era have amply demonstrated that the PRC party-state's pursuit of its policy goals was fraught with conflict and tension.[36] Conservation was no exception.

This book is based largely on archival documents in which local cadres and other state agents told their superiors how they had overcome local resistance and convinced villagers to participate in conservation schemes. Yet subsequent reports often contain accounts of local intransigence centered on the same problems and concerns that had supposedly been overcome. The misgivings of the masses never fully went away; resistance waned, only to reappear. Quotes from ordinary villagers frankly expressing their reservations and suspicions, often in coarse and colloquial language, appear throughout the investigations, work reports, meeting minutes, and other sources I have drawn on for this book, providing glimpses of how people understood conservation and its consequences. At the same time, quantitative data found in archives and published gazetteers make it possible to reconstruct the amount of time and effort that villagers devoted to conservation work and gauge the extent to which these projects improved—or failed to improve—their livelihoods by increasing access to food, fuel, and water.

Disputes over conservation were struggles over people's relationship with nature. Central and provincial governments, county leaders, and local cadres called on rural laborers to engage in conservation work rather than farming or other production activities. These demands pulled villagers in different directions, leading to contestation and conflict. Living in a world of risk and uncertainty, moreover, rural people had no way of knowing whether conservation would bring tangible returns. Some cultivators expressed an aversion to the large investments of backbreaking labor that these projects required and worried that they would hamper crop production. To be effective, conservation had to respond and adapt to the dispersed agencies of the natural world. But attempts to manage environmental unpredictability were rarely successful. People questioned the usefulness of conservation infrastructure that could not eliminate environmental hazards like drought and flood, which only worsened when poorly designed, built, and maintained dams and reservoirs failed. Although some villagers enthusiastically joined conservation campaigns and many more simply went along with them, others engaged in passive and active forms of resistance—from doing work in a perfunctory manner to verbally attacking local cadres.

Central authorities transmitted conservation policies through the party-state's administrative hierarchy of provinces, prefectures, counties, and townships, but they had to be carried out at the level of the village and the collective. Grassroots cadres and other local state agents mediated between their superiors in the party-state apparatus, who expected them to meet conservation targets, and the villagers who were their neighbors, coworkers, and kin. To fulfill their duties, state agents on the ground had to address villagers' concerns and persuade them to implement conservation measures. The documentary record indicates that the methods used to achieve compliance went beyond simple orders and threats. Local cadres disseminated propaganda, recalibrated remuneration systems, adjusted work schedules, and tightened supervision to gain popular participation. In 1956, households forfeited their landholdings to higher-level agricultural cooperatives that paid members work points in exchange for their labor. They also lost the right to withdraw from the collectives. At this point, reliance on material incentives to persuade villagers to do conservation work declined markedly. In the early stages of the Great Leap Forward, in 1958, propaganda that evocatively described the environmental and economic improvements that campaigns to conserve water and soil would bring about proved effective in mobilizing rural people to remake the land. Because villagers depended on collectives for their grain rations, those not won over by this vision had little choice but to capitulate and take part.

Between 2017 and 2019, I had the opportunity to conduct oral history interviews with elderly villagers in Dengjiabao who participated in Mao-era water and soil conservation campaigns. During our conversations, they recalled the origins and development of conservation programs in their village, the environmental and socioeconomic impact of these measures, and how the work of remaking the environment transformed their everyday lives. Oral histories also reveal that, due to gendered divisions of labor and resource use, men and women experienced these conservation campaigns differently. Archival documents and published sources sometimes offer fleeting glimpses of topics related to conservation's gendered implications for women, but these texts were mostly written by, for, and about men. Only in my interviews did the gendered dimensions of conservation become legible. This focus on gender-differentiated environmental experiences highlights, in the words of development studies scholars Melissa Leach and Cathy Green, "the ways that gender relations structure (and are structured through) environmental use and management" as mediated by divisions of labor and relations of power.[37] Exploring these topics in Mao-era rural China adds to recent efforts by environmental historians to demonstrate the importance of gender in human-environment interactions.[38]

My investigation of the uneven distribution of the costs and benefits of environmental management also engages in comparative dialogue with global environmental histories of water and soil conservation. As previous studies of Kenya, Lesotho, South Africa, and the American Southwest have documented, the introduction and enforcement of conservation policies that deprive the rural poor of control over natural resources to make them available for dominant groups frequently encounter opposition and resistance.[39] The local archives that I have consulted contain records of tensions and disputes related to conservation campaigns in rural Gansu, as well as how local cadres sought to resolve them. To be sure, the racism that pervades settler colonialism did not inform conservation in Wushan County during the Mao era.[40] Yet the parallels between conservation in twentieth-century China and colonial settings are more than superficial. The American adviser Walter C. Lowdermilk assisted in formulating plans to preserve water and soil in China during the 1940s, and environmental knowledge and practices derived from the United States informed conservation schemes implemented by colonial regimes in Africa as well.[41]

During the PRC's collective era, state accumulation relied on "mandatory, unequal exchange between the urban and rural sectors." The countryside functioned as what historian Jacob Eyferth calls an "internal colony" that provided cheaply priced raw materials needed to fund urban industrialization.[42] Discrimination based on socially constructed physical markers of rural identity that Jeremy Brown has termed "spatial profiling" justified this systemic exploitation of China's countryside.[43] In Mao-era China, like in colonial Kenya, Tanzania, and elsewhere, state-led conservation initiatives also intensified pressure on work time—especially for rural women. For the inhabitants of China's countryside, as for rural people in colonial settings, conservation was inseparable from an extractive mode of accumulation that entailed loss of access to resources and intensified exploitation. Employing a place-specific perspective, the chapters that follow assess how these social inequalities shaped quotidian experiences of environmental change and evaluate the unequal distribution of power, resources, and costs.

ONE

"Tianshui's Three Treasures"
Conservation in Wartime Gansu

When hiking up the steep, winding path to see the earthen bunds (also known as contour banks or ridges) built to conserve water and soil in the hills above Tianjiazhuang village, outside the city of Tianshui, a knowledgeable guide can point out the withered stands of black locust trees planted more than half a century ago. At the right time of year, if you know where to look, you can see sweet clover plants growing in terraced fields on the hillsides and ravines surrounding Tianshui. Together, the bunds, sweet clover, and locust trees gained a reputation during the 1950s among Chinese proponents of water and soil conservation as "Tianshui's three treasures" (*Tianshui san da bao*) for their efficacy in checking erosion.[1] The three treasures and their spread across the rural landscape of Gansu and elsewhere in northwestern China are an unacknowledged environmental legacy of World War II.

The Anti-Japanese War of Resistance of 1937–45, as World War II is known in China, did tremendous damage to the environment.[2] But the conflict was also the catalyst for water and soil conservation efforts undertaken by China's Nationalist government. Since the 1920s, Chinese agronomists, foresters, and water conservancy experts had been active in transnational exchanges about soil erosion and the best methods for alleviating it.[3] But it was not until the 1940s that the Nationalist regime launched China's earliest state-led programs to conserve soil and water in the Loess Plateau region. Walter C. Lowdermilk, assistant chief of the US Soil Conservation Service and a leading evangelist of soil conservation, directly influenced these programs as an adviser to the Nationalist government.

The emergence of water and soil conservation in wartime China was part of a transnational circulation of agricultural knowledge, environmental perceptions, and conservation practices that spurred state initiatives across the globe. Although recurrent droughts in Africa and Australia had previously caused concern about land degradation, the Dust Bowl that struck the

Great Plains of North America in the 1930s heightened other settler-colonial societies' anxieties about soil erosion. Canada and the United States initiated programs to conserve water and soil in the mid-1930s in response to dust storms on their dryland prairies. Building on earlier exchanges of agricultural personnel and publications, colonial states in East and Southern Africa drew on American conservationists' ideas about what caused the Dust Bowl to launch concerted soil conservation efforts. As historian Sarah Phillips has written, "The perceived threat of soil erosion on a grand scale, induced in large part by impressions of the denuded American plains, helped justify accelerated state interventions in African agriculture in the 1930s and 1940s."[4] The founding chief of the US Soil Conservation Service, Hugh Hammond Bennett, toured South Africa in 1944 and urged the state to undertake antierosion programs modeled on the US response to the Dust Bowl.[5] The steps taken by colonial governments in Africa to prevent erosion had far-reaching consequences: compulsory terracing schemes and grazing limitations imposed during Britain's "second colonial occupation" following World War II sparked resistance that lent impetus to independence movements.[6] In Australia, ecological damage caused by soil erosion in the 1930s led to the establishment of conservation agencies in New South Wales in 1938 and in Victoria in 1940, which gained further influence in the post–World War II period.[7]

The "agro-technical internationalism" of the 1930s and 1940s, as Phillips calls it, directly influenced the Nationalist government's water and soil conservation programs.[8] But such programs also grew out of conditions specific to wartime China. For Chinese conservation experts during World War II, the interlocking imperatives of harnessing scarce resources to resist the Japanese invasion, developing China's northwestern frontier, and strengthening the nation-state required limiting water and soil loss by rationalizing land use. The Japanese seizure of China's main economic centers after the outbreak of full-scale military hostilities in 1937 deepened the Nationalist regime's need to manage and develop the resources of China's unoccupied western interior to support economic mobilization.[9] The regime's Ministry of Agriculture and Forestry established the Tianshui Water and Soil Conservation Experiment Area (Tianshui shuitu baochi shiyanqu, hereafter referred to as the experiment area) in August 1942.[10] Tianshui's location

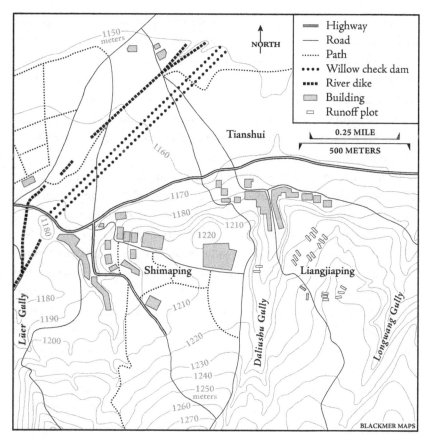

MAP 4. The Tianshui Water and Soil Conservation Experiment Area

as a central hub on the roadways that linked the Nationalist government's wartime capital in Chongqing with Northwest China's Loess Plateau during the 1940s made it an ideal site for this project. The agency still operates at the site where it was originally founded, now as the PRC's Yellow River Water and Soil Conservation Tianshui Management and Supervision Bureau/Tianshui Water and Soil Conservation Scientific Experiment Station (Huanghe shuitu baochi Tianshui zhili jianduju/Tianshui shuitu baochi kexue shiyanzhan).

In addition to examining how wartime mobilization informed the experiment area's early research, demonstration, and extension efforts, this chapter assesses the socioeconomic and ecological factors that shaped local responses to these state interventions. The outcomes were mixed. The priorities of the expert and the farmer did not always coincide, as when the socioeconomic and environmental constraints that prevailed in Gansu during the 1940s hampered the experiment area's plans to construct terraces and channels to limit water and soil loss. The experiment area's promotion of tree and grass species for conservation purposes, on the other hand, met with an enthusiastic response from the local populace.

By the early twentieth century, Gansu and the rest of the Loess Plateau was severely deforested, resulting in erosion as well as acute shortages of biomass for use as fuel and fertilizer.[11] Most rural residents had to eke out a meager and precarious existence from this degraded landscape. As one foreign author in Gansu noted during the 1940s, "Extensive areas are farmed which are not suited to cultivation. For want of fuel, animal manure and stalks of plants are burned for cooking and heat and these materials cannot be used to enrich the soil." The land soon became exhausted, and erosion intensified.[12] Villagers in Tianshui welcomed the experiment area's introduction of grass and tree species because they helped alleviate this resource scarcity and land degradation. Although conservation specialists aspired to rationalize human interactions with the land as part of a larger wartime drive to develop Northwest China, the success or failure of the measures they advocated depended on the extent to which they fit with place-specific socioecological conditions on the ground and spoke to the quotidian needs of the rural populace.

Conservation and Wartime Mobilization

With the Japanese invasion and occupation of China's coastal provinces in 1937, as a high-ranking provincial official in Gansu put it in 1940, "the Northwest suddenly emerged from an obscure border region into a vital base for prolonged resistance and national reconstruction." In Northwest China, Gansu "occupied a key position as the center of the region," largely due to its place "on the path of direct communication with Soviet Russia" via Xinjiang to the west. This strategic position made Gansu not only a "great pulse of China," but a "pivotal point linking Asia and Europe." The official wrote that Gansu possessed wide expanses of arable land and natural resources "of great value" to national defense, so it had "a significant role to play" in China's War of Resistance, as well as "good prospects for future economic development." Gansu had tried to increase production and feed its rapidly growing population, but due to what the official called "the ignorance of the peasants," farming methods remained "primitive" and output lagged. Much of Gansu was well suited for afforestation and animal husbandry, the official maintained, but they had been neglected in the past. Developing them required state intervention.[13]

Water and soil conservation featured prominently in this vision of agricultural development and improvement. Ren Chengtong (1898–1973), who worked for the experiment area as a technical consultant, articulated the connection between conservation and the larger goal of "reconstructing the Northwest." Writing in 1943, Ren held that China's Northwest was "the cradle of the Chinese race." Ancient ruins evidenced the past existence of "wealthy and flourishing capitals and ancient towns" in areas that had since been enveloped by the Gobi Desert. Desiccation and decline, Ren thought, "resulted from people of that time coveting immediate profits and excessively cultivating steep mountain slopes." Not only did growing numbers of farmers still clear inclined land for farming, which removed vegetation cover and accelerated erosion, but officials who advocated frontier development and land reclamation promoted it as well. As water ran off hillsides, aridity increased. "If this error is not actively corrected and continues to spread," Ren warned, "today's bustling cities will in the future turn into ancient cities beneath the desert." As it sought to reconstruct the Northwest and "open the frontier," the Nationalist regime had to "use water and soil conservation as the central principle in carrying out this work." The definition of conservation, Ren maintained, was simple: "It is only, based on various methods for exhausting the land's benefits, applying principles for sustaining the land's perpetual productive capacity" (*baochi tudi yongjiu shengchan nengli zhi yuanze*).[14] The Japanese had occupied vast swaths of farmland, so China had to attend to its food supply problem. Thus, "for the sake of the War of Resistance and for the sake of national reconstruction, forest reclamation and water conservancy (*linken shuili*) [were] sectors of urgent importance in economic reconstruction."[15]

As a prominent wartime agricultural development initiative, the experiment area gained support from China's international partners. On behalf of the Nationalist government's Executive Yuan, the Yellow River Conservancy Commission arranged for Walter C. Lowdermilk to come to China in 1942 as an agricultural adviser.[16] Lowdermilk was one of the many American agricultural experts who had ventured to China in the early twentieth century to impart the "universal truths" of agronomy, forestry, soil science, and agricultural economics.[17] From 1922 to 1927, he had taught at the University of Nanking's School of Agriculture and Forestry. Ren Chengtong was his student and collaborated with him on field studies of deforestation, streamflow, and erosion in North China.[18]

During World War II, as J. Megan Greene has shown, droves of scientific and technical advisers from the United States offered assistance and training programs in support of the Chinese Nationalist regime, America's wartime ally.[19] When Lowdermilk returned to China in 1942–43, he intended to "make a joint study of land use problems" in the Northwest, where, in his words, "erosion is most acute and affects decisively the problem of control of floodwaters in the Yellow River."[20] Along the way, Lowdermilk and a field staff of Chinese technicians would "designate a number of suitable areas for demonstration projects and put them on the land for technical men to see."[21] Water and soil conservation held critical importance in China's war effort, Lowdermilk believed, because food production was "the basis for efficient resistance of the people during war time and for rehabilitation, reconstruction and industrialisation during the post-war period."[22]

Writing in 1945, the experiment area's director, Ye Peizhong, also linked conserving water and soil to China's war effort: "During the War of Resistance, reconstructing the Northwest has been looked upon as important, and carrying out water and soil conservation to increase agricultural production has become an even more important program."[23] Wei Zhanggen, a technician at the experiment area, went even further by describing erosion in geopolitical terms: "If water and soil conservation and the work of maintaining land's productive capacity are not promptly carried out, then cultivated land will be eroded into gullies, good fields will turn into deserts, and it will truly be lost soil (*shitu*) that our nation will have no way to recover."[24] The specific term that Wei used to describe loss of farmland due to soil erosion—*shitu*—often refers to territories that have been lost to a rival geopolitical power and need to be recovered. By employing this vocabulary, Wei implied that erosion and foreign invasion had to be opposed with equal vigor. By rationalizing land use and slowing soil loss, conservation would thus further China's national defense.[25]

Trouble with Terraces

In concrete terms, what could be done? Lowdermilk acknowledged that farmers in Northwest China were "very skillful in terracing" and had practiced it for centuries, but he also stressed the limitations of inherited conservation techniques. In his words, "The old Chinese bench terraces were not systematically designed and very often are not on contour, so sheet erosion and gully erosion still go on." When terraces went uphill and downhill instead of following the contour line at a right angle to the slope, runoff from rainstorms flowed in an uncontrolled manner across the landscape and washed away the soil. For this reason, Lowdermilk recommended devising "an improved method of building bench terraces" on highlands with soil layers more than two meters deep. In Tianshui, he advocated planting strips of alfalfa, rye, or other grasses and legumes at proper intervals on sloping fields and digging "contour channels designed for adequate capacity" below the strips. The grass strips would hold soil that washed down the slopes and absorb runoff water; the channels would catch what the strips did not. This "contour-channel system" would feature adequate outlets and waterways for excess rainfall (figs 4 and 5). Annual plowing would level the fields between strips and build up banks along them.[26] Wei Zhanggen added that terraces, although Chinese farmers had been building them for centuries, had not been generally adopted. Existing techniques needed to be improved and implemented over a wider area to have a positive effect.[27] Wei echoed Lowdermilk by arguing that construction of improved systems of "terraces and channels" (*titian gouxu*) to intercept runoff and conserve water and soil would limit the threat of drought and flooding while also increasing yields.[28]

But before work could begin, somewhere had to be found to carry it out. The experiment area spent most of 1943 embroiled in a protracted dispute with local landlords, who refused to sell their land for use as a demonstration

FIGURE 4. Field planning in the experiment area. Lowdermilk on the left. W. C. Lowdermilk Papers, ca. 1912–1969, Bancroft Library of the University of California, Berkeley [BANC MSS 72/206, container 5].

FIGURE 5. Bank channel with strip crop sowed above. W. C. Lowdermilk Papers, ca. 1912–1969, Bancroft Library of the University of California, Berkeley [BANC MSS 72/206, container 5].

site.[29] Concern that altering the land for conservation purposes would damage or threaten ancestral graves animated this opposition (fig. 6). Lawsuits in rural China during the Qing period, as documented by Tristan Brown, often referenced geomancy (*fengshui*) in disputes over auspicious plots of land deemed suitable for gravesites.[30] Geomantic beliefs permeated land disputes well into the twentieth century, with households invoking possible harm to *fengshui*—and the misfortunes that it might cause—to protect their ancestral property. The tensions between the experiment area and Tianshui's local landholders that took place in 1943–44 were typical. The experiment area held that it had carefully demarcated all graves and agreed not to disturb any land that contained them. However, a petition from local landowners to the Nationalist government claimed that the land used by the experiment area contained "dozens of ancestral graves," which caused them "extreme fear."[31] A wealthy landlord whose "family trade was fortunetelling" (*jiaye fengjian*) challenged the experiment area's plans to purchase his land

FIGURE 6. View from ridge north of Tianshui with graves in foreground, city in midground, and experiment area to left of gully in the distance. W. C. Lowdermilk Papers, ca. 1912–1969, Bancroft Library of the University of California, Berkeley [BANC MSS 72/206, container 5].

by arguing that water and soil conservation would "transform the nearby topography" and damage *fengshui*.[32]

After provincial and county officials intervened and convinced the intransigent local elites to sell, personnel from the experiment area conducted topographical and soil surveys, and in spring 1944 the terrace and channel demonstration project got underway.[33] Yet gravesites and geomancy still sparked controversy. A report from May 1944 further noted that the experiment area's designs for terraces and channels along the contour did not impinge on existing gravesites. But powerful landholding families, due to their "geomantic beliefs" (*fengshui zhi shuo*), wanted to place new graves in land designated for terraces and thus asked that it be excluded from the demonstration project. Fearing similar problems in the future, the experiment area convened a meeting with the Tianshui County government. After conducting land surveys, county officials decided that whenever field engineering projects encountered a grave, the experiment area would set aside one *zhang* (3⅓ meters) in front, two *zhang* behind, and one *zhang* five *chi* (one *chi* is 33⅓ centimeters) to the left and right of the gravesite.[34] Conservation experts may have considered geomantic beliefs to be backward superstition or a pretext for local residents to refuse to sell their land, but they still had to be reckoned with.

Graves were not the only problem. Because farmers in Tianshui could build terraces and channels only during the agricultural slack season, the project initially made limited progress. As a later report explained, "To give consideration to farmers' cultivation activities, work had to be done when agricultural land lay fallow, so it proceeded slowly, with only 181.1 *zhang* (603.6 meters) of terraces and channels completed."[35] Government support eventually made it possible for the experiment area to recruit paid laborers and expand the demonstration project's scope. As one of the experiment area's technical experts, Yan Wenguang, later recalled, "In organizing work, in addition to a small area in which the county government enlisted civilian laborers from nearby townships to engage in construction, state investment was utilized over a large area to hire workers." By late 1945, the experiment area had constructed 16,500 meters of bench terraces and built small banks along roads to guide runoff water into channels and prevent it from accelerating erosion. These structures covered more than 2,000 *mu* (133.3 hectares) of land, or 80 percent of the experiment area's territory.[36]

Convincing farmers in Tianshui to adopt conservation techniques on a larger scale, however, was not easy. Constructing bench terraces required a good bit of labor, particularly to dig the contour channels. According to Lowdermilk's estimate, one man could construct, by hand, a channel with a cross section of 0.45 to 0.8 square meters and a length of 17 to 33 meters in one day. Fifteen to thirty workdays were required to build channels on one hectare of land, so a farmer with "medium-sized" holdings of 1.42 hectares "working at slack times of the year" would need two or three years to construct channels on their farm.[37] These labor requirements made terracing too costly for many poor households. As conservation specialist Wei Zhanggen wrote, "In light of most farmers' economic capacity, although they know that carrying out terrace and channel engineering projects could indeed improve the land's use value, they still do not have the capacity to construct them on their own and require government assistance."[38] Even when local people recognized conservation's potential benefits, they had to balance them against other considerations.

Along with economic constraints, the effectiveness of conservation techniques was uncertain. Although conservation experts claimed the technical and scientific high ground, the measures that they advocated often failed to realize their stated aims and purposes. With cultivation extending to steep slopes with gradients of over 30 percent, the experiment area's personnel added narrow drainage outlets to terraces and channel systems to divert runoff water, carry it away at a nonerosive velocity, and thereby decrease the burden on structures built further downhill. Yet, as Wei admitted, experimental results showed that the drainage outlets were costly, labor-intensive, and "yielded few results." More research was needed on the best way to manage steep slopes and whether farmers could make a living by foregoing crop production on steeply inclined land in favor of planting pasture grasses or engaging in other pursuits.[39]

Yan Wenguang's retrospective assessment went further in explaining the rural populace's ambivalence toward the "improved" terraces and channels championed by the experiment area. Farmers in Tianshui, as Yan recalled, "did not welcome and also did not reject" implementing conservation measures on their land. Most farmers thought "management measures made sense in principle and admitted that they were a good thing." But conservation techniques often left much to be desired, and their influence on agricultural production was not always positive. Some poor-quality terraces and "contour trenches" (*shuiping gou*) exposed less fertile "virgin soil, negatively influencing crop growth and decreasing production in some places. This aroused farmers' suspicions, and some also felt that digging a contour trench impeded cultivation, so after they were constructed, some people intentionally or unintentionally destroyed the engineering projects."[40] When building terraces and channels interfered with farming, ambivalence about conservation became outright opposition.

Yan admitted that after the first few years, despite making some achievements, conservation programs in Tianshui had encountered "quite a few problems worth paying attention to."[41] Although contour trenches dug on slopes were supposed to "impede runoff and sediment" so moisture would permeate the soil and benefit crop production, seedlings on terraced fields were often flooded or "killed by the sediment" (*yu si*). As Yan explained, "Especially when carrying out construction of terraces and contour trenches, not paying attention to the handling of surface soil, digging up bottom soil, and pressing down surface soil, thereby making the soil become poor, led to decreased production." These factors combined to make Tianshui's farmers "anxious" (*huailü*) about terraces.[42]

Local people recognized that conservation could potentially improve their land and livelihoods, but many could not afford the investments of time and labor it required. In other instances, cultivators saw that poorly planned and constructed infrastructure damaged crop production. As a result, Tianshui's farmers showed little enthusiasm for experimental terraces and channels that cost more than they could invest, inadvertently decreased soil fertility and submerged crop seedlings, and made cultivation more difficult. Such problems, it is worth noting, were not unique to China. In Southern Africa during the 1930s and 1940s, conservation measures mandated by colonial authorities required substantial labor inputs. At times, they interfered with the boundaries of farm plots, reduced the area available for cultivation, and collapsed because they could not withstand runoff from rainstorms.[43] Indeed, Kate Showers has argued that in colonial Lesotho, poorly designed and implemented conservation schemes did little to slow erosion and may have even promoted gullying by concentrating large amounts of water—and its erosive potential—at certain points in the landscape.[44]

In wartime Tianshui, the prevailing land tenure system also posed difficulties. Decades of erosion had made landholdings narrow and fragmented; terraces and channels further complicated the patchwork of boundaries between fields. As Wei Zhanggen explained, "If, after terrace and channel engineering projects along the contour line are planned, land becomes even more fragmented and it impedes cultivation, it will be difficult to make farmers willingly accept them." Because the tracts of land on which terraces were to be built often belonged to multiple households, farmers had to be persuaded to cooperate with one another. Implementing conservation schemes, in Wei's view, thus required re-demarcating landholdings. If re-demarcation consolidated holdings, then "cultivation will not be difficult, and land can be rationally utilized."[45] Moreover, tenancy arrangements gave cultivators little incentive to improve land that was rented from others. Much of the farmland on the outskirts of Tianshui belonged to landlords who lived in town, Yan Wenguang observed, so "it was impossible to mobilize farmers' enthusiasm for working the land to construct bench terraces."[46]

The experiment area did not have the capacity to alter land tenure relations, but it adapted some conservation techniques to make them more effective and appealing. A 1948 report indicated that the one-meter-wide grass strips that Lowdermilk had recommended planting along the edges of terraces did not grow well and the grass was not dense enough to retain sediment.[47] "Therefore," the report noted, "fertile soil from fields still pours into channels in large amounts, making surface soil gradually become infertile, while also increasing the onerousness and difficulty of channel repair work." Local people, meanwhile, rejected grass strips, feeling that they "occupied too much land," and so "did not willingly accept them, and when tilling they often destroyed them, so it is difficult to attain results in protection."[48]

Wei Zhanggen and Yan Wenguang favored replacing the grass strips with low earthen bunds (*digeng*, also called contour banks in English) of about 1.5 to 2 meters in width next to channels along the edges of terraced fields. By slowing and dispersing runoff, bunds increase water infiltration, enhance soil moisture, and limit erosion. In Tianshui, bunds proved more effective than grass strips for intercepting silt and occupied less cultivated land. Farmers, for their part, found this measure easy to implement, and accepted it.[49] After the CCP's assumption of power in 1949, Yan Wenguang and the experiment area's other personnel continued to promote the use of bunds. By 1956, approximately 3,562,200 *mu* (237,480 hectares) of bunds had been constructed in Tianshui Prefecture. During the first decade of prc rule, inclined terraces built using the bunds first tested by the experiment area became a primary component of water and soil conservation programs throughout Gansu.[50]

Treasure Grass

In contrast to terraces and channels, which met with early difficulties, promotion of certain species of vegetation to limit erosion and preserve water and soil saw rapid results. In 1944, under the direction of Ye Peizhong, a plant breeding specialist, the experiment area established a pasturage station that gathered hundreds of types of grasses from China, along with numerous foreign varieties, to identify potentially useful varieties for conserving water and soil.[51] Ye had only recently made his way to Gansu with the multitude of others who had fled Japanese-occupied eastern China. A native of Jiangsu, Ye graduated in 1927 from the Forestry Department at the University of Nanking, where he studied with Lowdermilk. He later joined the Lowdermilk-led investigation group that surveyed land use, erosion, and water conservancy in Shaanxi, Gansu, and Qinghai Provinces. Once the investigation concluded in 1943, Ye remained with the experiment area, and in 1945 he became its director.[52]

Ye focused on overseeing the experiment area's selection and breeding of soil-conserving plant varieties. Sweet clover (*caomuxi*), a nitrogen-fixing leguminous plant native to Eurasia that had been introduced in North America and elsewhere as a forage crop, was one of the most successful. Wild varieties of sweet clover grew throughout China, and from 1942 to 1943, while participating in Lowdermilk's investigation of Northwest China, Ye gathered over two thousand plant samples, including several types of sweet clover.[53] A report from 1945 described the experiment area's success in "discovering effective soil conservation plants" by collecting pasturage grass and tree species in Shaanxi, Gansu, and Qinghai, including areas around Tianshui. As the report explained, "In this locale we discovered a kind of *Melilotus alba* [sic] that is similar to American sweet clover." It was experimentally planted on infertile soil, and 160 liters of seeds and 800 kilograms of dry grass were harvested from every *mu*. As the report stated, "Fresh grass can serve as fodder. If dried grass is used as kindling, with each jin [500 grams] calculated as [being worth] 3 yuan, it can be sold for 4,800 yuan. This can solve the Northwest's fuel and fodder problems."[54]

Despite the availability of local varieties, the sweet clover promoted by the experiment area was mainly foreign. Cultivation of the plant did not attract sustained attention until after 1943, when Ye Peizhong oversaw the experiment area's planting of biennial white sweet clover (*baihua caomuxi*, *Melilotus albus*) and biennial yellow sweet clover (*huanghua caomuxi*, *Melilotus officinalis*), using seeds acquired from the United States Department of Agriculture and Soil Conservation Service. Although obtained via exchanges with the United States, these varieties were not native to North America either: biennial white sweet clover originated in Siberia, and biennial yellow sweet clover in Spain.[55] The circulation of these plant varieties between Europe, Asia, and North America exemplified the transnational character of the water and soil conservation practices implemented in China.

Regardless of their origin, the nitrogen-fixing capacity of these sweet clover varieties made them a valuable soil enhancer. Beginning in 1945, the experiment area added sweet clover to crop rotation experiments conducted in its runoff plots. Tests indicated that when sown as a cover crop on summer fallow land, sweet clover decreased runoff by 59–68 percent compared to other rotation systems and reduced soil erosion by 67 percent. In experiments comparing various types of soil-replenishing crops in 1948, sweet clover proved more effective than black or adzuki beans. Application of 62.5 kilograms of beancake fertilizer to each *mu* of land increased wheat production to 79 kilograms per *mu*, but when sweet clover was used as a cover crop, wheat yields were 26 percent higher, at 94.5 kilograms per *mu*.[56] Besides improving soil quality and boosting crop production when used for intercropping, sweet clover also provided feed for livestock and a source of nectar for honeybees. The plant's fast and robust growth gave it additional appeal: it grew tall; adapted well to inclined landscapes, clay soils, and saline-alkaline riverbanks; and flourished in upland areas like the hills around Tianshui, with elevations over 2,500 meters. Sweet clover's dense branches, leaves, and root structures also checked the loss of water and soil.[57]

Above all else, the rapid diffusion of sweet clover during the 1940s came from its ability to ameliorate the fuel scarcity that had long existed in Tianshui and the rest of Northwest China. Demographic changes during the war years, when refugees fled in the hundreds of thousands from occupied territories to China's interior, made the shortages more severe. As Ren Chengtong wrote in 1941, "In Tianshui County, since the beginning of the War of Resistance, many refugees from outside provinces have come, so a fuel famine (*chaihuang*) has occurred."[58] Fuel shortages led to more tree cutting and charcoal burning, which depleted woodlands as far as 50 kilometers from Tianshui's county seat, and the distance over which timber had to be imported increased 2.5 kilometers per year. Residents in some areas spent more money on fuel than food. Since fuel shortages led to destruction of vegetation cover, the problem had to be solved for water and soil conservation measures to succeed.[59]

The desperate search for heating fuel also decreased the availability of fertilizer and fodder. A 1946 newspaper article reported that Gansu suffered from shortages of fertilizer, with supplies of human excrement and livestock manure falling far short of the amount that farmers needed. The problem was that, though "lots of livestock manure could originally be fermented, decomposed, and used as fertilizer, since Gansu Province is extremely cold, lacks grasses, and has few trees, many poor people use livestock manure as fuel to defend against the cold. Because kindling and charcoal are also scarce, farmers also use grass roots and grain stalks as fuel."[60] Destruction of vegetation cover to obtain fuel, in turn, decreased the amount of fodder available for livestock and reduced their ability to produce additional manure. For the rural populace, the dearth of fertilizer, fuel, and fodder created a vicious cycle of resource scarcity, land degradation, low agricultural productivity, and poverty.

Tianshui's residents welcomed sweet clover because it supplied a much-needed fuel source in biomass-starved Gansu. Yan Wenguang, using language characteristic of the post-1949 period, later recalled the plant's significance: "Since the stalks were tall and large and had many branches, a lot of kindling could be collected from them and they burned vigorously, which was a good method for relieving the fuel difficulties of the masses, so without being promoted it spread on its own."[61]

Yet sweet clover's spread was not totally spontaneous. Agricultural extension and demonstration hastened its diffusion. The Tianshui Water and Soil Conservation Experiment Area planted sweet clover in grass strips along the terraces and channels it constructed for demonstration purposes. In the words of a 1947 report, "to encourage farmers to take an interest in planting grass strips," when sweet clover plants matured, the experiment area let them harvest it. After threshing, farmers could keep the stalks for their own use, but they had to give the seeds to the experiment area, which would distribute them to others. By the end of July 1947, farmers near Tianshui handed over approximately fifty kilograms of sweet clover seeds.[62] In 1948 the experiment area also took part in a local Farmer's Day festival and exhibited "outstanding soil conservation plant samples" and seed varieties, along with photographs and charts.[63]

Because sweet clover provided fuel, checked erosion, and replenished soil nutrients, it did not take long for the plant to gain popularity. When propagated on riverbanks near Tianshui at the mouth of Lüer Gully (Lüergou), farmers in the vicinity started coming to the experiment area to ask for seeds so they could plant it themselves.[64] According to a report from July 1947, villagers saw that "the sweet clover planted in this [experiment] area can prevent erosion on wasteland and can gradually restore its fertility. Moreover, its benefits are even greater than agricultural crops, so they come one after another to this area to request this kind of sweet clover to emulate it."[65] Farmers in one village planted sweet clover seeds that they obtained from the experiment area on 106 *mu* (7.06 hectares) of land.[66] By autumn 1948, that area expanded by nearly 60 percent as villagers had sown sweet clover on an additional 63 *mu* (4.2 hectares).[67]

As a report from 1948 related, "This experiment area's former director Ye Peizhong spared no effort in breeding soil-conserving plants, so after several years of research and experiments, they yielded results and attracted the attention of self-cultivating farmers, with many coming to the [experiment] area to ask for them." Among these forage grasses, the report identified sweet clover as the most popular due to its ability to "increase soil fertility and decrease erosion, while also providing fuel and serving as a preparatory crop for other agricultural crops that yields great results in terms of increasing production."[68] As more farmers saw the benefits of sweet clover, the experiment area gave out increasing numbers of seeds, and the plant's cultivation spread.[69]

Along with meeting local people's resource needs, sweet clover had enormous value as a commodity. In the late 1940s, villagers were willing to exchange a liter of grain for five hundred grams of white sweet clover that they used as fuel, fodder, and fertilizer. As Yan Wenguang recalled, people "had a deep fondness for it and called it 'foreign alfalfa' (*yang muxu*) and 'treasure grass' (*baobei cao*)."[70] Rural residents carried sweet clover stalks on their backs and went into the city to sell them. Because they were so combustible, sweet clove stalks fetched a price two or three times higher than other kindling. By end of the 1940s, farmers had planted more than ten thousand *mu* (666.7 hectares) on the outskirts of Tianshui.[71]

After 1949, sweet clover cultivation spread even more. In the 1950s, sweet clover was planted throughout Gansu, eventually extending to over one million *mu* (66,667 hectares) of land in the province. At the behest of the PRC's central government, Gansu sent five hundred thousand kilograms of sweet clover seed to twenty other provinces.[72] By the 1970s, according to one estimate, sweet clover grew on as many as ten million *mu* (666,667 hectares) across China.[73]

The King of Trees

The experiment area's research on "vanguard tree species" during the 1940s and its plans to encourage farmers to plant them on abandoned slopes and in gullies were equally successful.[74] Under Ye Peizhong's leadership, the experiment area planted over three hundred thousand trees of more than twenty different types at its Daliushu Gully (Daliushugou) and Longwang Gully (Longwanggou) demonstration sites, where erosion had caused landslides and clogged local watersheds with sediment. Black locust (*cihuai*, *Robinia pseudoacacia*), another foreign plant species, was the most favored.[75]

Black locust trees originated in the southern and central Appalachian Mountains of the eastern United States but first came to China in 1898 as part of afforestation programs in the German concession of Qingdao in northern China's Shandong Province. In the 1920s and 1930s, officials and commoners began planting these trees in Tianshui and other parts of Gansu, where they were known as "German locusts" (*Deguo huai*).[76] At first, the planting of these trees had nothing to do with slowing erosion. As Yan Wenguang explained, "Previously in the Northwest black locust was mostly a tree species that grew scattered in cities and rarely grew on dry abandoned gullies."[77] In 1944, Ren Chengtong and Ye Peizhong selected black locust seeds and raised saplings; they planted the first trees for conservation purposes in Daliushu Gully the following year.[78] Preliminary studies showed that black locusts formed dense, contiguous stands on collapsed slopes, stabilized gullies, and decreased the intensity of mudslides. Black locust trees planted on loess hillsides and gullies also held up well during heavy rainstorms. As Yan recalled, people in Tianshui praised it as "the king of tree species" (*wangpai shuzhong*) for its ability to grow quickly, protect soil, and provide fuel and building material.[79]

While the experiment area's personnel considered provision of fuel to villagers a secondary goal of afforestation, access to kindling from black locust trees held enormous significance for Tianshui's fuel-starved populace.[80] Archival documents are full of complaints about farmers from villages near the experiment area cutting down immature trees for fuel. A 1947 report complained that it was not easy to foster "the concept of loving forests" among local people. Officials urged nearby farmers to preserve trees, but it was hard to keep herders and woodcutters from damaging them, since locals desperately needed any vegetation they could find to heat their homes, cook their food, and graze their flocks. As the report stated, "The Northwest's fuel supplies are extraordinarily scarce, and in addition herders cannot store a lot of winter fodder, so protection and management are quite difficult." In the gullies near Tianshui's Shimaping village, small trees suffered damage, but near Daliushu Gully demonstration site "due to propaganda over the past few years" the damage was lighter.[81] It took persistent exhortations and careful monitoring to convince villagers that black locust trees were there to check gully erosion, not to be used as precious fuel.[82]

After 1949, black locust trees spread from Tianshui throughout eastern Gansu and neighboring provinces, eventually becoming the main tree variety planted for water and soil conservation purposes in the upper reaches of the Wei River and elsewhere in China.[83] Between 1950 and 2005, China's state-led afforestation programs planted black locust trees on over seventy thousand hectares of land throughout the Loess Plateau region.[84]

Unforeseen Consequences

Sweet clover and black locust trees had two qualities that made them particularly attractive to conservation experts and Tianshui's rural populace. They grew quickly, which made them useful for restoring vegetation cover on barren slopes, and their ability to fix atmospheric nitrogen enriched soil fertility and improved crop yields. The experiment area's desire to rapidly reforest denuded hillsides to slow erosion and increase agricultural output, along with the deprivation that existed in poor rural locales plagued by acute resource scarcities, explain their shared embrace of sweet clover and black locust trees. But from a longer-term perspective, the diffusion of these plant species had mixed ecological consequences.

Following their introduction and extension in the mid-1940s, white sweet clover and yellow sweet clover became established in twenty-two of China's provinces and municipalities. Their diverse habitats included fallow fields, grasslands, tree nurseries, and land along railways and roads, especially areas disturbed by construction, mining, or severe erosion. In the ecotones where the farmlands and grasslands of northwestern China meet and overlap, sweet clover has been disruptive: as an invasive species in prairies and steppes, sweet clover has degraded grasslands by overtopping and shading native plants that thrive on sunlight. Dissemination of sweet clover has thus altered the composition and structure of local vegetation in ways that reduce biodiversity.[85] A miracle plant became an invader as it moved from farmland to grassland. No one in wartime Gansu anticipated the consequences, however. Concerns about nonnative species did not exist at the time, and the short-term benefits that sweet clover brought to people who suffered from soil depletion and fuel shortages made it a treasure, not an ecological invader.

Black locust trees, heralded as the king of tree species for conservation, caused even greater problems. For several years after reaching maturity, black locust trees enrich soil nutrients, including nitrogen, and improve soil fertility. However, the tree requires a high volume of water, which often leads to the formation of a dry soil layer that is hazardous for other organisms and hampers replenishment of the water table. In China's arid Loess Plateau region, the spread of large-scale black locust plantations has aggravated water shortages and increased the risk of desertification. Current research even questions whether black locust trees protect against erosion. Rather than limiting soil loss, black locust plantations may decrease functional diversity by reducing the perennial herbaceous species that do the most to retard soil loss. Black locust trees thus have "negative implications for water recharge" in deeper soils and little benefit in terms of limiting soil erosion because of their effects on other plant life.[86]

Trees that once seemed indispensable allies in the war against erosion would eventually become a liability. Yet the experiment area's personnel, who had only limited experience with black locusts in the mid-1940s, could not have foreseen the problems that would result from their widespread cultivation. Given the experiment area's goal—forged in the crucible of long-term environmental degradation, resource scarcity, and wartime urgency—to reforest hillsides as rapidly as possible, its staff gave no thought to conducting the extensive studies needed to determine the effects of planting black locust trees in particular environments. And local people in desperate need of trees for fuel and fodder simply did not have the luxury of thinking about future consequences. The immediate benefits of growing black locusts were all that mattered.

Tianshui did not see combat during China's Anti-Japanese War of Resistance, but the conflict profoundly influenced the conservation programs undertaken there. World War II, as Simo Laakkonen, Richard Tucker, and Timo Vuorisalo have suggested, "synchronized global activities and generated surprisingly similar and simultaneous emergence and development of new environmental perceptions, organizations, and activities in the postwar world." The war's role as a "stimulus for nature conservation movements on different continents" made it "a major turning point in environmental policy making over the twentieth century."[87] We can see this is in the emergence of water and soil conservation in wartime China. During the 1940s, in dialogue with US advisors like Lowdermilk, the Nationalist regime adopted and promoted globally circulating environmental ideas and management techniques to further its agenda of developing the land and resources of the Northwest for wartime economic mobilization.

As in the settler-colonial societies from which it drew inspiration, conservation emerged in wartime China as a tool of state intervention that furthered the control of people and resources. Like their counterparts in Africa, North America, and elsewhere, conservation experts in wartime China trumpeted their knowledge and techniques as formulas for development and improvement. They also shared an unquestioning belief that conserving water and soil and maintaining their productivity required fundamentally changing rural people's relations to the land, whether they liked it or not. Concerns about geomancy and poor farmers' aversion to the risk that came with adopting untested cultivation techniques, in this view, were obstacles to progress. Joshua Nygren has written that conservation's advocates in the United States expressed a "technological optimism" that "considered technology—both physical equipment and associated practices—the key to conserving soil and soil moisture" and therefore sustaining agriculture.[88] Chinese conservation experts in the 1940s shared this belief. With technological optimism, in turn, came a marked tendency to see their technical solutions as panaceas that farmers needed to accept rather than tailoring conservation measures to meet local people's needs. The trained experts employed by the experiment area assumed that they alone should determine how to efficiently develop the land and its resources and that conservation required getting farmers to adopt the practices that they advocated. But the conservation schemes that scientific and technical elites had the most success enacting during the 1940s were those that aligned with the socioeconomic and environmental realities in Tianshui's countryside. Bunds, sweet clover, and black locust trees did not turn into treasures until they were accepted by the rural populace and woven into the fabric of rural society.

The Nationalist regime suffered defeat at the hands of the CCP in the Chinese Civil War (1946–49), but the Tianshui Water and Soil Conservation Experiment Area remained open after the government that founded it collapsed. Conservation specialists who had collaborated with Lowdermilk and served the Nationalists seamlessly shifted their allegiance to the

Communists and expanded the experiment area's research and extension programs with the newly founded PRC government's support. The PRC's adoption of plans to mitigate water and soil loss initially devised in Tianshui during World War II gave them significant and lasting results.[89] The CCP's programs of land reform and collectivization during the 1950s provided the organizational apparatus and mobilization techniques to implement water and soil conservation measures first formulated under the Nationalist regime on a far wider scale.

TWO

"Speak Bitterness to Floods"

Mobilization and Resistance in the Early 1950s

In 1949 the newly founded PRC regime took over the Tianshui Water and Soil Conservation Experiment Area. Despite several name changes, its efforts to remake rural people's interactions with the land continued unabated.[1] In the early 1950s, the scope of the experiment area's activities expanded from the small-scale experimental projects it had carried out under the wartime Nationalist government to more ambitious demonstration and extension programs that showed villagers in Gansu the importance of preserving water and soil and encouraged them to implement conservation measures. The same technical experts who had undertaken pilot conservation initiatives in the 1940s for the Nationalist government spearheaded efforts during the 1950s on behalf of the PRC. Even if the personnel remained largely the same, however, the context in China's countryside had profoundly changed. The CCP's land reform campaigns, undertaken between 1945 and 1952, had fatally weakened prerevolutionary local elites. Rural cadres, who were deeply enmeshed in local societies and, at the same time, had interests and identities closely tied to the new PRC regime, could be counted on to undertake tasks assigned to them by their party-state superiors. The CCP had a proven repertoire of mobilization strategies as well as agents on the ground that it could use to put water and soil conservation policies into effect.

In summer 1952, conservation expert Yan Wenguang traveled as part of a work team to Wushan County, about ninety-five kilometers west of Tianshui city, which was also part of Tianshui Prefecture. At the time, Wushan County had a population of approximately 180,000.[2] During the Mao era, as Elizabeth Perry points out, the CCP frequently used work teams as instruments of grassroots mobilization and policy implementation. Higher-level party-state organs appointed and directed these ad hoc units, which they dispatched for limited periods to advance a specific mission via mass mobilization.[3] The mission for Yan Wenguang's conservation work team, he later wrote, was to increase crop productivity and improve fields on inclined hills, thereby "creating prosperous and happy production conditions for the numerous people of the mountainous areas."[4] When Yan arrived in Wushan and explained the purpose of his visit to local authorities, Wushan's county head, Shen Manyuan, agreed about the county's suitability for conservation programs. They soon settled on Dengjiabao, a hillside village south of the Wei River in Wushan's Dongshun township, as the "key point" (*zhongdian*) for demonstration and extension.[5] In addition to the "representativeness" of Dengjiabao's erosion conditions, the work team selected the village because its proximity to Wushan's county seat and the railway line made it "convenient for leadership."[6] Adhering to what Sebastian Heilmann calls the CCP's "distinctive policymaking process" of disseminating model experiences drawn from local experimentation in particular settings for application in other jurisdictions, conservation experts and county officials wanted to see if the measures first tried out in the "point" of Dengjiabao could be extended to the "plane" of Wushan County.[7]

Several months after conservation efforts began in Wushan, PRC leaders confirmed water and soil conservation as a nationwide priority. In December 1952, on behalf of the PRC's government administrative council, Zhou Enlai issued a directive on "mobilizing the masses to continue to develop the campaign to defend against drought and resist drought, and vigorously carry out water and soil conservation work."[8] Stating that conservation of water and soil was of great urgency for controlling China's rivers and meeting the needs of agricultural production in mountainous areas, the directive identified several of the Yellow River's main tributaries, including the Wei River, as "key points" for conservation programs.[9]

As in other Mao-era campaigns, work teams and local leaders in Wushan County formed leadership groups and selected activists to implement the party-state's agenda.[10] Technical experts from the Tianshui experiment area, dubbed an "experiment station" in the 1950s, and officials in Wushan enlisted grassroots cadres and local activists to demonstrate the efficacy of water and soil conservation. However, cultivators displayed an aversion to adopting unproven techniques that might not yield favorable results. Concerned primarily with alleviating resource shortages and ensuring subsistence, local people doubted conservation's effectiveness, were uneasy about the amount of labor required, and suspected it would disrupt farming.

Villagers in Wushan deployed multiple vocabularies to articulate their resistance to water and soil conservation programs. Some criticized conservation in terms of religious and geomantic beliefs that questioned the human ability to transform the environment. Others couched their concerns that conservation might interfere with farming and decrease crop output in the PRC party-state agents' language of "production" (*shengchan*): propaganda asserted that conservation would increase agricultural production; skeptical villagers argued that conservation threatened it. Rural people appropriated hegemonic state vocabulary, which, in Gail Hershatter's words, they "wrenched out of its intended context and deployed in ways that would mock the intentions of state officials, even if unintentionally."[11]

County leaders and technical personnel who directed conservation during the early 1950s allayed some of these misgivings. Mutual-aid teams formed in Dengjiabao and elsewhere in Wushan presented tangible examples of conservation's benefits and carried out this work during slack farming periods to avoid interfering with farming. But even the most fastidious planning and organizational efforts could not alleviate environmental unpredictability. Drought led to harvest failures in summer 1953 and runoff from torrential rainstorms in summer 1954 burst dams built to manage gullies near Dengjiabao. The inability of conservation measures to prevent these catastrophes left villagers disillusioned with the party-state's calls to remake the land. Technical experts, county officials, and grassroots cadres had to convince rural citizens that conservation served their interests and persuade them to devote precious time and labor to it.

Conservation Comes to Dengjiabao

The village at the center of 1950s conservation programs in Wushan County, Dengjiabao, perches on a hillside directly south of the Wei River. Shortly after the founding of the PRC in 1949, the neighboring villages of Lijiaping, Majiashan, and Zhangjiabao combined with the "natural village" of Dengjiabao to form Dengjiabao administrative village. Denizens of the natural villages came from the same patrilineal descent groups. Those from Dengjiabao (Deng family fort), as its name suggests, had Deng as their family name. Villagers in Lijiaping (Li family plateau) had Li as their family name. Ma predominated in Majiashan (Ma family mountain), and Zhang was most common in Zhangjiabao (Zhang family fort).

In this chapter and those that follow, "Dengjiabao" refers to the larger administrative village unless otherwise noted. Dengjiabao had 91 households at the beginning of the 1950s and a total of population of 509 residents. It covered an area of 4.2 square kilometers, with about 2,200 *mu* (146.66 hectares) of cultivated fields. The elevation of the hillside village increased sharply from 1,540 meters at its lowest point to a height of 1,920 meters above sea level. Most fields had steep gradients of around 15 percent, but the incline on some farmland was well over 25 percent. Runoff from rainstorms, which fell mostly in summer, caused severe soil erosion on these slopes. By one estimate, the village's inclined fields lost about 16,300 cubic meters of surface soil annually.[12] As a popular saying in Dengjiabao went, "On the loess slopes, when rainstorms come, if they're light, they leave behind innumerable fine gullies, and if they're heavy, they wash away all three [things] (all the fertilizer, all the soil, and all the seeds); fields turn into roads and roads turn into gullies."[13] This erosion created the gullies and barren slopes that made up more than half of Dengjiabao's land area. Loss of water and soil also lowered crop yields. During the 1940s, output per *mu* in Dengjiabao varied from seventy to eighty *jin* (35–40 kg) per year at its highest and thirty to forty *jin* (15–20 kg) at its lowest. Most households lacked grain and other staple carbohydrates, like sweet potatoes, for three to four months a year. As a result, they had to make up for the shortfall by selling earthenware pots or doing short-term wage labor to earn money to purchase food from other areas.[14] Chronic erosion thus shaped both Dengjiabao's landscape and its residents' livelihoods.

These were the conditions that water and soil conservation aimed to ameliorate. In summer 1952, Yan Wenguang and his work team visited Dengjiabao and other nearby villages to, on the one hand, "learn from the masses" about their agricultural experience and, on the other, "organize and mobilize the masses" by explaining the intimate relationship between water and soil conservation and agricultural production.[15] Along with county head Shen Manyuan and a villager named Deng Madou, Yan oversaw construction of the same contour bunds (small ridges) that he had promoted in Tianshui during the 1940s as a demonstration project.[16] When I interviewed a man in

FIGURE 7. Villagers in fields with bunds along their edges. Chen and Ren, "Shui bu xia yuan, ni bu chu gou."

his eighties who was once Dengjiabao's local party secretary, he remembered Deng Madou as the pioneer of water and soil conservation in the village: "At that time ... our village had Grandpa Ma (*Ma yeye*). He was called Deng Madou. He made bunds on his parcel of steeply inclined land in the gully. This was the earliest beginning of water and soil conservation."[17] The productivity of Deng Madou's land increased after building the bunds, and cadres and villagers from Dongshun, Nanyu, and Yanchi—three of Wushan's more than forty townships—later came to Dengjiabao to view the measures that had brought about this improvement (fig 7).[18] In addition to persuading people to adopt similar techniques, touring Deng Madou's fields gave them a chance to see how it was done. Fostering local exemplars thus helped state agents make conservation meaningful to villagers.

Unfortunately for Yan Wenguang's work team and Wushan's county authorities, however, extension efforts in Dengjiabao initially garnered little support from grassroots cadres. As Yan wrote, conserving water and soil was a "new kind of work" that consisted mainly of constructing bunds, building terraces, and digging level trenches and water cellars. At first, local cadres did not understand what the unfamiliar term *water and soil conservation* meant, so they were "afraid that they could not grasp it and that it would not be easy to lead the masses." Cadres also feared that villagers would not accept conservation programs.[19] Their trepidation made them less willing to take the lead in organizing others.

Ordinary villagers had even greater misgivings, mostly related to water and soil conservation's potential effects on cultivation. As Yan put it, "some were afraid that building bunds and digging level trenches would occupy farmland; some were afraid that soil was too dry to build them well and that the work would be done for nothing."[20] People worried that the sediment that accumulated in trenches would destroy seedlings; some thought that covering fertile topsoil with subsurface virgin soil when digging up earth to build bunds would hamper crop growth, so conservation was "doing work in vain to serve no real purpose."[21] Many people insisted they were too busy with farmwork; others anticipated that runoff would wash away the bunds, so building them was pointless.[22]

Relations between local cadres charged with implementing conservation measures and other villagers grew tense. A county government report on the development of conservation work in Dengjiabao related that some villagers criticized cadres by saying, "For decades we didn't do water and soil conservation and managed just the same. You must have full bellies and nothing better to do to fuck with this shit (*cao de zhe gui*)." When cadres told other villagers that conservation could increase yields, they shot back that digging up the land would ruin it rather than increasing production. Other villagers objected to conservation programs because, in their words, "It's clearly doing useless work and making things look good for the government under the name of increasing production. Who'd do that?"[23] As another report noted, people in Dengjiabao initially believed that building bunds, digging trenches, and constructing terraces occupied land, did not aid production, and squandered labor. Conservation amounted to "keeping up appearances for the government."[24] Overall, Yan Wenguang observed that villagers "did not have interest or confidence in water and soil conservation work."[25] Consequently, according to another account, "the mood of unwillingness to build terraces was quite great."[26] This resistance resulted not from ignorance or innate conservatism, but from genuine anxieties about the effects of conservation techniques on land, labor, and livelihoods.

In response, Wushan's county leaders convened meetings with cadres from Dongshun, Nanyu, and Yanchi townships to, as Yan recalled, make them recognize that conservation's goal was to develop agricultural production and that it was "intimately related to peasants' immediate interests."[27] Regardless of whether township-level cadres found these arguments persuasive, the meeting signaled that their superiors considered conservation a high priority, so they needed to take it seriously. Once local cadres had come around, they conducted propaganda and education "to arouse the masses' recognition of water and soil conservation and used concrete and vivid local examples related to water and soil conservation to eliminate the masses' ideological misgivings."[28] The assumption was that if people understood that conservation did not pose a risk but could increase yields and improve their livelihoods, they would willingly take part. Local state agents had to convincingly make that case.

County officials and technical experts took responsibility for overseeing mobilization. In explaining how villagers' reservations and misgivings were overcome, a draft report from Wushan County on conservation efforts in Dengjiabao stated that "leaders personally got to work: In 1952, when it started, county head Shen Manyuan personally went into the fields to build earthen bunds."[29] Shen also visited villages to encourage the planting of sweet clover.[30] Technical personnel who came to Wushan from Tianshui as part of the conservation work team also offered guidance and assistance. In December 1953, technical experts from the Tianshui experiment station drew up a five-year plan for water and soil conservation in Dengjiabao (map 5). A conservation expert named Wang Zhiguo played a particularly active role: he and other experiment station personnel "often personally went to the fields to provide technical direction in building bunds and terraces and personally showed how it was done, which attracted all the village cadres to engage in study."[31] Wang moved to Dengjiabao for a time, helped villagers

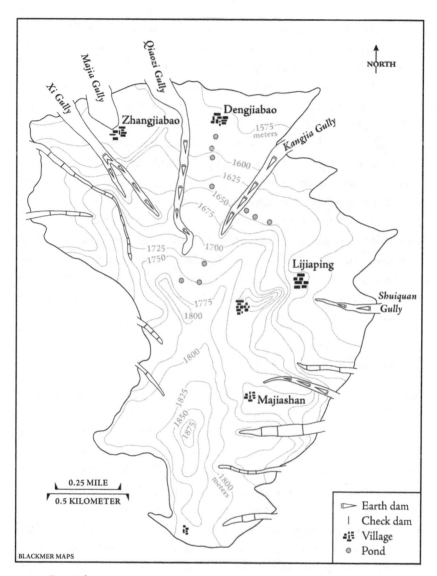

MAP 5. Dengjiabao

with farmwork, and discussed conservation with them in the evenings.[32] As the former party secretary in Dengjiabao recalled when I spoke with him, "Wang Zhiguo was a [water and soil conservation] cadre but his hands had more callouses than a peasant."[33] Technical experts did more than spout theory—they went into the fields with villagers and got their hands dirty. By living and working alongside local people, outside experts gained their trust and mediated between the party-state and grassroots society.

Formal training classes also taught cadres and officials about conservation techniques. In autumn 1953, over one hundred county, district, and township cadres from Wushan attended training classes put on by Tianshui Prefecture. In 1954 more than two hundred local "technicians" (*jishuyuan*) from Wushan underwent similar training, learning to build bunds and dig trenches so they could disseminate these techniques to their fellow villagers.[34] Along with technical experts deputed by higher-level agencies, newly trained local personnel sought to educate other villagers, overcome their trepidation, and convince them to take part.

Mobilizing Mutual-Aid Teams

The scale of conservation programs grew during the early 1950s alongside the social transformations that swept China's countryside. Before 1949, households in Wushan had implemented conservation practices like terracing in an isolated manner. The CCP's land reform campaign created the conditions to make conservation more widespread. From August 1951 to May 1952, land reform work teams in Wushan confiscated land, draft animals, and farm tools from landlords who did not farm (but lived off rents) and redistributed them to poor peasants, middle peasants, and hired laborers.[35] Once land reform had eliminated large landowners like those who had opposed water and soil conservation initiatives in Tianshui in the 1940s, local agents of the party-state had an easier time carrying out environmental projects.

Beginning in summer 1952, townships and villages in Wushan assigned a specified number of cadres to undertake conservation work via mutual-aid teams that were formed throughout China's countryside after land reform as the first step toward agricultural collectivization.[36] These groups regularized forms of mutual assistance that had long existed among relatives and neighbors in village communities, placing them under the supervision of team leaders who often shared kinship ties with other members. The members of mutual-aid teams voluntarily assisted each other with planting and harvesting. Households did not have to pay other team members if they exchanged equal amounts of labor. If the members of one household did less work than others, they had to compensate those who had assisted them. However, mutual-aid teams did not alter property rights: each household kept its crops and retained ownership of its land, farm tools, and livestock.[37]

A report on the development of water and soil conservation in Dengjiabao argued that mutual-aid teams encouraged conservation in several ways. First, "mutual aid and cooperation" made it possible to combine conservation with farming and allocate time and labor so that conservation did not adversely influence agricultural cultivation. Second, forming mutual-aid teams made it easier to instruct people about conservation techniques. Third, as the report put it, "only by organizing the peasantry is it possible to engage in planned intensive cultivation, increase grain output, and consolidate the confidence of the masses in developing water and soil conservation work."[38] A document outlining arrangements for conservation work in Wushan during the latter half of 1954 likewise explained, "Water and soil conservation is long-term work that requires a lot of labor. Individual peasants have great difficulty [with it]. Mutual-aid teams are a little bit better. Cooperatives would be even more advantageous for carrying it out."[39] Successfully conserving water and soil would increase production and income, thus strengthening mutual-aid teams. As a result, mutual-aid teams lent impetus to conservation and the development of conservation promoted mutual-aid and cooperation.[40] The two campaigns reinforced each other.

Wushan County leaders groomed three activists from Dengjiabao's two year-round mutual-aid teams—Deng Haihai, Deng Qingyi, and Deng Junjie—to demonstrate conservation techniques to villagers. All three men had attended the earlier meeting of cadres from Dongshun, Nanyu, and Yanchi townships.[41] Deng Haihai, a middle peasant and candidate for CCP membership who later joined the party, led a mutual-aid team and was head of Dengjiabao's peasant association (fig. 8).[42] Deng Haihai sought to drum up enthusiasm for conservation by imbuing it with revolutionary and geopolitical significance. Invoking the Resist America Aid Korea Campaign

FIGURE 8. Deng Haihai (right) and personnel from the Tianshui Water and Soil Conservation Experiment Station inspecting hemp planted on slopes in Dengjiabao. Gansu sheng shuiliting, *Jianshe shanqu de bangyang*.

(1950–53) that the CCP launched to maintain revolutionary momentum and consolidate its authority after China's entry to the Korean War, Deng Haihai told villagers that "to defend the fruits of victory from land reform, protect the motherland, and resist America and aid Korea, we have to do water and soil conservation well." Not only would conservation benefit villagers by increasing crop yields, but it would also, he argued, protect the railroad below the village against washouts, support industrial production, and "defend the motherland."[43] The thrust of these pronouncements was that conservation served the long-term interests of both rural households and the Chinese nation.

Deng Haihai and Dengjiabao's other local cadres and activists convinced a mutual-aid team member named Deng Junfu to build bunds on four *mu*

(0.26 hectare) of his land. After initially agreeing, Deng Junfu changed his mind and backed out, so conservation expert Wang Zhiguo brought in twenty young people who constructed bunds and trenches on two *mu* (0.13 hectare) of Deng Junfu's land to demonstrate the techniques. The next day, Deng Junfu's father scolded him, saying, "We didn't have anyone die—who're they digging this to bury?"[44] Trenches and embankments looked too much like graves for the old man's liking, so he insisted on filling in the inauspicious ditches. Unshaken, Deng Haihai instructed other team members to build bunds on their land and had cadres show them that the structures did not waste labor, were sturdy, and did not occupy too much farmland.[45] After the Wushan County government began its conservation efforts, according to a record of Deng Haihai's accomplishments, he built bunds and dug trenches on his steeply inclined land to check erosion and limit water and soil loss. Six days after he finished, heavy rains fell and no erosion took place, so "he further recognized that water and soil conservation could transform nature and increase grain production."[46] Deng Zicheng and Deng Hanjie dug trenches on their land as well. When runoff from heavy rains did not create any erosion rills in their fields, all the village's residents—even Deng Junfu's obstinate father—added bunds and trenches to their land.[47]

The example of these activists persuaded their fellow villagers to adopt other conservation methods as well. When the county government advocated planting sweet potatoes on small ridges with pits between them (a technique known as ridge tillage) to hold water and prevent runoff, most people rejected the idea, saying that it would require a lot of work, seeds were too scarce, and the sweet potatoes might not grow well. Skeptics maintained that their land was either too steep or too flat for ridge tillage to be worthwhile. To assuage their concerns, Deng Haihai's mutual-aid team planted sweet potatoes on a plot of inclined land using ridge tillage and gathered mutual-aid team leaders and other residents to observe. The demonstration won most of them over. That said, reports from a work team sent to Dengjiabao acknowledged that a few team members "still feared that seeds were scarce, there would be few potatoes, and it would require a lot of work."[48] Although Deng Haihai had persuaded some of his fellow villagers, misgivings persisted.

Furthermore, although planting sweet clover had gained popularity in Tianshui during the 1940s (see chapter 1), Wushan's residents had mixed reactions to its cultivation. When Wushan's county government directed cadres to conduct propaganda about sweet clover's advantages, some villagers welcomed the plant as a means of alleviating fuel shortages. In Wushan's Tianqu township, villagers were enthusiastic about sweet clover, remarking, "We lack fuel here so it's just right—it's great."[49] However, because they had never planted sweet clover before, most villagers in Wushan worried that introducing the plant would decrease yields of other crops. Some local cadres opted to wait and see what happened when others planted it. Although the government distributed large amounts of sweet clover seed in Wushan, a report on conservation work in the county from March 1954 noted that many people had returned the seeds or never bothered to plant them. Some villagers had assumed they could eat sweet clover like a vegetable, but when the sweet clover planted in 1953 sprouted, they found out that it tasted bitter, so they dug it up. Other reports indicated that people did not consider sweet clover's usefulness in replenishing soil nutrients, so they harbored an attitude of "half belief and half disbelief."[50] Soon after, cadres in Dengjiabao arranged for mutual-aid teams to plant sweet clover and invited other villagers to observe the results. When Deng Haihai planted sweet clover on two *mu* (0.13 hectare) of land, he obtained enough fodder to feed an ox for six months, convincing twenty-five households in Dengjiabao to plant five hundred *jin* (250 kg) of sweet clover seeds.[51]

In a speech given several years later, a Communist Youth League member named Li Xuding recalled that because villagers had never planted sweet clover before, they had misgivings when the government first called on people to cultivate it. "Some said: 'On land this poor, if you plant grain, you can only harvest a little. Who wants to plant grass as well?!' Some said: 'On our dry mountains and bare slopes, dew doesn't even stay put. How can sweet clover grow?'" Li also worried about how others might respond if the sweet clover he planted did not grow. But then a cadre said to him, "Xuding! Planting sweet clover can not only improve the soil and conserve water and soil, but it also has many [other] benefits. If our league members don't take the lead in responding to the party's call, who can be depended upon to do it?" Acting on this advice, Li planted sweet clover on a small plot of land that he attentively watered and weeded. Other people in the village followed his example, as Li informed his audience, planting sweet clover on more than fifty *mu* (3.33 hectares). This yielded a harvest of more than two thousand *jin* (1,000 kg) of clover plants, which provided local households with badly needed livestock fodder and fuel for cooking and heating. This favorable outcome persuaded everyone in Dengjiabao, and Li boasted that "the mountains and plains are green; the barren slopes of the past have become the world of sweet clover."[52]

In addition to demonstrating conservation's benefits, cadres and officials tried to engage villagers with propaganda that framed conservation in terms of their tangible life experiences, stressing the threat of floods and the importance of controlling them. Pointing to the frequency and destructiveness of flooding in Dengjiabao, where runoff from seasonal rainstorms turned roads into gullies, erosion caused subsidence in fields, and deluges sometimes killed livestock, cadres urged people to "speak bitterness to floods" (*xiang hongshui suku*). This rhetoric sought to move villagers to struggle against floodwaters the way they had struggled against landlords by speaking bitterness—denouncing their exploitative misdeeds—during land reform campaigns. Cadres warned villagers that the alternative was dire: "If we don't actively do water and soil conservation, after ten years we won't even be able to preserve the village." To further illustrate their point, cadres also called attention to the contrast between villagers who improved their land by conserving water and soil and those whose land still suffered from erosion and low productivity.[53]

Eventually, as conservation expert Yan Wenguang put it, the propaganda "broke through the masses' misgivings and they shifted from having an attitude of suspicion toward water and soil conservation to taking an interest in it."[54] In Yan's telling, demonstration and education gradually overcame the aversion that villagers had toward taking the risk of adopting untested methods. But other sources show that many obstacles remained.

Land reform had redistributed the property of landlords, but it had not targeted middle peasants who owned some land and engaged in farming or rich peasants who hired labor or rented out a portion of their land. As a result, land reform did not eliminate inequalities among villagers. With access to more or better land, labor power, and draft animals, some households remained better-off than others.[55] The middle peasants among the nine households in the Deng Daisheng mutual-aid team, who had many workers and livestock, suspected that poorer households in the team would not properly repay them for their services during the spring plowing. Better-off households, who typically had more human and animal labor power than poorer ones, wondered why they should do a day's work on someone else's land if they got less in return. Middle peasants responded by excluding poor peasants from mutual-aid arrangements to avoid having to subsidize households with fewer resources. As a result, middle peasants from the Deng Daisheng mutual-aid team worked only with middle peasants, and poor peasants worked with poor peasants. To mend these divisions and ensure fair compensation among members, the mutual-aid team enacted a "democratic management system" that rationally evaluated and recorded work and unified the allocation of labor and livestock.[56]

Other teams struggled as well. The Li Wanfu mutual-aid team, for instance, settled accounts to determine who owed what to whom only once between the planting of the sweet potato crop and the summer harvest. As a result, team members often ended up doing work for others without repayment. A peasant named Li Jincai, whose household had lots of labor power, "got the worst of it" and became unwilling to work for others because he was inadequately compensated.[57] For two days, Li Jincai and a man named Li Baoxu left the team and worked by themselves. The team had also set the value of a workday too low (four *jiao* when the summer harvest started) and did not evaluate work in a way that reflected the relative difficulty or urgency of different tasks. For instance, the first half of the day earned the same amount as the less arduous second half of the day. To keep other households from exiting the mutual-aid team, team leaders settled accounts more regularly to determine how much each member was owed, increased the value of a workday to five *jiao*, and counted the first half of the day as 60 percent of the workday and the latter half of the day as 40 percent.[58] Reconciling the interests of mutual-aid team members thus necessitated careful calibration of the value assigned to particular types of work.

Using the Gaps

Even when mutual-aid teams convinced their members that they would get fair compensation for their labor, grassroots cadres had to balance conservation with farming. Indeed, villagers' main reservations about conservation work centered on its potentially adverse impact on agricultural production. People were already busy farming, so they feared that if they devoted time and labor to water and soil conservation it would "delay cultivation." Some villagers claimed that when individual households had done conservation work in the past "it required great exertions but yielded few benefits."[59] Cadres thus had to ensure that conservation did not interfere with farming, and that it was "carried out in combination with the masses' immediate interests and with production."[60]

Attaining that goal meant carefully aligning work schedules. One of the most important times of year for doing conservation work came in early autumn, just after the summer harvest. At that point, villagers had harvested the summer wheat crop, much of the land lay fallow, and the relatively high levels of precipitation made the soil moist and well-suited for building bunds.[61] But people still had to tend fallow land, plow fields that would be sown with new crops, and do other farmwork. So as not to interfere with these tasks, cadres instructed mutual-aid teams to use mornings for farmwork and afternoons to build bunds and terraces or to plant trees. Another arrangement was for teams to send some of their members to till land in the morning while the rest worked on conservation projects. If rainfall made fields too wet to plow, everyone built bunds and terraces while the moist earth was easy to dig. Once the soil got too dry, teams switched to digging trenches and ponds.[62] When November arrived and the sun's rays weakened, bunds would not dry properly, and once the ground froze in winter they could easily collapse.[63] This made it imperative to finish building them in early autumn.

Later reports characterized the arrangements devised to attend to conservation work in autumn 1952 as "utilizing spare time during the gaps in agricultural production and after it rained, paying attention to combining work and rest." Villagers had previously taken a well-deserved break or done sideline production during the slack farming season; now they used this time "to carry out maintenance, do composting, and organize tools to lay the foundation for agricultural production. At the same time, they conserve water and soil and keep it from being lost." Official reports make no mention of the income that villagers lost by foregoing sideline production.

Conservation work was carried out according to a formula: "Grasp the slack agricultural season, utilize gaps in agricultural production, don't violate the farming season, and carry out assaults after it rains."[64] To avoid hampering crop growth, care was taken to set aside fertile topsoil and return it to the original location after bunds were built.[65]

Encouraged by cadres and officials, Yan Wenguang recalled that in autumn 1952 a "mass fervor" for building bunds and terraces emerged in Wushan County, with different townships competing to outdo one another. By late October 1952, residents had constructed bunds and terraces on 93.4 percent of the fields in the key-point township of Dongshun, where Dengjiabao was located, and on 44.8 percent of all the farmland in Dongshun, Nanyu, and Yanchi townships.[66] Inspection teams ensured the quality of the work by making the rounds to offer praise and criticism.[67] Dengjiabao organized four mutual-aid teams that completed bunds in three hundred *mu* (20 hectares) of fields that autumn.[68] Villagers in Dongshun, Nanyu, and Yanchi townships also planted walnut, almond, and willow trees, dug trenches and ponds to capture runoff, repaired collapses, and planted sweet clover.[69]

Given the shortages of biomass caused by long-term deforestation in Gansu, however, people's desperate need for fuel often outweighed concerns about conserving water and soil. Villagers throughout Wushan cut grass, dug up roots, and burned charcoal for fuel in upland areas. Stripping vegetation from hillsides alleviated fuel shortages but accelerated erosion.[70] At the same time, villagers in certain locales gathered medicinal plants like ephedra (*mahuang, Ephedra sinica*) and Chinese licorice (*gancao, Glycyrrhiza uralensis*) as a sideline employment instead of taking the time to maintain bunds, which jeopardized their integrity. Flooding washed out some bunds constructed in 1953, and those built using loose earth collapsed.[71] Conservation experts and local cadres passed along technical instructions to mutual-aid teams, but poor conception and execution limited effectiveness. Designs were not always appropriate for local conditions, and projects often suffered from shoddy work. As a result, they failed to preserve water and soil and sometimes even caused agricultural output to decrease.[72] Yet nature itself soon did even greater damage.

Drought and Disillusionment

During the spring and summer of 1953, drought struck Wushan. Water and soil conservation work made no progress for the first half of the year and "the mood of the masses was rather lax." Poorly implemented conservation measures only made things worse. In the previous year, some residents had dug trenches too deep and left infertile virgin soil on the surface. Lack of rainfall and loss of fertile topsoil had hampered crop growth, which angered villagers.[73] County authorities feared that more sinister opposition lurked in the background. The summary of a meeting of Wushan's labor models and mutual-aid team leaders in February 1954 warned that "landlord elements, counter-revolutionary elements, and sorcerers" (*wushen*) were relying on "the superstitious thought of the backward masses to manipulate a portion of the backward masses to carry out sabotage activities." During the drought in spring and summer 1953, the report warned, the phenomenon of "cursing the government" had emerged in some places, which "was unconsciously serving landlord elements and counter-revolutionary elements." County leaders called on everyone to heighten their alertness so as not to be taken in by these "bad elements."[74] Although the meeting summary does not offer specifics, it clearly indicates that at least some villagers did not accept the methods of transforming the environment that local agents of the party-state advocated.

Other sources suggest that popular religion inspired outright resistance toward water and soil conservation schemes. As one resident of Wushan's Zhaoping Township declared, "Heaven making the waters surge is all prescribed by Old Man Heaven (*tianye*). People can't do anything about it. Whoever wants to do [water and soil conservation work] can go do it. I'm not going. I'm not willing [to do it] and they can deal with me according to the law." From this perspective, divine entities created floods, and human attempts to use conservation or any other means to prevent them were futile. Reports also claimed that elderly people with some education expressed their incredulity about conservation by citing a famous passage from *Biographies of the Deities and Immortals* (Shenxian zhuan) by the classical writer Ge Hong (283–343 or 346): "The sages say the sea turns into mulberry fields and mulberry fields turn into the sea; high banks turn into valleys and deep valleys turn into steep hills. That's the cycle of heaven and earth." Environmental transformation, in short, unfolded according to cyclical patterns that humans could not alter. Geomancy also inspired apprehension about efforts to alter the landscape. People throughout China believed that invisible subterranean channels called earth veins (*dimai*) directed flows of energy or aether (*qi*) through the land; disrupting them could have negative effects.[75] When asked to do conservation work on the "main mountain" near a village in Wushan, residents complained, "If we dig, it will move the dragon's head and the vein's aether (*maiqi*) will go away."[76] Altering the topography of the hills, in other words, would disrupt the flow of auspicious energies through the local environment. These geomantic understandings cast conservation as futile and even harmful.

To allay the disillusionment that the drought caused in summer 1953 and prevent villagers from turning to religion as a solution, Dengjiabao's conservation work team conducted propaganda via mutual-aid teams to reassure villagers that conservation would do no harm and could increase crop production. The work team identified cultivators who successfully increased productivity by building bunds and organized observational visits to Dengjiabao attended by five hundred cadres and other residents to publicize their accomplishments. At the same time, Wushan County celebrated activists like Deng Haihai and Deng Hanjie, both of whom received awards as labor models. These local exemplars then called on others to lend their support. As Deng Haihai told his fellow villagers, "Building bunds and digging trenches can increase grain yields and it's work that we farmers should do. Before, we didn't understand what water and soil conservation was. Now the Communist Party has sent cadres to work for us. If we don't engage in production well, how can we be worthy of the Communist Party and Chairman Mao?" Once people learned about conservation's significance, as Deng Haihai stressed, they had a duty to put it into practice.[77] Eventually, this mobilization had the desired result. Later investigations found that the administrative village of Dengjiabao (which included Dengjiabao, Lijiaping, Zhangjiabao, and Majiashan natural villages) built bunds on three hundred *mu* (20 hectares) of land in 1952; in 1953 it had already built them on two thousand *mu* (133.33 hectares).[78]

Propaganda aside, villagers took part in water and soil conservation work in 1953 largely because it had helped to improve yields, as promised. Annual per capita production of grain and other staple carbohydrates in Dengjiabao increased from 188.5 kilograms in 1952 to 244.25 kilograms in 1953.[79] Villagers still battled hunger, to be sure.[80] But increasing agricultural production convinced more villagers to implement conservation measures and join the mutual-aid teams that were promoting them.

When the Dams Break

Focusing solely on production statistics, however, overlooks the setbacks and readjustments that conservation efforts underwent. Once they had built bunds beside fields to conserve water and soil, mutual-aid teams turned to gully management. Five large gullies cut through the landscape around Dengjiabao: Majia Gully (Majiagou) and Xi Gully (Xigou) to the west, Shuiquan Gully (Shuiquangou) to the east, and Kangjia Gully (Kangjiagou) and Qiaozi Gully (Qiaozigou) in the middle. The gullies covered 2,500 *mu* (166.66 hectares) of inclined land, 80 percent of which was cultivated.[81] In the early 1920s, as elderly villagers explained, Qiaozi Gully was less than seventeen meters wide and ten meters deep, with a path running through it. A decade later, torrential summer rains had collapsed most of the farmland on either side of the gully. The gully widened and deepened, destroying the path. By 1953, Qiaozi Gully had a width of over thirty-three meters in its widest section and a depth of about twenty-five meters at its deepest. Most rainfall created only a small flow of water at the gully's head, but runoff expanded and accelerated farther downstream. Locals related that the floodwaters from one torrential rainstorm had washed a mule from Dengjiabao all the way to the gully's mouth.[82]

When conservation efforts began in summer 1952, villagers started making small mounds of earth (*tudang*) in the gullies to slow runoff, reduce erosion, and retain silt. In 1953 they built more than twenty earth dams next to the paths that ran through Dengjiabao's fields, demonstrating that dams could impede runoff from hillsides and conserve water and soil.[83] Later that same year, villagers built 133 more dams near the heads of Kangjia Gully and Qiaozi Gully.[84] In 1954 the Tianshui prefectural commissioner's office called for additional tree planting, grass planting, and dam building in gullies near Dengjiabao to address the populace's critical fuel and fodder needs and promote comprehensive development of agriculture, water control, forestry, and animal husbandry. To that end, seven cadres from Tianshui Prefecture's agriculture, water and soil conservation, and forestry stations formed a Dengjiabao Agriculture, Water Conservancy, Forestry, and Animal Husbandry Key Point Work Team, which arrived in the village in early March and disseminated slogans related to gully management.[85]

Propaganda again focused on concrete local examples to assuage local people's concerns about conservation's risks and illustrate its practical benefits. Meetings that the key point work team held with grassroots cadres and other Dengjiabao residents stressed that gully expansion was an "inevitable trend" that only conservation programs could contend with. To illustrate, the key point work team pointed to a popular local saying: "When a person is small the gully is shallow; when a person is old the gully is deep." Building on people's awareness of gully expansion and the harm it did to crop production, the work team convinced villagers to "actively undertake operations." The Tianshui experiment station's propaganda about the benefits of gully management, according to a work team report, had also "heightened the confidence of the masses and set off a great mass fervor."[86] In March 1954, the key point work team made plans to plant trees and grasses and build more dams in Kangjia Gully, Qiaozi Gully, and Majia Gully.[87] Mass meetings encouraged villagers to use the slack farming season to concentrate labor power for afforestation, grass planting, and building dams at the gully heads. Management of other gullies would start during the slack season in autumn.[88]

As before, mutual-aid teams composed of villagers who voluntarily pooled their labor provided the organizational foundation for conservation work. The administrative village of Dengjiabao claimed thirteen mutual-aid teams in 1954, with a membership of 263 men and 247 women.[89] Following several mobilization meetings, the teams divided the gullies around Dengjiabao into sections. Each team planted trees and grasses in a designated area, adhering to the principle that "the team plants, the team protects, and the team benefits." Mutual-aid teams allocated benefits derived from the trees and sweet clover they planted to members based on how much land and labor they contributed. Teams compensated members for any farmland that planting vegetation and building dams removed from cultivation.[90] Starting from uncultivated land where management measures could be most easily applied, the key point work team advised mutual-aid team leaders to "bring around the ideology of households who own steeply inclined land in gullies on which crops are not grown and enter the land as shares."[91] A parcel of 0.4 *mu* (0.026 hectares) of privately owned "mature wasteland" next to a gully counted as one share for compensation.[92]

Workdays earned payment as well. Labor remuneration for gully management work employed the "dead points, living appraisal method" (*sifen huoping de banfa*).[93] Used throughout China, this system called for mutual-aid teams to engage in "democratic assessment" to decide on a fixed (i.e., "dead") number of points per workday for each member depending on their skill and productivity. Once the mutual-aid team determined a standard number of points per day for each member, that figure served as the basis for appraising their *actual* (i.e., "living") work points, which could vary from day to day. Each evening, the team conducted evaluations and added or deducted points from each member's standard daily work points depending on the quantity and quality of their work for the day.[94] This method allowed teams to assess and record work points "based on strength and weakness of labor power and superiority and inferiority of techniques," implementing "the principle that those who labor a lot receive a lot."[95] This system of distributing benefits based on the amount of labor and land contributed gave team members an incentive to carry out conservation work.

To ensure that trees and grasses took root, mutual-aid team leaders, cadres, and activists taught other team members proper planting techniques.[96] Gully management had a prescribed sequence: first male team members excavated earth and built dams, then men and women planted trees, and finally women planted sweet clover.[97] A total of 193 people from Dengjiabao, 125 men and 68 women, mobilized in spring 1954 to plant saplings and sow sweet clover.[98] The key point work team estimated that it would take ten days (from March 25 to April 5) to finish managing the gully. But efficiency and enthusiasm increased because, as the work team reported, "a rational division of labor between men and women was carried out (men first dug pits, then women planted trees and planted sweet clover), and competitions were launched that greatly brought labor activism into play," so the project took only five days.[99]

FIGURE 9. Earth dam construction in Dengjiabao, April 17, 1954. Gansu sheng shuiliting, *Jianshe shanqu de bangyang*.

Li Xuding recounted that when the CCP called on the people of Dengjiabao to build dams in gullies in 1954, his own mutual-aid team and the Li Wanfu team shared responsibility for managing the lower half of Kangjia Gully. When team members balked at working on the lower half of the gully, which had red sandy soil that made it difficult to manage, Li Xuding encouraged them by saying, "Things are done by humans and difficulties are also overcome by humans. If we work hard and sweat, no matter how great the difficulty, it will give way to us." Since the gully bottom did not have any soil in it, team members had to walk halfway up the mountain to get earth for building the dam and carry it down on their backs. When one person grew tired, another took over.[100]

Work plans also sought to ensure that diverting labor to building dams did not interfere with farming. According to the key point work team's 1954 summary report on gully management, the earth dam project started right when spring plowing was at its busiest.[101] As a result, cadres and mutual-aid team leaders had to wait to build dams until after it rained, "when there was a gap in farming." This timing avoided delays in crop cultivation and made it possible to build sturdier dams using wet soil (fig. 9). As it happened, large amounts of rain fell in 1954, so mutual-aid teams "used eight slack farming periods after it rained" to build 254 earth dams. When building the dams, villagers first filled in a layer of earth about one-third of a meter thick and used their feet to tamp it down. After adding more layers and tamping them down as well, people used shovels to tamp down the dam's inner and outer slopes. Finally, they planted sweet clover or other grasses on the top and sides of the dam to strengthen it.

After afforestation, grass planting, and dam building work was finished, the key point work team convened a discussion meeting with mutual-aid team leaders, local cadres, and several "experienced old peasants" to discuss the results. Those in attendance believed that the dams were properly designed and gully management was sure to be effective. The work team boasted, "Dams have been built all over the gullies, with each connecting to another and several small ones linking into a big one. The bottom of the gullies and their two sides have been planted with trees and planted with grasses. Three years from now, trees will have grown, and they will guarantee that rainwater is retained in the gullies section by section, and it will not flow out anymore." Attendees likewise reported that bunds kept rainwater in fields, so no runoff occurred. Local activist Deng Junjie did not miss the chance to drive home conservation's political significance: "Doing it this way makes the gullies look good. The words that Chairman Mao says are all to do things for the people. From now on, whatever he says, that's what we'll do." The visual appearance of gullies filled with rows of dams and trees, as Deng Junjie's words made evident, symbolized the transformation of nature through collective labor and affirmed the legitimacy of the PRC and its leader.

Beyond this political message, the meeting called attention to several concrete advantages of managing gullies. Water from summer downpours no longer ran down slopes, so runoff did not wash away soil. The soil also absorbed moisture more effectively, which increased drought resistance. After heavy rains, silt-laden water did not flow out of gullies, so floods would no longer threaten the flatlands below, damage nearby railroad lines, or silt up the river. When trees grew larger and sweet clover stalks matured, they provided sources of fuel. Villagers could cut sweet clover and other grasses as fodder for livestock as well. Once they had sufficient kindling, people could use livestock manure as fertilizer instead of burning it. Villagers could also apply sweet clover as crop dressing and turn it over into the soil as green fertilizer to add organic matter and nutrients. Finally, the silt-laden runoff deposited in the dams would become a convenient source of water for livestock, and residents could cultivate sediment deposits retained in the dams when water receded.

Despite the meeting's generally positive tone, however, participants also pointed out deficiencies. Mutual-aid team members used their feet to tamp down earth, so the dams were weaker than if they had used tampers. Villagers had not capped the joints where dams and gully walls came together, which made them less stable. Plans for planting trees and grasses had not taken livestock grazing into account: when mutual-aid teams planted trees on uncultivated land at gully heads and on slopes, other villagers complained that "planting trees is good, but the oxen and sheep don't have any paths to walk on." Finally, mutual-aid teams had not come up with a consistent method of evaluating work, recording shares, and distributing benefits. Some teams assessed the labor devoted to planting trees and grasses as shares, but not the work done building dams; others recorded all types of labor. This lack of consistency led to grievances among team members.

But these problems paled in comparison to the disaster that occurred shortly thereafter. During the summer and autumn of 1954, runoff from torrential rainstorms damaged or washed away 90 percent of the dams built in Dengjiabao and leaked through many bunds and terraces. Floods knocked over millet in fields and uprooted sweet potato crops. Erosion rills formed in fallow land; torrents cut off roads and the sediment they carried clogged springs.[102] Despite the confidence expressed at earlier meetings, conservation infrastructure had not withstood heavy seasonal precipitation. As a result, reports admitted, "The mood of masses was low for a time and complaints sprang up all over, [such as]: 'The government says water and soil conservation's important, but now we've done this work for nothing. The crops have been washed away and our lives are all in critical [condition]. [You] always have to rely on heaven to eat.' Some villagers grew pessimistic and disappointed, sobbing and sighing."[103] The disaster affirmed perceptions rooted in popular religion that questioned humanity's ability to master the environment. If dams could not withstand rainstorms, people believed conservation was futile.

Li Xuding later recounted that after a round of heavy rains washed out dams, some people remarked, "This is [like] Qin Shihuang [259–10 BCE] building the Great Wall, abusing people for nothing! Earth dams can't even stop floodwaters!" Li and other team leaders found that dams had washed out because they did not meet technical standards: they were built on an unstable foundation of sandy soil, had no water outlet channels, and were not built with the proper incline. Having learned this lesson, mutual-aid teams mobilized to rebuild the collapsed dams. "Not long after we started work," Li related, "Heaven seemed to be testing us on purpose. There was another heavy rainstorm, and the newly rebuilt dam broke again. This time, some people lost confidence, some just shook their heads without speaking; some just sighed and said, 'It's finished, it's finished, this time it's all finished.'"[104] In Li Xuding's account, repairing the dams was a clash between the heaven-sent forces of nature and the power of human will.

To confront this morale crisis, the head of Wushan County's construction section (*jianshe kezhang*) went to Dengjiabao to meet with local cadres and other residents. He explained "the great significance of struggling resolutely against various kinds of natural disasters" and reassured local people that such extreme catastrophes only occurred once in a long period of time. Cadres also stressed that the recent flood disaster had occurred not because water and soil conservation itself was not of any use, but because people had done the work poorly.[105]

Specifically, the 1954 dam failure resulted from four factors. First, the rains were heavy and prolonged. Second, Dengjiabao had not effectively combined different kinds of conservation measures to protect dams by slowing and conserving runoff. Some fields did not have fully completed bunds, some had no bunds at all, and some did not have trenches. Third, the gullies had a large catchment area but few engineering works to impede runoff, so water accumulated and increased the burden on the dams. Fourth, many dams were of poor quality.[106] The summer rainstorms destroyed only dams that did not meet proper specifications—they had overly steep inclines or water outlets that were too narrow or too shallow. Some lacked water outlets entirely. Dams broke when they were made of poor-quality earth, the earth was too loose, or laborers had not finished them. By contrast, good-quality dams with thick bodies did not incur any damage.[107] Building all dams in the proper manner, cadres and officials concluded, would prevent washouts and avoid wasting labor on failed projects.[108] Construction needed to proceed from the branch gullies and the tops of gullies, where runoff originated, to the main gully and the gully bottoms. After every rainstorm, residents had to conduct inspections and make repairs quickly to avoid prolonged damage from washouts.[109]

This explanation, reports stated, "rectified the disheartened mood of the masses and strengthened their confidence in struggling against nature." Mutual-aid teams mobilized to dig out springs clogged with sediment and restore transportation on washed-out paths. In three days, they repaired dams and salvaged crops from some sorghum and millet fields. Investigations revealed that ponds dug next to paths that ran through fields, in gullies, and on steeply inclined slopes had retained runoff, so the waters did not gather behind dams and increase the burden on them. As a result, villagers became more willing to adopt these measures.[110]

According to Li Xuding, after rainstorms caused dams to fail for a second time in autumn 1954, local party leaders called for an emergency cadre meeting at which they "used the story of the Red Army climbing snow-capped mountains, crossing grasslands, falling, and getting back up again during the Long March to educate everyone that we must be a 'Red Army' fighting against floodwaters." If dams washed out, they would rebuild them.[111] Invoking the ideals of military struggle and self-sacrifice was a powerful tool for mobilizing people to transform the environment.[112] Early the next morning, Li Xuding and other cadres went door-to-door to marshal their fellow villagers, but most did not listen. Leading by example, Li picked up a shovel and, with an eight-person group of cadres and other villagers, went to Kangjia Gully and started rebuilding a dam. When others saw Li's group at work, they came to help. In three days, Dengjiabao had rebuilt more than 170 dams and constructed 91 new ones out of stacked stone with soil bedding. In Li's words, "They were tall, solid, and good looking. No matter how big the floodwaters that come, they will surely be rebuffed and never think of washing them out again."[113] When heavy rains fell later in autumn 1954, none of the newly restored and consolidated dams washed out.[114]

Nevertheless, the influence of Dengjiabao's gully management experience was not entirely positive. When cadres from other areas toured Dengjiabao, the dams made a profound impression on them. After returning home, the cadres focused only on managing gullies and neglected the importance of taking a comprehensive approach that integrated multiple conservation techniques. In the words of one report on conservation work in Wushan County, "They only think highly of building dams and do not recognize that building bunds is the first link in water and soil conservation." Without bunds to retain water in fields, runoff from rainstorms flowed into gullies and threatened dams. To ensure the dams' stability, the report advised, cadres had to keep the lessons learned from Dengjiabao's earlier washout disasters in mind.[115]

Anxieties and Adjustments

Even though mutual-aid teams were typically composed of neighbors and kin, divisions within these groups complicated efforts to mobilize villagers for conservation work. Frictions existed between members with different amounts of land. In one village near Wushan's county seat, local cadres made a general call for everyone to build bunds, mobilizing 110 people regardless of how much land they owned. All the villagers had suspicions about how mutual-aid teams would evaluate and record work. Those with a lot of land worried about having to pay others for their assistance. Some landowners wondered, "With this many people working, who am I going to compensate for workdays? How much am I going to compensate them for workdays?" Those without much land questioned whether they would benefit from conservation measures at all. The day after bund building commenced, nine households in the village held back their most capable workers, sending youngsters of twelve or thirteen to do what they considered "unpaid corvee labor" (*zhi chaishi*).[116] In Tan'ge district, mutual-aid teams had not settled accounts and members doubted they would receive payment for the work that they had done for others. One peasant complained, "I'm so poor that I don't even have a speck of land on the mountain. I did seven days of work for nothing."[117] It made no sense for households to let their most valuable laborers work for the mutual-aid team if they did not know what—if anything—they would get in return.

In Guanping, in the township of Liyao, residents from the hamlets of Wangjiagou, Zhangjiagou, and Guanjiagou did gully management work for ten days, but mutual-aid teams had not calculated who owed what to whom for their labor contributions. In addition to these poor accounting practices, conservation plans sometimes focused on certain locales and neglected others. People from Zhangjiagou and Wangjiagou reported, "We carried grain on our backs to make things easier for Guanjiagou." Despite having done gully management work for three years, mutual-aid teams from Zhangjiagou and Wangjiagou had not managed gullies near their own homes, which they considered unfair. "No matter what," they said, "we're not going to do it anymore." In other cases, lack of payment resulted from team leaders taking advantage of other members. In Guanping village's Wang Tingjun mutual-aid team, a member named Shi Bingzhi spent three days building bunds for Wang Tingjun in 1954, but Wang did not record the work or compensate Shi for his services. For that reason, Shi said that Wang had forced him to "do unpaid corvee labor for three days."[118]

Elsewhere, the fear that conservation measures would interfere with agricultural production was vindicated. In Longquan district, broadcasts called on residents to construct bunds in the middle of the summer harvest, which gave rise to many complaints. In one village, local cadres who were eager to impress their superiors with how much conservation work they could complete called away people who were busy threshing grain to build bunds.[119] If villagers refused to do conservation work, they met with harsh consequences. Cadres in another township, for instance, urged people to build bunds, some of whom refused. To make an example of recalcitrant villagers, cadres used the humiliating punishment of parading them around in large hats as intimidation and accused them of being "resistant toward water and soil conservation and having ideological problems." The punishments backfired, however; villagers became even less willing to do conservation work.[120]

Members of mutual-aid teams who trusted that they would get fair compensation for their labor contributions were far more willing to participate. Team members wanted to work for what they considered adequate payment; assessment systems had to make them confident that they would receive it. Villagers remarked, "In the past [if you] cut a bundle of grass or gathered a bundle of kindling [you] could cook, [but] water and soil conservation didn't provide food to eat." But they were more favorably inclined toward conservation work after they felt that "evaluating points and recording work is actually accumulating pay for yourself."[121] Conservation initiatives had to address resource shortages and basic subsistence needs. Otherwise, villagers greeted them with indifference or suspicion.

Under the newly founded PRC regime in the early 1950s, water and soil conservation experts like Yan Wenguang promoted many of the same land management measures they had advocated in the 1940s under the Nationalist regime. But the conservation schemes undertaken by the PRC party-state differed significantly from those initiated by the Nationalist government. Although conservation experts employed by state agencies ventured into the field to oversee conservation work before and after 1949, under the PRC they carried out demonstration and extension programs with support and assistance from a party-state apparatus that extended down to local activists and mutual-aid teams in villages like Dengjiabao. This structure provided instruments of mass mobilization and policy implementation in rural society that did not exist under the Nationalist government.

When they went to Wushan's countryside during the 1950s, technical experts, county officials, and grassroots cadres relied on local activists and model peasants to demonstrate the efficacy of conservation measures to local people who were understandably wary of adopting unproven techniques that might not yield favorable results. Even with support from local agents of the PRC party-state, extension and mobilization efforts that began in Dengjiabao in 1952 could not overcome these misgivings. Many local people feared that conservation projects took too much labor and worried that they would be useless at best and detrimental to crop cultivation at worst.

Villagers in Dengjiabao and other parts of Wushan County used multiple vocabularies, old and new, to express their opposition. Both traditional ideas about the environment and discourses espoused by the PRC party-state provided languages of resistance. Villagers invoked popular religion and geomantic principles to dispute the claim, put forth in propaganda promoting water and soil conservation, that human action could conquer nature. In other cases, villagers appropriated the party-state's vocabulary of production and redeployed it to question official claims about conservation's utility and effectiveness. At the same time, environmental unpredictably undermined popular confidence in conservation and complicated the CCP's strategies of mass mobilization and policy implementation. For many villagers, the drought of 1953 and the dam failures that occurred in 1954 proved their misgivings correct. If conservation was no match for these acts of nature, what value did it have?

Local state agents had to address this question. Their answer was that the problem was not conservation as such; people simply did it wrong. Technical experts, county leaders, grassroots cadres, and local activists hastened to point out that failures of dams and other infrastructure had resulted from improper design and building techniques. They remained confident that making necessary adjustments and tightening quality control could prevent future disasters. The champions of conservation did not acknowledge that technological adaptation in the face of environmental challenges amounted to trial and error, and errors meant wasted labor, damage to crops, and more work for local people.

Those costly setbacks notwithstanding, by 1954 conservation in Dengjiabao and the rest of Wushan County had started to make headway. In addition to propaganda trumpeting the importance of conserving water and soil and all the benefits that doing so would bring, mutual-aid teams got their members to implement conservation measures by carefully adjusting evaluation and remuneration systems. Increasing crop yields in 1953 and 1954 lent credence to claims about conservation's advantages and persuaded villagers to take part. But frictions between the priorities of local people and conservation schemes motivated by the developmental agenda of the party-state had not disappeared. Collectivization and state extraction soon intensified them.

THREE

"Getting Organized Is Powerful"
Conservation and Collectivization

The first news article in *People's Daily* devoted entirely to Dengjiabao, published in August 1955, narrated how the village had eliminated the hazards caused by erosion. It reported that Dengjiabao had once endured poor harvests every year and was frequently threatened by drought and flood. No rain fell in early summer, but in late summer and autumn runoff from torrential downpours washed away "the three alls" (*san guang*): all the soil, all the fertilizer, and all the seedlings. Erosion made farmland less and less fertile, gullies grew wider and deeper, and runoff from highlands washed ever more sediment into the Wei River below the village. But over the previous three years, the article reported, Dengjiabao's residents had vanquished the threat of natural disasters and transformed their benighted landscape. They controlled water and soil loss by building bunds and terraces, planting vegetation, constructing check dams in gullies, and digging water-storage ponds and reservoirs. So many trees and grasses had been planted that, as the article described, "when looking into the distance from the village, hillsides are no longer bare like in the past, but are a swath of verdant green."[1]

The collectivization of Chinese agriculture entered a new stage in 1954, when the PRC mandated that mutual-aid teams across China transition into larger agricultural cooperatives. Mutual-aid teams initially undertook conservation work in Dengjiabao, but after the formation of an agricultural cooperative in late 1954, according to the *People's Daily* article, "the peasants' vigor in struggling against nature became even greater." Since 1952, agricultural output had increased by 40 percent. Originally, twenty-three of twenty-five households in the natural village of Dengjiabao did not have enough grain and other staples to eat. Two years later, the article claimed, twenty of those twenty-five households had sufficient clothing and food, and after the 1955 autumn harvest, two out of every three households would have surplus food.[2] The article's takeaway was that conservation had transformed an impoverished, disaster-ridden village into a prosperous one blessed with economic security.

When news of PRC State Council vice-chairman Deng Zihui's announcement of the Multipurpose Plan for Permanently Controlling the Yellow River and Exploiting Its Water Resources at the second meeting of the First National People's Representative Congress reached Dengjiabao, the *People's Daily* claimed "the peasants were all filled with exultation" and pledged to complete plans for building field engineering projects that autumn ahead of schedule.[3] The Multipurpose Plan called for the construction of large and small reservoirs for flood control, hydropower, and silt retention on the main course of the Yellow River, its tributaries, and in the gullies of the Loess Plateau. It also included plans to build 638,000 check dams to conserve water and soil, plant trees on twenty-one million *mu* (800,000 hectares) of land, and make other farmland improvements.[4] The CCP's vision of transforming the environment through mass mobilization and collective struggle had enriched Dengjiabao, the article suggested, and villagers had greeted the party-state's plans with jubilation and enthusiasm.

But evidence from local archives reveals that the transition from mutual-aid teams to cooperatives did not instantly bolster Dengjiabao's residents' dedication to conservation, nor did villagers greet central government plans with jubilation. Villagers expressed persistent dissatisfaction with the pressure that conservation placed on work time, ongoing concerns that conservation work would interfere with farming, and lingering doubts about its effectiveness. Confronted with entrenched antipathy toward conservation, cooperatives in Dengjiabao and other parts of Wushan had to devise intricate arrangements for evaluating, recording, and compensating members' labor contributions. It took these incentives to make people willing to engage in the arduous work that conservation required.

In the mid-1950s, moreover, the same grassroots cadres who directed conservation programs at the local level also became responsible for making sure that cooperatives fulfilled compulsory state grain procurements. After 1953, the PRC party-state's "unified purchase and supply" (*tonggou tongxiao*) system, which set procurement quotas for grain and other agricultural products, deprived households of control over the crops they produced.

Conservation may have increased crop yields, but this system of state extraction cut into rural people's share of the harvest and reduced the benefits they received for their labor.

Nevertheless, the priorities of rural people continued to shape the way conservation measures were implemented. County officials and grassroots cadres responded to popular intransigence by adjusting incentives and work schedules. Villagers, for their part, remained adept at using strategies that combined varying degrees of accommodation, negotiation, and resistance— both covert and overt—to navigate state directives.

The first section of this chapter outlines the remuneration systems that cooperatives in various parts of Wushan County employed to motivate villagers to do conservation work and the obstacles these arrangements faced. Through an in-depth examination of conservation efforts in Wushan's Guohuai township, the second section highlights the difficulties that accompanied conservation programs pursued by cooperatives and how local cadres and officials sought to address them. Returning to Dengjiabao, section three discusses the organization of tree and grass planting campaigns in the village. Section four examines attempts to mobilize Dengjiabao's residents to haul water from dams to irrigate fields during winter, demonstrating that even in this model village, people balked at conservation projects that demanded heavy labor expenditures without alleviating resource shortages or addressing their immediate needs.

Compensation for Conservation

In late 1953, PRC leaders hastened the transition to collective farming in China's countryside by calling for the formation of lower-level agricultural cooperatives. These new organizations varied in size but were usually made up of twenty to thirty households. Members still owned their land, livestock, and tools, but pooled them for collective use. Households earned a share of the harvest based in part on the amount of property they contributed and in part on work points earned in exchange for their labor.[5] In Dengjiabao, as in many other Chinese villages, dependable local cadres and activists spearheaded the formation of agricultural cooperatives. The mutual-aid teams of Deng Haihai, Deng Junjie, Deng Chenghai, and Deng Hongshan organized

Dengjiabao's first cooperative in November 1954, with the ever-reliable Deng Haihai serving as its director and Deng Junjie as its vice director. The cooperative enlisted twenty-four households (96 percent of the total) in the natural village of Dengjiabao and seven households from Lijiaping village as members. Dengjiabao had twenty-four mutual-aid teams in 1954, but only seven remained in 1955 after the co-op absorbed the rest.[6]

Cooperatives throughout China determined the compensation that their members received for conservation work and other forms of collective labor by "evaluating work and recording points" (sometimes rendered as "evaluating points and recording work"). When cooperatives in Wushan introduced this system at district training classes, cadres reported that many people displayed "a mood of resistance."[7] But local authorities were confident that a "mutually beneficial policy" could overcome their reservations and act as "a sharp-edged weapon for arousing peasants' activism in doing water and soil conservation."[8] Effective compensation, according to a report from one conservation training session, would "break down misgivings that the masses had because they feared suffering losses" and convince households to participate in conservation projects.[9]

As cadres and cooperative leaders searched for the right combination of incentives to motivate villagers, remuneration took a variety of forms. For field engineering projects like bunds and trenches, cooperatives evaluated work the same way they evaluated other labor, paying members a share of the harvest at the end of the year in which the work was done (*dangnian fenhong*).[10] When a co-op in Tielong township opted to make payments for work devoted to field engineering projects in the following year, some members refused to build bunds and went off to cut wheat instead.[11] Distributing payments in the same year, as county government reports explained, increased members' enthusiasm.[12] That said, not all conservation measures brought results in the year they were completed, so paying members in the same year resulted in lower compensation per workday than if co-ops waited to distribute them in the future, when they had actually increased harvest yields.[13] The value of work points and total income were higher if payments were spread out over future years in which gains were realized. However, villagers with few reserves did not have the luxury of waiting and were anxious about getting paid for the work they had done.

Not only were time horizons for realizing benefits complicated, but households of different socioeconomic status had conflicting interests. Paying members in the same year reduced compensation per workday, which disadvantaged households with more land and fewer workers vis-à-vis households with little land and more labor. Relatedly, if cooperatives issued more work points, the ultimate value of each work point decreased, which harmed households with more land and fewer workers more than those with more able-bodied laborers who could earn a larger number of work points. By the same token, if co-ops distributed benefits in the same year, their members received payment as a percentage of that year's profits. The problem was that these payments did not reflect the increase in the co-op's income that would occur in the following year, when conservation projects started to improve yields. Compensation for conservation work thus did not account for the improvements that resulted from it. When new members joined the co-op, by contrast, their share of the harvest included the increase in production that resulted from work done by other members in the preceding year. In that way, as a report on conservation work in Dengjiabao put it, "new cooperative members took advantage of old cooperative members."[14] In collectives made up of villagers who performed hard labor and did not have a large surplus to distribute, the resentment was visceral.

While older cooperative members felt newcomers unfairly benefited from labor that they had not performed, new members had their own concerns. Private investments from which households had not yet garnered returns proved especially vexing. Many villagers hesitated to implement conservation measures on their land until after they joined co-ops, since they thought they would not earn work points or receive compensation for work they did before joining.[15] Hence, as a report from October 1955 explained, when co-ops made payments in the current year, "peasants preparing to join the cooperative didn't actively build bunds."[16] Dengjiabao's work team noted that some residents preferred not to put in conservation measures on their land because they thought, "After autumn [we're] going to join the cooperative. Forget it! After [we] join the cooperative, there'll be people to do it. If [we] do it [now] it's work expended for nothing."[17] Holding out to get assistance from others made better sense than doing it by themselves.

At the same time, even though households retained property rights to their land after joining the cooperative, they would have to share the returns from investments made to improve their land with other members. In Guohuai township, people doubted that they would receive compensation for work done before they joined the cooperative and believed that "after they joined, the land would belong to the whole cooperative, and they wouldn't benefit." As some villagers put it, "We're joining the cooperative this year. What's the point of doing that [conservation work]?"[18] After weighing the pros and cons, many opted not to carry out conservation measures.

Compensation systems had to take all these considerations into account. In July 1955, district-level cadres in Wushan County investigated the possibility of cooperatives distributing payments for work done during the summer harvest in the current year and for work done afterward in the following year.[19] Thereafter, some co-ops started to stagger compensation for conservation work over several years. Payments were made in the current year for work that increased production during the same year, like building bunds during spring plowing time, and in the following year for bunds built after the summer harvest, which would not increase production until the next year.[20] If a cooperative distributed payments in the following year, it calculated payments for work done in the second half of the year as a percentage of all workdays spent on farming and sideline production. The co-op then multiplied a member's total workdays in the following year by that percentage to determine the number of workdays for which to compensate them. This arrangement ensured that old co-op members benefited exclusively from work done in the first part of the year and new members shared part of the benefits from work done in the latter part of the year. Reports stated that new and old members alike considered the system rational and satisfactory.[21]

A report on conservation work in Dengjiabao from October 1955 spelled out another arrangement, urging "agricultural cooperatives with a relatively good foundation in mutual-aid and cooperation" to spread payments over several years while also using a piece-rate system. Paying members over a period of three years for labor they contributed during any one year ensured that they received part of their compensation in the year when a conservation project generated actual benefits. If new members had implemented conservation measures on their land, co-ops compensated them in installments. Two-thirds of the compensation was received the year after they joined, and after three years the co-op no longer compensated them for the earlier improvements.[22] The piece-rate system separated tasks into categories and assigned work points according to their difficulty and importance. Co-ops gave members a predetermined number of work points for a task done to a minimum quality standard. The piece-rate method, as another report stated, could "overcome the phenomena of loafing on the job, rushing to earn as many work points as possible, and neglecting quality."[23] As Wushan County's water and soil conservation "key point," Dengjiabao piloted this system.[24]

By spreading payments out over several years, cooperatives assured people who had not yet joined that work they did after the summer harvest would yield benefits. As one report on conservation in Dengjiabao put it, this modification "overcame the passive mood of waiting to do it after entering the cooperative."[25] People readily accepted this method and local authorities favored it.[26] If the members of mutual-aid teams or self-cultivating peasants had already invested in field engineering projects, the co-op increased the estimated productivity of their land when they joined. Alternatively, if field engineering projects had not yet generated benefits, the co-op's leaders evaluated the new members' conservation measures and converted their value into work points rather than considering the land's estimated productivity.[27]

Cadres and officials hoped that implementing these compensation systems would make co-op members confident they would get fair returns on their labor. A man named Deng Erjie gave the desired response when, according to one work report, he said, "Now I'll do it well. Before, I was afraid that work points wouldn't be recorded. Now work points are recorded, grain is distributed, and fuel is distributed. Why wouldn't I do it?"[28]

Yet all the different ways of distributing payment could cause confusion. In some areas, cooperatives did not confirm the duration over which they would make payments. As a co-op member in Mahe township complained, "The full-time cadres said that pay for work done this year will be distributed this year; representatives at the specialized meeting that the county held said that the pay will be distributed when there are benefits. We still don't know what they're going to do." This uncertainty discouraged people, reports stated, and kept conservation work from developing on a large scale.[29]

To ensure fair and consistent remuneration, cooperatives classified farmland according to its soil type and slope gradient to determine the standard workday (*biaozhun gong*) for each category of land. These standards specified the expected quality and quantity (length, height, width) for field engineering projects done on every *mu* of land based on conditions in each locality. When existing cooperative members met these specifications, the co-op converted the value of the conservation projects to work points based on the standard workday and made payments as if they were labor contributions. When new members who had already completed conservation work on their land entered the co-op, it likewise classified their land according to type and quality. The co-op then recorded conservation measures that had met or exceeded standards as work points and distributed payments to new members in the current year.[30] If projects failed to meet prescribed standards, the co-op deducted the shortfall from new members' agricultural workdays.[31] By all accounts, defining the standard workday for each type of conservation project increased labor efficiency. Because co-op members expected a return for their effort and "work had a goal," this evaluation method decreased "work stoppages due to poor coordination and waste" and attained "mutual benefits." It also fostered unity between new and old members by eliminating old members' suspicions about newcomers taking advantage of them by benefiting from work done before they joined. Classifying tasks in a manner that reflected their actual difficulty incentivized members to work harder and proved effective in mobilizing people outside the cooperative to do conservation work.[32]

When building dams in gullies, after classifying land according to the severity of the flood damage it typically incurred, cadres and officials assigned gully management work to the households that stood to benefit. This ensured that everyone who would benefit was assigned work. Cooperatives had to complete this work in a certain amount of time according to specified standards and distributed work points among their members depending on how much labor they contributed.[33] When digging water-storage ponds, co-ops set standards based on the hardness of the soil and the difficulty of the work before apportioning labor responsibilities.[34]

Despite the effort that went into formulating compensation methods, they were not always effective. Sometimes policies simply were not implemented. When conservation work began in summer 1955, some locales issued a general call to rouse the populace to action, but "didn't evaluate work and didn't record points." In the township of Wenquan, leaders in one village called on residents to build bunds but did not properly record work points. This left cadres perplexed about how to handle remuneration and presumably made people angry about working without pay.[35] Other causes of nonimplementation derived from doubts about conservation's efficacy. As in the past, a report from a conservation work meeting explained, people still "feared that building bunds occupies land, delays work, and expends effort for nothing."[36] Some villagers complained that conservation, unlike tilling fields, did not provide them with grain, so it did not deserve their time. For this reason, people in a village in Mali district had built bunds in 1954, then plowed them under the next year.[37] Some claimed that steep hillsides could never become productive farmland. In the judgment of a man named Li Zijun, "Mountain land has no prospects and no future. [You] can't use tractors on it and there's no use for terraces."[38]

Many villagers continued to insist that other agricultural tasks left them no time for conservation. Nine representatives who attended a county government meeting in July 1955 made the "excuse" that they were too busy in summer to even think about doing conservation work.[39] As they put it, "We can't even finish regular things. Where's the time to pay attention to it? Building bunds can't be used as food." Others agreed that conservation was important, but claimed they were too busy to spare any labor for it.[40] Villagers preferred to devote their time to growing crops over moving dirt. Indeed, other kinds of nonfarm work were often far more lucrative. One report mentioned that a resident of Pogen village grumbled, "It was hard as hell this year and in the end, we didn't even harvest as much as before. [You] get more from making a few deliveries to the Gongjiamen train station."[41] In the view of villagers like this one, conservation demanded backbreaking labor but did not increase yields as much as cadres led them to expect. They preferred to opt out and do part-time labor instead.

Rural people's willingness and ability to participate also varied with the seasons and the agricultural cycle. In summer 1955, residents of several districts claimed they could not build bunds on dry soil and had to wait for rain. Investigators noted with concern that it would be impossible to meet conservation targets if they only launched "assaults" after rainy days. Accommodating disgruntled villagers and meeting demands from their superiors forced local cadres to adjust their approach. In some places, the summer harvest was finished by the end of July and people had already hoed fields planted with autumn crops. The report explained that the late summer and early autumn was a "gap when farming is slack" (*nongxian kongxi*). Leaders at every level had to prepare to seize that opportunity, "otherwise the autumn fields will soon be harvested, and winter wheat will have to be planted, the weather will turn cold, the masses will have a lot of excuses, and it will influence completion of the water and soil conservation mission."[42] To take advantage of this window of time, the Wushan county committee designated September as a "water and soil conservation assault month" and mobilized villagers to build bunds until the start of the autumn harvest.[43]

Regardless of these adjustments, some people continued to doubt conservation's value and resorted to passive resistance in various forms. Reports from a county-level conservation training meeting state that cooperative members in Mali district harbored "four fears": fear that conservation would occupy land, fear that it was a lot of work, fear that it would not increase production, and fear that it would delay farmwork. Co-op members tried to avoid conservation work by using the "three pushes": ordinary townships pushed conservation work on main-point townships, the south mountain (i.e., the southern part of the district) pushed it on the north mountain (the northern part of the district), and mutual-aid teams pushed it on cooperatives. Reports also spoke of the "five not-dos": people not doing conservation work during dry spells, when it rained, when they were busy with farming, when the south mountain was too wet, and when the north mountain was too dry.[44]

Since villagers found ways to shirk responsibility, conservation in Mali district made little headway. Every time it rained heavily, runoff created floods that threatened villages, flowed through courtyards and houses, and inundated government offices. When people trying to obstruct floods and protect their fields and homes diverted water onto the property of others, arguments flared. During one such fight, one of the men wielded an iron shovel, the other a hoe, and the fracas threatened to put lives in danger.[45] Cadres and activists in Mali took the lead in remedying this situation. Following the autumn harvest, a meeting report indicated, they dug ponds in the hills behind a village in the district. When torrential rainstorms fell in late August 1955, to everyone's surprise, floodwaters did not enter the village, which convinced local people of conservation's effectiveness.[46]

Unified Purchase and Supply

County officials and grassroots cadres in Wushan also needed to ensure that grain procurement quotas imposed by the party-state were fulfilled. The PRC government's unified purchase and supply system, first instituted in late 1953, did away with independent marketing of grain in China's countryside and made cooperatives deliver grain to the state at a fixed purchase price. The new procurement system was transformative. As Jean Oi explains, "Under collectivization, peasants increasingly lost control over the distribution of their harvest. . . . The definition of surplus became one crafted by the state, not defined by peasant or even collective needs. . . . Peasant producers no longer had legal right to the harvest; it belonged to the collective."[47] Cultivators could no longer decide what to do with the crops they grew. Nor could they ensure their subsistence needs were met before fulfilling procurement quotas. The party-state determined the price of grain and how much was retained for local consumption, while co-op members depended on the collective for their food rations. PRC authorities had inserted cooperatives between rural households and the harvest, using the collectives to siphon off their hard-earned grain as cheaply as possible.[48]

Local cadres responsible for finding out how much grain each household had available and convincing them to part with it had little time to direct conservation work. According to one report, a cadre named Ling Faxiang, in Guangwu township, gave "grain work" precedence over conservation. When the Wushan county committee's investigation work team contacted him, Ling responded that "with grain work this tight, if water and soil conservation is delayed a little bit it doesn't matter much."[49] As a 1955 report on conservation in Luomen district complained, "The thought of the masses is resistant. They think [they're too] busy [with other] work, and they don't have time. Cadres haven't acted. They think that the weather's dry, they're busy with grain procurements, and the mission's onerous."[50] Conservation work lagged as a result. In September 1955, Luomen solved the problem by

TABLE 1. Grain production and estimated consumption in Dengjiabao

	1952	1953	1954	1955	1956	1957	1958	1959	1960
Per capita grain production (kg)	188.5	244.25	267	275.75	385	343.25	312.25	263.5	196
Estimated per capita grain availability after government transfers (kg)	—	222	237	242	328	276	251	212	158
Estimated per capita consumption (kcal)	1395	1645	1750	1790	2425	2045	1860	1570	1170

combining grain procurements with cadre training to foster seven hundred individuals who could disseminate conservation techniques and promote grain work.[51]

From 1952 to 1955, in Dengjiabao and the rest of Wushan, agricultural output increased along with the scope of conservation measures.[52] Over those four years, the land area on which bunds and terraces had been constructed in Dengjiabao expanded sevenfold. As a result, the amount of surface soil lost to erosion decreased by 60.5 percent.[53] What did that mean for Dengjiabao's populace? If villagers achieved "self-sufficiency" by producing at least 275 kilograms of grain and other carbohydrate staples per person per year, Dengjiabao might have reached that level in 1955 with production of 275.75 kilograms per capita. After subtracting state transfers, however, estimated availability of grain and other staples decreased to only about 242 kilograms per head. Estimates derived from per capita output suggest that food energy availability from harvests in Dengbiabao was a meager 1,395 calories per person per day in 1952, when most households did not produce enough to make it through the year but relied on side employments and wage labor to earn money to buy additional food on the market. The unified purchase and supply system eliminated that possibility. Even after government procurements, however, estimated per capita consumption grew from roughly 1,645 calories per day in 1953 to 1,750 calories per day in 1954 and 1,790 calories per day in 1955 (table 1).[54] Food availability was improving, in other words, but it still fell below the threshold of sufficiency. Although conservation had contributed to increased output, state procurements substantially reduced the benefits that accrued to people in Dengjiabao, who still teetered precariously on the margin of subsistence.

Some rural residents in Wushan expressed an awareness that state procurements cut into the benefits they could obtain from conservation. A man named Li Haiqing shrewdly remarked that even if water and soil conservation increased production, the government was simply going to requisition more grain at a low price. To sustain people's willingness to do conservation work, local authorities issued a barrage of arguments for its importance. They reminded villagers of the harm caused by water and soil loss, invoking the language of land reform by mobilizing them to "speak bitterness to nature" and "speak bitterness to natural disasters."[55] Unchecked runoff caused floods that damaged production, they pointed out, while conservation increased yields.[56] Propaganda reiterated that water and soil conservation was "an effective measure for stopping harm from floodwaters, fundamentally controlling the Yellow River, and directly supporting national industrialization." It promoted "long-term construction of mountainous areas" and offered a "key method for increasing production in the current year."[57] But the reality was that, under the unified purchase and supply system, improving agricultural output through conservation served the developmental priorities of the PRC party-state more than the needs of the rural populace.

Guohuai Township

Wushan's Guohuai township, located about fifteen kilometers directly east of Dengjiabao, exemplifies popular unease about conservation as well as typical negotiations between recalcitrant villagers and local cadres and officials. The township had built only a miniscule number of bunds and trenches since

1949. Investigations by Wushan County authorities found that conservation had made little headway in Guohuai because, when higher-level directives arrived, local cadres put forth "general calls" but made few concrete arrangements and did nothing to assuage popular misgivings. They neither implemented a mutually beneficial remuneration policy nor made plans to combine conservation with agricultural production.[58]

To better comprehend the problems, Wushan's party committee surveyed sixty-four households in Guohuai's village of Fengjiazhuang. Investigators found that party and youth league members were willing to do conservation work, but they had not won over the masses. As a local party member put it, "I'm willing to do water and soil conservation; it's just that one hand clapping doesn't make a sound." Cadres needed popular participation, but most villagers considered conservation useless and merely paid it lip service. Households with little labor power saw building bunds as a lot of work and a large capital expenditure with no guarantee that production would increase. Households with little land and plenty of labor feared that if they did conservation work on other co-op members' land, they would receive nothing in return. As another man proclaimed, "If other people aren't willing to do it, I'm not going to do it for nothing." People who had not yet joined the co-op worried that if they did conservation work on their farmland before joining, the co-op would not compensate them for the improvements. For this reason, they wanted to wait until they entered the cooperative.[59]

Busy with farming and delivering state grain procurements, many villagers felt they had no time for conservation. As Guo Sishiwu put it, "The work of hoeing the land, planting rape, cutting hemp, soaking hemp, and unified purchases has to be done. Where's the time? Once we aren't busy anymore, we'll do it." People especially disliked the technique of banking up earth into "soft" bunds during dry weather and waiting until rain had softened the earth to tamp them down properly and make them sturdier. The two-part process, they felt, took too much time and effort. As a man named Pan Xiangrui said, "This is [like] taking off your pants to fart—doing twice the work for one job" (*zhe shi tuo kuzi fangpi de, yici zuogong liangci hua le*).[60] As the pungent metaphor made plain, people already had too much work to do and could not devote time to labor-intensive conservation projects.

After getting an understanding of these misgivings, the Guohuai township party branch held meetings to make sure party members recognized the importance of conservation. To ensure that each party member met their prescribed target by overseeing the completion of conservation measures, the party branch instructed them to pay attention to the "six compares, six looks, and six changes":

1. Compare propaganda, look at results, change party members' past tendency to understand policy but not propagandize, and eliminate misgivings by making the benefits of water and soil conservation known to every household.
2. Compare leadership, look at surroundings, and change the tendency of party members to dance alone in their work with no one responding, truly giving play to the function of the core [i.e., party members] taking the lead.
3. Compare activism, look at connecting with the masses, change party members' work methods that are simple, impetuous, and divorced from the masses, walk the mass line, and make it so that everyone embraces [the methods] and all approve.
4. Compare main points and look at the whole, change [the situation of] having a point but no plane, combine point and plane, and develop the whole.
5. Compare quantity, look at quality, change rough and slipshod work, and attain quantity to complete the mission, but with quality as number one.
6. Compare water and soil conservation accomplishments, look at combining them with other work, change one-track work to closely combine with other work, and carry out mobilization work in agricultural cooperatives and mutual-aid teams.[61]

With the "six compares, six looks, and six changes," the party branch acknowledged the misgivings that existed among the populace and called on party members to eliminate them. The six slogans instructed party members to connect with villagers, allay their concerns, and convince them of conservation's benefits so they would respond favorably to mobilization. The slogans also specifically directed party members to combine conservation with other work to address local people's fear that it would adversely affect agricultural production and their complaints that it would interfere with the acquisition of grain for state procurements. Implementing conservation programs, as the instructions make evident, required engaging with villagers and formulating strategies that took their concerns into account.

Beginning on August 4, party members designated Guohuai's seven cooperatives as the township's key points for conservation work. Guohuai's youth league branch dispatched its members and other young people to encourage their families to support conservation efforts. The youth league branch's secretary, Wang Tingjun, and committee member Guo Sishiwu led local youths in doing conservation work, while Wenjiasi village organized a conservation team. To sway Guohuai's populace, party members and activists also disseminated propaganda emphasizing conservation's importance in controlling the Yellow River, furthering national construction, and promoting production, as well as its local benefits.[62]

To address the belief that conservation was of no use, cadres resorted to "education by example." In the village of Guojiazhuang, they organized small group discussions about the father of a man named Guo Siyuesheng, who had received four *mu* (0.266 hectares) of steeply inclined fields during land reform. In the four years since Guo's father first implemented conservation measures, he made the land into level fields that had better wheat yields than the plots on either side. The co-op in Guohuai's Yefu village likewise boasted that it had done conservation work and limited water and soil loss during the previous year. Crop yields improved, convincing villagers that conservation could rapidly promote production.[63]

After spending a day building soft bunds, cooperatives in Guohuai brought people in for on-the-spot visits. Once they saw the demonstration, villagers realized that soft bunds could obstruct runoff and did not waste labor. Building soft bunds and tamping them down after it rained, they acknowledged, was less wasteful than they had imagined.[64] Once again, the report narrated how cadres and activists overcame resistance and persuaded villagers to accept conservation by presenting local examples that communicated its efficacy.

But propaganda and demonstrations were not enough. As always, labor allocation and work schedules required careful consideration. Poor planning had hampered the development of work in Guohuai; now, each cooperative determined the sequence of agricultural tasks based on their relative urgency. Co-ops first assigned workers to do the most urgent tasks, while mobilizing the remaining labor power for conservation efforts. The Guojiazhuang cooperative, for example, designated plowing fields and state grain procurements as most urgent; cutting hemp and preparing to plant rape also qualified as pressing tasks. On September 3 and 4, along with devoting their labor to plowing, co-op members launched an assault to "prepare government grain." From September 5 to 9, cooperatives continued allocating some labor to plowing and grain procurements while some workers built soft bunds. After September 9, most co-op members cut hemp, some plowed and prepared to plant rape, and specialized work groups did conservation work. This careful division of labor ensured that co-op members completed conservation projects without neglecting agricultural production and state procurements.[65]

When evaluating and recording work points, Guohuai's cooperatives and mutual-aid teams relied on a piece-rate system. After considering land type and slope gradient, they determined quantitative and qualitative standards for the various components of conservation projects and unified the recording of work. Depending on local conditions, constructing sixteen *zhang* (53.328 meters) or nineteen *zhang* (63.327 meters) of bunds counted as one workday. For terraces, building nine *zhang* (29.997 meters) counted as one workday. Cooperatives compensated members for the labor they devoted to conservation projects over a period of three years, as explained above. Former mutual-aid team members who did conservation work in the year they joined the co-op received the same compensation as other members. If people did conservation work in one year and joined the co-op during the next, the co-op distributed payment over two years and withheld one-third.[66] This system, according to one report, eliminated time delays caused by the complicated task of evaluating work and motivated nearly every household to take part.[67]

Conservation had to attain high quality standards as well as quantitative targets. To that end, technicians who had attended conservation training classes taught proper techniques to fellow villagers. It should be noted that *technician* here referred to a local person who was knowledgeable and competent in conservation techniques, not a trained expert of the kind employed by higher-level government agencies. These local technicians taught conservation methods to mutual-aid teams and cooperatives in their villages via practical demonstrations. Youths in Fengjiazhuang, for example, had tried building bunds with poor results, so they lost confidence. But after attending an instructional meeting held by a technician named Feng Qing, they did better-quality work. Grassroots innovations spread as well. Residents of Guojiazhuang improved efficiency by organizing groups of four or five people to build bunds. One person set aside the fertile topsoil and dug up the unfertile soil beneath, one banked the earth, one tamped it down, and another filled in the trench with the topsoil for planting.[68] At a township-wide meeting, young people from Guojiazhuang exchanged techniques with youths from other villages, and co-op members taught them how to use Guojiazhuang's bund-building group system.[69]

Yet improved planning, evaluation, and training did not fix everything. Some villagers made bunds too wide and too tall, which occupied cultivated land. For the sake of convenience, some did not set aside fertile topsoil or use it to fill in ditches when building bunds, which decreased crop production.[70] Some remaining mutual-aid teams that had not merged into co-ops found it impossible to settle accounts in a timely manner. Suspicion often existed among villagers in Guohuai, who were willing to do conservation work for members of their own mutual-aid team—typically composed of family members and neighbors whom they could count on for an equivalent amount of work or fair payment in exchange for their labor—but not for other teams.[71] Local leaders had not found a reliable way to motivate every villager to contribute labor to collectively organized conservation programs, let alone make sure their work met prescribed quality standards.

Afforestation in Dengjiabao

In addition to building infrastructure like bunds, conservation programs also involved planting trees and grasses. Dengjiabao, like other villages in Wushan and the rest of the Loess Plateau, had acute shortages of the "three materials"—fuel, fodder, and fertilizer. Due to deforestation, male villagers had to travel eighty to ninety *li* (40–45 km) to get firewood. Women cut grasses and dug up roots for fuel, which not only required a great deal of labor but also increased runoff and erosion by removing vegetation cover.

In spring 1954, Dengjiabao started to address these problems by planting trees in Majia Gully, Qiaozi Gully, and Kangjia Gully. That autumn, county authorities resolved disagreements caused by the prohibition of livestock grazing in newly planted forests by demarcating boundaries between forest areas and pasturage.[72]

Even when livestock were not eating or trampling trees, forests and other flora did not necessarily coexist harmoniously. Sweet clover and other grasses could deprive saplings of sunlight and nutrients. By late 1955, the tall grass that grew on previously bare mountain ridges and slopes near Dengjiabao was interfering with the growth of immature trees. To promote afforestation and alleviate fuel difficulties, as Dengjiabao's conservation work team reported, members of youth organizations and other villagers mobilized from October 30 to November 9 to tend saplings and plant new trees. People trimmed branches and rooted out grasses that grew around planting pits, collecting 11,290 *jin* (5,645 kg) of grass. In addition to harvesting sweet clover, they planted two thousand pits with Armenian plum (*shanxing, Prunus sibirica*), pear (*shanli, Pyrus ussuriensis*), white poplar (*baiyang, Populus tomentosa*), Siberian elm (*yushu, Ulmus pumila*), and black locust trees.[73] The afforestation drive mobilized 120 people from forty-four households in the villages of Majiashan and Zhangjiabao, including 28 boys and 12 girls, who invested 217.8 workdays.[74]

Tending trees and uprooting grass paid off in the form of badly needed fuel. Payments followed the principles that "the team plants, the team protects, and the team benefits" and "those who labor more receive more." Zhangjiabao village took care of twenty *mu* (1.33 hectares) of forestland in Majia Gully, while also investing 75.4 workdays to harvest grass on 3,776 *mu* (251.73 hectares) of land and plant trees in Majia Gully, Guandi Gully, and Xi Gully. Every workday earned 50.1 *jin* (25.05 kg) of grass as compensation. The household of Zhang Kejun invested 5.5 workdays and receiving 276 *jin* (138 kg) of grass. Zhang's household had nine members, each of whom consumed 27 *jin* (13.5 kg) of fuel per day, so the grass met their needs for ten days. Zhao Fansheng's household, which had two people, brought in 75 *jin* (37.5 kg). Majiashan village looked after around 60 *mu* (4 hectares) of trees and harvested 5,958 *jin* (2,979 kg) of grass, putting in a total of 101 workdays. Since Majiashan had more grass to distribute than Zhangjiabao, every workday earned 59 *jin* (29.5 kg) of grass. Lin Wanfu, who put forth the most labor, personally contributed 9.8 workdays and received 578 *jin* (289 kg) of grass. Lin had a family of nine, so the grass he earned alleviated their fuel difficulties for 21.5 days. Most households got around 300 *jin* (150 kg) of grass. Majiashan mobilized the village's young people to tend 18 *mu* (1.2 hectares) of trees and harvest 1,556 *jin* (778 kg) of grass. For their 61.4 workdays, they received 25.3 *jin* (12.65 kg) of grass per person.[75] Tending young forests thus partially alleviated Dengjiabao's fuel scarcity problem.

Confidence in afforestation, forest protection, and conservation in general grew as a result. People recalled that in the past they had cut down so many trees on nearby hillsides that they were "balder than a shaved head." Now, according to the conservation work team's report, villagers reportedly marveled at the amount of fuel that grass planting and afforestation provided: "Today we've harvested so much grass. In a few more years branches [from trees they planted] alone will be more than we can burn. This really is doing something good for the next generation of sons and grandsons." Whether these words reflected villagers' actual views or the work team's attempt to promote its own accomplishment is not certain. But it is noteworthy that, rather than referring to the cooperative or the party-state, the statement framed an abundance of vegetation and fuel in terms of what mattered most to the rural populace—the welfare of their own households—and expressed a hope that they would realize even greater improvements in the future.[76]

In a similar vein, the work team's report quoted the mother of a CCP member named Deng Daisheng to convey the significance of branches and blades of grass for villagers: "Fuel has sentenced people to death. In the past, [we] had to travel several dozen *li* to cut grass, leaving when the rooster crowed, returning in the middle of the night, and the fuel that we carried was only enough to burn for three or four days. Daisheng! Doing this little bit of work in the biting cold [winter] has earned [us] so much grass. Planting trees on the mountain really has benefits."[77] Planting trees and other vegetation on denuded hillsides might have alleviated erosion, but local people found the biomass that it provided even more appealing, since twigs and grasses alleviated their critical need for fuel.

The rural campaigns of the Mao era—from cultivating cotton to con-

FIGURE 10. Li Xuding. Gansu sheng shuiliting, *Jianshe shanqu de bangyang*.

serving water and soil—often used models whose exceptional abilities and achievements were presented by party-state authorities as exemplars for the wider populace.[78] Campaigns to improve vegetation cover were no exception. During a drive to plant trees and grasses in spring 1955, the CCP youth league member Li Xuding (fig. 10) led a group of young people who tended immature forests and completed Dengjiabao's planting mission for the year.[79] Li Xuding had already gained a heroic reputation when dams in Dengjiabao washed out in 1954 and he bravely jumped into surging floodwaters to close a breach before a dam collapsed (see chapter 2).[80] Li equated tree planting with the contributions of young people to the growth of socialism: "What we're planting today are youth forests and also socialist forests. If one tree is planted, it must be guaranteed that one tree lives."[81] Every tree that took root advanced China's socialist construction. Li Xuding soon became a model for young people throughout Wushan. When attendees at the county's Youth Water and Soil Conservation Activist Meeting (Qingnian shuitu baochi huodong fenzi hui) toured Dengjiabao in August 1955, Li spoke to them about his "model achievements" and the afforestation methods the

Dengjiabao youth league branch had used. Deng Haihai also gave a report to the young people in attendance. As labor models, Deng and Li described Dengjiabao's experience and helped participants draw up conservation plans for their own areas.[82]

The meeting's attendees made up just a fraction of the 3,785 people who visited Dengjiabao between 1952 and 1955.[83] In 1955 alone, 2,322 cadres, labor models, and other visitors from Wushan and elsewhere came to the village to take part in observation and study. After every county government meeting, participants toured Dengjiabao, and the head of the county's construction office was frequently stationed there to direct activities.[84] During these inspection visits, in the words of a report on conservation training work in Wushan, "the classroom was Dengjiabao and the instructors were Deng Haihai and [conservation expert] Wang Zhiguo," who combined demonstrations and practical study to teach visitors how to build bunds, manage gullies, and dig water-storage ponds.[85] But Dengjiabao's influence was not limited to Wushan or even Gansu. Li Xuding attended a Five Province (Area) Youth Afforestation Conference in Yan'an, about 650 kilometers northeast of Wushan in northern Shaanxi Province, to share Dengjiabao's conservation experience.[86] Events of this kind transmitted knowledge of conservation measures used in Dengjiabao throughout the nation.

Winter Irrigation

Observation visits presented Dengjiabao and its activists as models for everyone in Wushan to emulate, while national conferences and state media coverage publicized them to an even wider audience. But conservation did not always have local support. Efforts to convince villagers in Dengjiabao to transport water stored in dams to irrigate fields illustrate rural people's resistance to what they perceived as an unreasonable burden. Cadres and officials resorted to a mix of propaganda and incentive systems to persuade people to do this hard work.

In 1955, building on the previous year's efforts, Dengjiabao sought to prevent washouts by strengthening and improving its existing dams. During the heaviest rainstorms of 1955, dams filled with water and silt, but none broke. A few small dams with narrow drainage outlets sprang leaks, but the leaks did not threaten their integrity. In 1954, the 264 dams built in Dengjiabao retained 792 cubic meters of silt; the following year Dengjiabao had 312 dams that retained 1,000 cubic meters of silt. These dams protected farmland along the gullies around Dengjiabao as well as the railway line on the flatlands below.[87]

During the torrential rainstorms in summer 1954, some poorly dug ponds in Dengjiabao had failed. Runoff, instead of being retained in the ponds, accumulated behind dams and burst through them. The resulting floods taught cadres and other villagers that the locations of ponds, rather than their size, determined their effectiveness. For this reason, in 1955 they followed the principle that "it doesn't matter if ponds are big or small, the location [just] has to be chosen well." In addition to improving the existing ponds, villagers dug new ones on hillsides, beside fields and roads, and at gully heads to capture runoff, slow erosion, and conserve soil. After water levels fell in the winter, Dengjiabao's three cooperatives planted twenty-one *mu* (1.4 hectares) of wheat on the soil captured in twenty-eight of these ponds. In Deng Haihai's estimation, "The big ponds that we dug at the top of Majia Mountain this year were a waste of labor. In practical form, digging a few small ponds would've been of greater use." During a rainstorm in August 1955, Deng Haihai observed that the ponds functioned well. "If it weren't for that," he said, "you never know how many crops below the mountain would've been washed out! And the dams in the gullies also would've been in danger."[88]

But local leaders wanted to do more than prevent floods. In winter 1955, the Wushan County government attempted to mobilize people to use the water collected in recently built dams for irrigation. In the words of a county government bulletin, "places with conditions for developing water control were not fully utilized," which would result in losses in agricultural production.[89] Dengjiabao's conservation work team reported that although gully management significantly reduced water and soil loss, apart from livestock drinking water from a few dams located near villages, most water in dams was not rationally utilized. Drawing water from dams for irrigation, the work team's report claimed, would increase yields and reduce the water volume in dams to ensure their security after the winter freeze and spring thaw. "For this reason," the report stated, "to rationally utilize the stored water, decrease the burden on the body of the dams, and prevent excessive water from causing dams to collapse and leak, [we] mobilized the masses to carry water to irrigate fields."[90] Hauling water, in other words, would fully utilize it for irrigation and protect the dams.

To mobilize the local populace, the conservation work team first explained the goals of gully management, the importance of controlling the Yellow River, the disasters that could occur if dams had too much water behind them, and how to prevent such occurrences. Despite the official messaging, people in Dengjiabao chafed at the heavy burden that the winter irrigation campaign presented. Neither cadres nor other villagers considered the project feasible. Two of the four cadres in the work team remarked skeptically, "All this talk's unrealistic and removed from the masses. Carrying water isn't easy and the dams are fine. Not carrying it's also alright." Cadres and other villagers worried that dams had so much water in them that transporting it all would be difficult. Deng Daisheng put it bluntly: "Making people carry water from such big dams will kill them." Some people simply did not have enough strength for the task. The village's vice director, Ma Jinlu, objected, "I huff and puff so much that I can't even breathe. I can't carry water. What're we to do?"[91]

So negative were the villagers that cadres hesitated to spread propaganda for fear of people's imprecations. Even the typically enthusiastic and committed labor model Deng Haihai admitted, "When we give cooperative members assurances, they aren't convinced, and they curse us as well." Understandably, people had no desire to haul water in frigidly cold winter weather. As production team leader Li Baocai put it, "Carrying all the water from these dams will work us to death. Even if carrying poles break their shoulders and people freeze, they won't be able to carry it all." Some objected that they did not have time. As Zhang Kejun said, "According to the plan that we made, we've got to hoe the land and dig trenches. People are very busy. Where're the people to send to carry water?" The water in some dams had frozen, making it impossible to carry. Other villagers suspected that cadres simply wanted to make extra work for them during a slack farming season. Mutual-aid team leader Ma Shuangbao grumbled, "Cadres see that we're idle, and they intentionally find ways to make us not idle. Poor us! Whatever they say, we have to do it." Another villager complained, "Making earth dams worked people to death to block the water. Now there's water, and people have to carry it. [We] don't know what to do."[92]

Hoping to address these grievances, the work team held a meeting of Dengjiabao's local cadres to affirm their accomplishments leading conservation work and explain the goals and direction of gully management. They emphasized that transporting water to irrigate fields could both increase grain production and fortify the dams. They also "settled accounts and made comparisons" by pointing out benefits obtained by managing gullies and the income that Dengjiabao had earned in 1955 from harvesting sweet clover stalks and seeds.[93] Won over by these arguments, local cadres delegated work to natural villages within the cooperative and held meetings to stress that irrigation increased crop yields. Cadres espoused "the spirit that being able to irrigate one *fen* is one *fen*, being able to irrigate one *mu* is one *mu*; being able to irrigate a little is better than not irrigating anything." During discussions, the activist Deng Hongshan said, "This is good. Now if [we] can irrigate [farmland] once during the winter who knows how much grain production can increase. All of us need to work as one to do it. When [we] get up in the morning, we'll take advantage of [the time] when the land's frozen and carry all the water in a few mornings." Zhao Fansheng referred to China's participation in the Korean War to downplay the hard work and self-sacrifice involved: "The volunteer army on the battlefields in Korea battled together to the death against the enemy. What's difficult about us carrying a few carrying poles of water to the fields?"[94] In other words, doing conservation work in winter was nothing compared to the war Chinese soldiers were fighting against US imperialism in Korea, so villagers needed to stop complaining and start working. The invocation of military ideals again justified intense physical exertion to transform the environment.

Proper organization and leadership were necessary to avoid work stoppages and waste. Local cadres decided which land to irrigate with water from the dams and created a method of evaluating work points. In mid-December 1955, Majiashan and Zhangjiabao villages also founded agricultural cooperatives. By the year's end, eighty-six households—over 92 percent of the households in the administrative village of Dengjiabao at that time—had joined one of the three cooperatives.[95] Local cadres instructed co-ops to organize their members to haul water from dams in the gullies that they managed. Cooperatives assessed work based on distance traveled, the steepness of roads, and the implements used for carrying water. The Dengjiabao co-op, for example, decided that five trips of approximately two hundred meters carrying water in a wooden barrel, six trips using a wooden barrel and a ceramic jar, and seven trips using a pair of ceramic jars would each earn one work point.[96]

At first people used large ladles to scoop the water out, but it proved inefficient, and when their hands got wet, they froze. They switched to digging trenches around dams to draw out the water, which was more efficient and kept their hands dry. Pouring water directly into fields planted with winter wheat damaged the roots of the wheat seedlings; experience showed that placing the barrel on the ground and tipping it to let water flow out irrigated the fields evenly without harming seedlings.[97] For six mornings, beginning on December 2, co-ops mobilized eighteen people (including nine women) to make 4,149 trips carrying water from twelve dams. If one trip covered 200 meters, each co-op member transported water over 7.5 kilometers every morning. Most of the water came from a dam in Kangjia Gully, to which villagers made 1,094 trips to irrigate 3.5 *mu* (0.233 hectares) of land. In total they irrigated 13.8 *mu* (0.92 hectares) of wheat and one *mu* (0.066 hectares) of peppercorns.[98]

The work team concluded that education and the implementation of a piece-rate system for recording work had made co-op members more conscientious, and expecting members to complete tasks to certain quality specifications within a defined time frame made them more diligent. The promise of future payment, along with an awareness that they would earn less if their work was subpar, incentivized people to carry out the grueling labor. A female cooperative member named Lin Qiumei echoed the official message when she told her male counterparts, "If [you] carry more water now, in the future it'll pay more dividends."[99] Another co-op member named Li Yongqing reportedly went out to carry water before sunrise and earned seven work points in one morning.

Local activists made sure to remind villagers that collective effort accomplished far more than going it alone. As Deng Hanjie declared, "Getting organized is powerful. This morning, we didn't sleep in, and we already irrigated one *mu*. If one person carried [water], they wouldn't be able to irrigate as much in a month. This is the advantage of a cooperative." In the end, cadres stressed, the party deserved credit. Deng Kejun noted that whenever a dry spell occurred in the past, drinking water had grown scarce, but now things had changed: "The Communist Party led us in building dams in gullies, which not only conserve water and soil but can also irrigate fields." Even uplands areas were now irrigated, which, in Deng Kejun's words, was "really something people never would've imagined."[100] Mobilizing villagers to undertake that difficult work required compensation systems that gave them incentives to do it in addition to propaganda urging them to participate.

Propaganda slogans from Dengjiabao waxed lyrical about the rationale for water and soil conservation—specifically using water from dams to irrigate fields—and the power of collective labor to remake the environment. A cooperative member named Deng Hanming came up with this ditty, which workers likely would have sung in unison while they hauled water:

> The Communist Party leaders are truly great; [they have] good methods to transform nature.
>
> Digging ponds and building dams; water and soil conservation can defend against drought.
>
> Clear water is stored in several dams; the government calls upon [us] to irrigate fields.
>
> Irrigated land going up the mountain is not difficult; the power of getting organized surpasses heaven (*zuzhi qilai liliang sheng guo tian*).
>
> Men and women, old and young, going at it together; the irrigated winter wheat looks really good.
>
> [Dams] do not burst; next year increased production is guaranteed.
>
> Support the nation's industrialization; people's livelihoods will greatly improve.[101]

This song valorized the CCP for promoting economic development and popular welfare by organizing rural people and endowing them with the power to overcome the environment, referred to here as "nature" and "heaven." Cooperatives, under the party-state's guidance, had built dams and dug ponds, and could use water stored in them to eliminate drought and transform arid hillsides into irrigated fields. Organization and mass mobilization, the lyrics suggested, resulted in progress and improvement. Reading the song alongside evidence found in other archival sources, however, suggests that its optimistic message was intended to counter the mood of pessimism and resistance toward hauling water from dams in the dead of winter that prevailed among Dengjiabao's populace.

Villagers rejected conservation measures that required backbreaking labor and increased demands on their work time, or which they feared might interfere with agricultural production. County officials and local cadres in Wushan had to respond to these misgivings. Engaging in constant back-and-forth with the local populace, they carefully adjusted systems of compensation and evaluation and took pains to align conservation with the seasonal cycle of farmwork to persuade rural residents to take part. The flexibility that local agents of the PRC party-state displayed in implementing conservation programs derived in part from the fact that, in 1954 and 1955, rural households retained private property rights to their land and joined agricultural cooperatives voluntarily. Their right to opt out gave villagers the leverage necessary to push state agents to modify official policies to assuage their anxieties and suspicions.

The structure of official reports narrated a process in which cadres and officials heard local objections and responded by demonstrating the tangible benefits of conservation, adjusting work schedules to avoid interfering with farming, and putting incentive systems in place that convinced villagers to take part in conservation schemes. Despite the tidy narrative closure seen in official reports, however, the "misgivings of the masses" and examples of their passive and active resistance appear over and over in the documents.

Even if mobilizing villagers did not go smoothly, it got easier when, as state propaganda promised, conserving water and soil helped increase crop yields and gave rural people access to scarce resources. The *People's Daily* article cited at the beginning of this chapter did not mislead readers when it reported that conservation measures in Dengjiabao had slowed erosion and that, between 1952 and 1955, agricultural production had expanded by

40 percent. Food availability in Dengjiabao had, in fact, increased, and local people were enthusiastic about planting trees and grasses that supplied them with badly needed fuel.

The key detail that the *People's Daily* article and other propaganda did not acknowledge—but which villagers in Wushan clearly understood—was that state procurements cut into the benefits that rural people stood to gain from conservation. As the PRC's unified purchase and supply system extracted surpluses from the agricultural sector, agents of the party-state exhorted villagers to work harder on conservation projects for lower returns. The task of delivering state grain procurements placed additional strain on work time, and requisitioning decreased food supplies available to rural households that had barely risen above the margin of subsistence. Loss of control over distribution of the harvest added a new layer to the suspicions, fears, and resentments that many rural people harbored toward the party-state's calls to remake the land in the name of conserving water and soil.

FOUR

"Dams Have Really Worn Us Out"

Labor, Local Knowledge, and the 1956 Irrigation Campaign

In the mid-1950s, China needed to increase agricultural output to feed its growing population and generate income for the PRC party-state to invest in industrial development, but it had few ways to achieve this goal. With little uncultivated land to convert to farming, production could be increased only by intensifying inputs in areas that were already being farmed. China did not have the capacity to produce large quantities of synthetic fertilizers, and large-scale capital investments in agriculture went against the PRC's strategy of extracting surpluses from the rural sector to capitalize the rapid development of heavy industry. Given these constraints, using mass mobilization of labor to convert nonirrigated lands to irrigated fields was the most promising way to increase yields.[1] This reasoning informed the "high tide" of water conservancy that the PRC launched in 1955 to expand the amount of irrigated land.[2] Small-scale local irrigation projects would soon transform the agricultural landscape. In China as a whole, the area of irrigated farmland increased from approximately seventeen million hectares in 1949–52 to between twenty-seven and thirty-five million hectares in 1957. Stevan Harrell calls this dramatic growth through capturing and diverting surface waters "the most obvious and important change in Chinese agriculture during the early and mid-1950s."[3]

This high tide in irrigation coincided with a high tide in agricultural collectivization. Spurred on by Mao Zedong, in late 1955 PRC central leadership called for the formation of higher-level agricultural producers' cooperatives throughout the countryside. Higher-level cooperatives grew to ten times larger than lower-level cooperatives, with two hundred to three hundred households organized into production brigades of twenty to thirty households each. This "socialist upsurge in the countryside" fully collectivized agricultural production, taking ownership of members' landholdings, farm tools, and draft animals. Higher-level cooperatives eliminated the dividends that lower-level cooperatives had previously paid members for their contributions of land and other means of production. Instead, higher-level co-ops compensated members based primarily on the value of work points they earned in exchange for their labor.

At the end of each year, after paying taxes and making compulsory sales of grain and other crops to the state, higher-level cooperatives retained some seed for the following year, repaid any debts they had incurred buying inputs, calculated production expenses, and invested a portion in collectively controlled funds. They then distributed the remainder of the harvest among households according to the cash value of the work points their members had earned. Some grain and other staples were also distributed to each household during the year (apportioned according to household size), the price of which was deducted from its work points–based distribution. If the cost of this grain exceeded the value of the work points a household had earned, the household owed the collective money. By the end of 1956, nearly all rural households in China had enrolled in higher-level cooperatives, and at the end of 1957 the party-state revoked their right to withdraw.[4]

Small-scale irrigation and flood control projects took full advantage of the labor mobilization that higher-level agricultural cooperatives made possible.[5] During the winter of 1955–56, China's irrigated land area increased from 370 million *mu* (24.66 million hectares) to 480 million *mu* (32 million hectares), with the rural populace digging 4.5 million wells and building 27,000 small reservoirs.[6]

Wushan County joined the rest of China in this twin upsurge in collectivization and water conservancy. In late 1955, Wushan had 622 lower-level cooperatives with a membership of 31,149 households, accounting for 92 percent of the households in the county. In spring 1956, 74 percent of households in Wushan (around 26,100) had formed 120 higher-level cooperatives.[7] By the year's end, 98 percent of the county's households (32,880) had joined 160 higher-level cooperatives.[8] In Dengjiabao, 98 out of 105 households (93.3 percent) joined a higher-level cooperative.[9]

As these higher-level co-ops were getting organized, Wushan County launched a "two hundred thousand wells, ponds, dams, water cellars, and springs campaign" (*20 wan jing tang ba jiao quan yundong*, hereafter referred to as the irrigation campaign) to expand irrigation and meet its 1956 target of increasing grain output to seventy million *jin* (35 million kg).[10] As soon as they were created, higher-level cooperatives mobilized to reroute waters to irrigate land.

Initially, the irrigation campaign met with resistance from members of higher-level co-ops as well as grassroots cadres and activists. To persuade low-level cadres and ordinary villagers to take part, higher-ups in the party-state apparatus directly oversaw irrigation work, employed political education and propaganda, and publicized certain locales as "key points" to model the effectiveness of water conservancy measures so that others would follow suit. State agents also drew on local environmental knowledge and practice, which they described as "mass experience" (*qunzhong jingyan*).[11] Following a pattern seen in agricultural improvement programs throughout the Mao era, cadres in Wushan made concerted efforts to engage with "old peasants," learn from their accumulated experience, and summarize that knowledge into generalizable principles that could guide the irrigation campaign throughout the county.[12]

Yet this emphasis on local knowledge and experience did not empower the rural populace. The priorities of the party-state, not those of villagers, determined what counted as useful local knowledge and how it would be used. Furthermore, vernacular knowledge alone was often an inadequate substitute for technical guidance and expertise, which higher-level government agencies could not provide in sufficient quantities. To fulfill campaign targets, grassroots cadres rushed to finish wells, dams, and other projects without sufficient advance planning and with little regard for structural integrity or effectiveness.

Labor intensification—people working harder and more efficiently for longer periods—made it possible for higher-level cooperatives to mobilize their members for water conservancy and conservation projects without disrupting agricultural production. The irrigation campaign squeezed ever more work out of villagers, but dam washouts and collapses squandered labor and materials. The PRC party-state pursued its goals of environmental transformation, accumulation, and economic development at minimal cost by exploiting local knowledge as well as local labor. In the absence of higher-level support, the burden of the irrigation campaign's failures fell on the rural populace.

The High Tide of Irrigation

The irrigation campaign tried to alleviate the effects of the Loess Plateau's unpredictable precipitation regime. Like the rest of the Loess Plateau, Gansu experiences inconsistent rainfall from year to year, and most precipitation occurs during the summer months.[13] Cultivators in this rain-fed farming region depended on precipitation to water their fields, so summer storms during the peak growing season decisively influenced annual harvests. When summer rains fell on bare loess soil with no vegetation to retain it, much of that precipitation turned into runoff that caused floods and left little moisture behind.[14] The well-being of the flora and fauna on the Loess Plateau and of the humans who rely on them, as Ruth Mostern observes, "hinges upon the amount of rain that falls during a single season each year."[15] Water conservancy measures intervened in the hydrologic cycle by influencing what happened to rain after it hit the ground. Wells, ponds, dams, and water cellars captured and stored runoff to solve the problem of too much water in one season and not enough in others.

The consequences of a disjuncture between the hydrologic and agricultural cycles were all too real. Since 1949, Wushan County had experienced two drought-related disasters. The first came in spring 1953, when lack of rain and swarms of locusts following the wheat harvest decreased crop output in summer and autumn (see chapter 2). Little rain or snow fell in winter 1955 and the dry weather persisted into spring 1956, again threatening crops. Wushan's county committee called "ten years, nine droughts" the defining feature of agriculture in the county, and county leaders saw promoting water conservancy to reduce or eliminate the threat of droughts as the only way to increase crop production.[16] The call for "two hundred thousand wells, ponds, dams, water cellars, and springs" first appeared in Wushan's 1956 water conservancy plan. The county committee originally set out to irrigate a modest thirteen thousand *mu* (866.66 hectares) of land that year, but in early February increased the goal to forty-six thousand *mu* (3,066.66 hectares). Targets skyrocketed in March, when Wushan convened a special meeting on water conservancy. After determining each cooperative's potential, county authorities resolved to irrigate one hundred thousand *mu* (6,666.66 hectares) of mountainous land via channels and make another three hundred thousand *mu* (20,000 hectares) into "point-irrigated land" (*dianjiaodi*) where people carried water to pour on crops—more than thirty times the original target. These water conservancy and conservation projects, county leaders anticipated, would preserve groundwater, irrigate arid land, defend against drought, and increase yields.[17]

In the first two months of 1956, members of higher-level cooperatives in Wushan managed branch gullies by constructing check dams, digging trenches, and building terraces on hillsides. Soon cooperatives mobilized for the irrigation campaign as well. As a February 1956 report put it: "All over the mountains and plains they are actively searching for water resources to dig wells and springs. For this reason, the mountains and plains are full of the laboring multitudes."[18] This mobilization altered the seasonal rhythm of work in the countryside, where the winter months had previously brought a respite from farming. In the past, after the autumn harvest, "fields were empty, and some [people] had nothing to do but rest for the winter and celebrate the Lunar New Year."[19] But in winter 1956, the irrigation campaign made conservation part of the festivities: a notice from Wushan County instructed cooperative cadres to compose songs about water and soil conservation and its benefits to be performed in villages during Lunar New Year, calling on them to "vigorously conduct propaganda in combination with the Spring Festival and spring plowing to vigorously promote work."[20]

In addition to preparing for spring plowing, co-op members in Wushan had to manage gullies, build dams, and dig wells to capture surface water. They spent mornings gathering fertilizer; when the ground thawed in the afternoon, they launched "water and soil conservation assaults."[21] Successfully combining water conservancy, conservation, and farming—expanding irrigation while maintaining agricultural production—was impossible without labor intensification.

Local Experience and Experimentation

The trajectory of the irrigation campaign adhered to the CCP's distinctive process of disseminating policies drawn from experimentation in one locale (the point) for application over a wider area (the plane).[22] The Wushan county committee selected Dongshun township, where Dengjiabao was located, as its point and sent a work team to direct cadres and villagers in digging wells and springs.²³ Responding to Wushan County's call for the township to increase grain production in 1956 and expand irrigated land area, Dongshun's township party branch organized residents to prepare for spring plowing, collect fertilizer, and do other winter farmwork while also launching a "campaign to dig wells and springs."²⁴ Local cadres justified the additional labor that the campaign created for villagers by stressing that it would improve their living conditions. In addition to providing irrigation, the party branch assured villagers that digging wells and springs would "solve the drinking water difficulties of people and livestock in mountainous areas," facilitate drainage, improve the soil, and supply water for brickmaking.²⁵

Despite the promised benefits, however, reports on the irrigation campaign from Dongshun's party branch observed that cadres and villagers were displaying what it called "ideological resistance" (*sixiang dichu*) toward spending their winter digging wells and springs. Some lower-level cadres and villagers harbored what reports called the "three fears": they feared that the work would be too hard, that if they were not able to strike water the masses would curse them, and that they would "waste labor and suffer from the cold."²⁶ Even Dengjiabao's celebrated labor model Deng Haihai sighed and refused to speak because he was afraid that other villagers would upbraid him if the wells that he encouraged them to dig came up dry. The co-op's supervisory vice director, Deng Hanjie, who was selected to lead well-digging work, also worried about incurring the wrath of other villagers if they did not strike water. Deng Zicheng, whom Deng Haihai had persuaded to build bunds back in 1952 (see chapter 2), complained about having to go through the motions and do what he considered pointless work to meet irrigation targets and satisfy county authorities. His advice was for villagers not to put forth too much effort: "It's wasting labor but [we] have to waste it; [when you] do it just don't breathe too heavily."²⁷

Not only did local people resent having to work all winter digging wells that might come up dry, reports from Dongshun township related, but they also expressed anxieties about the campaign's consequences for agriculture. Some villagers spoke of "two difficulties," griping that "when the ground freezes it'll be difficult to dig wells and springs, and when water freezes it'll be difficult to prospect for water sources."²⁸ The "one complaint" among villagers in Dongshun was that "digging springs and wells is the Party's policy [so we] have to do it."[29] They also had "six misgivings."[30] The first was that sending cadres to dig wells and springs would divert their attention from handling the cooperative's "substantive problems." Second, diverting labor to dig springs and wells could interfere with spring plowing. Third, people preferred to dig springs and wells in spring, summer, and autumn rather than in winter. Fourth, villagers thought they did not have the skills needed to dig them successfully. Fifth, because the ground was frozen in winter, they worried that the wells and springs they dug would collapse after the spring thaw. Sixth, some elderly people maintained that "digging wells and springs won't be of any use for irrigating land."[31]

Indeed, the dearth of water in mountainous areas made many villagers question the logic of the campaign. One co-op member in Dengjiabao announced, "I've lived for several decades, but [I've] never seen the mountain top have water. You've set up the cooperative and have nothing better to do than to purposely look for trouble (*guyi zhao mafan*)!"[32] According to Deng Madou, the old man who pioneered conservation work in Dengjiabao by building contour bunds in 1952 (see chapter 2), "During the hottest time in the fifth and sixth [lunar] months, Dengjiabao doesn't even have water to cook noodles. Now [they] want to dig wells and springs to irrigate land. This is [like] cutting a fart to blow out a lantern (*zhi pi lai chui deng*)."[33] People called digging wells and springs "foolish messing around" (*shagua hurigui de*).[34] Two men, Lin Gaisheng and Lin Jinwa, thought the campaign was a joke because, as they told Deng Hanjie, nobody had ever heard of digging wells on mountainsides.[35] Low groundwater levels in upland areas made it difficult to strike water. Even Deng Hanjie worried that "this time, if digging wells and springs doesn't succeed it'll make the masses curse us to death." These concerns, township reports observed, were a serious impediment.[36]

Successfully mobilizing for the campaign required educating both low-level cadres and ordinary villagers. A report from the Dongshun township party branch revealed how this was done.[37] First, the party branch conducted "ideological mobilization" among party and youth league members, local cadres, and activists to convince them of the importance of digging wells and springs. Dependable "backbone" cadres visited production brigades to lead and set an example for others. The party branch devised slogans to spur on the effort to transform the landscape: "To change mountain land into irrigated fields, digging wells and springs is key. To change the mountain land into irrigated fields, everyone come dig wells. When mountain land is irrigated once, grain [yields] will increase by half. Where there are mountains there must be water; how high the mountains are is how high the water [can be]." Invoking central orders that called for accelerating collectivization and technical improvements in agriculture, other slogans declared: "The great [Seventeen-Article] Directive [on Agriculture] and the Central Political Bureau's [Forty Article Outline] Program [for Agricultural Development] resplendently shine, illuminating our courageous advance to dig wells and springs." The propaganda had a clear message: by following the CCP's guidance and collectivizing agriculture, villagers could find water anywhere, remake the landscape, and generate economic prosperity.

These mobilization strategies won over some villagers, who encouraged others to support the campaign. As a production team leader in Dengjiabao stated, "If there's no water, then we have to look for water."[38] Deng Haihai had a change of heart about the campaign, spurring on fellow co-op members by telling them, "No matter how great the hardship, it can't impede the power of the people. I'll definitely achieve results digging wells and springs and report them to Chairman Mao!"[39] Despite their earlier trepidation, local cadres and activists conveyed the party-state's message to recalcitrant villagers and persuaded them to participate.

It would be inaccurate, however, to see the campaign as an entirely top-down affair. Grassroots cadres looked to local environmental knowledge for water conservancy techniques. Villagers knew where to look for water, and state agents used their experience as a guide. Dongshun township's party branch visited elderly villagers and convened "old-peasant discussion meetings," at which they "summarized [their] experience searching for water sources." These discussions indicated that water could be found in places where snow melted quickly, where lotus leaves and patches of grass grew, in places that stayed humid in dry weather, in ruptures in gullies that had water vapor in them, in places with lots of worms and ants, and wherever grain and grasses were especially lush.[40]

The township party branch also conferred with party and youth league members, cooperative cadres, and activists to select pilot sites for twelve wells and springs, deputing over thirty cadres and "experienced old peasants" to "use assault-style methods and act as the vanguard." This strategy, reports claimed, overcame the misgivings of cadres and other villagers.[41] At a meeting with youth league members and other young people, the party-branch mobilized over 90 youths to function as "shock brigades" for digging wells and springs, some of whom earned certificates of merit as labor models.[42] After activists from Dengjiabao dug wells and springs in Qiaozi Gully and struck water three times in succession, cooperative cadres and villagers from Majiashan came to observe and study these techniques.[43] By February 7, led by Deng Hanjie, Li Xuding, and Zhao Fansheng, Dengjiabao had dug twenty-four wells and springs that were capable of irrigating 590 *mu* (39.33 hectares).[44]

Using local know-how to figure out where to sink wells, Dongshun's party branch selected five people to form a survey group led by the township head to look for places where they could strike water. The group's members first dug a hole three *chi* (1 meter) deep, put a bowl at the bottom, and covered the hole with straw. The next day, they took out the bowl; if there were beads of water in it, they had discovered a spring. The survey group identified over 120 spots where water existed, then organized 150 people into a shock brigade to dig wells and springs. Each took five to fifteen days (twelve days on average) to complete, and they found water in 67 of the 71 the spots they dug. Reports from cadres in Dongshun played up their successes, claiming that by February 8, in addition to building 78 *mu* (5.2 hectares) of terraces, the township had dug fifty-one springs and twenty wells that irrigated 1,278 *mu* (85.2 hectares) of land.[45]

To prevent the irrigation campaign from interfering with agricultural production and the formation of higher-level cooperatives, the township party branch divided cadres and villagers into three groups: one group oversaw planning and administrative work, another handled "substantive farm problems" and took responsibility for labor and production, and the third dug wells and springs. To direct the campaign, the party branch outlined what it called the "four educations," the "one prepare," and the "three attentions."[46] The four educations consisted of teaching personnel to pay attention to safety, establishing "the collectivist ideology of taking the cooperative as the household," vigilantly guarding against "enemy plots and sabotage," and maintaining wells after digging them. The one prepare referred to preparing a shovel, a hoe, a new hemp rope, a basket for carrying earth, and a wooden bucket for carrying water before starting to dig a well. By preparing this equipment in advance, workers did not have to waste time gathering tools. The three attentions meant ensuring rational labor arrangements, strengthening labor management, and organizing an effective teamwork system. Generally, three people could dig a well or spring, but not all teams worked efficiently. One production team sent twenty-seven people to dig a single well, resulting in "severe under-utilization and waste" of labor. With no work to do, some people "slept or took a rest; some smoked or ate hot noodles; some people chatted and sang mountain folk songs," but the township party branch assured the county government that it had rectified the problem.

In conjunction with grassroots cadres, the Wushan county committee's organization bureau head and Dongshun township's party secretary traveled to mountainous areas to oversee the digging of wells and springs.[47] With higher-level support and encouragement, Dongshun became Wushan's "advanced front" in the irrigation campaign.[48] Township leaders pledged to personally organize "experienced old peasants and backbone cadres" to find water and sink one hundred wells and one thousand springs, while also levelling 60 percent of Dongshun's inclined land.[49] Expressing the aspirations of local people who had suffered from years of drought, the township party branch reported that villagers had exclaimed, "With high-level [cooperativization] (*gaojihua*), we're very enthusiastic. With all our hearts, we want to turn Dongshun's mountainous land into irrigated fields, turning an arid township into an irrigated township with one hundred wells and one thousand springs."[50]

Alongside these bold proclamations, however, the sources allude to persistent difficulties. Township reports recommended that local leaders, backbone cadres, and technically proficient individuals should direct the digging of wells and springs to avoid accidents, implying that lack of proper oversight had resulted in mishaps. The party branch also pointed to the need for realistic assessments of soil quality, topography, irrigation feasibility, and available water resources to "overcome a blindly optimistic and careless mood in work."[51] But as the campaign gained momentum, few heeded this advice.

Quantity over Quality

Beginning in late February, Wushan's county committee publicized Dongshun's achievements in other locales and had them send people to the township for observation and study. Districts and townships, in turn, established their own points and organized observation visits to extend water conservancy methods to other villages. Emulating strategies devised in Dongshun, state agents throughout Wushan continued to rely on local knowledge. To figure out how to find water and prevent "work stoppages due to poor coordination and waste," cadres made home visits to interview "experienced peasants" and summarized telltale signs of where water could be found.[52] To the indicators collected in Dongshun, they added mountain bends and curves in slopes, places where coltsfoot (*donghua, Tussilago farfara*) plants grew, anywhere tradition held that water existed, places with names containing the measure word for wells (*yan*), and places where they reckoned that aquifers converged.[53]

Throughout Wushan, county leaders organized young people to serve as the campaign's driving force. The county youth league, in conjunction with water conservancy and water and soil conservation organs, held a meeting in late March that was attended by 700 youth league cadres, model members, and activists. The meeting conducted "thorough ideological mobilization" to inspire youths to become "shock troops and dagger companies," with each young person responsible for digging five springs and every five youths expected to dig one well.[54] The county organized 875 shock brigades with over 28,000 adolescent girls and boys assuming a "battle posture."[55]

But even with mobilization in full swing, digging wells in upland areas with low groundwater tables drew ridicule. Local people jeeringly remarked that "digging wells in high mountains is [like] a blind person carrying a lantern—a waste of time," "digging springs and wells doesn't do any good," and "digging wells in mountains is [like] kids playing around."[56] Other villagers considered sinking wells and building dams a form of "technical work" that "uncultured peasants" could not do. Some cadres adopted a "wait and see attitude" and, disregarding instructions from their superiors, delayed and refused to act. Political pressure overcame this hesitation. County authorities interpreted overt or covert opposition to the irrigation campaign as "a reflection of rightist ideology" and held meetings to denounce such attitudes. Some county leaders also came under fire: the astronomical increase in Wushan's water conservancy mission for 1956 was the result of the county committee "criticizing its own rightist tendencies." The possibility that they, too, would be attacked as rightists if they did not dig wells and springs compelled virtually everyone in Wushan to join the campaign, and each day tens of thousands of people mobilized to look for water throughout the county.

Keeping this irrigation work from hampering crop production required careful labor allocation. The expansion of the campaign's scope coincided with the busy spring plowing season, so "the work mission in villages was extremely onerous." Wushan's county committee advised co-op leaders not to neglect water conservancy or agricultural production. County leaders had co-ops organize their members into three "forces": one to plow, another to do water conservancy work, and a third to collect fertilizer and do other farmwork. Although "during the spring planting period a lot of farmwork was piled up together," this division of labor ensured that farming and water conservancy work mostly proceeded smoothly.[57]

At the same time, the irrigation campaign shifted attention away from other conservation measures. Local cadres came under pressure from higher-level authorities as a result. An urgent directive from the Wushan county committee on February 28 observed that leaders in some areas had neglected field engineering projects like building terraces. Local leaders claimed they lacked the technical know-how needed to direct work. Grassroots cadres asserted that terracing was "inconvenient and expends a lot of labor" and people were not accustomed to it. The committee's directive accused local cadres of not propagandizing about the importance of terraces or urging people to construct them. Although a few places had built some terraces, they did not summarize or extend their work methods. According to the committee, neither lower-level cadres nor township-level leaders made terracing a priority. "For this reason," the directive claimed, "they only firmly grasp wells, ponds, dams, and water cellars. Firmly grasping this work is necessary and correct, but some cadres are paying no heed to the work of constructing level terraces." As a result, Wushan risked falling short of its target for building terraces that year.[58]

When the irrigation campaign reached its height in March, as a former member of Wushan's county committee recalled, it possessed an unprecedented boldness, vigor, and zeal.[59] But when people "rushed into action," as reports from 1956 stated, they focused on quantity rather than quality.[60] Due to "subjectivism" in their work, some cadres did not consider "natural characteristics and technical conditions." Rather, they "desired quantity and size, and were too eager to complete the mission."[61] In the context of "higher-level cooperativization and criticizing rightist conservative ideology," leaders "only saw organized peasants' production activism and labor enthusiasm and neglected that changing the face of nature is long-term and arduous work."[62] Leaders did not recognize that the labor force was limited, so they mobilized everyone to build dams and manage gullies. Cooperatives did not select sites well or adhere to proper technical specifications; many projects failed due to lack of surveying and poor design. Localities strove to generate statistics that met the campaign's prescribed targets with little concern for the structural integrity of what they built.[63] One villager captured prevailing attitudes when he remarked, "Who cares if three times seven is twenty-one. Just build the dam and forget about it."[64]

Numbers may have looked impressive, but the quality of work was poor. Dams constructed on land covered in thin layers of ice shifted once the ground thawed, which weakened them. Failure to properly tamp down dams, clear loose earth at abutments, carefully measure a dam's incline, and leave drainage outlets led to further damage.[65] The outcomes met with derision. When a dam made of adobe and loose earth in Yuanyang township collapsed as soon as waters arrived, villagers jabbed, "Y'all be careful and watch the dam; my ox is about to take a piss (*wo de niu yao jiao niao le*)."[66] Many wells, ponds, dams, and water cellars not only failed to store water but interfered with cultivation. Residents of a village in Tan'ge township dug ponds next to fields, which made it hard for people and livestock to walk through the fields and obstructed plowing. Frustrated villagers complained, "These aren't water storage ponds, they're pits for horses to fall into."[67] People in another village referred to water cellars dug beside roads as "donkey-scaring pits."[68]

Urgency won out over judicious planning, with damaging results. Inattention to local conditions, preoccupation with large projects, and overzealous pursuit of targets resulted in structures that, as a report on conservation work in Wushan during 1956 put it, "not only did not function to store water and conserve soil, but also caused serious erosion and runoff, making work go down the wrong path, and making the masses incur losses."[69] The report admitted that villagers offered a "fitting appraisal" when they remarked that "things get done, few are done well; the investments are large, the benefits are few." Focusing solely on managing gullies led people to overlook management measures on plateaus, so runoff from rainstorms caused washouts. Medium-sized dams became clogged with silt, and check dams and small dams burst, leaving villagers disillusioned.[70] When dam failures caused floods, people in Songshan township scathingly expressed their dissatisfaction: "Everything about the Communist Party is good, except dams kill people (*zhi you ba ba ren haisi le*). One [dam] washing out leads to ten more washing out. Small waters turn into big waters, and floodwaters kill people."[71]

Building dams that did more harm than good placed even heavier labor demands on Wushan's rural populace. As another conservation work report observed, "In many places work incurred losses, seriously exhausting the people and draining the treasury." A line crossed out in the original draft of the document read, "The creation of these serious problems is inseparable from our cadres not caring about the masses' hardships, not cherishing the masses' labor power, and lofty bureaucratic methods."[72] By redacting these words, county leaders apparently sought to avoid being held responsible for their subordinates' misdeeds.

Workers building a dam in one gully criticized local leaders, complaining that "going back and forth to build a dam runs people to death, carrying earth makes them die of hardship, at night they die from staying awake, stacking rocks scares people to death, and family members are worked to death (*wei da ba laiwang ba ren paosi, bei tu kusi, wanshang aosi, fang shitou ba ren xiasi, jiazhongren caosi*)!" Cooperative members had to travel far from their homes to do backbreaking and dangerous work well into the night so that they could fulfill dam-building targets without leaving farmwork undone. Certain cadres, moreover, "did not deal with things according to actual conditions and made coercive commands." During the harvest, a cadre in one co-op had members stop cutting wheat and do conservation work, "which made the masses dissatisfied."[73]

Clearly, the irrigation campaign had negative unintended consequences. As of late 1956, an article in *Gansu Daily* reported, the incomes of 38 percent of the members of Simen township's Xinguang cooperative had declined since its formation more than ten months earlier.[74] Men from sixteen households in the co-op had stopped farming and gone out to do wage labor. Women refused to take part in agricultural production and wanted to learn how to sew instead. Nearly all the cadres in the co-op wanted to resign. Usually, villagers focused on spring plowing after the Lunar New Year. But in early 1956, with spring farmwork at its busiest, higher-level authorities instructed the cooperative to "mobilize all power to launch a 1,000,000 [*sic*] wells, ponds, dams, cellars, and springs campaign." Worried that missing the spring plowing season would result in poor harvests, members asked to be able to plant crops before turning to farmland construction. Higher authorities rebuked their requests as ideologically backward and conservative and issued "mobilization orders to militarily advance against drought." County and district leaders made telephone calls to township-level cadres to demand numerical results and spur on work. Male and female co-op members labored during the day and at night (presumably with illumination from lamps) for more than two months, and some built dams until the summer harvest. The 403 households in the co-op devoted twelve thousand workdays to the irrigation campaign. But 80 percent of the dams, springs, and wells they built were "wasted goods." Many washed out during rainstorms, so villagers complained that they had done large amounts of labor for nothing. Labor shortages delayed planting, and even when planting was done on time the work was shoddy, decreasing yields and incomes.[75]

The summary of a training meeting for technical cadres in Wushan held in November 1956 related, in a moment of self-criticism, that the irrigation campaign earlier that year "had great momentum and came on too vigorously." Despite its achievements, it also caused "many problems." Ineffective projects wasted labor and materials; washouts left people disheartened and caused "great discontent." After a dam broke and unleashed a deluge that threatened fields, villagers in the village of Chaijiaping complained, "Dams, dams, dams—they make people afraid" (*ba, ba, ba, re de ren haipa*)." An attendee from Baiquan township echoed the sentiment: "This year dams have really worn us out." Another meeting attendee from Panlong commented on the large quantity of resources that dam building had consumed by quipping that his village had "poured more than forty thousand *jin* of cooked noodles onto the dam. I alone poured in three or four *dou*."[76] That month, *Gansu Daily* reported that Wushan County held a meeting of cooperative directors, who openly criticized "subjectivism"—failure to formulate policy based on actual conditions—in leadership. During spring plowing season, higher-level leaders made urgent demands to develop water conservancy plans and plant trees on barren hillsides, which caused many co-ops to miss the planting period. Dams washed out, wells were "wasted goods," and most of the trees they planted died, which squandered funds and labor. Co-op directors pointed out that higher-ups rarely came to mountainous areas to conduct investigations, so they advocated inappropriate methods that caused this litany of difficulties.[77]

Because large-scale water and soil conservation and irrigation projects did not yield immediate benefits, some co-ops could not afford to remunerate the work points that their members earned toiling on dams, which decreased people's incomes. "To a definite extent," as a county report noted, "this harmed peasants' labor enthusiasm in doing water and soil conservation."[78] A cooperative in Yanchi, for example, did not compensate its members for half of the over 4,000 workdays devoted to building a large dam. Furthermore, investment in construction cut into the pool of funds available for co-ops to distribute in exchange for work points. One man in Yanchi racked up over 460 workdays for the year, but over 70 had been spent doing unpaid basic construction and compulsory labor.[79] When projects involved "unified organization" by multiple districts or townships, some co-ops reaped benefits, but others did not, leading to "uncompensated requisitioning of labor power between accounting units."[80] As a result, co-op members sometimes worked for other collectives without pay.

Many projects had disappointing results. But local cadres, who wanted to impress their superiors by meeting campaign targets, reported only successes. Higher authorities rarely heard about failures until it was too late. In July 1956, county-level investigations found that, despite earlier reports that Wushan had completed over 51,000 wells, ponds, dams, water cellars, and springs, the real number was only 18,700. Poorly built "wasted goods" accounted for 9,124 of these projects. Of the more than 500 irrigation channels that had reportedly been built, only 369 existed. Nine townships claimed to have irrigated all their farmland, but "in actuality most projects were all labor done to no effect."[81]

The irrigation campaign took place alongside a push to increase agricultural output in Wushan by expanding cultivation of high-yield maize varieties, both of which demanded large amounts of labor.[82] Since the workforce was limited, the two campaigns inevitably interfered with one another. With "wasted goods" influencing maize cultivation and other farmwork, there was "a lot of discussion" among cadres and the masses; everyone was "in a hubbub," and "there was great indignation" (*da you buping zhi qi*).[83] Failures of dams and other water conservancy structures, as a county government planning document noted, made people view the irrigation campaign unfavorably: "The bad influence among the masses has not yet been eliminated and the mood of resistance that this has caused still impedes work's smooth development."[84]

Accidents caused further resentment. A former county committee member recalled how people "said that a donkey fell into that place's well and died, a sheep drowned in that place's pond, in that place a child fell into a dam and lost their life, etc." Some residents completely repudiated the irrigation campaign, chiding that "there're dams built in every gully, [but] every dam washes out; there's loss of labor and materials, [but] there's no compensation."[85]

The Xianghe Gully Project

The fate of dam construction in Wushan's Xiang River Gully (Xianghegou) exemplifies the irrigation campaign's shortcomings. The construction of a medium-sized dam in the middle of Xiang River Gully at Huaguoshan started early in the campaign, on March 17, and the workforce quickly expanded from 550 laborers sent by six higher-level cooperatives to 653 laborers from ten co-ops. Supply offices at the site made sure these workers had adequate food and access to tobacco and tea.[86] By July 7, the labor force had spent 132,306 workdays building a dam twenty meters high (five meters lower than originally planned) using over two hundred thousand cubic meters of earth.[87]

County leaders oversaw construction at Xiang River Gully, and temporary party and youth league branches mobilized laborers at the worksite.[88] A Xiang River Earth Dam Project Committee organized workers into teams that were given specific tasks. In allocating labor, the project committee reportedly "paid attention to the different work customs and special characteristics of peasants from the mountains and the plains, which also heightened work effectiveness." Political and safety education ensured that, "especially when rushing to attend to dangerous sections on rainy days and working overtime during assaults at night, the mood of the project's civilian laborers was enthusiastic from start to finish." Except for two serious injuries, from which the victims recovered, accidents caused only minor scrapes. Cooperative members worked well into the night, but the project committee gave the impression that they did so willingly and that the intense work schedule did not jeopardize safety.[89]

The dam's fate tells a different story. Due to a leak in the stone culvert on the dam's western side and a poor abutment with the gully slope, water broke through on June 28, creating an opening on the western edge that eventually widened to nearly 10 meters.[90] This was not the only disappointment. Initial plans called for building three smaller dams approximately 12 meters high in the western gully. Work started on two of them: a stone dam at Shuiliandong and an earthen dam at Zhonglou. On June 18, after 19 days of work, the Shuiliandong dam, which, though only 8.5 meters high, took 1,800 workdays to build, washed out due to problems with the stone used for construction, poor work techniques, and failure to open its spillway.[91] By early July, floods caused by rainstorms made work difficult. During summer, moreover, "farmwork was busy and labor power gradually decreased."[92] The Xiang River Gully project stopped on July 7, and work shifted to preventing floodwaters from harming the existing dam structure.[93] The workforce at the site fell from over 1,500 laborers to around 100.[94] Elsewhere in Wushan, the construction of three other medium-sized dams also stopped midway due to lack of technical guidance, poor planning, and insufficient labor.[95]

Reflecting on this outcome, the Xiang River Earth Dam Project Committee confessed that it had failed to make proper surveys or designs prior to starting work and had not drawn up "accurate labor power and time plans and materials and supply plans." Rather than having technical personnel survey and design the dam, administrative cadres held "discussion meetings with peasants" and made observations with the naked eye to calculate floodwater volume.[96] Wushan County's requests for technical cadres equipped with levels and tape measures to direct surveying and design fell on deaf ears. The "blindly determined" estimates of the labor, time, and earthworks needed to construct the dam proved inaccurate, so the project committee had to lower its planned height first from forty meters to thirty-three meters and then to twenty-five meters. A water-release culvert was built of stacked stones, which violated technical standards and jeopardized the body of the dam. The project committee had not surveyed the spillway but "roughly fixed" it on the gully's eastern slope. Rocky ground and a shortage of explosives made digging inefficient, so it was not completed before flood season arrived. Tools had to be made while work was going on, causing further delays.[97] Bunds had not been built to check erosion upstream at the gully head, which led to sedimentation of check dams and caused many to wash out. The site of the small stone dam at Shuiliandong lacked usable stone materials and sufficient earth for construction, which contributed to its collapse. The location of the earth dam at Zhonglou was better, but its small storage capacity did little to reduce the volume of water and silt transported to the larger dam downstream.[98]

Labor mobilization plans, the project committee acknowledged, "did not accord with reality, so after the originally planned labor power was transferred [elsewhere], the project was still not complete, which gave rise to many contradictions."[99] One production team had assigned only seven of its twenty-two laborers to plant crops, while the rest worked on the Xiang River dam project. Dissatisfied elderly villagers griped, "We're making young people all go treat the dam like it's food to eat (*ba ba dang fan zhe chi qu*)!"[100]

Although the invocation of local knowledge lent legitimacy to water conservancy efforts, it was not always adequate. During the initial stage of dam construction in Xiang River Gully, as a report from the project committee stated, it had "relied on the wisdom of the masses and conferred with the masses to solve quite a few problems related to cleaning the foundation, tamping, and constructing water interception channels and inclined cores." But the report also acknowledged that a lack of guidance from cadres with technical expertise resulted in defective work. The foundation of the medium-sized dam at Huaniaoshan, for instance, consisted of deep, highly permeable sand. The upstream toe of the dam should have had an impermeable clay bedding, but it did not, and work had to stop when floodwaters entered the reservoir. To increase speed, the project committee admitted, it had "neglected project quality and did not build the dam to its full height, which gave rise to regrets." Rock fragments at the dam's western edge were not cleared away, abutment grooves where the dam connected with gully slopes were not dug or tamped down properly, and a leak in the culvert pipe caused a breach. Worksite personnel had not persuaded local people of the project's value and importance. For this reason, "the phenomena of workers being afraid to expend labor, administrative cadres rushing, and technical personnel not being able to lead" had been serious."[101]

Lack of "rational planning" to coordinate earth digging with other work, the committee's report noted, led to long periods when workers did not have the materials needed to build and fill in the dam. Due to poor communication within the project committee, techniques were not properly implemented. Living arrangements for laborers were also inadequate. After the number of workers increased, some lived over eight *li* (4 km) from the worksite, traveling almost twenty *li* (10 km) roundtrip each day, "which influenced [their] rest and work."[102]

In October 1956, after dam construction had been stalled for more than three months, Wushan County appealed to higher-level administrative authorities in Gansu for assistance, arguing that favorable circumstances for resuming work had arrived. The county reported that surveys had been conducted, the Tianshui experiment station had nearly finished new dam designs, and preparations for restarting work were underway. In late autumn, the flood season had passed, agricultural production was entering a slack season, and the weather was nice, so it was "a good time to start work."[103]

For cooperative members, making their labor available to resume construction of the dam required getting agricultural work done in less time. Despite the setbacks that had occurred earlier, Wushan County leaders claimed that villagers living near the gully "urgently asked for [its] management." Other locales in Wushan, they stated, were also prepared to offer support. Villagers had started to put in overtime to get farmwork done quickly so they could devote their time to dam building. Members of several co-ops, according to the county report, in order "to transfer large amounts of labor power to the dam, have recently lit gas lamps at night and rushed to harvest autumn crops." Gaikou cooperative, for instance, transported manure to apply to wheat fields as fertilizer in just three days (seven days faster than previous years) so it could assist in restarting work. Upstream, Guaner cooperative had already built thirty-six check dams over three meters high to protect the large dam. All co-ops in the county had "recently been rushing to plant wheat and were busy harvesting autumn crops, constantly preparing to transfer the labor power needed for the Xiang River project." Work on the dam needed to restart, the county advised, "otherwise it will leave behind a bad influence among the masses, which will make future construction work difficult."[104]

Wushan's report pointed to the Xiang River Gully project's sunk costs as another reason to resume construction. In the first half of 1956, the project had cost ¥200,000 (including labor costs); protecting the dam against floods after work stopped consumed three thousand workdays and cost over ¥1,000. Recently, workers had removed broken rocks from places where problems had occurred on the western slope and dug five connecting channels. The provincial government had sent fifty-eight tons of cement and thirty-three iron pipes to the worksite, and additional living quarters for workers had been prepared.[105]

Wushan County authorities did not deny that "a situation of work being done blindly and lacking technical guidance in the first half of the year" resulted in some of it being done improperly: the dam's foundation was crudely prepared, and part of its body contained sand. However, the report concluded that since "[we've] already mounted the horse and it's hard to dismount," higher-level leaders in Gansu Province and Tianshui Prefecture should assist the project's completion by offering technical support, materials, and equipment. Wushan pledged to strengthen leadership, manage plateaus upstream, organize the county's workforce, and acquire all the supplies it could. The report requested prompt approval of the dam design so that work could restart in mid-October and finish before the ground froze that year.[106]

After making several visits to Xiang River Gully and examining materials sent by the Tianshui experiment area, known then as the Tianshui Water and

Soil Conservation Scientific Experiment Station (Tianshui shuitu baochi kexue shiyanzhan), Gansu's Water Conservancy Bureau advised against restarting work. It found that dam repairs were poorly planned and did not "combine with the masses' current production benefits." Gully slopes and upstream plateaus had not been effectively managed, so torrential runoff had caused washouts. The project's cost raised concerns, and doubts about its effectiveness remained. Concentrating labor power in "this small point," the provincial Water Conservancy Bureau observed, would hinder agricultural production and conservation work more widely. In the first half of 1956, the Water Conservancy Bureau warned, "blindness in the work of building dams has already given us great lessons. For this reason, the Xiang River Gully earthen dam project, which washed out and resulted in enormous losses of labor and materials, should be considered especially carefully."[107] Although Wushan County said that co-ops would provide the necessary workforce, the provincial Water Conservancy Bureau cautioned that "in the end [we] must carefully consider the problem of rationally allocating labor power for agricultural production and basic construction."[108]

The Xiang River Gully project consumed more than one hundred thousand workdays only to end in disappointment. Turning Wushan County's argument on its head, Gansu's Water Conservancy Bureau replied that the project "not only lost labor and materials but also created a bad influence among the masses." The economic benefits of managing the gully had to be considered alongside the drawbacks, "seeking to combine the immediate benefits and long-term benefits of the masses." If work resumed without proper design or sufficient technical guidance, another collapse was possible. With slopes and branch gullies unmanaged, floodwaters increased during rainstorms, as did the amount of sediment they carried, and rapid siltation threatened to shorten the dams' lifespan. Should they fail again, the Water Conservancy Bureau cautioned, "then the masses will blame us even more," which would make it harder to mobilize for large-scale conservation work in the future. If local enthusiasm for building dams was high, the Bureau recommended, the Tianshui experiment station and Wushan County should explain to cadres and other residents why work could not resume.[109]

The provincial government's decision coincided with a county-level reassessment of the irrigation campaign. After the 1956 autumn harvest, the

Wushan county committee convened a meeting of county, district, and township cadres to summarize the "two hundred thousand wells, ponds, dams, water cellars, and springs" campaign's results. Leaders encouraged participants to voice their assessments without fear of retribution and selected speakers with different points of view. In the end, everyone agreed on the correctness of the campaign and the importance of "changing the arid face of mountainous areas." The problem, as a participant recalled, was that leaders' aspirations had "surpassed practical possibilities, raising matters that simply could not be done in a short time, and this could not help but give rise to the problems of rushing, not paying attention to quality, or over-reporting." Everyone believed that agricultural production in Wushan had no way forward without water conservancy, so they could not let the 1956 campaign's shortcomings make them give up on irrigation. Instead, they had to learn from the experience, affirm the campaign's achievements, and move forward. In 1957 the county settled on a more modest "develop one thousand ponds, one hundred wells, and ten thousand water cellars and canals campaign" to expand irrigation and combat drought.[110]

Flood Defense and Farmwork in Dengjiabao

Even after the irrigation campaign subsided, cooperatives had to maintain the dams they had already built. To protect dams against floodwaters during the 1956 summer rainy season, as outlined in a report from a conservation work team member named Kong Fengzhong, Dengjiabao adhered to the principle of "first earthen dams, then field engineering, then tending [trees]." Newly organized "water and soil conservation restoration shock brigades" repaired damaged infrastructure in gullies. Production groups looked after dams, while children, women, and the elderly pulled weeds and tended newly planted trees. This division of labor made it possible to restore dams, bunds, ponds, and springs; fill collapses; and add water-drainage outlets to earthen dams in gullies. To publicize conservation's importance, the work team wrote slogans and goals in red clay around the village and on gully cliffs.[111]

Seeking ways to "rescue earth dams" after torrential rains and ensure their safety, the work team engaged in informal discussions with Deng Haihai and other villagers. They indicated that previously, whenever flash floods occurred, villagers rushed to protect dams by using earth to heighten them in places where there was overtopping. But the earth washed away when the volume of runoff grew, causing dams to fail. To solve this problem, villagers sealed gaps with a more porous mixture of hay and mud. This repair method allowed runoff to flow out gradually without washing away the earthworks. The force of floodwaters thus did not increase as they gathered behind the dams, so the structures held. The technique, which co-op members in Dengjiabao had devised after two serious dam failures, Kong Fengzhong stated, proved effective and was "worth trying out in each area."[112]

Yet nature had no regard for conservation and production plans, as prolonged rains impeded all types of work. The Dengjiabao brigade had tended only 37.5 percent of maize fields and hoed a mere 20 percent of its millet. Barley had gone to seed and nearly blighted. Wheat, barley, and bean fields were almost ready to be harvested, but still it rained. Forty men from Dengjiabao went to work as short-term laborers at Wushan's train station while waiting for the weather to improve. When the rain stopped, all sorts of work would crowd together, Kong Fengzhong advised, so the cooperative needed to make plans to avoid having to rush and neglecting important tasks. While it rained, rather than resting or doing hired labor, Kong urged co-op members to do what he called the "five checks": making sure tools (scythes, grinding stones, shoulder poles, ropes, and back frames) were prepared, that labor was adequate, that everyone contributed to the division of labor, that food was ready, and that cadres were properly assigned. To coordinate farming and conservation work, co-op leaders served as "summer harvest command post heads," with female cadres directing female members. Production teams acted as "command teams," with team leaders or party members in charge. Teams also established "three groups and one program": each team devised a water and soil conservation direction program; formed a shock group to harvest grain; established a women's shock group to hoe the autumn fields, weed, and select seeds; and formed another group to direct emergency repairs, inspection, and defense of the dams.[113]

This regimented structure ensured that no tasks were left undone. Teams made summer harvesting and autumn hoeing top priorities. Transporting fertilizer and building bunds were secondary. They waited for gaps in farming and rainy days to "launch all-out assaults" on bunds and gullies. Kong Fengzhong described "taking advantage of gaps [in farming] to organize power" in this manner as a crucial part of the summer harvest.[114] Balancing agriculture and conservation work did not allow for any downtime.

Labor intensification meant that the total workdays devoted to water and soil conservation in Dengjiabao boomed from 289.2 in 1952 to 1,820 in 1953. They dipped slightly to 1,712 in 1954 before increasing to 2,160.2 in 1955 and 3,700 in 1956.[115] Data at our disposal indicate that labor intensification ensured that the additional time and energy devoted to conservation did not adversely impact agriculture. Output per capita of grain and other staples in Dengjiabao grew by nearly 40 percent, from 275.75 kilograms in 1955 to 385 kilograms in 1956. Mobilization for irrigation projects did not interfere with planting and harvesting. Even after taxation and compulsory sales, grain availability exceeded the benchmark for self-sufficiency at around 328 kilograms per head. Estimated per capita consumption increased from roughly 1,790 calories per day in 1955 to 2,425 in 1956 (see table 1). However, there were already warning signs that villagers could not maintain the level of physical exertion needed to both farm and do conservation work.

The Limits of Local Mobilization

To further promote "water conservancy-ization" (*shuilihua*), Dengjiabao's conservation work team began digging a water retention reservoir at the head of Tiaozi Gully to stop its expansion and store runoff for irrigation. Water would not enter the gully after the reservoir's completion, the work team anticipated, making it possible to plant sweet potatoes and other crops on the land. By turning gully land into level fields, the project would thus move "from only managing gullies to managing gullies to increase agricultural production."[116]

Making sure that diverting labor to building the reservoir in Tiaozi Gully would not influence winter production took careful coordination. Dengjiabao organized a designated number of co-op members into two shifts: the first and fourth brigades took one, the third and second brigades took the other, and they switched every two days. Two brigades spent their shift working on the reservoir while the other two gathered fertilizer, and vice versa. This rotation, as the work team reported, proved "advantageous for digging the reservoir and also advantageous for gathering fertilizer, so neither is neglected."[117]

The work team outfitted the construction site with a boiler so co-op members had potable water. Explaining the significance of the reservoir for co-op members' livelihoods and stressing the importance of winter production during rest periods reportedly had a "profound influence" on the quality of work. Activist workers garnered public praise or had their achievements written on a blackboard for all to see, and this "praise and evaluation by comparison" roused enthusiasm. In addition, co-op members spent the last two hours of each two-day shift at meetings where they summarized "battle results," praised activists, affirmed accomplishments, pointed out shortcomings, and presented outstanding workers with honors and material rewards.[118]

Building the reservoir had not been easy. Because the cost of construction fell on the cooperative and because it would take time for the reservoir to benefit crop production, the work team requested government funds to compensate laborers and acquire materials. The livelihoods of co-op members in some places were still difficult, and digging the frozen ground had damaged tools. Under these circumstances, the work team asked higher-level state agencies for a subsidy of two *jiao* per labor power, for a total of ¥120, and an additional ¥200 for materials. "Although this requires some investment," the work team argued, "the effects will be great."[119]

However, the Tiaozi Gully reservoir was not the only project that needed support. Starting on December 3, a nine-person project committee comprising party members, full-time cadres, and local activists prepared to construct a bypass irrigation channel for the dam built in Kangjia Gully.[120] A report from Dengjiabao's conservation work team quoted Deng Kejun as saying that previously he and others had not believed that building dams was useful, but after Dengjiabao irrigated 65.5 *mu* (4.36 hectares) of land that winter, he saw that "irrigated land going up the mountain" had come to fruition, and with "state investment," he would have "unparalleled confidence" in doing this work.[121] To give the impression that local people were selflessly dedicated to water conservancy efforts, the work team announced that, when washing gravel in the Wei River, Deng Kejun and Zhang Zixiang, "paid no attention to their cold feet" and stood in the water all day, and Li Wanwan "went out first thing in the morning" to search for gravel "and didn't return home until 6:30pm."[122]

When construction of the bypass channel began on December 9, Wushan County projected that it would take 1,400 workdays. Providing this labor was a strain on local people. As county leaders cautioned, "If turning out for work is entirely obligatory (*quanbu yiwu chuqin*), it will be difficult for the masses here in Dengjiabao to take responsibility for joining in the common effort, and their livelihoods will be influenced to varying degrees." What they called "obligatory" work was little more than a euphemism for forced labor. Instead, county authorities asserted that those who worked on the bypass channel needed compensation. To get funds to pay workers, Wushan asked the Tianshui experiment area (which had changed its name to the Tianshui Water and Soil Conservation Work Extension Station in late 1956) for a daily subsidy of ¥0.8 per laborer, ¥1,100 in total, and another ¥2,000 for materials.[123]

Without higher-level assistance, mobilizing workers for the Kangjia Gully bypass channel and the Tiaozi Gully reservoir at the same time posed a dilemma. A comment jotted on the cover page of Wushan County's report on the bypass channel warned that arrangements had to be made to provide labor power to that project as well as the reservoir, "otherwise [we] will attend to one and neglect the other."[124] Cooperatives had a finite workforce, and conservation projects were stretching it to the limit.

But higher-level state agencies refused to assist. The Tianshui extension station responded to Wushan's request for funds for the bypass channel by stating that the regulations of Gansu's Water and Soil Conservation Committee stipulated that all investments for earthen dams ten to twenty meters high should rely on "civilian management and government assistance" (*min ban gong zhu*). Cooperatives supplied labor and the government provided materials such as cement, lime, and piping. Since the Kangjia Gully dam was only eleven meters high, the government would not provide subsidies for its workforce. Along with forty-five meters of porcelain piping already sent, it would provide ¥880 to pay for lime and cement.[125] The PRC party-state's developmental model during the 1950s involved extracting surplus from the countryside, not investing in it, so the cost of conservation fell on rural residents.

The "two hundred thousand wells, ponds, dams, water cellars, and springs campaign" aspired to alleviate chronic water shortages and low agricultural productivity by capturing uneven seasonal rainfall for irrigation, but it encountered resistance from the start. Villagers resented having to do irrigation work during the frigid winter months, when they customarily got a respite from farm labor, and they doubted its effectiveness. Grassroots cadres feared running afoul of neighbors and kin if irrigation projects failed. It took direct intervention by county and township authorities to change the minds of local state agents, who persuaded other villagers to take part. By promoting Dongshun as the key point for the campaign, county leaders gave other townships a blueprint for how to overcome local opposition and conduct mobilization.

That blueprint drew directly on local environmental knowledge and "mass experience," which grassroots cadres summarized and higher-level authorities disseminated to other locales for emulation. But local people could not select the purposes for which their knowledge was used. The 1956 irrigation campaign confirms Victor Seow's assertion that, even if expertise during the Mao era drew from a "broader cast of characters" than scientifically and technically trained elites, "their expertise still served narrow statist ends." Whether in the name of production, conservation, or a combination of the two, local knowledge was only deemed useful if it furthered "the advancement of the state."[126] Knowledge and practices rooted in the experiences of "old peasants" had value only if they aligned with the irrigation campaign's goals. By contrast, campaign leaders dismissed the knowledge of villagers whose experience led them to question the wisdom of looking for water in upland areas. Heeding that local environmental knowledge, which often proved to be correct, could have averted the waste of time and energy that resulted when wells and springs came up dry. Instead, the campaign extended experience drawn from the point that served the state's priorities uniformly across the plane.

In terms of advancing the irrigation campaign's goals, local environmental knowledge only went so far. Mass experience was no replacement for engineering expertise and technical precision. Lack of proper surveying, faulty design, and poor planning led to costly dam failures that squandered labor, caused serious flooding, and fanned popular discontent. The pressure to achieve rapid results made it impossible for project plans to pay adequate attention to adapting measures to local conditions. In recklessly pursuing unrealistic targets, the irrigation campaign put speed and quantity over deliberation and quality. Construction of shoddy and unstable structures proved worthless or even harmful, but problems did not come to the attention of superiors, who received false reports of exaggerated achievements. Some people in Wushan spoke out against the physical toil that the irrigation campaign demanded, the labor that was squandered on poor-quality projects, and the damage that resulted when dams collapsed. But voices of criticism and dissent were denounced as "rightist conservative ideology."

Throughout the irrigation campaign, higher-level cooperatives turned to regimentation and labor intensification to ensure that mobilizing the entire workforce for conservation did not hamper agricultural production. Total workdays devoted to conservation increased in the mid-1950s along with crop yields. Even with the share of the harvest that went to state grain procurements, villagers in Dengjiabao had more to eat in 1956 than before. But records related to the Xiang River Gully dam, Tiaozi Gully reservoir, and the Kangjia Gully bypass channel suggest that the irrigation campaign was pushing the rural workforce to its limit. Villagers often toiled literally day and night to attend to farming, irrigation projects, and conservation work, often with little or no compensation. Cadres and officials voiced concern that sending laborers to construct dams and reservoirs would interfere with crop cultivation. Disrupting this precarious balance between conservation and farming would have dire consequences.

FIVE

"Learn from Dengjiabao"

Conservation Militarized and Aestheticized

With the Great Leap Forward, Mao Zedong and his supporters endeavored to make China into a nation on par with the world's major economic powers by mobilizing its vast rural population to develop industry and agriculture. Villagers joined people's communes that consolidated landholdings, working to raise agricultural yields and remake China's landscape. Throughout the Great Leap, PRC leaders cast production as a military operation that required devoting all available resources to accomplishing miraculous feats of environmental and economic transformation. Collectives organized workers into quasi-military units and deployed them to combat nature.[1] Commune members marched in ranks to the fields each morning, accompanied by gongs, drums, and banners.[2] The militarization of organization and language transferred "the urgency, the discipline, and the heroism of wartime struggles to the task of building socialism in a time of peace."[3]

In this atmosphere, the village of Dengjiabao came to symbolize the successful use of militarized ideals and organization to alter the biophysical landscape to conserve water and soil. By publicizing Dengjiabao's experiences, the party-state encouraged other locales to remake the environment in a similar fashion. Dengjiabao's model status predated the Great Leap Forward, but because in Gansu the Great Leap focused on water conservancy and soil conservation, the movement amplified Dengjiabao's significance.[4] The PRC's larger developmental priorities explain the timing: the party-state wanted to limit erosion on the Loess Plateau and siltation in the Yellow River's lower reaches after 1957 to extend the life of the Sanmenxia dam and reservoir, on which construction commenced that year.[5]

To promote conservation, everyone needed to become more like Dengjiabao. In the spring of 1957, Wushan County initiated a "one hundred Dengjiabaos campaign" that called on other collectives to emulate its achievements. In early 1958, just after the start of the Great Leap Forward, Gansu launched a "ten thousand Dengjiabaos campaign," increasing Dengjiabao's influence by orders of magnitude. As a party branch secretary in Dengjiabao informed me during one of my visits, "Dengjiabao was like a propaganda phrase contrived to arouse popular feeling (*gudong renxin de xuanchuanyu zhi lei de*); it was related to the construction of water and soil conservation. ... At that time, Dengjiabao was a place that people in this vicinity really yearned [to be like]."[6]

The campaign soon transcended Gansu, with stories of Dengjiabao's conservation achievements reaching audiences throughout China. An article published in October 1958 in *People's Daily* trumpeted the village as the epitome of what mass mobilization under the people's communes made possible.[7] The article posed the question: "When all is said and done, what counts as aiming high?" The imperative to "aim high," drawn from Mao's exhortation to "go all out, aim high, and achieve greater, faster, better, and more economical results in building socialism," was a ubiquitous refrain during the Great Leap Forward. The article's author had traveled to Shaanxi and Gansu looking for examples of how to "aim high," and he cited Wushan as one of the most advanced counties he had visited. Among Wushan County's other accomplishments, Dengjiabao's experience conserving water and soil made it a "red flag that had risen to national prominence," charting a path for others as they, too, aimed high in conservation work.

Practically speaking, learning from Dengjiabao meant mobilizing rural people for conservation campaigns characterized by militarized rhetoric and organization. Language equating environmental transformation with warfare implies immediate and serious threats, the need for quick and forceful action, increased state intervention, and mobilization of resources. Making conservation the moral equivalent of war justified and drove the extreme labor intensification needed to rapidly transform the biophysical landscape. By urging administrative units and rural collectives to engage in labor competitions, the campaign to learn from Dengjiabao also increased the scale and intensity of conservation work, with armies of laborers exhorted to toil over vast areas with little respite.

This militarization of conservation also had a profoundly romanticized aesthetic dimension. Slogans, songs, poems, and other cultural products that animated the Dengjiabao campaign of 1957–58 rhapsodized about the mobilization of labor to remake the environment in grandiose, heroic terms reminiscent of epic sagas. Propaganda material lavishly extolled the aesthetic dimensions of the improvements that victory in these battles would bring—the beauty of clear water, lush green trees, and the curving parallel lines of terraces on hillsides.

William Thomas Okie has coined the term "aesthetic inhabitation" to recover "beauty as an important but underappreciated way of knowing the world," while also recognizing that "knowledge comes not merely by seeing and thinking but also by inhabiting the world with our whole bodies."[8] Because aesthetic experience is "full-bodied not just visual," it indexes connections between humans and nature. Opie observes that "this embodied sense of aesthetic experience is participatory. We make it even as we enjoy it."

During the early stages of the Great Leap Forward, campaign slogans and propaganda summoned reserves of popular enthusiasm and self-sacrifice by deploying aestheticized descriptions of the rural landscape that conservation promised to create. This discourse moved many villagers to join the struggle to transform the environment and create a better future. Wushan's rural populace labored to bring that aesthetically pleasing environment into existence during the Great Leap. Their experiences of the material world largely emerged from work.[9] People did not know the beauty of an idyllic pastoral environment as scenes before their eyes; they toiled to create it with their hands, feet, backs, and brains. And while the aesthetics of conservation inspired enthusiasm in some, others resented the demands that mass mobilization for the war against erosion put on them.

Competing to Conserve

To get conservation back on track after the disappointments of the "wells, pools, dams, and water cellars" campaign of 1956 (see chapter 4), Wushan County called for every locale to follow the example set by Dengjiabao. A training meeting held in November 1956 instructed attendees to take Dengjiabao as their direction by doing conservation work according to "the principle of suiting measures to local conditions." Mountainous areas in Wushan were to emulate Dengjiabao by building bunds and check dams, digging trenches, and combining planting trees and grasses for "integrated management from top to bottom." A report on the meeting quoted one cadre as saying, "Dengjiabao is our model. From now on, [we] definitely have to learn from Dengjiabao."[10] After returning home, Deng Hanjie and others from Dengjiabao who attended the county training meeting transmitted its message to an assembly of party members, youth league members, and cooperative leaders.[11] They then convened a general assembly of Dengjiabao's co-op members and "explained that all townships in the county are working hard to catch up with Dengjiabao, and if we don't work harder, there's a possibility that we'll fall behind." Everyone in attendance took a pledge to "work harder and plant the red flag in Dengjiabao forever."[12]

Before the winter freeze arrived, Dengjiabao planned to add bunds and trenches to autumn fields and dig ponds to capture runoff from roads. Dengjiabao's residents would repair existing bunds and fill collapses, while prohibiting people from digging up turf on inclined slopes to prevent further loss of water and soil. The co-op also planned to build three more earthen dams of five to eight meters in height in Tiaozi Gully and Kangjia Gully. Each production team mobilized more than ten people, some forty-five in total, for conservation work daily. The local cadres and activists from Dengjiabao who had attended the county training meeting—Deng Hanjie, Deng Kejun, Li Wanwan, Li Xiuyun, and Zhang Zixiang—oversaw work to ensure that labor was not squandered in making bunds and ponds that turned out to be "waste products." To push its members to work longer and harder, the co-op organized labor competitions between teams and groups. One production team coined the slogan "if the ground isn't frozen, don't stop work" to guarantee completion of the mission, which "set off a high tide in water and soil conservation work in the whole cooperative."[13]

Competition with other locales amplified the scale of the campaign. Dengjiabao announced that all its co-op members had "hundred-fold confidence" that they could complete their conservation mission before the winter freeze and challenged the entire county to do the same.[14] Wushan authorities then disseminated a copy of Dengjiabao's challenge to other cooperatives. In a notice sent to township party committees and co-op directors, county leaders asserted that Dengjiabao's conservation plans for the winter were well devised, the mood of its members was high, and their enthusiasm was "worth studying." When Dengjiabao guaranteed that it would complete the mission without delaying production, county authorities expressed a hope that other co-ops would issue similar challenges to their neighbors.[15] Instigating this competition generated a ripple effect, in which collectives spurred on and sought to outdo each other.

Let One Hundred Dengjiabaos Bloom

In July 1957, just two months after Wushan launched the hundred Dengjiabaos campaign, *Gansu Daily* reported that the county boasted fifty-three villages "like the nationally famous water and soil conservation key point village—Dengjiabao." Wushan County resolved to turn a hundred more villages into "Dengjiabaos" by the year's end.[16] Labor intensification was key to meeting that goal. Wushan's Mahe township, for example, had organized three hundred young, able-bodied laborers into shock brigades during the slack farming period prior to the wheat harvest. In the impossibly short period of seven days, they claimed to have made the village of Changjiawan into a Dengjiabao. An article in *Wushan News* reported that shock brigades had controlled water and soil loss by digging trenches, fish-scale pits, springs, and ponds; building terraces and check dams; and planting sweet clover. Local leaders then gathered participants to summarize their experience and select labor models. The claim that Changjiawan had controlled erosion in a week was clearly exaggerated, but other villages refused to be outdone. Inspired by Changjiawan, Mahe township's residents pledged to "grasp the military advance" against water and soil loss by completing six more Dengjiabaos within the year.[17]

Propaganda exhibitions staged by Wushan's county government curated the hundred Dengjiabaos campaign by celebrating the benefits that would result from conserving water and soil. Throughout the Mao era, museums and exhibitions turned material artifacts into what Denise Ho terms "object lessons" that imparted messages about history, the nation, and revolution. This "participatory propaganda" prompted observers to partake in practices that legitimated state power and galvanized political movements.[18] During the hundred Dengjiabaos campaign, exhibitions presented material objects as microcosmic representations of conservation's potential benefits. An exhibition held in Wushan in October 1957, for example, featured a set of paintings titled *A Nationwide Flag in Water and Soil Conservation* alongside a small model of a landscape "with crisscrossing pathways between fields, and flowers and fruits as far as the eye can see."[19] An article about the exhibition in *Wushan News* noted that the display attracted many visitors, who stood looking at it for a long time.[20] The objects were not necessarily faithful representations of Dengjiabao's environment, but that was not the point. By offering idealized depictions of Dengjiabao on a miniature scale, the paintings and model sent viewers a clear message about the landscape that conservation could bring into existence.

The exhibition presented observers with a narrative of environmental improvement and socioeconomic progress. Even though Dengjiabao was renowned for its conservation work, the article explained, in 1949 villagers could not have imagined the improvements that lay in store. During the "old times," Dengjiabao was a "famously desolate place with crisscrossing gullies and precipitous mountains." From afar, the article related, its landscape looked "barren and as red as flames," resembling a "cone-shaped sorghum bun" due to the red sand that covered its slopes. Runoff from rainstorms eroded this sandy soil and caused it to flow down hillsides. Locals described the village's past conditions as "drought in sunny weather and disaster in rainy weather." This erosion and aridity hampered crop yields and led to immiseration. The article noted that when drought and famine struck in 1929, forty-eight villagers starved to death, thirty fled, and countless more had to beg to survive. Even in normal years, crop yields were poor and most villagers lacked food and clothing.

The article went on to boast of the myriad improvements that conservation had wrought since the founding of the PRC. After describing present-day Dengjiabao's "unscathed land with verdant mountains and clear waters, crisscrossing pathways, and flowers and fruits everywhere," the author declared that people could bring about "marvelous achievements." Under the party-state's leadership, residents had "repaired mountains and controlled waters." Dengjiabao was now a "beautiful mountain village" with irrigated land, levelled gullies, terraced slopes, and trees covering its hillsides. Runoff no longer eroded the soil. "Among those who go up the mountain," the article asked, "Who could not be enchanted?" Hillsides where sand and gravel had once been exposed now supported flowers, crops, and trees. Ducks swam in water stored in five large reservoirs. The "enchanting scenery" that was visible everywhere had "brought the people an unimaginably fortunate life." The article hyperbolically claimed that yields had risen almost fourfold between 1952 and 1956, with output per *mu* on some land reaching 411.5 *jin* (205.75 kg). Village households had escaped poverty, and in 1956 alone they sold 24,141 *jin* (12,070.5 kg) of surplus grain to the state. Agricultural output had, in fact, risen only about half as much as the article claimed, but that was not the point. This propaganda piece sent the message that agricultural collectivization had given people in Dengjiabao an existence they had once prayed for, and other locales in Wushan should strive to emulate their achievements.[21]

The article's triumphalist narrative was not completely inaccurate. Several years of conservation work had altered Dengjiabao's environment in ways that benefited the local populace. Agricultural output and food availability had increased. Ducks did swim in reservoirs. But Dengjiabao was by no means a rural utopia. The article embellished the results of conservation schemes and conveniently omitted the difficulty of implementing them. But this propaganda piece, like the exhibition it described, was intended to persuade audiences that, by following Dengjiabao's example, they, too, could live in a veritable paradise of environmental abundance.

Dengjiabao was not alone, the article pointed out, for 109 other places in Wushan County matched it in the scale and quality of their conservation work. Over twenty cooperatives had "already basically achieved beautiful landscapes in which water does not go down plateaus, silt does not go out of gullies, all land has fields, bunds are connected, all gullies have dams, all slopes have grass, fruit trees have grown into forests, and greenery covers mountains." As a result, the county had controlled water and soil loss on 60 percent of its land. Many areas had dispatched "water and soil conservation consultants" to Dengjiabao and drawn on its experience to manage slopes and gullies, "so that new Dengjiabaos continuously appear in more and more areas throughout the county."[22]

In Tianshui Prefecture, valorization of Dengjiabao likewise emerged in response to the disappointments of the 1956 irrigation campaign. When called on to labor through winter in 1956 despite the frigid weather, according to one prefectural report on water conservancy and conservation work, disgruntled residents asked, "How many tens of thousands of people are going to catch colds?" Some people called it "a waste of 150,000 civilian workdays" and "making a futile effort to no avail." Others likened the irrigation campaign to "the First Emperor of Qin tormenting the people" and considered it "exhausting the people and harming finances." Widespread popular disillusionment kept Tianshui from meeting its irrigation and conservation targets for 1956 and hindered planning for the coming year.[23]

To recover from this setback, Tianshui adopted a classic CCP mobilization strategy by turning to the promotion of models. Prefectural authorities organized trips to observe the "advanced experiences" of Shanxi's Daquan Mountain (Daquanshan), made famous when Mao Zedong commented on it favorably in an essay about how conservation had transformed its appearance, and other exemplary locales.[24] Following these visits, as the prefectural report concluded, Tianshui obtained the true "scripture" (*jing*) of "integrated management, continuous management, and comprehensive management," and raised the "red flag" of Dengjiabao as its model for how to effectively preserve water and soil.[25] As we have seen, conservation campaigns in Dengjiabao did not always go smoothly. But prefectural leaders, who saw only carefully crafted county-level reports that related how cadres and activists in Dengjiabao overcame obstacles and successfully mobilized villagers to preserve water and soil, had little awareness of the messy circumstances on the ground.

Nationwide Notoriety

Adulation for Dengjiabao did not stop at the county or prefectural level. In late October 1957, *People's Daily* published a short piece about how conservation measures had enabled Dengjiabao to check erosion, prevent drought, increase yields, and overcome poverty. The article was accompanied by five photographs depicting Dengjiabao's terraced fields, water-retention ponds, newly planted trees, and happy men and women reaping abundant harvests.[26] In December, an illustrated full-page article in the *Gansu Daily*—replete with photographs of conservation projects, portraits of labor model Deng Haihai and conservation expert Wang Zhiguo, and drawings of terraced fields, women planting trees, and ducks swimming in a newly built reservoir—dubbed Dengjiabao "a model for the construction of mountainous areas."[27] State media coverage made Dengjiabao's conservation efforts and the idyllic pastoral scenery they had created into an example not only for the province, but for the entire nation.

A 1958 article in *People's Daily* repeated this narrative, describing how Wushan County, once desolate and backward, had undergone a fundamental transformation and garnered praise from Gansu's party committee. In the past, the article stated, people in the county "did not have the habit of conserving water and soil." But after Dengjiabao's emergence as a model, more than twenty thousand visitors listened as its residents "explained the methods of water and soil conservation, the process of ideological struggle, and economic circumstances before and after water and soil conservation." As a result, new "Dengjiabaos" were appearing all over Wushan. With frequent observation visits taking place, "the practice of honoring the advanced, learning from the advanced, and mutual competition" had taken shape throughout the county.[28]

At the Second Nationwide Water and Soil Conservation Conference held in Beijing in December 1957, the Tianshui Water and Soil Conservation Experiment Station, Wushan County, and Dengjiabao received awards from the PRC's National Water and Soil Conservation Commission.[29] At the conference, Wushan's county head, Bao Haizhen, gave a speech describing how this success had been realized. With different types of conservation work designated for each season, cooperative members in Wushan had to labor on them all year long. Combining the spring planting with field engineering projects, Bao said, ensured that conservation would "yield actual results for production in the current year." In May and June, co-op members managed barren slopes and prepared land for planting trees. After the summer harvest, co-op members plowed fields while building bunds and terraces. Following the autumn harvest, they constructed engineering works in gully bottoms and managed slopes. From mid-October to January of the following year, Bao recommended devoting 50 percent of the labor force to water conservancy for three months, which would "give play to the beneficial results of irrigation in the coming year's production."[30]

In addition to conserving water and soil on land farmed by their own cooperatives, people were often asked to work in other areas as well. Wushan County had adopted what Bao Haizhen called "mutual aid between mountains and plains." In spring, when residents of mountainous areas with a shorter growing season had not yet started to plow their fields, upland inhabitants went to assist with agricultural production on the plains, where farms were busy. In autumn, when farming was busiest in upland areas, laborers from the plains went to the mountains to assist. These labor transfers resolved the "contradiction" of mountainous areas having a large "basic construction mission" and few people while the plains had a small mission and many people. Sharing the workforce addressed "the problem of population distribution in the mountains and plains being extremely uneven."[31] Bao never mentioned what compensation—if any—laborers received when they worked for other cooperatives.

When Wushan had first mobilized the local populace to plant trees, Bao Haizhen admitted, many villagers did not want to do it. But after county authorities promoted the planting of sweet clover, which "preliminarily controlled water and soil loss and solved fuel and fertilizer difficulties," people were happy to plant grasses and began to see the importance of afforestation. Similarly, once Dengjiabao had successfully carried out field engineering projects, people "naturally asked to manage slopes and manage gullies." However, local leaders had to demonstrate the tangible, short-term benefits of conservation practices to persuade rural people to embrace them. Having members of other co-ops visit Dengjiabao and compare its circumstances with their own served this purpose.[32]

Since rural localities could not expect material or financial support from the state, Bao Haizhen recommended that small-scale conservation projects "depend on the masses" and that large ones "take the masses as primary, with the government subsidizing them." Never mentioning the assistance given to Dengjiabao as a "key point" since the early 1950s, Bao claimed that the government had invested a mere ¥700 in conservation efforts in Dengjiabao, and Wushan's experience showed that state support should come only after the local populace had acted. If the government provided money as soon as projects started, Bao warned, it would only "give rise to an ideology of dependency among the masses."[33] The model of Dengjiabao not only exemplified the benefits of conservation, but also instilled the value of local self-reliance in pursuit of objectives defined by higher levels of the party-state.

The accolades showered on Dengjiabao at the Second Nationwide Water and Soil Conservation Conference bolstered its influence. A campaign to "forever maintain Wushan County's red flag on the battlelines of water and soil conservation" reportedly gave rise to 500 more Dengjiabaos in the county in a single month.[34] From October to December 1957, Gansu claimed to have created 1,168 Dengjiabaos where no runoff occurred when thirty millimeters of rain fell in half an hour. The province's various prefectural governments pledged to create 13,000 more in the coming year.[35] In January 1958, Tianshui Prefecture called for the creation of 3,202 Dengjiabaos, construction of bunds on all inclined land, and management of 30,000 gullies.[36] Tianshui authorities dictated that to become a Dengjiabao, a locale with an area of two square kilometers had to achieve "centralized and integrated management" within a year, control runoff and erosion so that 70 percent of water and soil could be retained if forty millimeters of rain fell in thirty minutes, and increase grain output by an average of fifteen to twenty *jin* (7.5–10 kg) per *mu*.[37]

At the fifth session of the First National People's Conference on February 10, 1958, Gansu's second party secretary, Huo Weide, announced the province's "ten thousand Dengjiabaos campaign."[38] With conservation "rapidly making a great leap forward," Gansu claimed to have created 2,518 Dengjiabaos that "achieved concentrated management, integrated management, completed engineering measures, and basically controlled water and soil loss."[39] By the end of February, prefectural and municipal leaders throughout Gansu promised to establish another 15,000.[40] Gansu's third party secretary, Li Jinglin, explained in April that "making fifteen thousand Dengjiabaos bloom" throughout the province would guarantee completion of that year's conservation mission.[41]

The influence of Dengjiabao even reached China's most powerful national leaders. Zhou Enlai, in a letter to Mao Zedong dated June 29, 1958, regarding plans related to the Yellow River and problems with the Sanmenxia project, referred to Dengjiabao as one of the earliest and most successful "typical models" (*dianxing*) for water and soil conservation.[42] Zhou described the environmental and socio-economic improvements that the conservation model had realized and commented favorably on Wushan's Dengjiabao campaign.

How to Learn from Dengjiabao

To make it easier for other areas to emulate Dengjiabao, Tianshui's Water and Soil Conservation Committee prepared a summary of Dengjiabao's work methods in spring 1958, which it sent to all administrative units under its jurisdiction. Conservation in Dengjiabao expanded from small to large projects, managed fields before gullies, promoted concentrated management, and combined biological measures (i.e., planting trees and grasses) with engineering measures to prevent gully heads from advancing. Its principles, according to the document, were to manage branch gullies before main gullies, proceed from high ground to low ground, and divide land into sections to intercept runoff and sediment.[43] Tianshui's summary spelled out Dengjiabao's work methods in only the most general terms; sources from other locales detailed how they were implemented.

When conservation work began in Gansu's Qingshui County, about 160 kilometers east of Wushan on the border with Shaanxi Province, residents of Qingshui's Hongfu township expressed concerns much like those that had been voiced by people in Wushan. Villagers feared that bunds made of dry soil would collapse, so building them would waste labor. They worried that trees planted in dry red soil would not survive. They "feared that conservation measures would decrease production and feared [that they] wouldn't be able to manage deep gullies and large floodwaters." Some complained that "water and soil conservation is distant water that can't quench nearby thirst. We can't count on it." Residents with limited financial means believed conservation required state support. "If it has to be done," they argued, "the government needs to invest in it."[44]

As in Dengjiabao, local leaders found ways to quash people's doubts. A notice sent from Tianshui's Water Conservancy Bureau to the townships and other organs under the prefecture's jurisdiction related that, during mobilization in Hongfu township, "the [party-branch] secretary planted the flag, cooperative heads directed battle, brigade leaders fought at the vanguard, and party and league activists served as crack troops, dividing into teams to make a military advance on the northern mountain."[45] This account made it clear how cadres and activists in other locales should conduct mobilization. They were also to conduct political struggle. Cadres and activists in Hongfu township held "large debates"; criticized rightist, conservative, and parochial thought; and "established a new air of collectivism." Township authorities pointed to the successful management of one gully in the township to inspire residents to believe they could transform nature, setting off a "water and soil conservation high tide." In practice, this meant that people worked harder and longer. Hongfu township mobilized over 2,400 men and women to toil day and night, "waking up early and going to bed late to make a military advance on the northern mountain." Able-bodied youth lived at the worksite—ten *li* (5 kilometers) from their homes—to avoid having to travel back and forth, "persevering until there was victory in the struggle." Township leaders organized workers into "two columns of military advance" that attended to production and conservation, ensuring that "everyone has things to do, everything has people to take care of it, and no village has any idle people." One column was a "great agriculture and sideline employment army" of around 1,200 women and old men, who accounted for nearly 30 percent of the township's workforce. The remaining 70 percent was a "great water and soil conservation army" of more than 2,400 able-bodied men. For five days after these columns were formed, "socialist construction competitions" inspired people to create six Dengjiabaos and control water and soil loss on 12.5 square kilometers of land.

As in the actual Dengjiabao, conservation in Hongfu followed the principles of "comprehensive planning, suiting measures to local conditions, concentrated management, continuous management, integrated management, and simultaneously managing slopes and gullies, although slopes were primary." Field engineering projects preserved water and soil, defended against drought, increased crop production, leveled inclined land, and consolidated fields to facilitate mechanized plowing in the future. Inspections and evaluations through comparison monitored work quality. Echoing descriptions of the transformations that had taken place in Dengjiabao, local leaders reported that, thanks to conservation measures, "water doesn't go off plateaus, soil doesn't go down slopes, and sediment doesn't go out gullies." Hongfu township realized what leaders dubbed "five changes in the face [of the land]": fields had bunds, slopes had ditches, roads had pools alongside them, trees and grasses greened gully slopes, and gully bottoms became fields. The report declared that conservation work had not interfered with farming or sideline production and, by preserving water and soil, had "guaranteed increased grain production and conquered the threat of flood disasters."[46]

In Qin'an County, northeast of Wushan, militarized campaigns to "change the arid face [of the landscape], develop mountainous area production, improve people's livelihoods, and fundamentally control the Yellow River" likewise earned numerous locales the coveted title of Dengjiabao. Starting in early November 1957, as the Qin'an county government reported to Tianshui's prefectural leadership, Qin'an launched a "great leap forward campaign in production" focused on water conservancy, soil conservation, and fertilizer collection. Over three months of "arduous battle," the report stated, one hundred thousand people spent twenty days planting trees, irrigated land area expanded, and water and soil loss came under control. Regardless of the veracity these claims, rural people labored intensively: the amount of conservation work done in Qin'an during this three-month period exceeded that done from 1953 to 1957.[47]

And the campaigns did not end there. After planting more trees in spring 1958, a fifteen-day conservation assault made 124 more of Qin'an's villages into Dengjiabaos, reportedly controlling water and soil loss over an area of more than 400 square kilometers. By May 1958, according to the county government report, conservation efforts had managed 84.9 percent of the land in the county—1,235.6 square kilometers—that was affected by water and soil loss. These figures were undoubtedly inflated, of course. During winter 1957 and spring 1958, one report grandiosely asserted, Qin'an's populace had, "through the activity of transforming nature, even more clearly recognized that developing water conservancy and water and soil conservation are the most basic [forms of] construction for agricultural production, the lifeline for constructing mountainous areas, and an important, inseparable, and long-term link in socialist construction." This realization, the report claimed, motivated people to increase grain production to four hundred *jin* (200 kg) per *mu* and embark on another campaign to create 150 additional Dengjiabaos.[48] Inspiring the rural populace to transform the environment through conservation, the report stressed, was the path to economic progress.

Even if its achievements were exaggerated, Qin'an County's commitment to the Dengjiabao campaign made it a conservation model. In April 1958, Gansu's party secretary, Li Jinglin, instructed leaders throughout the province to emulate Qin'an, which now had 420 Dengjibaos. In Qin'an, Li related, the county head and party secretary personally "took command at the frontlines." Qin'an's entire workforce had been mobilized to "take part in battle," combining spring plowing, irrigation, and water and soil conservation.[49]

As these examples show, learning from Dengjiabao meant pursuing labor intensification through military-style mobilization. Not only did ideals of military regimentation, mobilization, and struggle inform this campaign to transform the environment, but leaders employed military-style organization to bring it about. Armies of workers advanced into battle, launching assaults to transform nature and conquer water and soil loss. The same militarization, both rhetorical and organizational, characterized all aspects of the Great Leap Forward.[50]

The Great War in Dengjiabao

The wave of mobilization that the Dengjiabao campaign had stirred up soon pushed residents of Dengjiabao itself to renew their dedication to remaking the land. Seeking to expand on past achievements and prevent complacency, Wushan's county committee introduced a new slogan: "You cannot simply mark time but must advance forward in great steps! Dengjiabao should go up another level!"[51] Now that other parts of Gansu were catching up, Dengjiabao had to redouble its efforts. In summer 1958, the county committee organized over twenty-five thousand people on three occasions to wage a "great war in Dengjiabao" (*da zhan Dengjiabao*). Propaganda described this workforce as an army of heroes in a struggle to conquer nature.[52] Before starting work, villagers attended meetings at which they swore oaths and pledged their determination to accomplish their mission like soldiers heading off to war (fig. 11). Battles involved digging soil from mountaintops to fill in gullies, building check dams and terraces, and planting shelterbelts.[53] Dengjiabao exhorted its residents to "make Dengjiabao's advancement more advanced and raise Dengjiabao's red flag higher and higher!" Other slogans urged co-op members to "launch satellites, ride rockets, and fight bitterly for three days and nights to overtake (Shanxi's) Daquan Mountain!"[54]

During an interview, a man who had been secretary of Dengjiabao's youth

FIGURE 11. "Under the party's leadership, the masses' vigor bursts through the heavens as they rally to pledge determination to conquer nature. The heroes waging war in Dengjiabao swear to raise Dengjiabao's red flag higher and higher." Gansu sheng renmin weiyuanhui, *Gansu sheng de shuili shuitu baochi*.

league branch in 1958 informed me that the secretary and deputy secretary of the county committee oversaw the conservation campaign, while the director of Dengjiabao's water and soil conservation station served as "the commander-in-chief of the great war in Dengjiabao."[55] The youth league secretary and other local cadres gave the commands, directing work through darkness and wet weather.[56]

News reports announced that by splitting mountaintops, leveling gullies, and connecting land into parcels, co-op members were preparing the way for irrigation and eventually mechanized cultivation with tractors. The people of Dengjiabao's "magnificent undertaking" to "conquer nature" had "pointed out a direction and established a paragon for thoroughly changing the face of mountainous areas." Impelled by the slogan "Dengjiabao's glory is the glory of the entire county's people!," twenty-eight co-ops in Wushan's Dongshun, Chengguan, and Simen townships, with the "lofty ideological style of communism and the spirit of great cooperation," sent more than 5,200 workers to Dengjiabao to assist. Traveling from as many as a dozen kilometers away, the workers brought their own tools and food and slept on the mountainside.[57]

The "struggle to conquer nature" by controlling gullies and terracing hillsides expressed confidence that collective labor could improve the environment and generate economic prosperity. An article in *Gansu Daily* described winding rows of laborers stretching from the foot to the top of the mountain, with "countless red flags fluttering in the wind, and the sound of young people and women singing rising one after the other." A large red flag planted on the peak was emblazoned with the words "the Great War in Dengjiabao." The slogan on another flag compared the ongoing conservation campaign to a popular Chinese story cycle about a filial son who freed his mother from her imprisonment under a mountain: "Chenxiang split the mountain to save his mother; we split the mountain for good fortune."[58] County and township leaders "went to the front," took part in labor, and slept outdoors with other workers, "which did even more to rouse the labor enthusiasm of the masses."[59]

People expressed their "resolute determination and grand hopes" by carving poems onto hillsides. One verse exhorted co-op members to "turn high mountains into terraces, tamp deep gullies flat and plant trees, call on barren slopes to grow green trees, order the land to catch up with Jiangnan."[60] Conservation of water and soil, the poem promised, could make arid, eroded hillsides become like Jiangnan, China's most productive and prosperous region. Another verse read: "Split mountains and fill gullies so land connects into parcels, bunds will change into mulberry orchards; tractors will speed round the mountain; grains, fruits, and vegetables of all sorts will be produced in abundance."[61] These slogans later appeared on the cover of *Gansu Daily* below a drawing of Dengjiabao's landscape.[62] By remaking the environment, backward villages could produce abundant fruits and grain. New technologies would turn barren landscapes into thoroughly modern yet idyllic pastoral spaces.

Further governmental recognition intensified the campaign. The PRC's central government selected Wushan County as the site of the Third Nationwide Water and Soil Conservation Conference, held in September 1958, further solidifying its status as a national model. To prepare for the conference, Wushan mobilized what contemporary sources described as a "great labor army" of "a hundred thousand people" to gather in the steep hillsides girding the banks of the Wei River and do conservation work.[63] In mid-July, a group of thirty thousand laborers "established barracks" at Dengjiabao and two other "base points."[64] The total of nearly eighty thousand people from Wushan ultimately took part in this work—albeit smaller than the number described in propaganda slogans—accounted for over 40 percent of the county's population.[65]

Wushan's campaign to control the Wei River coincided with the formation of people's communes throughout China's countryside. In late summer and autumn of 1958, communes made up of thousands of households replaced higher-level agricultural cooperatives. During this "wind of communization," people's communes took control of all property and resources within their boundaries and could appropriate labor and materials as they saw fit. PRC leaders anticipated that the communes' gigantic scale would facilitate mobilization for huge hydraulic engineering and construction projects.[66] In August 1958, Dongshun township—of which Dengjiabao was a part—joined six other townships to form the Hongxing (Red Star) People's Commune, with 12,607 households and 63,347 people.[67]

Militarization characterized all forms of production and labor management under the newly formed communes. In Wushan, as elsewhere in China, commune members participated in "large-scale cooperation" in "theaters of operation," with tens of thousands of workers from different locales deployed to "do battle" on a project.[68] The scale of the war against erosion grew to encompass wider areas and larger populations. When Wushan "raised troops" to control the Wei River in summer 1958, "people burst through the old ideological constraint of 'minding your own business' and territorial boundaries," taking part in what one news article called "great cooperation" in the use of labor and materials between cities and villages, between industry and agriculture, and among counties, townships, and communes.[69]

In anticipation of the Third Nationwide Water and Soil Conservation Conference, Tianshui's party committee formed a leadership group to coordinate with cadres at all levels, held on-site "evaluation by comparison meetings" with collective leaders, and sent out inspection teams and delegations headed by the prefecture's party secretary. This high-level encouragement set off "a mass water and soil conservation campaign on a scale greater than any other year" that sought to greet the conference with new and outstanding successes. The populace was "militarized, with field armies and regiments imbued with a spirit of daring that conquers mountains and rivers." After Wushan raised its "great labor army" numbering in the tens of thousands, 700,000 laborers from seven adjoining counties joined the struggle against the Wei River. In total, some 1,210,000 people throughout Tianshui were mobilized for conservation work.[70]

A slogan proclaiming that "with a great army of one hundred thousand in battle formation, the Wei River's banks will improve their appearance" lent inspiration to the campaign.[71] Another slogan doubled as the title of a song that romanticized conservation as a heroic struggle: "Wushan's People Remake the Earth."[72] Its lyrics described armies of "lords" from the county's populace who fought monstrous and demonic adversaries to conquer drought, erosion, and flooding.[73] The song cast the grinding work of diverting waters to irrigate upland areas, leveling land by filling in gullies, controlling the Wei River, and planting trees as part of a grand battle.

> High-spirited and majestic,
> Wushan's people remake the earth;
> conquering the south and battling the north,
> the momentum is like a bullfight.
> The first column transferred lords (*zhu hou*)
> to behead the demon and catch the water's head,
> opening the mountains and changing the course,
> making the waters reverse their flow.

An "expedition" of workers diverted waters up mountain slopes to irrigate fields. As a result, they had subdued the "drought demon" and made the mountains green. Fish and ducks swam in reservoirs and rice grew on mountainsides. Fighting an "endless battle," the people of Wushan harnessed rivers and remade the earth. With waters irrigating upland fields, even when droughts occurred, they would still enjoy abundant harvests.

> The second column transferred lords
> to carry mountains and fill ten thousand gullies;
> the concave and convex are made flat,
> and iron oxen run across the land.

Water and soil no longer flowed out of gullies, waters ran clear, and terraced fields ascended "straight to highest heaven."

> The third column transferred lords
> to greatly remake the Wei River;
> if it continues to act recklessly,
> slice it at the waist and cut off its head.

With the Wei River harnessed, wherever it flowed would become rich and its banks would turn into islands of wet rice fields.

> The fourth column transferred lords
> to finely embroider the earth,
> planting trees on barren mountains and in gullies,
> plains and plateaus becoming oases.

Wushan's people had reshaped the earth, "relying entirely on their own two hands," so that good fortune would never end.[74] With this language, the song turned backbreaking toil into an epic saga in which bold and daring acts of collective labor remade an environment plagued by drought, erosion, and floods into a verdant, irrigated, and flourishing agricultural landscape. Wushan's rural populace became the hero in a war against nature in which victory brought environmental abundance and human flourishing.

These cultural productions energized the campaigns to conserve water and soil. Continuing the mobilization that had started in June, Dengjiabao became one of the "main battlefields" in Wushan County's war to manage the Wei River and a beneficiary of "great cooperation."[75] From July 16 to July 24, ten thousand people from Wushan's Longtai, Tan'ge, Longquan, and Dongshun townships arrived in Dengjiabao and "started a full-scale offensive against the high mountains, deep gullies, and barren slopes." During the day, they worked in temperatures of over thirty degrees Celsius; at night they "lit red lanterns and struggled against the darkness.[76]

Once Wushan's county committee issued the mobilization slogan "control both mountains and water, tame the Wei River," people from every township "immediately rushed to the two banks of the Wei River, and from early August they were arrayed on the battlefield, enduring wind and rain to engage in assault warfare." The "great army of one hundred thousand" in Wushan "launched a campaign against mountains and went to war against water" for more than twenty days, completing conservation projects on 150 square kilometers of land on both sides of the Wei River.[77] In describing the environmental improvements that would be achieved, *Gansu Daily* stressed their aesthetic dimension. At the campaign's completion, hillsides would resemble nothing less than a "celestial landscape" in which "high mountain forest belts reflect green in the sky, in deep gullies the flowers and fruits are fragrant, terraces are flat as gold bars, crisscrossing canals flash with silver light, roads have changed into tree-shaded avenues, villages are a land of the immortals, tractors speed around mountains, maize and mulberry grow everywhere, droughts and sandstorms are no longer feared, and storehouses burst with grain and national wealth."[78] The article thus presented aesthetic markers of the landscape's vibrance, life, and abundance—the verdant trees, level terraces, sparkling water, shady streets, bumper crops—as evidence of the campaign's success.

Aesthetics over Agriculture

China's Third Nationwide Water and Soil Conservation Conference opened in Wushan on September 2, 1958, with an address given by the National Affairs Council Water and Soil Conservation Committee's secretary, He Jili, on behalf of its director, Chen Zhengren, who could not attend in person. He Jili asked rhetorically, "Why is this meeting convening in Wushan?" The answer was that it was thanks to the "advanced water and soil conservation model" of Dengjiabao.[79] The speech then described Dengjiabao as "one of the most prominent and best water and soil conservation models nationwide" and "the best and most practical water and soil conservation university nationwide." A Soviet water and soil conservation advisor in attendance remarked that he had heard of Dengjiabao, but what he observed there surpassed anything he could have imagined. Dengjiabao, as he put it, was "an extremely good model for the comprehensive transformation of nature."⁸⁰

People's Daily published a poem by a representative at the conference from Guangdong titled "Feelings on an Observation Visit to Dengjiabao" that extolled the results of the "great war in Dengjiabao" for readers across China:

> Yesterday mountains were poor and gullies dangerous,
> yellow sand and red water overflowing,
> how much grief and how much sorrow,
> how many broken cliffs and walls?
> The war in Dengjiabao
> split mountains to store water and fill gullies,
> fruits fragrant and grains ripe to celebrate an abundant harvest,
> the earth is newly embroidered.⁸¹

Dengjiabao sent representatives to Beijing to attend the Nationwide Agricultural Socialist Construction Advanced Work Unit Representative Conference that December, where it received a certificate of merit signed by Zhou Enlai.⁸²

During the summer of 1958, the pageantry surrounding the war against erosion in Dengjiabao inspired popular fervor. Female residents with good voices sang into megaphones while "people with a lot of physical power worked."⁸³ Dengjiabao hosted one of three film projection teams in Wushan County; propaganda teams and cultural troupes came from near and far. As a former party branch secretary remembered, "Some of them [city folk accustomed to flat land] didn't even dare to walk down the mountain slopes."⁸⁴ Propaganda teams from other locales came to Dengjiabao to entertain and inspire workers with their singing and dancing. A song composed by two natives of Longtai township titled "Do Not Let the Wei River Cause Any More Trouble" (*bu rang Weihe zai daodan*) captured the atmosphere:

> Set to work and break through the sky,
> with work wisdom rivaling that of the immortals;
> if the Wei River causes trouble,
> cut it in half with a knife.

> In the sixth month, the hottest days,
> a hundred thousand troops march high into the mountains,
> not afraid of wind and rain, not afraid of heat,
> to mightily battle with nature (*zhan ziran*).
> A hundred thousand troops march together,
> everywhere the singing is like the roar of the wind;
> determined to make mountains into plains,
> transforming nature and conquering heaven
> (*gaizao ziran shengguo tian*).
> In Dengjiabao they are arrayed,
> the sound of shovels and the noise of gongs and drums;
> high mountains and deep gullies turn into fertile farmland;
> village roads are flower orchards.[85]

Elderly villagers with whom I spoke recalled the slogans that people wrote in big characters on surrounding cliffs and the exhibition hall set up by the county government in Dengjiabao to accommodate the many visitors.[86] The spectacle of mass mobilization made the worksite seem like a festival. As an elderly woman reminisced, "At that time, the commune members were very enthusiastic. The local people were all very happy. They sang as they worked."[87]

However, enthusiasm alone could not sustain the level of physical effort the campaign required or keep it from interfering with crop production. As one elderly villager recalled, "Once the higher-ups said to work at Dengjiabao, we worked there. [People from] all the brigades in Wushan County came to Dengjiabao to work. To wage a great war in Dengjiabao. It was 1958. It exhausted the people and harmed finances.... Entire families took part. Everyone here took part. People from other counties also took part. Mass mobilization. Men and women all took part. Old people took care of the kids."[88] Another man recollected that "when building terraces, when the moonlight was very bright, we still kept working. You had to sneak in a rest under the cornstalks."[89]

Shifting the entire workforce from farming to conservation affected food supplies when people neglected the harvest. As another villager told me, "When we waged the great war [in 1958], the crops were still doing well.

Crops were harvested, thrown on the ground, and no one paid attention to them anymore."[90] The former youth league secretary likewise commented on the "formalism"—emphasis on appearances rather than actual results—that existed during the campaign: "Just digging to fill in gullies. I said, 'This is nonsense' (*hu'nao de*). The potatoes hadn't been harvested. There was a lot of rain at that time; we also worked in the rain. The rain was pouring, and everyone was outside. It was all for people making observation visits to look at." People dug earth for weeks at a time, "holding a shovel in the fields, singing at the top of their lungs." Yet the spectacular enthusiasm concealed an undercurrent of popular resentment. As the former youth league secretary confided when I spoke with him, "The great war in Dengjiabao actually wasn't welcomed by the masses. In the dark, [they] followed the commander-in-chief. When it was raining, [they were] still in the fields. It lasted for dozens of days and then subsided."[91] Despite the campaign's rhetoric and the better future it promised, villagers were loath to toil in the rain and dark.

The great war in Dengjiabao created an aesthetically pleasing environment for visiting dignitaries, conference attendees, and outside observers at the cost of agricultural production. The available data show that the balance between conservation and farming had reached a tipping point. Total workdays devoted to water and soil conservation in Dengjiabao more than doubled, from 3,700 in 1956 to 8,600 in 1957, before more than doubling again to 20,000 in 1958. This amounted to a 540 percent increase in only two years.[92] Between 1957 and 1958, the land on which level terraces were built increased by 370 percent.[93]

At the same time, however, the trend toward higher agricultural output and increasing caloric consumption seen between 1952 and 1956 decisively reversed. Per capita production of grain and other staples in Dengjiabao dipped from 385 kilograms in 1956 to 343.25 kilograms in 1957. After state procurements, estimated caloric availability fell from 2,425 to 2,045 calories. Grain availability remained barely sufficient at around 276 kilograms per head. Consumption exceeded pre-1956 levels, but a decline was clearly taking place. Circumstances worsened in 1958, when per capita output slid to 312.25 kilograms. After subtracting state grain procurements, average grain availability per person in Dengjiabao in 1958 dipped below the threshold of sufficiency to about 251 kilograms and consumption decreased to an estimated 1,860 calories a day (see table 1). The ratio of workdays devoted to agriculture to workdays spent on water conservancy, soil conservation, and afforestation decreased from 12.37:1 in 1957 to 2.36:1 in 1958, which helps explain the decline in crop output and food availability.[94] Conservation, instead of increasing yields, was now impinging on agricultural production.

Tongwei County, located directly north of Wushan, had been a vanguard in the campaign to catch up with Dengjiabao. Unfortunately, mass mobilization for conservation work in Tongwei had similar consequences. In August 1958, writes historian Yang Jisheng, "just as the crops were turning golden," people in Tongwei had to ignore the harvest so workers could prepare for a visit by a central government inspection team from the Third Nationwide Water and Soil Conservation Conference in Wushan. Some fifty thousand workers (51.4 percent of Tongwei's labor force) festooned sixty kilometers of road with "festive bunting, fluttering red flags, and oceans of big-character posters, filling the streets with a deafening clamor of gongs and drums and carrying out some last-minute soil and water conservation work." In October, Tongwei deployed more than twenty-five thousand people for additional conservation projects.[95]

During the Great Leap Forward, the appearance of the landscape became proof that the war against water and soil loss was being won, evidence of "aesthetic colonization" and mastery over nature.[96] But terracing hillsides and filling gullies to make a well-ordered agrarian landscape of level, parallel fields and green trees took precedence over harvesting grain. In Tongwei and Wushan counties, the resulting disruption of agricultural production would help precipitate a subsistence crisis of horrific proportions.

The aesthetic features of rural landscapes usually derive from the uses for which they were designed. Terraced hillsides, for instance, were initially intended to facilitate agriculture by conserving water and soil. But aesthetic and practical or utilitarian considerations can also "come apart" and exist in tension, with one subordinated to the other.[97] As James Scott has pointed out, "visual representations of order and efficiency" that may have made sense in their original context can become "detached from their initial moorings" as aesthetics take precedence over function: "The fact that they look right becomes more important than whether they work; or, better put, the assumption is that if the arrangement looks right, it will also, ipso facto, function well."[98] Preserving water and soil and increasing agricultural productivity were the original rationales for building terraces and other conservation infrastructure, but creating a well-ordered landscape did not necessarily further those goals. As conservation campaigns gained momentum in 1957–58, local cadres and officials mobilized rural people to make the landscape conform to an aesthetic ideal that outside observers recognized and praised. Maintaining crop production became a secondary concern. The relationship between aesthetics and utility became inverted as grandiose battles against nature pushed aside the mundane routines of farmwork.

FIGURE 12. Deng Fenqin and her husband. Chen and Ren, "Shui bu xia yuan, ni bu chu gou."

SIX

"Water Has Aroused the Girls' Hearts"
Gender and Conservation

I first went to Dengjiabao in 2017 to investigate how local CCP cadres persuaded rural people to implement conservation measures in the 1950s and how they championed their village as a nationwide model. While doing fieldwork, I interviewed an elderly woman named Deng Fenqin, whose image appeared in a lavishly illustrated 1957 article on Dengjiabao's water and soil conservation achievements that was published in the high-profile national journal the *People's Pictorial* (fig. 12). Deng Fenqin had not known that *People's Pictorial* had published a photograph of her and her late husband. When I showed it to her, it moved her to tears, and her family crowded around to see it. After several interviews with Deng Fenqin, I realized that it is impossible to understand water and soil conservation in Mao-era China without considering its gendered dimensions.[1] Efforts to alter people's relationship with the land, as her recollections made clear, were deeply connected with changes in gender relations and shifting conceptions of women's work. They also had far-reaching effects on child-rearing, food security, and other aspects of rural women's lives.

Campaigns to control water and soil loss had distinctive consequences for women. At the same time, official publications that praised Dengjiabao's achievements in the 1950s presented conservation in highly gendered terms, asserting that improvements in environmental conditions and living standards would reconfigure gender relations by helping unmarried men in poor, resource-starved villages like Dengjiabao find wives. However, a dissonance existed between this gendered vision of a good life and the experience of conservation for rural women, who had to balance the heavy physical work of remaking the land with their domestic responsibilities. My interviews with Deng Fenqin make it possible to trace the impact of the conservation campaigns in terms of women's embodied experiences of work, hunger, and affliction.

From imperial times until the early twentieth century, although women often helped with agricultural tasks, prevailing gender norms in rural Han Chinese communities dictated that men should farm outdoors while women engaged in handicraft production and domestic work inside. After the founding of the PRC in 1949, the party-state encouraged women to move from supposedly "unproductive" handicrafts and household labor into "productive" collective agriculture.[2] As in the Soviet Union, women in China's countryside bore the "double burden" of collective farmwork and the work of child-rearing, food acquisition and preparation, clothing production, and other household duties.[3] Conservation reflected this trend. Throughout the 1950s, efforts to conserve water and soil depended on the female workforce. Mass mobilization for large-scale conservation campaigns undertaken during the Great Leap Forward made female labor even more important and heightened the burdens on rural women.

Water and Wives

The heroic narratives of environmental improvement found in official sources and the accolades that Dengjiabao gained in the 1950s do not fully capture the local significance of water and soil conservation or its complex meanings, especially for rural women. Local environmental conditions and social constructions of female labor meant that women shouldered much of the work involved in acquiring scarce water and fuel resources for their households. Environmental degradation thus had a profound influence on the lives of female villagers. Both men and women in Dengjiabao and surrounding villages viewed carrying water as the work of women and children, but it was no easy task.[4] To obtain drinking water, women typically had to walk three to three and a half kilometers to mountain springs or trek down to the Wei River and haul the water back uphill on shoulder poles.[5] At the two springs near Dengjiabao, they had to wait in line to "use a metal dipper to scoop it up drip by drip."[6] After two rainless weeks, even the muddy water in springs and wells ran out, so female villagers had to carry heavy loads of water several kilometers up steep hillsides from the river below.[7]

Water scarcity, in turn, affected gender relations. The arduous task of obtaining water created such terrible working conditions in Dengjiabao that it made women hesitant to move to the village, depressing the local marriage market. As in most of China, the local custom was village exogamy, with women marrying outside of their own village. But due to the physical toil of carrying water over long distances, up and down steep slopes, parents did not want their daughters to marry Dengjiabao men. A popular saying in Wushan County advised: "If you have a girl, don't marry her to Dengjiabao. Going down the mountain to carry water is truly a hardship" (*you nü bu jia Dengjiabao, xiashan tiaoshui shizai ku*).[8] As result, Dengjiabao was notorious as a place where "getting a wife was most troublesome" and the village had a larger population of unwed men than elsewhere.[9] Young women from Dengjiabao, meanwhile, could not wait to marry out to villages on the plains.[10]

Conservation efforts in Dengjiabao, along with other improvements like erecting a windmill to grind grain, made it far more attractive to young women from nearby villages. The windmill was a novel spectacle, and it meant that women and other residents did not have to turn heavy millstones. During one of my visits, Dengjiabao's party secretary recited a popular local proverb from the 1950s: "A windmill is behind the village, hemp stalks grow to two or three *zhang*, and girls from the plains run up the mountain."[11] (Two or three *zhang* is between 6.7 and 10 meters, thus the proverb is likely hyperbole.) At that time, he explained, Dengjiabao was admired by people throughout Wushan County. Publications from the 1950s cast the windmill as an indication that Dengjiabao had attained a "perfectly satisfied life" and become a "fortunate socialist new village."[12]

Underscoring the extent of conservation's benefits, Dengjiabao's supporters pointed to its "four rarities" (*si xihan*): "irrigated land going up the mountain, wet rice and hemp going up the mountain, ducks in reservoirs, and land in connected parcels."[13] Official propaganda quickly picked up on these changes. State-sponsored publications credited conservation with changing how people perceived Dengjiabao and attracting young women to marry into the village. Propaganda conveyed the message that conservation did more than increase crop yields by limiting water and soil loss and facilitate irrigated fields and duck ponds: it also improved bachelors' marriage prospects.

As they crafted their message to raise the profile of conservation work, state agents paid close attention to local conditions, and their propaganda linking marriage to conservation reached a wide audience. An article that appeared in the *People's Daily* in 1956 described the woeful situation that had existed at the start of the decade: "At that time, if a Dengjiabao man wanted to marry a girl from another village it was like marrying a celestial maiden from heaven (*tianshang de xiannü*), because girls were afraid that if they married into this poor mountain village not only would they go hungry, but they were also afraid they'd suffer thirst."[14] The article recounted the tale of a young man from Dengjiabao and a young woman from another village who took a liking to each other, but "because the girl's father and mother disliked that Dengjiabao lacked water, the two lovers could not get married."[15] Now, the article said, conservation projects had improved conditions in the village so much that families who had left Dengjiabao because of its lack of water had started coming back.

This propaganda gave environmental management policies immediate significance at the level of familial and marital relations. A publication from 1958 reported: "The era of 'if you have a girl, don't marry her to Dengjiabao' has already gone away, never to return. Girls from the plains have seen Dengjiabao's construction achievements and construction prospects, and they have fallen in love with this place. In the past two years, eighteen girls have already come up the mountain to get married to youths here, and there are also many other girls from the plains who ardently love Dengjiabao youths and are preparing to come up the mountain to settle down and make a home."[16] The reversal in marriage patterns reportedly led people to exclaim that "water is the key link in mountainous area construction; water has aroused the girls' hearts" (*shui shi shanqu jianshe de gang, shui dadong le guniangmen de xin*).[17] This romanticized rhetoric reinforced the PRC's New Marriage Law, promulgated in 1950, which prohibited arranged marriage in favor of free choice, as these women were marrying into Dengjiabao households out of affection, not obligation.[18] Implicitly at least, state-sponsored publications sent the message that conservation could make young women fall in love with other poor, marginal villages and the men who lived in them. Dengjiabao was not alone: official sources drew similar connections between environmental improvements and a better marriage market to promote water conservancy projects in other parts of Wushan County as well.[19]

The *People's Pictorial* article featuring Deng Fenqin presented her experience as concrete evidence of the connection between water and weddings:

"In the past, girls from the plains were not willing to marry up the mountain [to Dengjiabao]. They thought that if they did not die of hunger they would die of thirst. However, over the past five years [1952–57], fifteen have gotten married [to young men from] here. Deng Fenqin (right), the wife of cooperative member Li Baoxu (left), is one of them."[20] Even more women came to the village as new brides soon thereafter.

The illustration cast Deng Fenqin in the role of a diligent and attentive wife, caring for her husband by giving him water from a new vacuum flask while he took a break from his work in the fields. Presenting marital relations in this manner reinforced conventional notions of masculinity and femininity. At the same time, the image appealed to male readers by promising that conservation could alleviate the shortages of both water and wives.

It was no coincidence that *People's Pictorial* selected Li Baoxu and Deng Fenqin as the model married couple for promoting conservation, as both had strong CCP connections. Deng, who grew up in a nearby village on the plains, informed me that she knew of Dengjiabao's renown when she was introduced to Li Baoxu as a marriage partner. She happily accepted the proposal in 1956 at the age of 18.[21] Party networks played a role in the matchmaking process. Deng had recently become a CCP member, and when she married Li Baoxu she joined the family of one of Dengjiabao's most prominent CCP activists. Baoxu's older brother was none other than Li Xuding, the party cadre, labor model, and deputy director of Dengjiabao's agricultural cooperative.[22] Li Baoxu and his brother passed away long ago, but during our interviews, Deng Fenqin confirmed the appeal that Dengjiabao had for young women in Wushan during the first decade of the PRC. Implicitly contrasting Dengjiabao's past prominence with its current marginalization even within Gansu, one of China's poorest provinces, she explained: "Lots of women from the plains married into this place, but now I can't recall their names. At that time, they thought that Dengjiabao was all the rage. When Dengjiabao built a windmill for grinding grain they thought Dengjiabao was great." At the time, as Deng related, she and seven or eight other women from the plains came up the mountain to marry men in Lijiaping, one of the natural villages that formed the administrative village of Dengjiabao. She remembered their arrival as a dramatic break from the old pattern in which women from upland villages married men on the more prosperous plains.[23]

By easing the scarcity of resources that had afflicted Dengjiabao, water and soil conservation made women's work at least a bit lighter. Deng Fenqin related that obtaining adequate drinking water was persistently difficult during the 1950s, although construction of a dam and reservoir in one of the gullies near Dengjiabao alleviated it somewhat: "At that time, in Dengjiabao some places on the mountain had natural spring water, but after that it wasn't enough to drink, and we drank water from the reservoir."[24]

In addition, planting trees and grasses for conservation purposes made gathering wood as biofuel (the most important source of rural domestic energy) less difficult. Acute shortages of what locals termed the "three materials"—fuel, fodder and fertilizer—plagued Dengjiabao, like much of Northwest China.[25] As a 1955 report on tree planting noted: "Dengjiabao is a mountain village in which the 'three materials' are all scarce. In a year, men frequently go to places eighty or ninety *li* [40–45 km] away to obtain kindling. Women also cut sod and dig grassroots to solve fuel difficulties. This not only wastes a lot of precious labor power, but also leads to serious soil erosion."[26]

Deng Fenqin recalled that during the late 1950s, "Mostly we could find branches from sea buckthorn plants (*suanci, Hippophae rhamnoides*) as kindling to burn." These plants have vicious thorns, but in the 1950s, some female cooperative members specialized in cutting and gathering the plants for fuel, earning work points for their labor.[27] A report published in the late 1950s asserted that planting sea buckthorn, in addition to consolidating inclined slopes and improving soil fertility, "did a great deal to solve the fuel problems of the masses."[28] By making it easier to obtain water and fuel, conservation measures carried out in Wushan during the mid-1950s thus appear to have brought about an improvement in the lives of local women.

Women's Work to Conserve Water and Soil

Women did not merely reap the benefits of conservation schemes, however; their labor made such schemes possible. Women doing agricultural work, especially in the busy farming season, was nothing new in rural China, even though in most villages the norm of female seclusion gave women's fieldwork the stigma of poverty and public disapproval. But in the 1950s, the PRC party-state encouraged women to take part in collective agriculture year-round to boost productivity and free male workers for other enterprises.[29] Mobilizing female workers overcame the problem of insufficient labor, by which leaders meant scarcity of male laborers. During the irrigation campaign in early 1956, *Gansu Daily* quoted the director of an agricultural cooperative in Wushan who said that because most male co-op members were busy doing conservation work, only women were available for agricultural labor, so the co-op did not finish its spring plowing and sowing on time.[30]

When cooperatives in Dongshun township began to build irrigation channels in early 1956, cadres and other villagers feared that they had too much work and too few people to do it. To alleviate these concerns, according to a report from the township party branch, the party helped cooperative cadres settle "the account of comparing women's participation in labor and doing work last year and this year" to show residents how much the workforce could accomplish when fully mobilized.[31] Excluding the ill, elderly, and weak, a typical production team in Dongshun had thirty female laborers. In 1956, all the women participated in labor, but the previous year only eighteen of them had done farmwork. Previously, female co-op members had done relatively light work like clearing and weeding fields. For fear of grinding their hands and getting blisters, women did not strip thatch—blackened by smoke and filled with nutrients—from houses, crush the nutrient-rich adobe bricks, and return these materials to fields to replenish soil fertility. But in 1956, women stripped houses, crushed bricks, and transplanted wheat seedlings; they also made potash fertilizer and planted maize and sweet potatoes. The township party branch stressed that female participation in collective agriculture had eliminated concerns about labor shortages related to irrigation projects: "That is to say," a party branch report concluded, "most farmwork is undertaken by women. How can labor not be diverted to open channels?" Higher-level cooperatives no longer compensated members with dividends for their contributions of land, moreover, so households could not support adult members whose labor did not earn work points. As a result, the report asserted, "Women who in the past were lazy and reliant upon men (*guoqu toulan kao nanren de nüren*) also actively participate in labor." One co-op's assistant director remarked, "This year women participating in labor has increased and their labor attitude is better than in past years." One female

FIGURE 13. Women tending contour strips planted with trees and grasses. Gansu sheng shuiliting, *Jianshe shanqu de bangyang*.

villager who had earned a total of three work points the previous year had already earned 130 work points by the tenth day of the second lunar month.[32]

When male cooperative members in Dengjiabao repaired earth dams that had been damaged during the summer rainy season of 1956, women, children, and the elderly hoed fields planted with autumn crops, weeded, and tended trees (fig. 13). Female cadres directed a "women's shock brigade" that did this work. When there was too much work to finish in daylight hours, women and men toiled into the night. As a report from Dengjiabao asserted, "Using moonlit nights to mobilize women to weed and men to quickly carry [earth] on their shoulders or backs" made it possible to combine preparation for the summer harvest and conservation work without neglecting either.[33] An article on Wushan County's conservation achievements reported that cadres had women replace men in raising livestock, plowing, seeding, hauling manure, and composting to ensure the availability of able-bodied men for conservation campaigns. In the winter of 1957, women's farm labor enabled Wushan to mobilize sixty thousand male laborers for water conservancy projects without affecting the transport of fertilizer or other crucial agricultural work.[34]

Beyond freeing up men's labor power, women also participated in large-scale conservation campaigns. In 1956, Wushan authorities resolved to "grasp full-scale mobilization, especially of the broad [majority of] women, making them display a great function in water and soil conservation."[35] Official publications pointed to full exploitation of the female workforce as integral to conservation's success. Noting that "during the spring plowing season women's power is idle (*chungeng shi funü liliang xian*)," an agricultural cooperative in Wushan mobilized women for conservation work during that period. In spring 1957 alone, women and children built over nine hundred *mu* (approximately 70 hectares) of bunds.[36] A report on Dengjiabao published in 1958 advised cadres "also [to] pay close attention to giving full play to women's activist function" by employing them in conservation work. The rate of women's participation in collective labor reached nearly 100 percent in Dengjiabao that year, and women took on almost all the work of afforestation, digging level trenches, and building earthen bunds.[37]

Deng Fenqin recalled that she and other female members of her household regularly engaged in conservation work during the first decade of the PRC: "All the women took part at that time. Some were especially outstanding and were selected as labor models and the like." Women like Deng also attended the many meetings held to mobilize residents for conservation campaigns. As she proudly said, "Starting in 1956 in Dengjiabao, whenever there was a meeting I was there."[38] As Gail Hershatter has shown, the PRC party-state reconfigured social space during the early 1950s, making it acceptable, and eventually compulsory, for women to leave their households and gather in worksites and meeting grounds.[39]

Cooperatives in Wushan County calculated the number of workdays that male and female laborers could expend in the entire year, which they then "rationally allocated to the work of basic construction and water and soil conservation (agriculture, forestry, and animal husbandry each occupying a certain amount) and side employments."⁴⁰ This not only made it possible to complete each kind of work, "but also solved the problem of [having] lots of people and little land, and surplus labor power not being able to find an outlet," achieving the goals of "every person having work to do" and "every matter having someone to attend to it."⁴¹ Collectives thus mobilized both female and male workforces, albeit with a gendered division of labor. Male workers in Dengjiabao built reservoirs, dams, and wells, while women worked on all other conservation projects alongside men—building terraces and bunds, digging ponds, planting trees and grasses, and leveling fields.⁴² When planting trees and grasses in gullies, Dengjiabao carried out a "rational division of labor" between men and women, with men digging pits and women following behind them to plant trees and sweet clover. This gendered division of labor increased the effectiveness of afforestation and grass planting.⁴³

Afforestation gained greater urgency when the PRC's draft 1956–67 National Program for Agricultural Development, announced in January 1956, stipulated that "in twelve years, starting from 1956, all barren land and barren mountains that can be greened will be greened. Trees should be planted in a planned way beside all houses, villages, roads, and waterways and on barren land and on barren mountains wherever possible."⁴⁴ On February 17, 1956, an editorial in *People's Daily* lent impetus to this tree-planting campaign by calling on China's populace to "make green the fatherland" (*lühua zuguo*).⁴⁵ The labor of rural women was instrumental in this drive.

CCP women's organizations spearheaded the campaign by mobilizing members to plant trees. On January 31, 1956, three thousand co-op members from Dongshun township assembled for an oath meeting (*xuanshi dahui*), at which they swore to Chairman Mao and the people of the Chinese nation that within two years they would green their township by planting trees on barren slopes, in gullies, next to roads, near villages, and on riverbanks. In seven years, they pledged to make Dongshun into "a great garden with shade-giving trees and flowers and fruits in full bloom."⁴⁶ The township women's federation and youth league branch, along with women and young people from each village, wrote guarantees and took oaths to fulfill their mission. The women's federation pledged to plant 30 *mu* (2 hectares) of "women's forests" in five places. Each woman had targets for gathering seeds, raising seedlings, and planting trees.[47] Cooperatives also organized female members to collect peach pits from village households for planting.[48] Acting on a directive from Wushan's county committee, the township party branch designated March 15–21 as "Dongshun township afforestation assault week," calling on residents to plant a total of one million trees and one hundred *mu* (6.66 hectares) of saplings. The campaign's "battle slogan" exhorted township residents to "launch a military advance against 'barren mountains,' 'dry mountains,' 'gullies,' and 'riverbanks,' and make them wear green clothes."[49] As part of this effort, on March 16–17, the township party branch mobilized 1,400 women, students, and other youth to plant trees along the southern bank of the Wei River.[50]

The call to plant more trees intensified the labor demands on women and young people. At the beginning of the afforestation campaign, people had "mistaken ideologies and misgivings": for instance, they said that they had already planted so many trees that there were no good places left to plant them. Some pointed out that their other tasks left little time for afforestation: "The work of spring plowing, water conservancy, and gathering fertilizer is so intense, where's the time to plant trees?" Voicing exasperation with the additional tree-planting obligation, one co-op head remarked, "It's really making [us] way too busy; busier than [we] can deal with."[51] To spur the campaign on, party and youth league branches in Dongshun formed five "youth afforestation shock brigades" comprising sixteen small groups with over six hundred male and female members to "serve as the core and the power in afforestation."[52] The township party branch set planting targets and roused young women and men with slogans. Another township formed production groups in which "young adult [males] prepared the land, experienced old people planted trees, and women watered them."[53]

Campaign rhetoric cast women's achievements in afforestation as a signifier of female empowerment. As Cheng Li and Yanjun Liu observe, "Tree planting could demonstrate the growing power and ability of women, an agenda that Mao's government eagerly promoted."[54] Women who planted trees in Wushan's Tan'ge district welcomed International Women's Day on March 8 by singing: "Carry out inspection and careful planning, struggle across the barren mountains, every person planting at least one *mu*, trees must be planted beside buildings and roads. The fragrant flowers are most fortunate. All the women mobilize to make an assault for three days to become labor models." A "great mass fervor" arose as cooperatives, teams, young people, and women held "challenge competitions," vying to see who could plant the most trees.[55]

Without appropriate planning and clear directives, however, "blindness" (*mangmuxing*) plagued afforestation. As one report noted, "As soon as tree-planting starts, men, women, old, and young all go up the mountains and plant trees anywhere that is empty. After finishing planting, they disperse in a hubbub, which results in waste of labor power and materials."[56] People planted lots of trees, but no one made sure that they survived and took root. Trees planted in inappropriate locations like fields later had to be uprooted. The question of how to compensate cooperative members for afforestation work also posed difficulties. Forestry did not factor into cooperatives' production plans, the report stated, so "the labor power needed for tree-planting and labor compensation have not been rationally solved. Some even see forestry production as a burden, fearing that it will occupy lots of work points, decreasing agricultural income and work point standards." In other words, members worried that if co-ops assigned work points for afforestation, which, unlike other agricultural labor, did not directly contribute to crop output, the average value of a work point would decrease, cutting into their overall incomes. When planting trees, some cooperatives "did not allocate appropriate labor power and only mobilized women and children." Many considered tree planting "volunteer work" and did not assign work points for it, which left members in low spirits and "influenced the activism of the masses in tree planting and tending saplings."

To systematize afforestation activities, in autumn 1956 county authorities made every township and cooperative responsible for planting trees in specifically demarcated sections, "with each agricultural cooperative giving the greening mission over to production teams, youth teams, and women." At the same time, each township's forestry personnel organized "youths and women to utilize gaps in the slack farming season to tend [saplings] and guarantee the results of tree-planting."[57]

As with other aspects of conservation, Dengjiabao's experience mobilizing women to plant trees became a model for other locales. Dengjiabao assigned 120 young men and women in fall 1956 to form four "land preparation assault vanguard groups." Led by local cadres, the teams dug pits and trenches for trees whenever rainfall made it impossible to plant winter wheat or harvest autumn crops. On October 7, 1956, Dengjiabao also sent every woman and 30 percent of the male workforce—some two hundred people in all—to the lower sections of Kangjia Gully and Lijiaping to "undertake a military advance against barren mountains and start greening."[58]

Dengjiabao exhorted people in other locales to follow suit. On November 27, 1956, Wushan County leaders forwarded an open letter from Dengjiabao's youth league branch and its female residents to Wushan's other agricultural cooperatives. The letter challenged them to respond to the CCP's call to "green the fatherland in twelve years" and surpass the county committee's call to "green the entire county in five years" by striving to realize the county's five-year goal in only *three* years. In addition to digging small furrows in winter wheat fields to conserve rainwater and ensure crops had sufficient moisture, women and young people in Dengjiabao resolved that every person would plant 450 trees that autumn—150 more than the target that the county had set for them. Dengjiabao's four production teams, "using the youth league branch and women's representatives as leaders and using youth as the core," organized four "tree-planting assault tiger brigades." Technical cadres conducted patrols, made inspections, and directed work "so that quantity exceeds quotas and quality is number one," while also overseeing field preparation and planting. Local leaders made sure to "pay attention to labor attitude and compare excellence in quantity and quality, compare mutual benefit, and make commendations from time to time to promote work." The letter from Dengjiabao's women and youths guaranteed that they would complete their afforestation mission for that autumn and raised a "friendly challenge" for other localities in Wushan to do the same.[59]

In October 1957, a directive from Gansu's provincial women's federation to women's federation branches throughout the province called on rural women to participate in water conservancy and fertilizer collection campaigns that winter and the coming spring. As the directive put it, "Women are an indispensable power in agricultural production. To complete various missions to increase production, [we] must give full play to women's labor potential, mobilizing women to actively participate in developing water conservancy, water and soil conservation, and fertilizer collection campaigns." The provincial women's federation advocated propagandizing to rural women about the significance of water conservancy and water and soil conservation, discussing central and provincial directives with them, stressing the favorable conditions for the campaign that winter, and "affirming [their] confidence that humans can conquer heaven and transform nature, stimulating the mass of women to use their brains, think of methods, and raise suggestions."[60]

When it came to collecting fertilizer, the provincial women's federation instructed, cooperative members had to criticize the "right-wing conservative ideology that 'fertilizer sources have all been dug up,'" and mobilize women to obtain fertilizer by making livestock pens so that manure could be more easily gathered, scraping soot from kangs (raised, heated platforms that rural households used for sitting, entertaining and sleeping), burning clods of soil, sweeping courtyards and roads, gathering wild animal droppings, and collecting nightsoil and potash. In addition to gathering fertilizer from their own households, women also had to participate in collective fertilizer-gathering activities such as digging out mud from reservoirs, disassembling kangs, and tearing down old walls.[61]

The directive from the Gansu women's federation recommended that agricultural cooperatives conduct "unified planning of water conservancy projects and male and female labor power" and "do the utmost to allocate work that is suitable for women, such as digging small channels and ponds, building bunds, carrying earth, and digging earth, to women; look after women's special characteristics; and pay attention to women's safety and health." Properly arranging conservation, fertilizer collection, side employments, and domestic responsibilities would result in more women joining the campaign. The directive also recommended that women "study knowledge and techniques related to water conservancy and water and soil conservation to lay the foundation for further developing water conservancy work in the future."[62]

The directive pointed out that townships and cooperatives could give female co-op members quantitative targets for collecting fertilizer and hold fertilizer-gathering competitions between co-ops and production teams to compare quantity, quality, and work turnout. Women's "fertilizer-gathering inspection small groups" at the brigade or team level would investigate and summarize the results, urge the women on, give timely praise, and strengthen direction to ensure that women completed their missions. Finally, the directive called on all women's federation cadres to take part in labor alongside other women.[63]

Archives from the 1950s suggest that this large-scale mobilization of female labor for conservation campaigns also aroused anxiety and discontent. A report on water conservancy and water and soil conservation work in Tianshui Prefecture, for instance, indicated that during the "one million wells, cisterns, reservoirs, and water cellars" campaign of 1956, disgruntled residents had asked, "How many women are going to have miscarriages (*funü liuchan duoshaoren*)?"[64] Their concern indicates that the campaign mobilized women for heavy labor regardless of their personal situation, which often put pregnancies at risk.[65]

Local leaders put social and political pressure on women who did not join in collective agriculture and conservation work. A planning report from Dengjiabao disapprovingly noted in October 1956 that "some women still do not participate in autumn harvest work." The wife of a man named Deng Huangqing was over twenty years old and, "apart from caring for children and sleeping," she did not go to the fields to take part in production at all.[66] A writer who visited Dengjiabao in 1958 observed a big-character poster emblazoned with the headline "Embroidery girls please come downstairs (*qing xiunü xialou*)." The point was not just to criticize young unmarried women for staying in their houses and sewing but to persuade them to give up their "unproductive" lifestyle and take part in "productive" collective labor. The poster read: "Cooperative members, everyone look, one team has three female idlers who idle about and do not go outdoors, go to the fields, or take part in production.... If you give up your embroidery girl airs and engage in production, if you want to be a labor model, it will not be difficult."[67] From the perspective of CCP cadres, "feudal" practices like female seclusion, regardless of how much work women did in their homes, amounted to idleness and a backward-looking adherence to gender roles associated with class enemies. In the new China, women were expected to go outdoors and participate in collective production. At a mass meeting, the three women in question swore that they would take off their "idler hats" and take part in productive labor, a pledge that they fulfilled.[68] The poster makes it clear that, for some women, leaving the home to do agricultural labor was not exciting or liberating. It took explicit devaluation of the work they performed in the home and a degree of shaming to alter the older gendered household division of labor and induce all women to participate in conservation work.[69]

During militarized conservation campaigns like the "great war in Dengjiabao," women were conscripted alongside men. As Deng Fenqin recalled, "At that time, when leveling land, if there was a large-scale battle, we went out very early to work and only came back after it got dark. When it snowed [we] still leveled land as usual. . . . Anyway, at that time if they said to go in the daytime [we] went in daytime. If they said to go in the evening, we went in the evening."[70] Another elderly woman who had been called on to level inclined land during the Great Leap Forward recalled that "the snow was deep, but we all had to go. Only when the stars were shining brightly could we rest."[71] Conservation took priority over everything else, and people labored under all conditions to complete their missions.

Deng Fenqin also spoke of the sheer enthusiasm with which many villagers initially greeted this militarized campaign to transform the environment. "The great war was waged at that time. While doing work, when the masses lined up, Chairman [Mao]'s portrait was carried at the front as they walked." Upon arriving, they posted Mao's portrait at the worksite. According to Deng Fenqin, "After they went, when the work was finished, the chairman's portrait was carried back at the front [of the ranks]. Those who could sing would sing songs. There were a lot of songs that they sang. . . . Then, when they lined up, those who could sing stood in front, and those who couldn't sing stood at the rear. I can't sing, so I stood at the rear."[72] Even without joining in the singing, as a party member, Deng Fenqin played a leading role in conservation work.[73] During the Great Leap Forward, as she said proudly, "It was often propagandized that party members were at the front. I worked at the front and that's how it was."[74] Conservation campaigns, under the leadership of grassroots cadres and activists, mobilized everyone—male and female, young and old—to do their utmost to remake the land.

Making a "Three-Eight Dengjiabao" in Kangle County

In 1957, when Gansu's party leaders launched the ten thousand Dengjiabaos campaign, they encouraged other localities to mobilize their female workforces to conserve water and soil. During this campaign, the model of Dengjiabao had a direct influence on efforts to intensify female labor. In March 1958, for instance, the party branch of the Nianpu cooperative in Dangguan township, Kangle County (about 170 km northwest of Wushan), endeavoured to convert an erosion-prone gully into an exemplary Dengjiabao. Supported by the township party branch, the local women's federation mobilized 120 women to "advance militarily" against the gully for ten days and eight nights to construct terraces and other conservation infrastructure. However, female co-op members expressed dissatisfaction with the campaign. According to an official report, some women complained, "This year all the male labor power is constructing irrigation channels." Without men to assist them, the women claimed, they could not do the work. Some found it too difficult to climb the slopes; others said, "We don't have the strength to construct anything."[75]

Local cadres initially responded with propaganda that stressed how water and soil conservation increased production for the collective. Invoking the date of International Women's Day, March 8, they asserted that if women did conservation work at night after completing their household tasks, they could turn the gully into a "beneficial 'March 8 Dengjiabao'" (*zaofu de "sanba" Dengjiabao*).[76] These exhortations got the campaign started, but during its most critical stage the number of women who turned out for work fell by 50 per cent. According to the report, "Some women did not come because they had small [that is, bound] feet and the hills were steep, so it was difficult to walk at night. Some women did not come because there was no one to look after their children. Some women believed that 'Doing a little work at night isn't any use.'"[77] The impediments created by the custom of foot binding and childcare responsibilities made many women unwilling or unable to take part in the conservation campaign, which affected the progress of work.

To overcome this challenge, local authorities formulated two principles to maximize output from women's work. First, they rationalized plans for female labor power. Pregnant women and women with "weak bodies" were assigned lighter tasks; younger and stronger women were assigned heavier work.[78] Elderly women with bound feet were assigned to gentle slopes and younger women with unbound feet worked on steeper land. No matter if they had difficulty walking, everyone had a job to do. Secondly, cadres and officials recognized that they had to "pay attention to women's special circumstances." Mothers with infants needed time to nurse their children and could go home for meals. Childless women took their meals in the gully to avoid losing work time by going home to eat.[79]

With these arrangements in place, "women's enthusiasm for labor surged rapidly" and old women of seventy years of age took part alongside girls of thirteen.[80] Even women who had previously refused to participate went out to work. Some women did not want to come late, so they skipped breakfast and brought some steamed bread to eat at the worksite. Official reports lauded women for working at night in freezing weather. Some women declared, "The snow has permeated our clothes, but it has not permeated our hearts. We resolve to struggle against hardships, treat moonlit nights as daylight, and do two days' work in one day."[81] They would not "go back down the hills," they declared, until they created a Dengjiabao. Not only did their performance "arouse the confidence and resolve of the broad masses of women in constructing socialism," but men praised female workers for surpassing the martial heroine from the Northern Song period (960–1127), Mu Guiying.[82] By finding ways to accommodate women's specific circumstances, whether bound feet or young children needing care, and putting them to work, the campaign met its goals. Learning from Dengjiabao meant exploiting female labor to the utmost extent.

From Reproductive to Productive Labor

Although archival sources leave no doubt that female labor was essential for conservation campaigns during the 1950s, they offer only fleeting glimpses of how women experienced them. Oral history interviews help fill in the gaps in the written record. Deng Fenqin's recollections bring the household-level effects of conservation to the forefront, revealing what military-style mobilization to fight water and soil loss meant for rural women and how it changed the contours of their daily lives. Deng recalled that she had previously attended to household work, but during the conservation campaigns, "when they said that party members and cadres should take the lead we didn't hesitate and ran [to do it]. When we went, we were very happy. We just did it, not paying attention to anything in the household. At that time, we worked hard.... Whatever they said, we only paid attention to doing it."[83]

When cooperatives sent mothers to engage in conservation work, they could not look after their children. Like all rural women in China during the 1950s, Dengjiabao's female residents worked regardless of whether childcare was available.[84] According to Deng Fenqin, "When there was the great war, which was in 1957 and 1958, at that time the adults all went out to do work." As a result, mothers and most other adult family members could not look after small children. Older siblings helped by taking infants out to their mothers where they were working in the fields. As Deng Fenqin put it, "After the students were dismissed from school, they took the [infant] children to their mothers to feed them milk." She laughed when she remembered how some babies got better treatment than others: "The adorable ones kept getting carried away [to be played with and looked after], but no one took the ugly ones." But combining domestic responsibilities like childcare with agricultural labor could meet with disapproval. Some local leaders worried that higher-level cadres and officials, all men, might consider the presence of children at worksites unseemly and an impediment to work. According to Deng, "Sometimes if [they] took the children to the mountain and then someone came to inspect it looked bad, so they left the children at home and made the old folks watch them."[85] Although mothers tried to provide care for infants and toddlers in the fields and hills, they often had to rely on school-age children and elderly people to fulfill this task, due in no small part to a male presumption that taking care of children did not qualify as labor.

Sometimes parents who could not find anyone to take care of their young children had no choice but to leave them at home unattended. Children who could sit up and walk were left to roam around on their own. For infants between six months and a year of age who were crawling, busy parents often simply tethered them to the family's *kang*. Deng Fenqin recalled a horrible accident that occurred due to this practice. Usually, parents measured the rope carefully based on the length of the *kang*, making sure the rope was short enough that the baby would stay safely on the platform. If they did not measure properly, however, the child could fall off the *kang* with the rope tangled around their neck. One family made this mistake, and "when they came home the child had already been strangled to death."[86] In her study of rural women in Shaanxi during the 1950s, Hershatter tells of similar tragedies that occurred when family members left infants tethered to the bedside.[87]

In most instances, however, mutual-assistance networks and collective childcare organizations kept families from having to leave their little ones home alone. As in other parts of China, collectives in Wushan organized nurseries to look after young children while their parents worked. An article in *Wushan News*, for instance, reported that Wushan's Zhongliang cooperative had "realized that women being encumbered by children led to losses in production," so on March 25, 1957, the local women's federation branch established a "childcare group."[88] During a three-month trial period, "they organized various types of childcare organization to solve the pressing difficulties of the broad [majority] of female cooperative members."[89] These groups built on informal parenting networks that families and neighbors had already devised. By July 1957, the co-op had formed three childcare groups and fifteen "field babysitting groups," in which women took turns looking after children while doing farmwork, while forty-five households assisted one another by looking after the children of relatives and neighbors. These collective arrangements took care of a total of 551 children, "solving the difficulty of being encumbered by children for 106 mothers and increasing their work turnout rate."[90] One mother, who had only worked four shifts in three months, put in more than thirty workdays in a little over a month after her children entered the childcare group. Whenever she met someone, the woman happily told them, "If the childcare group hadn't been organized, in a single year I wouldn't have been able to earn all these work points."[91]

As useful as the childcare groups were, mothers did not receive work points for taking care of their own children, so the devaluing of household labor had material consequences. When the Zhongliang co-op initially began organizing childcare groups, many women had misgivings, fearing that people from outside their family would not take good care of their children. Mothers were also unhappy that caregivers would be given work points for childcare, while they received no remuneration for caring for their own children and had to do farm labor to earn work points. In response, the cooperative organized two types of childcare groups. Children over two years old who had not yet entered school received care from relatives and neighbors who provided mutual assistance or from groups organized by brigades that selected "ten elderly people who are public-minded and selfless and have experience in taking care of children to be responsible for looking after them" in exchange for "rationally determined" compensation.[92] In Deng Fenqin's recollection, the childcare centers set up in Dengjiabao during the Great Leap Forward had no real facilities and did not depart much from ad hoc arrangements that parents had already worked out: "Actually it [the nursery] just found a few old folk to watch the children."[93]

The Zhongliang cooperative also organized "production groups" that took 150 children under two years of age into the fields, with mothers taking turns to watch them. Ten women from one brigade organized a production group, took their young children to the fields, and arranged shade tents, sheepskins, and other utensils needed to care for them. Female co-op members indicated that the childcare organizations had three good points: "children could be nursed in a timely fashion; mothers were relieved that caregivers were taking good care of them; and they could earn [points for] workdays, so their livelihoods improved."[94] By systematizing childcare networks that parents had devised on their own, cooperatives let mothers balance their concern for their children's safety with the need to take part in collective labor. Yet the arrangements also increased the amount of work that mothers had to do in the fields, as they farmed and looked after children at the same time. Fathers did not share this burden.

In Wushan, as in other parts of China in the late 1950s, collective dining halls were established to free women's labor for production by reducing their cooking responsibilities. To save time and labor power for the summer harvest, as early as July 1957 the Dongshun higher-level agricultural cooperative, of which Dengjiabao was a part, borrowed cooking utensils from its members and set up a "busy farming season dining hall" (*nongmang shitang*) to prevent women from "being pestered by household duties" and ensure that single men could go to the fields. Each day over forty people ate at the dining hall, exchanging tickets for their meals and settling accounts afterward. According to cooperative members, as *Wushan News* reported, the dining hall had two main benefits: "1) Single men and women can participate in production on time and none of them are encumbered. 2) Collective eating and collective production; in families, men do not have to wait for the women and women do not have to wait for the men; whenever they arrive, they eat, which is extremely convenient."[95]

In summer 1958, Wushan's county committee expressed concerns that from July to September, local industry, the summer harvest, management of autumn crops, deep plowing, fertilizer collection, and "various kinds of field engineering projects and basic construction" would require 12,630,000 workdays. In three months, at the normal work turnout rate, the county's 133,000 laborers could put in only 5,060,000 workdays, which would fall short of anticipated requirement by 6,710,000. One of the measures that the county adopted to address this problem was to "carry out collective livelihood benefit measures to thoroughly liberate women's labor power." By late July, co-ops in Wushan had set up 1,853 dining halls, where 70 percent of their members ate, and established 221 nurseries and 1,119 childcare groups. Co-ops also formed sewing groups outfitted with three hundred sewing machines so that women could devote less time to making clothing for their families. As a result, an article in *Gansu Daily* estimated, over sixty thousand female co-op members could be "thoroughly liberated from household labor" and the efficiency of male and female laborers would increase.[96]

Similarly, when villagers in Wushan voiced concern that labor shortages would make it impossible to attend to autumn production in 1958, county leaders held a meeting of over two hundred party branch secretaries and production team leaders to instruct collectives to "rapidly solve the childcare problem and liberate women's labor power" and "resolutely implement the principle that if weak labor power can do it do not let strong labor power do it, and if women can do it do not let men do it." A "technical instruction campaign" to teach women to harrow and plant crops would "make them able to take on various kinds of farmwork."[97]

Engaging with the gendered aspects of environmental history demonstrates that fully understanding how the lives of rural Chinese women changed during the Mao era requires sustained investigation of their everyday encounters with the environment, as well as of how social, economic, and political developments modified those relationships. Environmental degradation, like conservation, meant something different for women than it did for men. As the history of water and soil conservation in Dengjiabao and other parts of Wushan County during the 1950s makes evident, these gender-differentiated experiences of environmental change had a direct bearing on women's lives.

In northwestern China, as in many other parts of the world, the gendered division of labor dictated that women and girls did the daily work of gathering fuel and fetching water.[98] Costs associated with the depletion of these essential resources thus fell disproportionately on rural women, as the acute scarcity of biofuel and water forced them to devote more time and effort to fulfilling these basic needs. Conservation initiatives undertaken in Dengjiabao during the early 1950s, which made fuel and water more available, undoubtedly improved the lives of rural women.

Implementation of conservation measures would have been impossible without women's labor, and Deng Fenqin took evident pride in her contribution to these efforts. But what may initially have been an exciting new opportunity for women to join in collective labor outside the home soon became a burden. In Mao-era China, as in colonial Kenya and Tanzania, state-led conservation schemes intensified pressure on women's work time.[99] Even if they brought environmental improvements, by the mid-1950s the demands of conservation programs had started to weigh on rural women, who experienced this increased labor burden in gendered ways. Despite the formation of collective childcare organizations and dining halls, mobilization for conservation campaigns made it more challenging for women to fulfill the domestic labor obligations that ensured social reproduction within their households. Female labor played a vital role in remaking China's environment for the sake of conserving water and soil. But that is not all. Environmental changes witnessed during the 1950s left their traces on the biophysical landscape as well as on the bodies and minds of rural women.

SEVEN

"Conservation Was Primary, Farming Was Secondary"
The Great Famine and Its Aftermath

In April 1960, *People's Daily* published a speech by Gansu provincial governor Deng Baoshan in which he trumpeted people's communes as "the basis for high-speed development of water and soil conservation."[1] Previously, conservation initiatives in Gansu managed only one gully and slope at a time. But, as Deng proclaimed, the formation of communes at the start of the Great Leap Forward in 1958 had completely transformed the relations of production, developed productive capacity to an unprecedented degree, and ushered in a new phase of large-scale management of mountain ranges and watersheds. Communes provided comprehensive planning and an "organizational guarantee" that conservation plans could be realized. Dengjiabao was the proof. In eight years, Deng asserted, it had managed only 10 square kilometers of land. In winter 1959 and spring 1960 alone, he claimed, Dengjiabao's brigade members had managed an unbelievable 240 square kilometers of land, 80 square kilometers of which attained the high standards seen in Dengjiabao itself. As he explained, "With people's communes, it is possible to better mobilize labor power, organize large-scale battles and large-scale cooperation, and carry out powerful and dynamic mass campaigns." Large-scale cooperation meant channeling thousands of people from a wide area who focused their efforts on a single project, as had occurred in summer 1958 during the great war in Dengjiabao. Before the formation of communes, Deng said, the labor power mobilized for conservation campaigns was usually no more than several hundred people from a few agricultural cooperatives. Now a water and soil conservation battle like the great war in Dengjiabao involved several communes or counties cooperating, with thousands or tens of thousands of people "going to the front."

Not only were the accomplishments described in Deng Baoshan's speech incredibly exaggerated, but he never addressed the impact these conservation battles had on agricultural production. Between 1958 and 1960, yields of grain and other staples in Dengjiabao decreased by over 36.5 percent. Per capita production in 1960 had fallen by nearly 50 percent from its peak in 1956.[2] During the Great Leap Forward, mobilization to conserve water and soil drew labor power from farming and disrupted agricultural output, leading to a precipitous decline in harvests and food availability (see chapter 5). The losses in Dengjiabao paralleled trends throughout China. The Great Leap Forward sought to accelerate economic development through mass mobilization of rural labor, endeavoring to raise agricultural yields while also initiating local industries like backyard steel furnaces. Since commune members employed in steel production, water conservancy, or other Great Leap projects could not farm, harvests declined. In the charged atmosphere of the time, cadres hesitated to admit they had not met production targets and reported exaggerated yields to their superiors. When one collective reported record output, another tried to outdo them by claiming even more inflated achievements. Basing their numbers on wildly overblown production figures, state procurements extracted grain from the countryside to feed cities and supply the industrial sector. Urban party members, industrial workers, and the military received food rations from the state; rural dwellers did not. The PRC government requisitioned over 17.4 percent of China's total grain output in 1957, 20.9 percent in 1958, 28 percent in 1959, and 21 percent in 1960.[3] Plummeting harvests and rapacious grain procurements led to famine. Death rates shot up while birth rates plummeted. Across China, the resulting catastrophe took between fifteen and forty million lives.[4]

In Dengjiabao, conservation campaigns launched during the Great Leap Forward played a major role in bringing about this subsistence crisis. Along with inclement weather, large-scale diversion of labor to conservation projects—often with little or no compensation—and prioritization of the aesthetics of the rural landscape at the expense of farmwork disrupted agricultural production. Under these conditions, state grain expropriations further jeopardized rural people's food entitlements.

The evidence from Dengjiabao shows that men and women experienced this ecological catastrophe differently. During interviews conducted by personnel from the Tianshui Water and Soil Conservation Experiment Station in 1961, men in Dengjiabao spoke primarily about the damage the

Great Leap Forward conservation battles did to agriculture, as well as the importance of restoring grain production and striking a balance between conservation and farming. Male villagers, however, were silent about how the catastrophe affected social reproduction: the work of giving birth, raising children, and feeding family members. During my fieldwork, I learned about how conservation campaigns and the horrific famine to which they contributed burdened women in ways that affected their domestic lives, threatened their families' subsistence, and left enduring effects on their bodies. The subsistence crisis reduced female fertility and birth rates and subjected women to long-lasting ailments.

The hardships of famine subsided after 1961, when local authorities in Wushan County followed central government directives and implemented policies to undo the Great Leap's worst excesses. Food gradually became more available, but the steps that desperate villagers took to recover from the famine had environmental consequences that damaged many of the conservation measures undertaken over the previous decade.

Waging the Great War in Dengjiabao

In the oral history interviews I conducted in Dengjiabao, elderly villagers who lived through the Great Leap Forward vividly described the militarized mobilization for conservation campaigns. In 2019, one man described the commitment of all available labor power to the war against water and soil loss: "1958. The Great Leap Forward. Terraces. Leveling land. At that time, it was human-wave attacks (*renhai zhan*). There wasn't any machinery like now and no handcarts. Just human-wave tactics."[5] Commune leaders deployed Dengjiabao's entire workforce, along with commune members deputed from elsewhere in Wushan County, to remaking the land.

Even if commune members were initially enthusiastic about the conservation campaigns launched in 1958, this mass mobilization did not benefit the local populace. As communes prioritized remaking the land and meeting conservation targets during the initial stage of the Great Leap, agricultural production became secondary. Communes frequently appropriated labor and resources for conservation projects from subordinate units without compensation.[6] Because "able-bodied labor power" (i.e., male laborers) and key local leaders left to work on conservation and hydraulic engineering projects, as one Wushan County official recalled, those who remained to do farmwork "were mostly old people, women, and disabled people, and they were not equal to the task."[7] Nature made cultivating the land harder when three years of drought and inclement weather descended on Wushan from 1959 to 1961.[8] Conservation work, by diverting labor away from agriculture, only aggravated the harvest shortfalls.[9]

A former People's Liberation Army soldier from the Dazhuang production brigade in Chengguan commune named Wang Haicheng took leave from his job at a commercial bureau in Xinjiang in spring 1959 to visit his family back in Wushan. In a letter addressed directly to Mao Zedong, Wang described the alarming conditions he found in his native place. "When I returned home," he wrote, "I saw that the lives of commune members in Wushan and Tongwei Counties were relatively bitter."[10] Most commune members ate only four to ten *liang* (200–500 grams, or around 700–1750 calories) of grain and other staples per day. Wang explained the dire effects of this meagre food intake: "Commune members' mood is extremely low. In terms of production, this year most of the land has not been planted." Livestock had died in large numbers, and many commune members had fled. Local people expressed indignation toward the people's communes and the CCP leaders who championed them. "At the same time," Wang wrote, "some commune members openly say that Chairman Mao isn't even letting us get enough food to eat (*Mao zhuxi lian fan dou bu jiao women chibao*). More importantly, some commune members see communes as not as good as going it alone. Some say that if [we] work [we] can't even stay alive, and if [we] don't work [we] can't stay alive either." Collective labor had led only to food insecurity, so local people saw no reason to take part. Wang attributed this disillusionment to commune cadres who displayed "bureaucratism" and were "repressing democracy." During the previous year, cadres had not informed commune members about grain production targets before putting them into effect. At year's end, when the targets had not been met, the cadres assembled commune members and demanded to know what they had done with the grain. At the same time, Wang reported, cadres cursed commune members and subjected them to struggle sessions, "so when commune members had objections, they didn't dare raise them."

Available statistics bear out his assessment. In Wushan County, total grain production in 1961 had fallen by around 60 percent compared to its peak in 1956 and was 24 percent below 1949 levels.[11] Output in Dengjiabao declined similarly. Per capita production peaked in 1956 at 385 kilograms per capita, falling to 196 kilograms per capita in 1960. Food energy availability per capita in Dengbiabao decreased from a maximum of around 2,425 calories per day at its height in 1956 to a mere 1,170 calories per day in 1960 (see table 1).[12]

Per capita output in Dengjiabao in 1960 may have been higher than it was in 1952, but government grain procurements reduced food availability to critically low levels. Prior to 1953, moreover, villagers engaged in handicraft production or did seasonal wage labor to earn money for purchasing additional food. Even if Dengjiabao's harvests could feed its residents for only eight or nine months of the year in the early 1950s, the ability to buy food on the market enabled them to survive. With the imposition of the PRC's unified purchase and supply system and the formation of people's communes, which eliminated markets for labor and grain in the countryside, this was no longer an option.

In Tianshui Prefecture, the administrative unit to which Wushan County and Dengjiabao belonged, average per capita output of grain and other staples for 1960–62 was 157 kilograms; after subtracting government procurements and withholding by collectives, average per capita availability came to a meagre 123 kilograms—less than one thousand calories per person per day.[13] In addition to the available statistical data, evidence from archival documents and oral history interviews confirms that, as in many other parts of China, government grain seizures pushed food consumption well below the margin of subsistence. Driven by the expectations of the Great Leap, collective leaders inflated crop yields to boost their reputations, and the party-state extracted grain based on their exaggerated reports. Cadres pressed other villagers hard to deliver government grain, leaving scarcely any behind for local consumption.[14]

The result was famine. According to Yang Jisheng, Wushan County experienced 11,374 famine-related deaths in 1958 (1.98 percent mortality), 9,420 in 1959 (1.63 percent mortality), and 28,253 in 1960 (a staggering 5.21 percent mortality rate).[15] Dengjiabao's population fell from 605 in 1958 to 560 in 1961, decreasing 7.43 percent during the "three hard years."[16] The

Great Leap's promise of environmental improvement, increased agricultural production, and rural prosperity brought catastrophic famine-related mortality.

Local Views of Conservation

How did people in Dengjiabao who took part in these conservation campaigns understand and evaluate them? How did they experience the collective drive to transform the environment during the Great Leap Forward and the famine to which it contributed? Archival documents help answer these questions. In late 1960 and early 1961, the PRC central government's partial acknowledgement of the nationwide crisis caused by the Great Leap triggered official inquiries into its consequences. In this context, personnel from the Tianshui Water and Soil Conservation Experiment Station returned to Dengjiabao in spring 1961 to investigate the status of recent conservation initiatives. Their records, held at the Yellow River Conservancy Commission Archives in the city of Zhengzhou, contain notes from conversations between investigators and members of production teams in Dengjiabao. In these discussions, male villagers reflected on the conservation campaigns of the Great Leap and their impact. These notes are unedited, quickly jotted down by hand. Along with interviews I conducted in Dengjiabao, the notes reveal the acute contradictions that emerged between the party-state's conservation agenda and the subsistence priorities of rural villagers.

Investigators from the experiment station interviewed Li Xuding, who was Dengjiabao's brigade leader and a nationwide labor model, along with other production team members from Lijiaping, one of the natural villages that constituted the Dengjiabao brigade. As these villagers explained, "Water and soil conservation's pretty good (*shuitu baochi hao shi hao*), but for the past few years grain rations have been low (*kouliang di*) and life's been tight, so we simply couldn't pay any attention to doing water and soil conservation work."[17] During the subsistence crisis that struck in 1959 and 1960, finding food and staying alive mattered far more to villagers than slowing erosion. That said, the production team members had no objection to implementing conservation measures under normal circumstances. "In fact," they said, "everyone loves flat land and dislikes steeply inclined land." If conservation work made land easier to farm by turning slopes into level fields, they were all for it.

Villagers clearly preferred some forms of conservation over others. Production team members in Lijiaping liked building terraces and bunds, since they gradually leveled land and had the potential to increase yields, noting that "they'd rather cultivate one *mu* of flat land than cultivate ten *mu* of steeply inclined land."[18] Members of another production team added, "Building bunds is the best. It can impede runoff and can increase production. In places with trenches, it not only accumulates fertile soil, but it can also promote crop production." Fertility improved in the sediment that accumulated along the bunds, increasing yields by 20 to 50 percent.[19] Villagers also liked planting trees and grasses because they provided desperately needed fuel, solidified bunds, retained water and soil on slopes, and preserved soil moisture.[20] Intercropping sweet clover and alfalfa with grains or potatoes likewise enriched soil fertility and markedly increased yields.[21] People could consume alfalfa and sweet clover when there was nothing else to eat in addition to using them as fodder for livestock.[22] During the famine, according to Lijiaping residents, "alfalfa kept many people alive."[23]

Other conservation measures were less popular. Constructing dams and reservoirs required extensive labor and lacked tangible benefits—or did more harm than good. Villagers said, "Dams aren't good. They have no benefits, they waste labor, and water isn't stored up."[24] When there was little rain, dams were empty; when rain was plentiful, dams washed out. Badly built dams broke during rainstorms, unleashing stored water and creating harmful deluges. At the same time, villagers felt that dams were of little use when it came to capturing sediment to create fields in gullies and leveling the land.[25] Reservoirs and water cellars held either too much water or not enough: "When it rains, water accumulates and even the fields are saturated. When there's slight drought and crops need water, wells and reservoirs don't have water in them either."[26]

Making matters worse, Great Leap conservation campaigns hampered production by drawing labor away from farming. In Leijiashan, a village that was also part of the Dengjiabao brigade, local leaders sent the entire workforce to take part in the great war in Dengjiabao during the busy farming season in August and September of 1958, so commune members could not weed or loosen soil for the broomcorn millet crop.[27] According to Li Xuding and his comrades, "Doing battle in large military units (*da bingtuan zuozhan*) isn't good. In 1958, when ten thousand people waged a great war in Dengjiabao, they didn't look after their own crops. Once labor power was recklessly transferred, it wasted labor power and wasted grain."[28] A former production team leader named Li Jianyuan agreed: "Water and soil conservation's pretty good. [But] large-scale warfare for water and soil conservation and chaotically opening irrigation canals transferred away labor power, and for this reason agriculture was neglected." With much of the workforce sent to conservation projects, cultivators had to plant wheat without plowing under the stubble from the previous season's grass and broomcorn millet, so the wheat did not grow well. As Li Jianyuan recalled, "Night and day [we] waged a bitter war digging in gullies, filling in gullies, digging irrigation channels, constructing step fields, and planting trees, placing agricultural production in a secondary position."[29]

Gathering armies of workers for "large-formation warfare" and large-scale cooperation damaged crops in places that provided labor as well as where projects took place. When communes transferred people to other places to work, "wherever they went was where they ate," so sites of high-priority conservation projects like Dengjiabao had to support large influxes of outsiders.[30] At the same time, commune members deployed to other areas for large-scale cooperation did not put forth their full effort because the projects did not directly benefit them. They simply went through the motions and did the assigned work in a careless manner. As Dengjiabao residents concluded, "Large-scale cooperation wastes labor power." People transferred from Zhang County, directly east of Wushan, to participate in the great war in Dengjiabao "had the ideology of being guests and a mission point of view, so they weren't able to suit measures to local conditions."[31] When outsiders came to Dengjiabao, their work was perfunctory, and their limited knowledge of local circumstances made them less effective. Loss of agricultural labor, as villagers observed, "influenced production per unit of area [in places that sent workers to Dengjiabao], and at the same time the work units that benefited didn't welcome it either."[32] Large-scale cooperation burdened everyone involved.

Even if local leaders managed Dengjiabao relatively well, focusing all labor power on a single project and neglecting everything else diminished harvests.³³ Production team members from Majiashan village reported that when people went to Dengjiabao, they left their own crops untended. After they arrived in Dengjiabao, as production team members put it, outsiders "had a mission point of view and made a mess." Another problem was that conservation campaigns had sacrificed farmland to construct as many terraces and dams as possible. Villagers said that when tens of thousands of people "waged war" in Dengjiabao "it wasn't good," because they "dug up crop land, and land that shouldn't have been dug up was built upon and changed into other types of land."³⁴

Following the disasters of the Great Leap, villagers emphasized that collectives had to ensure that conservation did not interfere with farming. Without denying that conserving water and soil was good, production team members in Dengjiabao thought it "should be done gradually and must utilize the slack season." By contrast, the war waged in Dengjiabao in 1958 had extended into the busiest farming season and interfered with agriculture. As interviewees told investigators, "Crops hadn't been harvested and [we] went to struggle in Dengjiabao. Farmers rely on farming to eat. It made water and soil conservation primary and agriculture secondary."³⁵ They advised that large-scale assaults should take place only during slack periods in the spring, after the summer harvest, in winter, and when it rained.³⁶ Launching assaults at these times meant villagers had to work all year long, however, which also took its toll. Communes devoted any available time to conservation work, so when farming duties slowed down, villagers could not relax or engage in sideline production. Extreme labor intensification decreased labor effectiveness. In recent years, according to production team members from Majiashan village, "work and rest weren't combined well. Winter idleness changed into winter busyness and no distinction was made between winter and spring. That way, in winter people couldn't rest well and in spring they couldn't work well."³⁷ Commune members were reaching the point of exhaustion.

The number of workdays devoted to water and soil conservation projects in Dengjiabao increased from 3,700 in 1956 to 8,600 in 1957 and 20,000 in 1958 before declining somewhat to 16,000 in 1959 and falling to only 600 in 1960.³⁸ Not coincidentally, the upsurge in time and effort devoted to conservation projects in 1958 and 1959 coincided with falling yields and the decline of Dengjiabao's population due to famine-related mortality.

Even as the war in Dengjiabao negatively affected crop yields, local cadres exaggerated production reports. A former party branch secretary was open about the prevalence of this practice during the Great Leap Forward: "It had an influence; at that time, there was exaggeration (*gao fukua*). There wasn't that much [grain]. There were situations in which grain was plowed over into the land. At that time [following the war in Dengjiabao], there wasn't any grain."[39] When asked what the great war in Dengjiabao had achieved, he insisted that "most of it was exaggerated. It was bragging (*chui niupi de*)."[40] He added that, in contrast to the situation between 1952 and 1957, Great Leap conservation campaigns had minimal benefits. "At that time, production wasn't increased.... Water and soil conservation preserved water and soil, but grain [output] didn't increase. That is to say, it was bragging.... At that time, everything was overblown. Exaggerated. The land wasn't truly leveled.... Not much. Not much land was leveled.... During the great war in Dengjiabao people came from the whole county. It was exaggerated. [Even] if it was level land [already], they leveled it (*yaoshi pingdi, jiu nong ping le*)."[41] The scale of exaggeration could be mindboggling. Cadres and officials claimed that yields in some places reached an astonishing one thousand *jin* (500 kg) per *mu*, but local people admitted to investigators in 1961 that this was untrue. To "convey that vigor was great," as production team members from Majiashan put it, cadres "emptily reported numbers" and inflated output. The steps taken to present visitors who came to Dengjiabao with a rural landscape that had the appearance of abundance also damaged crop production. As a way "to welcome inspections and for photographs," cultivators moved seedlings from several parcels of land into a single field to make crop growth appear more impressive and give the impression that an abundant harvest was on the way.[42] Unfortunately, moving the seedlings killed them. Li Xuding likewise told investigators that to "welcome observers and appraisals" and "launch satellites and seize a red flag"—garnering praise from visitors who believed they had made astronomical achievements—people "took crop seedlings from several fields and moved them into one field. They could launch big satellites, [but] as a result, grain couldn't be harvested and [they] just went hungry."[43]

In other instances, conservation cut directly into food supplies. According to two men named Li Tongtong and Li Fusheng, "In 1958 when waging the great war in Dengjiabao, to build step fields in the gully, over ten *mu* [0.66 hectare] of unripe potato fields were completely dug up to fill in the gully."[44] Other commune members also reported that "the great war in Dengjiabao took unripe potatoes and dug them up before they'd sprouted." The campaign put conservation first and agriculture second, "firmly grasping water and soil conservation and slackening in agriculture."[45] Commune members had "exchanged experiences" with people in other places, but many of the planting techniques they adopted had proven unsuited to local conditions, which also caused yields to decline.[46] Hillsides covered with level terraces came to matter more than growing food and ensuring subsistence.

Even after agricultural production had clearly decreased, political pressure led people to continue to inflate yields. As production team leaders in Majiashan explained, "When commune members were asked if they could do it, they said they could. If they said it wasn't possible, [other people] said they had rightist tendencies and were also conservative. Cadres at each level were all unwilling to tell the truth, otherwise they'd get the worst of it." Even in 1961, many villagers hesitated to criticize China's highest leaders. Production team members held that "the party central and Chairman Mao's policies are correct" but were quick to point out that "cadres below executed them badly."[47]

When I interviewed Dengjiabao's former party branch secretary, he recalled one production team leader who engaged in "blind commandism" and claimed to have grown apple and peach trees alongside maize sprouts. When presenting the apples and peaches to Wushan County leaders, a waist-drumming team (*yaogu dui*) led a parade of production team members to an elementary school in the county seat, where the county committee greeted them with steamed wheat buns—an incredibly rare treat. But, unbeknownst to county leaders, the production team had actually borrowed fruits from neighboring villages on the plains. As the former party branch secretary told me, "We took the apples and peaches to report the good news to the county, saying that the apples and peaches were grown in Dengjiabao, but actually at that time we didn't grow apples here."[48] The miraculous achievement was fake.

Beneath the facade and despite the grand aspirations that accompanied the formation of people's communes, conservation campaigns during the Great Leap Forward jeopardized food security. As Li Xuding and his fellow production team members told investigators, by 1960 "there was no grain to eat, which created problems." On the one hand, some team members acknowledged that conservation measures slowed erosion: "Ten thousand people waging a great war in Dengjiabao had its benefits. The achievements were great and made it so that silt didn't go out of gullies and water didn't go down plateaus."[49] On the other hand, the cost of that accomplishment was too great, and the resulting food shortages appeared to betray the promises of the revolution.[50] As some villagers complained, "During land reform, propaganda said that under socialism you'd never eat a meal without meat." Now they "couldn't even eat grain." In their view, "making a big scene at the Wei River" in summer 1958 to greet the Third Nationwide Water and Social Conservation Conference in Wushan (see chapter 5) had done more than anything to cause their deprivation. In their words, "abandoning the crops in the fields and having to move to Dengjiabao led to great hunger and drove [people] to their deaths."[51]

Circumstances in 1958, according to Li Xuding and his comrades, differed from those between 1952 and 1955, when Dengjiabao transitioned from individual production (*dan gan*) to mutual-aid teams and agricultural cooperatives. In those years, villagers combined farming and conservation, prioritizing agricultural production. Mutual-aid teams and co-ops had built bunds and filled in gullies to level land during slack seasons and on rainy days, which promoted production. But things changed in 1958 with the formation of people's communes and the Great Leap Forward: "Only paying attention to form, to strive for a red flag and to welcome observers and appraisals, [we] dropped agriculture to do water and soil conservation."[52]

An elderly villager I interviewed recalled the negative impact on farming and food supplies. People went hungry unless they harvested crops, and when large-scale mobilization for conservation campaigns made farmwork all but impossible, production collapsed. Without food to eat, people gave up on both conservation and farming. As he explained, "In 1960, the last year, grain wasn't harvested, and the maize was all abandoned in the fields." The problem, in his view, was that government policies "managed people too strictly." Even though no one had food, villagers did not dare touch the harvest before the collective determined how to distribute it. Consuming grain would bring accusations of theft. In his words, "Grain was scarce, and people went hungry. The wheat was still growing in the fields and rain turned it black. No one dared move it and no one looked after it. Then the grain was ruined and that made grain rations tight. It was the government's policy, and no one dared move it. If a household had cooking smoke, [other people] went in to inspect where the things [they had to eat] had come from."[53] Anyone who had food was suspicious, and evidence indicates that grain theft did take place in Dengjiabao during the famine. Contemporary sources referred explicitly to "the problem of commune members stealing grain" from the collective fields and pointed to increasing grain output and boosting food rations as the only ways to stop the malfeasance.[54] In Dengjiabao, as elsewhere in China, famine victims did whatever they could to survive.[55]

By 1961, lack of food left Dengjiabao's residents unable to do any work at all. In the words of Li Jianyuan, "Now grain rations are too low, and production can't be increased. Cooperative members don't have enough to eat; water and soil conservation simply can't be carried out. Not even farmwork can be done." Resumption of conservation work had to wait until agricultural production, grain rations, and labor power recovered.[56] Li Tongtong and Li Fusheng echoed this sentiment: "Grain ration standards are low, and life isn't good. People don't want to do it. Farmwork can't even be carried out. They simply don't have the strength to carry out water and soil conservation." Villagers stressed that making conservation primary and agriculture secondary during the Great Leap was the reason. Inability to combine farming and conservation "became a reason that agricultural output has decreased by the year over the past several years."[57] Other Dengjiabao residents recommended that collectives temporarily stop assigning laborers to conservation projects: "Only after increasing agricultural production and increasing grain rations should water and soil conservation be carried out. [We] must firmly grasp building bunds, [but] farming well is the foundation."[58] People needed to have food to survive, let alone work, so farming had to come first.

A man named Ma Xingwu, previously an accountant in Dengjiabao's higher-level agricultural cooperative, expressed similar views. Conservation was necessary, he said, but low food rations made it impossible. In the past, whenever light rain fell, everyone went out to make emergency repairs to

"CONSERVATION WAS PRIMARY" 195

dams and terraces. Now no one had the strength to make repairs; they could only "squat at home" In Ma's estimation, the Great Leap had been counterproductive: "The achievements of the past have all been damaged by last year and this year. Agricultural production and water and soil conservation have both been damaged." Inadequate rations left people hungry, so they stole unripe crops from fields.[59] "Life hasn't improved (grain rations are too low). Agricultural production can't advance; water and soil conservation simply can't be carried out."[60]

The scale of the collective units that organized and directed conservation work and farming was crucial. Whether for agricultural production or conservation, as Li Xuding and his fellow production team members explained, "based on the lessons of the past, the masses all believe that the forms [that existed] at the time of the lower-level cooperatives and higher-level cooperatives are best." Larger-scale collective organizations had only caused harm. When communes mobilized their members for conservation projects, they got little if anything in return, leaving them overworked and hungry. As Li Xuding and other men from Lijiaping remarked, "Appropriation from subordinate units kills people (*pingdiao haisi ren*). The masses want to go to Dengjiabao to settle accounts and seek compensation for their labor power and work accounts from large-scale cooperation."[61] People from all over Wushan County had done conservation work in Dengjiabao; after 1961 those who had survived the famine wanted fair payment for services rendered. Li Jianyuan, for his part, stressed that conservation had to be done in a way that did not take labor away from farming, "[We] can't, as in the past, wage large-formation warfare. [We] have to, like in the cooperative period, carry it out during slack farming season and on rainy days."[62] Smaller-scale cooperatives had managed labor more efficiently, villagers reported, so after cultivating fields everyone could spare some time to build bunds, manage gullies, and plant grasses.[63] Villagers preferred to rely on local production brigades and teams instead of communes with thousands of people.

Gender and Disaster

The interviews conducted by the Tianshui Water and Soil Conservation Experiment Station in 1961 offer rich insight into local perceptions of conservation, but they have a serious limitation: the investigators spoke only with Dengjiabao's male production team members. Women's views are totally absent. Despite all the CCP had done since 1949 to challenge the traditional norm of female seclusion, in 1961 the idea of letting male outsiders be alone with local women to conduct interviews may have struck villagers and investigators as inappropriate. Only in my interviews with Deng Fenqin, a woman who lived through the conservation campaigns of the Great Leap Forward, did I learn about their gendered dimensions. This oral history helps make legible the impact of conservation on women's embodied experiences of work, hunger, and affliction.

Once they were formed, the people's communes fundamentally altered systems of labor compensation in ways that were partly intended to make local women able to take part in collective enterprises. In the first stage of the Great Leap Forward, the PRC government eliminated the work-point system. Instead, communes determined part of their members' compensation (usually 30–40 percent) based on work attendance and a predetermined wage grade. Communes distributed a larger portion of compensation (typically 60–70 percent) through a free supply system that allocated grain and other staples according to need, promising all members free food from dining halls.[64] Income was no longer linked to labor contributions.

The communal dining halls, which fed everyone in the commune from "one big pot," were expanded across China during the Great Leap to lighten women's domestic workloads. PRC leaders believed that the dining halls would relieve most women of cooking duties and release their labor for collective production. Some women initially welcomed the communal dining halls, but few of the dining halls functioned effectively.[65] During Dengjiabao's great war to conserve water and soil in 1958, Deng Fenqin was tasked with managing provisions in the collective dining hall.[66] From the start, dining hall managers like Deng had to cope with acute supply shortages of necessities like grain, oil, and salt. Of all of them, in the words of a former vice secretary in the Wushan county committee, "The fuel problem was the biggest. There was no kindling to burn."[67] Dengjiabao's fuel supplies, which met 77.2 percent of its residents' consumption requirements in 1958, decreased to 49 percent of need in 1959 and 23 percent in 1960.[68] As a result, dining hall personnel had to cut down trees, including those planted for conservation purposes, to cook.

Deng Fenqin recalled the collapse of crop production during the Great Leap Forward and the severe food shortages it caused: "It didn't rain for three years [1959–61]. Everything was dried out. Before that, the crops were doing well, but then they all dried up."[69] Even before the drought began, she said, people had neglected the harvest to join the great war in Dengjiabao. Eventually, with crops unattended and drought worsening, food became scarce. She said, "The plains could be irrigated. The mountains were dried out. Grain rations were tight.... Grain rations were paralyzed. After grain rations were tight, no one paid attention to Dengjiabao anymore."[70] Disruption of farmwork and persistent drought caused food shortages that ground all conservation work in Dengjiabao to a halt.

Deng Fenqin was proud of her ability to keep her fellow villagers alive, recalling that even during the horrific famine of 1959–60, when she oversaw the dining hall, "not a single person in Lijiaping ever starved to death."[71] Population data from Lijiaping attest to her claim. While the Dengjiabao brigade's population fell from 606 in 1957 to 560 in 1961, the Lijiaping production team's population did not decline during the "three hard years."[72]

But even if people did not perish during the famine, what they ate offered little nourishment. In keeping with the trend throughout much of China in 1960, Deng Fenqin fed everyone who came to the dining hall two ladles of gruel made from beets (*tiangen*) and potatoes, staple foodstuffs of the day, along with a few pieces of yellow radish or other root vegetables. Today, as villagers informed me, people would never think to eat beets, and they do not even feed them to their pigs. "At that time," Deng recalled, "if you ate some coarse grain, buckwheat, or bean flour and the like, [you] thought it was pretty good. There basically wasn't any wheat flour."[73] As Lijiaping's male production team members explained to investigators from the Tianshui Water and Soil Conservation Experiment Station in 1961, common people "disliked the dining halls. They didn't get enough to eat. In food grain distribution, and perhaps in all other forms of distribution, there must be distribution based on labor. Food grain should be distributed to the household. [We] don't want dining halls."[74]

Hoping to get their families through the subsistence crisis, women scavenged for plants. Around 1960, when grain and other staples grew critically scarce, Deng Fenqin went with other women into the mountains to pick wild vegetables, dig for roots, or strip tree bark as food substitutes. Willow buds soaked in water for a few days to reduce their bitter flavor and then made into preserved vegetables (*suancai*) averted hunger but did not offer much nutritional content.[75] Gender norms dictated that it must be women who kept their families alive, either by cooking or gathering food, even when they also did communal labor.

Lack of food and fuel, combined with greatly increased labor burdens during the Great Leap, took a great toll on rural women. For Deng Fenqin, the arduous work of scavenging for food coincided with the arrival of her first son, in 1960. After giving birth, Deng, like Chinese mothers even today, would have expected to eat unusually well and rest in the house for a month to regain her strength.[76] But famine made it impossible for her to observe this postpartum custom. As she related, "In that year, I gave birth to him. Even before the one-month lying-in period ended (*haimei zuoguo yuezi*), I'd already gone to the mountains to pick alfalfa."[77] Since she later had several other children, Deng Fenqin seems to have made it through this ordeal without serious reproductive health concerns. Other rural women suffered miscarriages, uterine prolapse, and other health problems when they had to return to work too soon after giving birth.[78] Like many women who lived through China's collectivization era, Deng reported that the strain of childbearing and the struggle to survive the famine left her with painful and lingering embodied memories: "Because of that time, my legs hurt all the time now and I can't do any work (*ganhuo*)." And she repeated, "Seven or eight days after giving birth to a child, I had to go out to gather wild vegetables."[79] Having to return to work immediately after giving birth deeply hurt Deng's identity as woman and mother, a trauma she experienced and expressed in terms of her enduring bodily afflictions.

The Great Leap famine also took a heavy toll on overworked and underfed men. Indeed, evidence indicates that men died in larger numbers than women. Data from Wushan during the famine suggests the typical male-to-female excess sex ratio in rural China shifted to a female-to-male excess sex ratio from 1959 to 1962, suggesting a higher death rate for males.[80] This is typical in the global history of famines. Although the reasons for the female mortality advantage in times of famine remain poorly understood and controversial, some experts believe it may relate to women's comparatively high reserves of body fat.[81] But just because fewer women died does not mean they suffered less. In addition to the trauma of losing male family members, when men died women would have taken on their work.

Not surprisingly, given the famine's impact on women's health and well-being, female fertility appears to have decreased during the disaster. Although I have not found data on birth rates for Wushan County, Yang Jisheng indicates that in Gansu Province the birth rate fell from 3.15 percent in 1958 to 1.93 percent in 1959, 1.55 percent in 1960, and 1.48 percent in 1961.[82]

The scattered available evidence suggests a similar decline in Wushan. According to a report from October 1961, the birth rate fell by 61.2 percent in the Mulin commune in Wushan's Yanjing district between 1958 and 1960. Child mortality also seems to have increased. The report indicates that in two communes in Yanjing district, one child died in 1958, two in 1959, and fourteen in 1960. It also found that in the Mulin, Hualin, and Yuchuan communes, children aged seven and below accounted for 13.08 percent of the population in 1961, 12.10 percent below the 1959 national average. The famine's impact on child mortality is demonstrated most strikingly by the fact that children aged three and below made up just 3.08 percent of the three communes, 10.62 percent below the 1959 national average.[83]

Recovery after Famine

Life for villagers in Dengjiabao, whether male or female, did not improve until 1961, when the PRC central government adjusted its agricultural policies. Moves to modify and stabilize communes in spring 1959 were followed by an attempted revival of Great Leap policies in 1960, then a final retreat from them the next year. In response to low morale and declining work efficiency, in early 1959 the government made the brigade the basic accounting unit, reimplemented the work-point system, and limited the proportion of grain distributed through the free supply system. Yet work points had essentially no value if brigades had no grain for which to exchange them. By summer 1959, brigades and production teams differed little from the earlier agricultural cooperatives, except that they had to support projects undertaken by the people's communes. Following the disputes between Mao Zedong and other high-level leaders at the Lushan Conference in July–August 1959, however, the government once again made the commune the basic accounting unit. After agricultural production declined further and the famine became more severe, in early 1961 the basic accounting unit shifted back to the brigade. Then in autumn 1961, the CCP Central Committee settled on the smaller production team as the basic accounting unit and reduced the size of communes and brigades. Production teams revived the system of paying work points to members depending on the quantity and quality of their labor contributions. When the Great Leap ended in 1961, collective organization, labor management, and income distribution systems differed little from those that had existed under the lower-level cooperatives in 1955, except households did not receive dividend payments for privately owned land.[84] Communal dining halls were phased out and, as Deng Fenqin put it, the collective "distributed [to] every household grain to eat separately, and from then on we started to make food for our own families to eat."[85]

As the central government adjusted its policies toward rural collectives, cadres and officials in Wushan County began to address local problems caused by the Great Leap. During a meeting of cadres from the Dengjiabao brigade and its subordinate production teams on May 29, 1961, county leaders addressed the impact of recent conservation campaigns on agriculture production and food security. The notebooks from the Tianshui Water and Soil Conservation Experiment Station's investigation contain a detailed record of the meeting. County authorities openly acknowledged the dissatisfaction and disillusionment of the local populace. Conservation campaigns had diverted enormous amounts of labor and resources to Dengjiabao, "but when rectifying the phenomenon of exaggeration, the masses cursed this red flag to death [saying that] it was worthless."[86] People had an antipathy toward reservoirs, dams, and wells because "past arrangements were inappropriate." Conservation measures had not started from the "perspective of production." Instead, they sought "to grasp red flags and welcome observers and appraisals." During the Great Leap, appearances mattered more than utility. Rather than being suited to local conditions, reservoirs, dams, and wells had been built beside roads to show them off to passersby. Furthermore, the commune had expended far too much labor power constructing reservoirs and dams. If that labor had been used to construct terraces, "the masses would definitely have been delighted."

Especially since the Great Leap Forward started in 1958, conservation had been overemphasized: "It squeezed out agriculture. It was like water and soil conservation was primary and agriculture was secondary. As a result, production decreased."[87] The masses would only support building bunds and terraces if the work was "closely combined with production" so that crop output increased. Weighing the achievements and shortcomings of conservation, Wushan's county head, Li Zhichang, gave a speech urging the cadres in attendance to educate the local populace and convince them to identify and overcome their own insufficiencies while expanding and heightening past achievements.[88] As these statements show, local officials were willing to respond to the grievances of male production team members by realigning conservation with agriculture.

To alleviate the Great Leap Forward's excesses, county head Li Zhichang stressed that Dengjiabao had to emphasize agricultural production and "resolutely implement [the principle of] taking grain as the key link."[89] Uncompleted terraces could be finished later. Integrating sweet clover into the crop rotation system would increase yields and solve the problem of collectives having inadequate labor to gather and transport fertilizer. Training more technicians would increase the quality of conservation work. Tending private plots, which the government allowed after the famine, and increasing output would solve the problem of commune members pilfering grain and other food crops from collective fields. As Li Zhichang put it, "Only when grain rations increase will no one steal." Finally, Li stressed the importance of reconciling short-term and long-term benefits: "These few years [we] have only paid attention to long-term benefits and haven't paid attention to short-term benefits. The masses don't like it. Distant water can't quench present thirst." Addressing many of the complaints voiced by local people, Li acknowledged—albeit implicitly—that reckless pursuit of conservation during the Great Leap had been detrimental to their livelihoods.

In another speech given in late 1962, Wushan's vice county head, Wu Guobin, said that in agricultural and water conservancy work since 1959, "the communist wind blew relatively severely" and the "wind of uncompensated requisitioning of resources" by communes had also grown quite serious. Implementation of conservation policies had serious shortcomings and errors, Wu Guobin averred, exemplified by "overextending scale, pulling the battle lines too long, prioritizing the large and looking down on the small, prioritizing construction, and looking down on management." Although these tendencies were more pronounced in some areas than others, their negative influence was pervasive. Irrigated land had dried out and crop production had decreased for successive years.[90] Dengjiabao's celebrated conservation projects had been "completely damaged."[91]

Some of the strategies local people had employed to recover from the famine contributed to the destruction of vegetation cover. When I interviewed him, an elderly villager described how, after the Great Leap Forward, people in Dengjiabao took to reclaiming uncultivated land on steep slopes: "People dug up the land. Some people dug up several hundred *mu* of land. At the time, it was all wasteland. On the mountain. It was all wasteland." Once the Great Leap ended, "people could reclaim wasteland and plant it. Whoever cleared it, it belonged to them.... Whoever planted it harvested it, and then their bellies could be filled."[92] Deng Fenqin also recalled that after the famine villagers began to "reclaim wasteland on a large scale" and planted potatoes on the newly cleared fields.[93] While this increased output by extending cultivated area, which gave households access to crops and kept them from going hungry, it also damaged vegetation cover and accelerated erosion.

Along with the felling of trees to fuel dining hall stoves and backyard furnaces during the Great Leap Forward, postfamine land clearance reversed years of successful afforestation and grass planting. Since 1952, villagers in Dengjiabao had planted trees and grasses on barren mountains and gullies. In the early 1950s, a mere 2,300 trees grew in Dengjiabao. By 1960, according to a report from the PRC central government's Water and Soil Conservation Inspection Work Team, the Dengjiabao brigade had planted 800,000 fruit trees and 1,140,100 "kindling and lumber trees" on around 2,200 *mu* (146.52 hectares) of land. While it is impossible to gauge the accuracy of these numbers, tree planting had clearly made great strides. Not only did afforestation and grass planting limit erosion and increase local people's incomes, but trees and grasses provided badly needed fuel and fodder. The inspection report stated that the entire Dengjiabao brigade required 1,480,000 *jin* (740,000 kg) of kindling per year and its hundred head of livestock required 600,000 *jin* (300,000 kg) of grass as fodder, but crop stalks only produced 1,420,000 *jin* (710,000 kg). Planting trees and grasses made up for the shortfall and alleviated fuel, fodder, and fertilizer shortages. Equally importantly, acquiring fuel from trees and grasses saved over three thousand workdays that women had previously spent trekking long distances to gather kindling.[94]

However, the Great Leap Forward and the ensuing famine made it impossible to maintain the improved vegetation cover. To alleviate the large-scale damage to trees and grasses that occurred in Wushan in the wake of the subsistence crisis, during the May 1961 cadre meeting Li Zhichang recommended delegating management and protection of forests and grasslands to production teams; a portion of the benefits from trees and grasses would belong to individuals and a portion to the collective. If production teams took responsibility for managing and protecting forests and grasses, Li proposed, they could increase sideline income and solve their fuel problems.[95] Yet the question of which collective units had property rights over the trees planted during conservation campaigns was vexing. Brigades (*shengchandui*) had planted, managed, and maintained trees, but it was not clear whether ownership and future benefits from them should accrue to the commune or to its subordinate units. This uncertainty decreased brigade members' enthusiasm for afforestation because, as a report on conservation in Dengjiabao from late 1960 observed, "they feared doing work without any benefits" (*pa bai chugong wu shouyi*).[96] Who had responsibility for maintaining the projects built and the trees planted during the "large-scale cooperation" of the Great Leap Forward, when commune members had traveled to other areas to do work, and who would enjoy their benefits was also uncertain. Dengjiabao eventually decided that management of trees, grasses, and engineering projects was the duty of production teams (*xiao dui*), which provided labor and reaped the rewards.[97]

But even when labor obligations aligned with resource claims, there was deforestation. One county-level report on forestry work indicated that after 1949, the village of Dengjiabao, one of the natural villages that formed the larger Dengjiabao brigade, had planted 349,532 trees, but by 1962 people had cut down 340,823, or 97.5 percent, of the previous total, leaving around 9,700 trees behind. People also felled protective forests that had been planted along transportation lines, canals, and riverbanks. Between the Wushan and Luomen railway stations, only three trees remained within a zone three *li* (1.5 km) to the south of the railway line, which, the report stated, hurt water and soil conservation and the safety of building projects. Villagers had cut down trees as fuel for backyard iron furnaces during the Great Leap, as firewood for communal dining halls, to strip their bark to consume as famine food, and to convert forested land to agricultural cultivation as part of post-famine recovery efforts.[98]

This deforestation prompted many residents to write "co-signed letters to the government requesting a stop to the illegal practice of indiscriminate felling."[99] Some people cut down trees because their livelihoods compelled them to do so or because they had no other way to obtain fuel. Others, including some "bad elements," felled trees to "make huge profits and get rich." A system of rewards and punishments did not govern forest protection, the report observed, and it received neither rational compensation nor "material and spiritual encouragement." Some people cursed forest protection personnel, "bad elements" who refused to mend their ways after repeated violations went unpunished, and "forest-damaging elements" physically assaulted cadres who tried to stop their behavior. In Laojun Mountain (Laojunshan), thugs attacked and injured three forest-protection personnel, and cadres' fears of such attacks were increasing.[100]

After the famine, according to a published oral history, "orchards had been destroyed, water and soil conservation engineering works were in disrepair, and tree groves experienced serious damage."[101] Wushan County's conservation mission thus centered on stopping land reclamation and tree felling, protecting existing projects, and restoring "key points" such as Dengjiabao. To combine conservation with agricultural production, commune members would fill in dry springs, repair gullies, renovate flood channels, and plant trees and grasses whenever rains made farming impossible. Regulations strictly forbade destroying forests, converting uncultivated areas to farmland, and other activities that were detrimental to the conservation of water and soil. County authorities also prohibited bringing slopes with a gradient of over twenty-five degrees under cultivation and instructed local cadres to try to persuade people not to farm steeply inclined land that they had already reclaimed.[102]

Water and soil conservation in Dengjiabao started to get back on its feet after 1962, when cadres oversaw renewed afforestation efforts. Tree planting improved access to fuel, while construction of irrigation systems during the 1960s and 1970s improved access to water.[103] Without sustained higher-level support, however, these measures did not last. By the 1980s, although terraces still sculpted the land around Dengjiabao, other water conservancy infrastructure constructed during the first three decades of the PRC, such as ponds and reservoirs, had decayed due to wear and neglect. At the same time, Dengjiabao's growing population cleared trees and other vegetation to cultivate steeply inclined gullies and converted waterless dams into fields. The area of land under cultivation expanded, but agricultural productivity declined due to a lack of irrigation.[104] Springs and reservoirs dried up as well. Villagers turned to building percolation trenches (shallow excavated trenches designed to capture runoff and enable it to infiltrate the groundwater aquifer), but they did not capture enough water. Residents devoted any time not spent farming to trying to find water. As in the early 1950s, the sight of women lined up for hours at wells became common. Households invested in water cellars that used plastic tarps to gather groundwater, but during dry weather villagers had to find money to hire automobiles, tractors, or mule carts to transport water from the flatlands. As a result, wrote an observer, "the farmers cherish water as if it were oil."[105]

Although crop yields recovered to prefamine levels in the mid-1960s, per capita production basically stagnated until the late 1980s. Although we do not have comprehensive data on post-1961 agricultural production in Dengjiabao specifically, per capita output in Wushan County was 239 kilograms in 1953 but stood at 215.4 kilograms per person in 1964; in 1982 per capita production was only 211.7 kilograms.[106] In Tianshui Prefecture as a whole, per capita production of grain and other staples was 262 kilograms in 1952 and 250 kilograms in 1957. From 1965 to 1988, per capita output fluctuated between 325 kilograms (1975) and 201 kilograms (1980).[107] Despite the prc party-state's extraordinary mobilization of rural people to conserve water and soil and the hardships they endured to remake the landscape, conservation programs did not bring them enduring benefits during the collective era.

Between 1952 and 1956, mutual-aid teams and agricultural cooperatives in Wushan County found ways to circumvent local ambivalence toward water and soil conservation and combine these activities with farming. Evidence indicates that conservation measures helped increase agricultural output in Dengjiabao for a time, although the central government's unified purchase and supply system cut into the returns that local people derived from higher yields. As male production team members in Dengjiabao stated repeatedly during interviews with investigators from the Tianshui Water and Soil Conservation Experiment Station in 1961, conservation measures had value when they facilitated cultivation by leveling steeply inclined slopes and boosting productivity or when afforestation and grass planting supplied the biomass they desperately needed for fuel and fodder. As male villagers in Dengjiabao understood it, conservation was valuable if it promoted local welfare by making it easier to farm, increasing food availability, and providing access to scarce resources.

Circumstances changed markedly in 1958 with the start of the Great Leap Forward. Many commune members seem to have initially greeted the campaign with enthusiasm. But when mobilization reached a fever pitch, Dengjiabao's entire workforce, along with laborers from elsewhere in Wushan County, threw all their efforts into conservation campaigns at the expense of farmwork. The costs were considerable. When diversion of all available labor to conservation projects caused people to neglect farming and the state extracted grain procurements based on exaggerated production reports, food shortages and famine followed. The burden of conservation fell squarely on the rural populace, jeopardizing their food entitlements and physical well-being. With people too hungry to work, conservation projects ground to a halt by 1960. Some cadres saw this outcome as a betrayal of revolutionary ideals. Du Yinghua, a Wushan county secretary connected to the underground dissident journal *Spark* (Xinghuo), asked, "The revolution was victorious, and what did we bring the peasants? Starvation! And death!" This statement resulted in Du's arrest during the anti-rightist turn that followed the Lushan Conference of 1959 and his eventual execution.[108]

Male production team members in Dengjiabao spoke openly with investigators about the adverse effects of Great Leap Forward conservation campaigns on agriculture, criticized large-scale mobilization and uncompensated labor requisitioning, and aired grievances about the inadequacy of food rations. But these records tell only half the story. Conservation of water and soil depended on the female workforce throughout the 1950s, and mass mobilization for large-scale conservation campaigns launched during the Great Leap Forward made female labor even more important. Even before the start of the Great Leap, the demands of conservation already weighed heavily on rural women, who experienced this labor intensification in gendered ways. The conservation campaigns of the late 1950s subjected women to even heavier labor obligations, forcing them to balance farming and conservation work with domestic responsibilities. The Great Leap famine, in turn, forced women to devise ways to keep their families alive and damaged their health and well-being.

This subsistence crisis, along with efforts to recover from it during the early 1960s, jeopardized the benefits of earlier conservation schemes. Felling trees, whether as a survival strategy during the famine or to clear inclined land for crop cultivation in its wake, damaged vegetation cover and threatened to bring back the scarcities of fuel, fodder, and fertilizer that planting trees and grasses had helped to alleviate. Much of the water conservancy infrastructure that people had worked so hard to build during the 1950s—the wells, the dams, the reservoirs—crumbled over the ensuing decades, leading to the return of acute water shortages. Wushan County and Dengjiabao never regained the nationwide prominence they attained during the Great Leap Forward. After 1963, the name Dengjiabao, once a frequent subject of state media coverage, completely vanishes from *People's Daily* and other prominent national publications. The conservation red flag had faded into obscurity.

EPILOGUE

After the founding of the PRC in 1949, Chinese conservation experts who had previously served the Nationalist regime joined CCP cadres and officials in seeking to remake rural people's relations with the land in the name of conserving water and soil. For state authorities and technocratic elites to make this environmental vision a reality, however, their interventions had to overcome the friction posed by the local populace in places like Wushan County and the environments with which they were enmeshed. That responsibility fell to local state agents, who acted as intermediaries between their fellow villagers and higher levels of the PRC's party-state apparatus.

Grassroots cadres and activists who spearheaded conservation programs in Dengjiabao during the 1950s garnered acclaim as labor models. But the overwork and stress that came with alleviating the misgivings of other villagers while also meeting the expectations of their administrative superiors took a heavy toll. The model mutual-aid team and agricultural cooperative leader Deng Haihai, a heavy smoker, died in 1964 at the age of fifty-seven after suffering from a chronic respiratory ailment for several years. Upon Deng's passing, his doctor remarked that, by always striving to take the lead in collective labor, he had "let the government worry him to death" (*rang gongjia ba ta caoxinsi le*).[1] He was not alone. Former youth league leader Li Xuding perished in his late forties from a sudden brain aneurysm while working in Dengjiabao's apple orchard. Wushan County held a memorial service to honor the labor model after his passing.[2] Deng Fenqin, Li Xuding's sister-in-law, enjoyed far greater longevity, but she suffers from ailments caused by her physical toil during the Great Leap Forward, when she led female villagers in the "great war in Dengjiabao" and famine forced her to go out and search for food shortly after childbirth.

As prominent local leaders passed away, conservation efforts in Dengjiabao lagged, and the village faded back into obscurity during the 1960s, the Dazhai brigade in Shanxi's mountainous Xiyang County garnered a level of fame that far surpassed Dengjiabao's. Following serious floods in August 1963, Dazhai's local party secretary, Chen Yonggui, refused to accept official aid, declaring that his brigade would not only rebuild entirely on its own but also contribute grain to the state. Although Dazhai received state support behind the scenes, official propaganda painted the brigade's effort to make good on Chen's guarantee as a model of self-reliance. In early 1964, *People's Daily* urged others to follow the "Dazhai Road" by using collective will and revolutionary commitment to transform the environment; in the following year, Mao Zedong instructed all of China to learn from Dazhai.[3] As Judith Shapiro writes, "Dazhai was initially promoted as an embodiment of the spirit of independence, hard work, and close relations between Party leaders and ordinary peasants, who were depicted laboring together to terrace mountainsides and fill gullies with earth."[4]

Like Dengjiabao before it, Dazhai was praised for turning rocky, barren hillsides into productive fields by building terraces that conserved water and soil on steeply inclined land; state propagandists exhorted other locales to emulate these feats. During the campaign to learn from Dazhai (1964–78), people across China could read about the brigade's legendary exploits and see images of its accomplishments in state publications. Throngs of visitors traveled to Dazhai to witness all it had achieved. The PRC party-state's promotion of the Dazhai model often led to what Shapiro calls "dogmatic uniformity," in which applying a single approach regardless of its suitability to local conditions brought disastrous ecological consequences.[5] Building terraced fields on slopes that were too steep to cultivate increased erosion and sedimentation; turning lakes and rivers into farmland resulted in ecosystem imbalances and worsened flooding. In other instances, as Sigrid Schmalzer has shown, Dazhai's association with the principle of self-reliance served as inspiration for local actors who resisted the inappropriate imposition of outside models and argued for policies that were suited to local conditions.[6]

Everyone in China had to "learn from Dazhai in agriculture" during the 1960s and 1970s, but some Dengjiabao residents claim that Dazhai learned everything it knew about conserving water and soil from them. As a former party branch secretary insisted in one of our interviews: "Water and soil conservation developed, and the land was leveled. Didn't Dazhai come to study Dengjiabao? Dazhai only started doing it after they came to study Dengjiabao" (*Dazhai lai xuexi Dengjiabao zhihou cai gaoqi de*).[7] Among the tens of thousands of people from all over China who came to learn from Dengjiabao in the 1950s, I have not found concrete evidence of visitors from Dazhai. But that is not the point. For Dengjiabao's elderly inhabitants, their village's influence on Dazhai imbues the environmental transformations that they worked to bring about in their younger days with enduring significance.

The rest of China has largely forgotten about Dengjiabao and Wushan County, but the PRC party-state's commitment to conserving water and soil has not flagged. To address environmental damage caused by agricultural expansion between the 1950s and 1980s, the PRC piloted the policy of "returning farmland to forest" (*tuigeng huanlin*)—commonly known as "grain for green"—in Gansu, Shaanxi, and Sichuan in 1999 before starting the program in other provinces the following year. By the late 1990s, China's central government leaders came to see the collective-era drive to increase grain production by expanding the amount of land under cultivation as unproductive. Much of the steeply inclined farmland added between the 1950s and the 1980s was now deemed marginal for agriculture and susceptible to runoff and erosion. By retiring sloping land from cropping and instead planting trees on it, the policy of returning fields to forest aimed to restore the "ecosystem services," such as erosion and flood control, that this land could provide. Regardless of this marginal land's low productivity, however, the inclined fields generated income for rural households, who needed at least temporary compensation if they could no longer farm them. For this reason, the PRC's grain for green program paid farmers to take marginal farmland out of cultivation and plant trees on it, while also paying them an annual subsidy to compensate for lost income.[8]

Although ostensibly a form of payment for ecosystem services, according to an evaluation of the early stages of the program by economists Jintao Xu and Ran Tao, the grain for green program was, "in practice, just another top-down, campaign-style program."[9] Participation was technically voluntary, but, as with the conservation campaigns of the Mao era, its implementation often did not respect that principle. A significant portion of households reported they had little or no choice about whether to take part. In Gansu, only 31 percent of households surveyed felt they could decide to participate or not.[10] And, as in the collective era, rural households continued to shoulder the burden of conservation, as payments for converting land did not offset the cost of participation. In Gansu, costs to farmers tended to outweigh the value of state compensation, and nearly half of households enrolled in the farmland conversion program incurred economic losses.[11]

Impoverished villages in remote parts of Wushan County that converted farmland to forests, for example, depended on land conversion subsidies for their income. During the early stages of the process of returning farmland to forests, however, households that retired inclined land from cultivation had to invest large amounts of capital in planting trees, and subsidies did not cover these costs.[12] Alluding to the fact that households had little choice about whether to take part in the farmland conversion scheme and did not always benefit from it, one report advised that Wushan County should follow the principles of "voluntariness, autonomy, and mutual benefit" to "encourage ordinary farmers to increase their income" and maintain their enthusiasm for planting trees.[13]

Lack of labor also hampered the program. Unlike the days when the household registration system tied peasants to agricultural collectives and kept them in the countryside, by the 2010s rural households in Wushan depended on nonfarm wage labor as their main source of income. Most young men worked outside their native villages as hired laborers, while young women earned money taking care of children on the plains. From 1999 to 2014, the government offered a subsidy of ¥2,000 over a period of sixteen years for each *mu* of farmland that was converted to "ecological forests" planted for conservation purposes and ¥800 over five years for each *mu* of "economic forests" like fruit orchards. After 2014, the government began providing three payments totaling ¥1,200 per *mu* for all types of forests. Since it took only ten days for a wage laborer to earn ¥1,200, working-age people had no incentive to take part in the sloping land conversion program. Elderly people who remained in the villages had difficulty planting saplings, weeding, loosening soil, applying fertilizer, and watering the immature trees. As a result, many saplings did not survive, and tree planting efforts generally had poor results.[14]

To meet targets for returning farmland to forests and ensure the delivery of state subsidies, local governments across China tended to overreport tree survival rates or had households replant trees on land where they had not taken root prior to upper-level inspections. In many parts of China, even when trees were replanted, lack of water made it impossible to guarantee that they would take root. Low survival rates and frequent replanting reduced the program's effectiveness and increased implementation costs.[15] To boost their income, some households in Wushan planted crops like wheat, maize, flax, and rapeseed among trees on land that they had ostensibly converted to forests and did not leave enough space for saplings to grow. Immature trees withered when crops robbed them of water and fertilizer. Once subsidy payments ceased, moreover, many households converted the land on which trees had been planted back to agricultural cultivation.[16] Monitoring and supervision of tree planting by county authorities was "superficial" and did nothing to prevent these outcomes.[17] Due to lack of official oversight and local people's lack of incentives to convert farmland to forests, remote sensing studies found that, while forest cover in Tianshui Prefecture as a whole had increased from 1988 to 2015, Wushan County's forested area actually *declined* during that period.[18]

Even when saplings survived, tree planting did not always have the intended ecological consequences. Trees need much more water than grasses or shrubs, so large-scale afforestation sometimes hampers water retention in soil.[19] Black locust trees, which were promoted by the Tianshui Water and Soil Conservation Experiment Area in the 1940s and are now the third-most-prevalent afforestation or reforestation tree species in the world (behind eucalyptus and poplar), have especially adverse effects. Black locust monocultures tend to grow poorly, reduce streamflow due to their high demand for water, impede regeneration of other tree species, decrease biodiversity, and damage native ecosystems.[20]

While calling the PRC's support for environmental initiatives "encouraging," Xu and Tao find that "large-scale campaign-style programs are not the way to reverse adverse environmental outcomes stemming from a complex combination of factors."[21] The goals of environmental amelioration and poverty alleviation, in their view, can only be realized by combining the grain for green program with "an array of policies focused on the rural economy."[22] Longer-term investments in agriculture, balanced with the development of nonagricultural sectors of the rural economy and migration out of the Loess Plateau's most ecologically fragile regions, they assert, "might do as much or more to relieve pressure on sloping, marginal cropland than a campaign-style government program advertised as the final solution to high soil erosion."[23]

These recent efforts to turn farmland into forests share obvious similarities with Mao-era campaigns to conserve water and soil. Whether in the 1950s or the 2010s, local cadres and officials who want to bolster their performance evaluations by impressing their superiors with numerous short-term "administrative achievements" pay insufficient attention to the quality of work, often leading to poor results. Rural dwellers with little choice about whether to participate in these top-down environmental management campaigns shoulder their costs. Even with the far-reaching transformations witnessed in China since the Mao era, the burden of conservation still falls on poor and disadvantaged rural populations.

To what extent have the sacrifices that Dengjiabao's residents made in the name of conservation improved environmental conditions in the village? When I visited Dengjiabao between 2017 and 2019, its dry landscape featured no trace of the ponds and reservoirs in which ducks once swam. Water conservancy infrastructure that local people devoted so much time and effort to building and maintaining in the 1950s, like Dengjiabao's renown as a model in the PRC's battle to preserve water and soil, has disappeared. So have Dengjiabao's human inhabitants. Most people have left the village and moved to a new residential area on the flatlands several kilometers away, trading old houses with timber frames and earthen walls for brick and tile buildings with corrugated metal roofs and concrete courtyards. This move took place as part of the PRC's New Socialist Countryside program, initiated in 2006, which responded to rural poverty by consolidating and relocating villages to provide residents with modern housing and better access to services.[24]

As in the many other "hollow villages" found throughout China's countryside today, much of Dengjiabao's working-age population has migrated to towns and cities, leaving grandparents behind to care for small children. Only part of the workforce, including Deng Fenqin's sons, has stayed in the countryside to engage in agriculture. In addition to cultivating flatlands near the new residential areas, the remaining farmers drive three-wheeled carts up a steep road that winds along the edge of precipitous gullies to tend fields and orchards that grow on terraced hillsides close to the old village.

Although Dengjiabao and Wushan County have long since fallen from fame, not all changes have been for the worse. Like China's rural populace in general, villagers enjoy far better living standards today than they did during the Mao years. When I asked Deng Fenqin if things were better in the Mao era or the present, she answered unequivocally: "It's definitely better now. Now it's socialism (*xianzai shi shehui zhuyi le*)! [We're] very fortunate now. Now it's really good.... At that time, when leveling land, when waging the great war [in Dengjiabao], [we] went out early and didn't come back until it had gotten dark. When it snowed, [we] still had to level land. Now [we're] especially fortunate and enjoy life all the time. [We] really longed for good fortune at that time, but now [we're] really fortunate."[25]

Contrasting the traumas she endured during the Great Leap Forward with today's good fortune, Deng Fenqin creates a narrative distance between her past hardships and current comforts. Her words give little sense that she thinks the former made the latter possible. During the arduous conservation campaigns of the 1950s, she and her fellow villagers could only dream of the life that her family currently enjoys, with a small but comfortable home in the new residential area and a plentiful variety of food. They can show guests hospitality by offering them tea, snacks like flatbread and cookies, and cigarettes. When Deng moved to Dengjiabao in 1956, she and other villagers longed for the "fortunate" life that the CCP assured them would arrive in the socialist future. Those aspirations, which eluded Deng and so many rural people throughout the Mao years, have become a reality in the age that most outsiders call China's "postsocialist" era.

On the other hand, although livelihoods in villages like Dengjiabao have greatly improved, rural and urban incomes and living standards have continued to diverge since the collective era, with a chasm of staggering inequality separating cities from the countryside. Rural areas are a world apart from China's thriving, cosmopolitan urban centers. The lifestyles of rural people and the opportunities available to them, especially in poor provinces like Gansu, pale in comparison to those enjoyed by most urban dwellers. Rather than being the inevitable outcome of the PRC's post-1978 economic development, as Nick R. Smith has written, this urban-rural inequality derives from "the party-state's own administrative separation of urban and rural areas, a policy that systematically excludes rural areas and populations from many of the benefits of urban development."[26] That binary system, which has formed the "bedrock of Chinese society" since the 1950s, has allowed "extraction of resources from rural areas to support urban development, resulting in both supercharged urbanization and incipient rural collapse."

The history of water and soil conservation in modern China cannot be understood in isolation from these patterns of state extraction and uneven development. Environmental management initiatives, as this book has argued, must be evaluated in relation to the networks of interest and inequity to which they are related and which they frequently reinforce. Conservation served the PRC party-state's developmental agenda more than it did the needs and aspirations of China's rural populace. Campaigns to conserve water and soil imposed heavier workloads on rural people, while state grain procurements deprived them of control over the harvest and reduced the benefits they got in return for their work. Although per capita food consumption and fuel and water availability in Dengjiabao increased from 1952 to 1956, mobilizing all available labor for militarized conservation campaigns at the expense of agricultural production during the Great Leap Forward was catastrophic. After consumption of grain and other staples returned to prefamine levels during the early 1960s, villagers did not see real gains in per capita consumption to compensate for their intensified labor throughout most of the collective era.

The epigraph to Donald Worster's classic history of the Dust Bowl on the southern plains of the United States during the 1930s quotes Marx's famous adage that "all progress in capitalistic agriculture is a progress in the art, not only of robbing the laborer, but of robbing the soil."[27] Progress in state-socialist accumulation based on the extraction of agricultural surpluses from China's rural sector to capitalize industrialization perpetrated similar ecological larceny. The PRC's developmental agenda during the collective era, to borrow Gramsci's language, effectively "subjugated" China's rural areas and "reduced them to exploitable colonies."[28] The key difference was that, during the late 1950s, China's rural households, unlike the farm families uprooted by the Dust Bowl, essentially lost the ability to migrate. Although agricultural collectivization deprived rural people of the means of production, it did not force them off the land. Instead, the PRC's household registration system eventually made it all but impossible for rural dwellers to exit agriculture. People classified as peasants became tied to rural spaces, where they tilled collective fields and fulfilled compulsory state grain procurements. For the party-state to extract surplus from the countryside, members of agricultural collectives had to grow crops and extract surplus from the land. To contend with the accelerated erosion of fragile loess soils that came about as a result, rural communities had to devote even more of their time and energy to conservation work. This cycle exacerbated the marginalization of China's countryside vis-à-vis its cities that persists to the present day.

In his assessment of the PRC's Third Front campaign to construct military and industrial infrastructure in China's interior during the 1960s and 1970s, Stevan Harrell argues that, even if they contributed to the growth of China's heavy industrial complex, Third Front projects "brought pollution and environmental degradation to local areas, illustrating the environmentally unjust relationship between national-scale growth and local-scale pollution so characteristic of heavy industrial development." Third Front industries exploited the resources of China's interior "for the benefit primarily of the urban areas in China Proper, setting up a classical kind of environmental injustice characteristic of extractive colonialism."[29] The uneven relationship between China's urban centers and the rural areas from which the state siphoned off agricultural surpluses to capitalize heavy industrialization constituted another form of "extractive colonialism" that generated its own environmental injustices.

The work of conserving water and soil imposed considerable burdens on rural people, but the environmental improvements it brought to places like Dengjiabao have been fleeting. A group of investigators who studied Dengjiabao in the early 2000s found it indistinguishable from other villages in Wushan County. When the deputy director of the county's water and soil conservation station took them to see the gullies where, half a century earlier, Dengjiabao's residents had planted six hundred *mu* (40 hectares) of trees, the investigators found that not even six *mu* (0.4 hectares) of trees remained. During the Great Leap Forward, the deputy director told them, people had cut down almost all the trees to obtain fuel and building materials for backyard steel furnaces and dining halls. He commented that, starting in the 1960s, villagers in Dengjiabao no longer paid attention to conserving water and soil.[30]

With vegetation cover significantly reduced, by the first decade of the twenty-first century, Dengjiabao's soil had poor moisture retention capacity and low rates of effective rainwater utilization. The village experienced severe soil erosion and chronic water shortages. If anything, investigators noted, "slopes here are steeper, there are more gullies, floodwaters are larger, and water and soil loss is more serious than elsewhere!"[31] Deteriorating environmental conditions, in turn, hastened the outflow of Dengjiabao's population, as "many villagers who lacked confidence in Dengjiabao's ecological environment dejectedly left their hometown."[32] The deputy director regretfully observed, "The lesson Dengjiabao has taught us today is that it's easy to destroy an enterprise, it's difficult to start an enterprise, and it's even more difficult to maintain an enterprise!"[33]

Contrasting Dengjiabao's past prominence with its current poverty and marginalization, the elderly folk I interviewed spoke nostalgically about the days when cadres from their village had the honor of attending conferences in Beijing, shook hands with Zhou Enlai, and saw Mao Zedong in person. Young men speak longingly of the days when conservation of water and soil shifted the marriage market in Dengjiabao's favor. While heads of households in other parts of Wushan, like Deng Fenqin's parents, willingly sent their daughters to marry men in Dengjiabao after better access to water and fuel eased the workload of female villagers in the mid-1950s, that pattern has long since come to an end. As a local party branch secretary explained to me during one of my visits, "Now the girls from the mountain all want to get married down the mountain. In the past, girls from down the mountain wanted to get married up here, and it was only that way for Dengjiabao."[34]

The intensified ecological hazards from climate change expose further inequalities. Higher temperatures and precipitation extremes have made areas like Tianshui and Wushan even more susceptible to droughts as well as flood-inducing rainstorms.[35] A recent study found that Gansu has higher levels of sensitivity and exposure to climate change, as well as greater vulnerability to water scarcity and natural disasters, than any province in western China. These hazards disproportionately affect the health and wellbeing of poor and marginalized populations in ecologically fragile regions whose livelihoods depend on climate-sensitive resources like water and soil. People who inhabit villages like Dengjiabao have far less capacity to prepare for and respond to these environmental stressors than inhabitants of more economically developed and affluent regions in eastern China.[36]

This book offers a reminder that the benefits and costs of actions taken in response to climate change—or any environmental problem—are unevenly distributed across social hierarchies, and that these environmental inequalities cast relations of power in stark relief. Instead of shifting the burden of conservation onto vulnerable, marginalized peoples and depriving them of the benefits, environmental protection must uphold their dignity, respect their priorities, and further their interests and aspirations. Maximizing long-term environmental well-being cannot compromise the goal of creating equitable societies in which healthy and decent lives are possible for everyone. If solutions to environmental problems are to be truly sustainable, they also need to be just and humane.

GLOSSARY OF CHINESE CHARACTERS

20 wan jing tang ba jiao quan yundong 20万井塘坝窖泉运动

ba, ba, ba, re de ren haipa 坝, 坝, 坝, 惹的人害怕
ba ba dang fan zhe chi qu 把坝当饭者吃去
baihua caomuxi 白花草木樨
baiyang 白杨
Bao Haizhen 包海珍
baobei cao 宝贝草
baochi tudi yongjiu shengchan nengli zhi yuanze 保持土地永久生产能力之原则
biaozhun gong 标准工
bu rang Weihe zai daodan 不让渭河再捣蛋

cao de zhe gui 肏的这鬼
caomuxi 草木樨
chaihuang 柴荒
Chaijiaping 柴家坪
Changjiawan 常家弯
Chen Yonggui 陈永贵
Chen Zhengren 陈正人
Chengguan 城关
Chenxiang 沉香
chui niupi de 吹牛皮的
chungeng shi funü liliang xian 春耕时妇女力量闲
cihuai 刺槐

Daliushugou 大柳树沟
Dangguan 党关
Daquanshan 大泉山

da bingtuan zuozhan 大兵团作战
da you buping zhi qi 大有不平之气
da zhan Dengjiabao 大战邓家堡
dan gan 单干
dangnian fenhong 当年分红
Dazhai 大寨
Dazhai lai xuexi Dengjiabao zhihou cai gaoqi de 大寨来学习邓家堡之后才搞起的
Dazhuang 大庄
Deguo huai 德国槐
Deng Baoshan 邓宝珊
Deng Chenghai 邓成海
Deng Daisheng 邓代生
Deng Erjie 邓儿杰
Deng Fenqin 邓粉琴
Deng Haihai 邓海海
Deng Hanming 邓汉明
Deng Hongshan 邓宏山
Deng Huangqing 邓尪清
Deng Junfu 邓俊福
Deng Junjie 邓俊杰
Deng Kejun 邓克俊
Deng Madou 邓麻豆
Deng Qingyi 邓清义
Deng Zihui 邓子恢
Dengjiabao 邓家堡
Dengjiabao yundong 邓家堡运动
dianjiaodi 点浇地
dianxing 典型
digeng 地埂
dimai 地脉
donghua 冬花
Dongshun 东顺
Du Yinghua 杜映华

Feng Qing 冯青
Fengjiazhuang 冯家庄
fengshui 风水
fengshui zhi shuo 风水之说
funü liuchan duoshaoren 妇女流产多少人

Gaikou 改口
gaizao ziran shengguo tian 改造自然胜过天
gancao 甘草
ganhuo 干活
gao fukua 搞浮夸
gaojihua 高级化
Ge Hong 葛洪
Gongjiamen 巩家门
Guaner 观儿
Guangwu 广武
Guanjiagou 管家沟
Guanping 管坪
gudong renxin de xuanchuanyu zhi lei de 鼓动人心的宣传语之类的
Guo Sishiwu 郭四十五
Guo Siyuesheng 郭四月生
Guohuai 郭槐
Guojiazhuang 郭家庄
Guoli Xibei jishu zhuanke xuexiao 国立西北技术专科学校
guoqu toulan kao nanren de nüren 过去偷懒靠男人的女人
guyi zhao mafan 故意找麻烦

haimei zuoguo yuezi 还没坐过月子
He Jili 何基礼
Hongfu 红富
Hongxing 红星
Huaguoshan 花菓山
huailü 怀虑
Hualin 桦林

Huanghe shuitu baochi Tianshui zhili jianduju / Tianshui shuitu baochi kexue shiyanzhan 黄河水土保持天水治理监督局 / 天水水土保持科学试验站
huanghua caomuxi 黄花草木樨
hu'nao de 胡闹的
Huo Weide 霍维德

jianshe kezhang 建设科长
jiaye fengjian 家业风鉴
jing 经
jishuyuan 技术员

kang 炕
Kangjiagou 康家沟
Kangle 康乐
Kong Fengzhong 孔凤忠
kouliang di 口粮低

Laojunshan 老君山
Leijiashan 雷家山
Li Baocai 黎保才
Li Baoxu 黎保蓄
Li Fusheng 黎复生
Li Haiqing 李海清
Li Jianyuan 黎建元
Li Jincai 黎进才
Li Jinglin 李景林
Li Tongtong 黎仝仝
Li Wanfu 黎万福
Li Wanwan 李万万
Li Xuding 黎绪定
Li Yongqing 黎永清
Li Zhichang 李治长
Li Zijun 李子俊
Lijiaping 黎家坪
Lin Gaisheng 林改生

GLOSSARY OF CHINESE CHARACTERS

Lin Jinwa 林进娃
Lin Qiumei 林秋梅
Ling Faxiang 令发祥
linken shuili 林垦水利
Liyao 李窑
Longnan renmin nonglin shiyanchang 陇南人民农林实验场
Longnan renmin nonglin shiyanqu 陇南人民农林实验区
Longnan shuitu baochi shiyanqu 陇南水土保持实验区
Longnan shuitu baochi tuiguangzhan 陇南水土保持推广站
Longquan 龙泉
Longwanggou 龙王沟
Lüergou 吕二沟
lühua zuguo 绿化祖国
Luomen 洛门

Ma Jinlu 马进禄
Ma Shuangbao 马双保
Ma Xingwu 马兴务
Ma yeye 麻爷爷
Mahe 马河
mahuang 麻黄
maiqi 脉气
Majiagou 马家沟
Majiashan 马家山
Mali 马力
mangmuxing 盲目性
Mao zhuxi lian fan dou bu jiao women chibao 毛主席连饭都不叫我们吃饱
min ban gong zhu 民办公助
Mu Guiying 穆桂英
Mulin 木林

Nanyu 南峪
Nianpu 廿舖

nongmang shitang 农忙食堂
nongxian kongxi 农闲空隙

pa bai chugong wu shouyi 怕白出工无收益
Pan Xiangrui 潘香瑞
Panlong 盘龙
pingdiao haisi ren 平调害死人
Pogen 坡跟

Qiaozigou 桥子沟
Qin Shihuang 秦始皇
Qin'an 秦安
qing xiunü xialou 请绣女下楼
Qingnian shuitu baochi huodong fenzi hui 青年水土保持活动份子会
Qingshui 清水
quanbu yiwu chuqin 全部义务出勤
qunzhong jingyan 群众经验

rang gongjia ba ta caoxinsi le 让公家把他操心死了
Ren Chengtong 任承统
renhai zhan 人海战

san guang 三光
shagua hurigui de 傻瓜胡日鬼的
shanli 山梨
shanxing 山杏
Shen Manyuan 沈满源
shengchan 生产
shengchandui 生产队
Shenxian zhuan 神仙传
Shi Bingzhi 史炳直
Shimaping 石马坪
shitu 失土
shui shi shanqu jianshe de gang, shui dadong le guniangmen de xin

水是山区建设的纲，水打动了姑娘们的心
Shuiliandong 水濂洞
shuilihua 水利化
shuiping gou 水平沟
Shuiquangou 水泉沟
shuitu baochi 水土保持
shuitu baochi hao shi hao 水土保持好是好
si xihan 四稀罕
sifen huoping de banfa 死分活评的办法
sixiang dichu 思想抵触
Songshan 嵩山
suancai 酸菜
suanci 酸刺

Tan'ge 滩歌
tiangen 甜根
Tianjiazhuang 田家庄
Tianqu 天衢
tianshang de xiannü 天上的仙女
Tianshui san da bao 天水三大宝
Tianshui shuitu baochi kexue shiyanzhan 天水水土保持科学试验站
Tianshui shuitu baochi shiyanqu 天水水土保持实验区
Tianshui shuitu baochi tuiguangzhan 天水水土保持推广站
tianye 天爷
Tielong 铁笼
titian 梯田
titian gouxu 梯田沟洫
tonggou tongxiao 统购统销
Tongwei 通渭
tudang 土档
tuigeng huanlin 退耕还林

Wang Haicheng 王海诚
Wang Tingjun 汪庭俊

Wang Zhiguo 汪治国
Wangjiagou 王家沟
wangpai shuzhong 王牌树种
wei da ba laiwang ba ren paosi, bei tu kusi, wanshang aosi, fang shitou ba ren xiasi, jiazhongren caosi 为打坝来往把人跑死，背土苦死，晚上熬死，放石头把人吓死，家中人操死
Wei Zhanggen 魏章根
Wenjiasi 文家寺
Wenquan 温泉
wo de niu yao jiao niao le 我的牛要浇尿了
Wu Guobin 吴国彬
Wushan 武山
wushen 巫神

xiang hongshui suku 向洪水诉苦
Xianghegou 响河沟
xianzai shi shehui zhuyi le 现在是社会主义了
xiao dui 小队
Xibei nongxueyuan 西北农学院
Xigou 西沟
Xinghuo 星火
Xiyang 昔阳
xuanshi dahui 宣誓大会

yan 眼
Yan Wenguang 闫文光
Yan'an 延安
Yanchi 盐池
yang muxu 洋苜蓿
Yanjing 盐井
yaogu dui 腰鼓队
yaoshi pingdi, jiu nong ping le 要是平地，就弄平了
Ye Peizhong 叶培忠
Yefu 冶扶

you nü bu jia Dengjiabao, xiashan tiaoshui shizai ku 有女不嫁邓家堡，下山挑水实在苦
Yuchuan 榆川
Yushu 榆树
yu si 淤死
Yuanyang 鸳鸯

zaofu de "sanba" Dengjiabao 造福的"三八"邓家堡
zhan ziran 战自然
Zhang 漳
Zhang Kejun 张克俊
Zhang Zixiang 张自祥
Zhangjiabao 张家堡
Zhangjiagou 张家沟

Zhao Fansheng 赵反生
Zhaoping 赵平
zhe shi tuo kuzi fangpi de, yici zuogong liangci hua le 这是脱裤子放屁的，一次做工两次花了
zhi chaishi 支差事
zhi pi lai chui deng 止屁来吹灯
zhi you ba ba ren haisi le 只有坝把人害死了
zhongdian 重点
Zhongliang 中梁
Zhonglou 钟楼
zhu hou 诸侯
zuzhi qilai liliang sheng guo tian 组织起来力量胜过天

NOTES

Abbreviations

GPA	Gansu Provincial Archives
IMH	Institute of Modern History Archives
QCA	Qin'an County Archives
TMA	Tianshui Municipal Archives
WCA	Wushan County Archives
YRCC	Yellow River Conservancy Commission Archives

Introduction

1. Gansu sheng shuiliting, *Jianshe shanqu de bangyang*.
2. Residents of the village refer to it as "Dengjiabao" when speaking in Mandarin, but the character "bao" in Dengjiabao is also pronounced "bu" in the local dialect.
3. Interviews, May 2018 and September 2019.
4. Brown and Johnson, *Maoism at the Grassroots*, 1.
5. Mostern, *Yellow River*, 37–44; He et al., "Winter Wheat Yield," 1169–78; Kimura and Takayama, "Loess Plateau," 23–33.
6. Mostern, *Yellow River*, 121.
7. Mostern, *Yellow River*, 134.
8. Mostern, *Yellow River*, 43.
9. Bray, *Science and Civilisation*, 125–26; Xu, "Zhongguo titian wenjian lu," 48.
10. Pietz, *Yellow River*; Ding, "Yellow River."
11. Huanghe shuili weiyuanhui Huanghe zhongyou zhiliju, *Huanghe shuitu baochi zhi*, 111; Xin and Jiang, *Zhongguo shuitu baochi gailun*, 7.
12. Wang et al., "Recent Changes in Sediment Delivery"; Wang et al., "Stepwise Decreases of the Huanghe"; Wu et al., "Reservoir Regulation"; Syvitski et al., "Earth's Sediment Cycle"; Syvitski and Kettner, "Sediment Flux."
13. Eyferth, "State Socialism"; Goldman, "Introduction."
14. China's urban-rural divide is brilliantly discussed in Brown, *City versus Countryside*.
15. Cohen, "Cultural and Political Inventions," 158. On intellectual debates on "the peasant" in China since the 1980s, see Day, *Peasant in Postsocialist China*.
16. Li et al., "Agricultural Vulnerability"; He et al., "Diverse Responses of Winter Wheat."
17. Anderson, "Depression, Dust Bowl" 327.

18. For examples of these continuities, see Muscolino, *Fishing Wars*; Pietz, *Engineering the State*; Pietz, *Yellow River*; Ding, "Yellow River."
19. An et al., "Agriculture," 66–67.
20. Heilmann, "Local Experiments."
21. Mosley, "Common Ground," 919.
22. Blackbourn, "Environmental History," 20.
23. Shapiro, *Mao's War*. The environmental destruction that occurred during the Mao era is also described in Smil, *Bad Earth*. For a far more balanced account, see Harrell, *Ecological History*.
24. Schmalzer, *Red Revolution, Green Revolution*; Li and Liu, "Selling Forestry Revolution"; Songster, *Panda Nation*; Goldstein, *Remains of the Everyday*.
25. Schmalzer, "Layer upon Layer."
26. Impetus for these questions derives from Blaikie and Brookfield, *Land Degradation and Society*, 64.
27. Peet and Watts, *Liberation Ecologies*.
28. Sze, *Sustainability*.
29. My discussion of the gendered dimensions of conservation builds on Gail Hershatter's monumental study of rural women during the collective era, as well as more recent work by Jacob Eyferth. See Hershatter, *Gender of Memory*; Eyferth, "Women's Work"; Eyferth, "State Socialism."
30. The literature on the Great Famine is voluminous, but outstanding histories of the disaster include Wemheuer, *Famine Politics*; Yang, *Tombstone*; Manning and Wemheuer, *Eating Bitterness*; and Thaxton, *Catastrophe and Contention*.
31. Ash, "Squeezing the Peasants."
32. Eyferth, "State Socialism," 236; Eisenman, *Red China's Green Revolution*.
33. This typology of strategies draws inspiration from Fitzpatrick, *Stalin's Peasants*.
34. Schmalzer, *Red Revolution, Green Revolution*, 148.
35. Schmalzer, *Red Revolution, Green Revolution*, 148.
36. Friedman et al., *Chinese Village, Socialist State*; Brown and Johnson, *Maoism at the Grassroots*.
37. Leach and Green, "Gender and Environmental History," 351.
38. Important exceptions notwithstanding, historical relationships between gender and environment remain an under-developed realm of inquiry. Some pioneering works include Merchant, *Death of Nature*; Merchant, "Gender and Environmental History"; Leach and Green, "Gender and Environmental History"; Scharff, *Seeing Nature through Gender*; MacKenzie, *Land, Ecology and Resistance*; Weisiger, *Dreaming of Sheep*; Unger, *Beyond Nature's Housekeepers*; Morgan and Cook, "Gender, Environment and History." Gender has received even less attention in work on China, a relative newcomer on the environmental history scene. Studies of Chinese environmental history that consider gender include Finnane,

"Water, Love, and Labor"; Muscolino, *Ecology of War*, ch. 5; Muscolino, "Girls' Hearts."

39. Anderson, "Depression, Dust Bowl,"; Mackenzie, *Land, Ecology and Resistance*; Showers, *Imperial Gullies*; Beinart and Hughes, *Environment and Empire*, 284–88; Beinart, *Rise of Conservation*, 346–53; Mulwafu, *Conservation Song*; Shanguhyia, *Population, Tradition, and Environmental Control*; Weisiger, *Dreaming of Sheep*.

40. For an illuminating discussion of settler colonialism's consequences for people and the environment, see Voyles, *Settler Sea*. Wushan County was overwhelmingly Han Chinese. During the late 1950s, its ethnic minority population consisted of two households (six people in all) from the Hui ethnic group. Wushan xianzhi bianzuan weiyuanhui, *Wushan xianzhi*, 153.

41. Phillips, "Dust Bowl"; Dodson, "Soil Conservation Safari"; Anderson, "Depression, Dust Bowl,"; Beinart, "Introduction"; Showers, "Soil Erosion and Conservation."

42. Eyferth, "One Country," 195. See also Eyferth, "State Socialism." This perspective differs from that of Alvin Gouldner, who characterized Stalinism in the Soviet Union as "internal colonialism" but contrasted it with China's experience under Mao. Gouldner, "Stalinism."

43. Brown, "Spatial Profiling." See also Cohen, "Cultural and Political Inventions," 154–55.

ONE "Tianshui's Three Treasures"

1. Dong, "Jiefang qianhou Tianshui shuitu baochi keyan shiyan gongzuo," 379; Gao, "Zhongguo shuitu baochi shihua," 64.
2. Muscolino, *Ecology of War*.
3. Muscolino, "Wasteful Nations."
4. Phillips, "Dust Bowl," 246.
5. Phillips, "Dust Bowl," 260–61. See also Dodson, "Soil Conservation Safari."
6. On soil conservation and colonial development, see Anderson, "Depression, Dust Bowl"; Beinart, "Soil Erosion"; Mackenzie, *Land, Ecology and Resistance*; Showers, *Imperial Gullies*; Showers, "Soil Erosion and Conservation"; Hodge, *Triumph of the Expert*; Beinart and Hughes, *Environment and Empire*, 284–88; Beinart, *Rise of Conservation*; Mulwafu, *Conservation Song*; Shanguhyia, *Environmental Control*.
7. Robin, "Radical Ecology," 191–208.
8. Phillips, "Agro-Technical Internationalism."
9. Muscolino, "Refugees."
10. Dong, "Jiefang qian Tianshui de shuitu baochi gongzuo," 113–21; Dong,

"Jiefang qianhou Tianshui shuitu baochi keyan shiyan gongzuo," 376–84; Yang, "1940 niandai de Tianshui shuitu baochi shiyanqu shulun"; Mo, "Zhongguo shuitu baochi de faxiangdi."

11. The history of deforestation on the Loess Plateau is covered in Shi, "Lishi shiqi Huanghe zhongyou de senlin," 232–313. See also Mostern, *Yellow River.*

12. Food and Agriculture Organization of the United Nations, *Training Rural Leaders,* 9.

13. "Cradle of China's Civilization Caught Up in Surge of North-West Provincial Development Movement," *China Weekly Review* (March 1941), 452–53. On wartime construction of transport links with the Soviet Union that passed through Gansu, see Baker, "Soviet Aid."

14. Ren, "Jianshe Xibei yu shuitu baochi," 470. In late 1940, Ren tried to start China's first water and soil conservation research organ, the Longnan Water and Soil Conservation Experiment Area (Longnan shuitu baochi shiyanqu), also based in Tianshui, on behalf of the Yellow River Conservancy Commission, but it quickly folded due to lack of funds and bureaucratic infighting. After 1943, Ren worked as an advisor to the Tianshui Water and Soil Conservation Experiment Area. See Ren, "Pingzhi shuitu zaofu renlei," 237–49; Zhongguo kexue jishu xiehui, *Zhongguo kexue jishu zhuanjia zhuanlue,* 156–67. On Ren's earlier career, see Muscolino, "Wasteful Nations."

15. Ling and Ren, "Xibei shuitu baochi shiye zhi sheji yu shishi," 85.

16. W. C. Lowdermilk, "Preliminary Report," 1943, YRCC; Lowdermilk, *Water Conservation and Reclamation,* 379–413.

17. Stross, *Stubborn Earth,* 13.

18. On Lowdermilk's earlier research in China, see Muscolino, "Wasteful Nations"; Lowdermilk, "Surface Run-Off."

19. Greene, *Building a Nation.*

20. Lowdermilk, "Preliminary Report," 4

21. Lowdermilk, "Preliminary Report," 6.

22. Lowdermilk, "Preliminary Report," 3.

23. Ye Peizhong, "Xu."

24. Wei Zhanggen, "Titian gouxu zhi sheji yu shishi," 59. Unfortunately, I have not found biographical information on Wei Zhanggen.

25. Wei, "Titian gouxu zhi sheji yu shishi," 59.

26. Quotations from report written by Lowdermilk and published as Food and Agriculture Organization of the United Nations, *Soil Conservation,* 89.

27. Wei, "Titian gouxu zhi sheji yu shishi," 59.

28. Wei, "Titian gouxu zhi sheji yu shishi," 60.

29. For a detailed discussion of this land dispute, see Muscolino, "Wartime Water and Soil Conservation."

30. Brown, *Laws of the Land*.
31. "Chao yuan cheng." Attached to notice from Administrative Yuan, December 15, 1943, IMH.
32. "Nonglinbu shuitu baochi shiyanqu cheng," February 25, 1944, IMH.
33. Muscolino, "Wartime Water and Soil Conservation."
34. "Nonglinbu shuitu baochi shiyanqu sanshisan nian wu yuefen gongzuo jianbao biao," June 1944, IMH. According to Brown, custom in various regions of China during the Qing dictated that a similar "zone of protection" should exist around graves. Brown, *Laws of the Land*, 21.
35. "San nian lai zhi Tianshui shuitu baochi shiyanqu," in *San nian lai zhi Tianshui shuitu baochi shiyanqu*, ed. Nonglinbu shuitu baochi shiyanqu, 3.
36. Yan, "Minguo shiqi shuitu baochi zhi zui," 73. See also Wei, "Titian gouxu zhi sheji yu shishi," 72; Mo, "Huanghe shuili weiyuanhui Tianshui shuitu baochi kexue shiyanzhan zhanzhi," 124; Tianshui shi difangzhi bianweihui, *Tianshui shizhi*, 1111–12, 1115; Tianshui shi kexue jishu zhi bianjibu, *Tianshui shi kexue jishu zhi*, 611–12. Born in Xi'an in 1920, Yan Wenguang joined the experiment area in 1944 after graduating from the water conservancy section at National Northwest Technical School (Guoli Xibei jishu zhuanke xuexiao). Yan continued working at the experiment area for forty years and served as its director for a time. Xiang, "Gansu shuitu baochi gongzuo de jiwei kaichuangzhe," 150–69; Mo, "Huanghe shuili weiyuanhui Tianshui shuitu baochi kexue shiyanzhan zhanzhi," 220.
37. Food and Agriculture Organization of the United Nations, *Soil Conservation*, 89–90.
38. Wei, "Titian gouxu zhi sheji yu shishi," 73.
39. Wei, "Titian gouxu zhi sheji yu shishi," 73.
40. Yan, "Minguo shiqi shuitu baochi zhi zui," 73.
41. Yan, "Minguo shiqi shuitu baochi zhi zui," 73.
42. Yan, "Minguo shiqi shuitu baochi zhi zui," 74.
43. Beinart, "Introduction," 145–46, 160; Beinart, *Rise of Conservation*, 353.
44. Showers, *Imperial Gullies*, 172–75.
45. Wei, "Titian gouxu zhi sheji yu shishi," 73–74. See also Yan, "Minguo shiqi shuitu baochi zhi zui," 74.
46. Yan, "Minguo shiqi shuitu baochi zhi zui," 74. On difficulties that landlord-tenant relations posed for conservation work, see also "Nonglinbu shuitu baochi shiyanqu sanshiliu niandu shang ban nian gongzuo jindu jiantao baogao biao," July 1947, GPA.
47. The report indicated that planting grass strips on the edge of terraces exposed a wider area to sunlight and air, which caused moisture to evaporate and dried the soil. For that reason, grass did not grow well. "Nonglinbu shuitu baochi shiyanqu sanshiqi niandu shang ban nian gongzuo jindu jiantao baogao biao,"

August 1948, GPA. The same report appears in "Nonglinbu shuitu baochi shiyanqu sanshiqi niandu zhengji bijiao biao," January 1949, GPA. See also Mo, "Huanghe shuili weiyuanhui Tianshui shuitu baochi kexue shiyanzhan zhanzhi," 24.

48. "Nonglinbu shuitu baochi shiyanqu sanshiqi niandu shang ban nian gongzuo jindu jiantao baogao biao." See also "Nonglinbu shuitu baochi shiyanqu sanshiqi niandu zhengji bijiao biao."

49. Mo, "Huanghe shuili weiyuanhui Tianshui shuitu baochi kexue shiyanzhan zhanzhi," 124–25.

50. Tianshui shi difangzhi bianweihui, *Tianshui shizhi*, 1115; Mo, "Huanghe shuili weiyuanhui Tianshui shuitu baochi kexue shiyanzhan zhanzhi," 124–25.

51. On the pasturage station, see Li, "Minguo Tianshui shuitu baochi shiyanqu mucao pinzhong de xuanyu."

52. For a biography of Ye Peizhong, see Zhongguo kexue jishu xiehui, *Zhongguo kexue jishu zhuanjia zhuanlue*, 199–214.

53. Mo, "Caomuxi shihua," 102.

54. "Cheng Xingzhengyuan," January 9, 1945, IMH.

55. In the 1930s, the Yellow River Conservancy Commission, the Northwest Agricultural Institute (Xibei nongxueyuan), and other research organs had introduced other European varieties of sweet clover, but they did not have a lasting influence. Quanguo mucao pinzhong shending weiyuanhui, *Zhongguo mucao dengji pinzhong ji*, 151. See also Mo, "Woguo caomuxi de yinzhong tuiguang jingguo," 67; "San nian lai zhi Tianshui shuitu baochi shiyanqu," 8.

56. Mo, "Caomuxi shihua," 102; Tianshui shi kexue jishu zhi bianjibu, *Tianshui shi kexue jishu zhi*, 609.

57. Yan, "Minguo shiqi shuitu baochi zhi zui," 72–73. See also Mo, "Caomuxi shihua," 102; Dong, "Jiefang qian Tianshui de shuitu baochi gongzuo," 119–20.

58. Ren, "Gansu shuitu baochi shiyanqu zhi kancha," 7.

59. Ren, "Gansu shuitu baochi shiyanqu zhi kancha," 7.

60. Wen, "Gansu de jiupin gongzuo." On the impact of fuel demand on forests and other vegetation, see Shi, "Lishi shiqi Huanghe zhongyou de senlin," 303–5.

61. Yan, "Minguo shiqi shuitu baochi zhi zui," 72–73. See also Mo, "Caomuxi shihua," 102; Dong, "Jiefang qian Tianshui de shuitu baochi gongzuo," 119–20.

62. "Nonglinbu shuitu baochi shiyanqu sanshiliu nian qi yuefen gongzuo jianbao biao," August 1947, GPA.

63. "Nonglinbu shuitu baochi shiyanqu sanshiqi niandu zhengji bijiao biao." See also "Nonglinbu shuitu baochi shiyanqu sanshiqi niandu shang ban nian gongzuo jindu jiantao baogao biao."

64. Mo, "Caomuxi shihua," 102.

65. "Nonglinbu shuitu baochi shiyanqu sanshiliu nian qi yuefen gongzuo jianbao biao."

66. "Nonglinbu shuitu baochi shiyanqu sanshiliu nian qi yuefen gongzuo jianbao biao." See also Mo, "Caomuxi shihua," 102.
67. "Nonglinbu shuitu baochi shiyanqu sanshiqi nian jiu yuefen gongzuo jianbao biao," October 1948, IMH.
68. "Nonglinbu shuitu baochi shiyanqu sanshiqi niandu zhengji bijiao biao." See also "Nonglinbu shuitu baochi shiyanqu sanshiqi nian jiu yuefen gongzuo jianbao biao."
69. "Nonglinbu shuitu baochi shiyanqu sanshiqi nian jiu yuefen gongzuo jianbao biao." See also Mo, "Caomuxi shihua," 102.
70. Yan, "Minguo shiqi shuitu baochi zhi zui," 72–73. Other sources state that one *sheng* of grain could be traded for one *sheng* of sweet clover. See Mo, "Caomuxi shihua," 102.
71. Mo, "Caomuxi shihua," 102.
72. Dong, "Jiefang qian Tianshui de shuitu baochi gongzuo," 119–20; Gao, "Zhongguo shuitu baochi shihua," 64. See also Mo, "Caomuxi shihua," 102–3.
73. Mo, "Woguo caomuxi de yinzhong tuiguang jingguo," 67.
74. "Nonglinbu shuitu baochi shiyanqu sanshisan niandu zhengji bijiao biao," January 1944, GPA.
75. Yan, "Minguo shiqi shuitu baochi zhi zui," 72.
76. Wan, "Jiefang qian de Tianshui linye," 88; Tianshui shuitu baochi kexue shiyanzhan, "Tianshui diqu de yanghuai gougu zaolin"; Jiang, "Yanghuai zaipei jingyan ji qi shuitu baochi xiaoyi de ceyan," 181; Jiang and Zhang, "Weihe shangyou yanghuai shuitu baochi lin yanjiu baogao," 124.
77. Yan, "Minguo shiqi shuitu baochi zhi zui," 72. See also Wan, "Jiefang qian de Tianshui linye," 88.
78. Tianshui shi kexue jishu zhi bianjibu, *Tianshui shi kexue jishu zhi*, 606.
79. Yan, "Minguo shiqi shuitu baochi zhi zui," 73. See also Gao, "Zhongguo shuitu baochi shihua," 64.
80. "Nonglinbu shuitu baochi shiyanqu sanshiqi niandu shang ban nian gongzuo jindu jiantao baogao biao."
81. "Nonglinbu shuitu baochi shiyanqu sanshiliu niandu yuan yuefen gongzuo jianbao biao," February 1947, GPA.
82. "Nonglinbu shuitu baochi shiyanqu sanshisi niandu zhengji bijiao biao," January 1946, GPA; "Nonglinbu shuitu baochi shiyanqu sanshiliu nian er yuefen gongzuo jianbao biao," March 1947, GPA; "Nonglinbu shuitu baochi shiyanqu sanshiliu nian san yuefen gongzuo jianbao biao," April 1947, GPA.
83. Gao, "Zhongguo shuitu baochi shihua," 64; Wan, "Jiefang qian de Tianshui linye," 88.
84. Kou et al., "*Robinia pseudoacacia* Afforestation," 147.

85. Chen et al., "Invasion of Farmland-Grassland Ecosystems," 1012–16.
86. Kou et al., *Robinia pseudoacacia* Afforestation," 157.
87. Laakkonen et al., "Hypotheses," 323.
88. Nygren, "Save the Plains," 203.
89. This assessment of the long-term influence of Lowdermilk's activities in China differs from that of Greene, *Building a Nation*, 240–41.

TWO "Speak Bitterness to Floods"

1. The Tianshui Water and Soil Conservation Experiment Area merged with other agricultural agencies in Tianshui in 1949 to form the Longnan People's Agriculture and Forestry Experiment Area (Longnan renmin nonglin shiyanqu; after 1951, Longnan renmin nonglin shiyanchang), which changed its name in 1953 to the Longnan Water and Soil Conservation Extension Station (Longnan shuitu baochi tuiguangzhan). In 1954 it became the Tianshui Water and Soil Conservation Extension Station (Tianshui shuitu baochi tuiguangzhan) and in 1956 it became the Tianshui Water and Soil Conservation Scientific Experiment Station (Tianshui shuitu baochi kexue shiyanzhan). See Mo, "Huanghe shuili weiyuanhui Tianshui shuitu baochi kexue shiyanzhan zhanzhi," 60; Dong, "Jiefang qian Tianshui de shuitu baochi gongzuo," 378–79; Mo, "Zhongguo shuitu baochi de faxiangdi," 174–77.
2. According to land reform investigations, Wushan had a population of 178,749 in 1951; the PRC census of 1953 found that the county had a population of 188,207. Wushan xianzhi bianzuan weiyuanhui, *Wushan xianzhi*, III, 154.
3. Perry, "Making Communism Work," 537.
4. Yan, "Wushan xian Dongshun xiang shuitu baochi gongzuo shi zenyang kaizhan de," 76.
5. Yan, "Wushi niandai Wushan Dengjiabao gao shuitu baochi de huiyi," 152; Yan, "Wushan xian Dongshun xiang shuitu baochi gongzuo shi zenyang kaizhan de," 76–77. See also Wushan xianzhi bianzuan weiyuanhui, *Wushan xianzhi*, 328; Tianshui shi difangzhi bianweihui, *Tianshui shizhi*, 1114, 1115.
6. "Wushan xian shuitu baochi gongzuo kaizhan qingkuang," 1955, WCA. See also Wushan xian renmin weiyuanhui, "Wushan xian Dengjiabao san nian lai shuitu baochi gongzuo jiben zongjie," September 26, 1955, WCA.
7. Heilmann, "Local Experiments." See also Schmalzer, *Red Revolution, Green Revolution*, 33, 41, 43–44.
8. "Zhongyang renmin zhengfu zhengwuyuan guanyu fadong qunzhong jixu kaizhan fang han, kang han yundong bing dali tuixing shuitu baochi gongzuo de zhishi," 394–97.

9. "Zhongyang renmin zhengfu zhengwuyuan guanyu fadong qunzhong jixu kaizhan fang han, kang han yundong bing dali tuixing shuitu baochi gongzuo de zhishi," 394–97.

10. Perry, "Making Communism Work," 550.

11. Hershatter, *Gender of Memory*, 25.

12. Wushan xianzhi bianzuan weiyuanhui, *Wushan xianzhi*, 328; Yan, "Wushi niandai Wushan Dengjiabao gao shuitu baochi de huiyi," 153; Wushan xian renmin weiyuanhui, "Wushan xian Dengjiabao san nian lai shuitu baochi gongzuo jiben zongjie." Figures for elevation and soil loss from "Dengjiabao shuitu baochi dianxing diaocha baogao (chugao)," June 1961, 1, 14, YRCC.

13. Yan, "Wushi niandai Wushan Dengjiabao gao shuitu baochi de huiyi," 153.

14. Wushan xianzhi bianzuan weiyuanhui, *Wushan xianzhi*, 328; Yan, "Wushi niandai Wushan Dengjiabao gao shuitu baochi de huiyi," 153; "Dengjiabao shuitu baochi dianxing diaocha baogao," 1–2.

15. Yan, "Wushi niandai Wushan Dengjiabao gao shuitu baochi de huiyi," 152.

16. Yan, "Wushi niandai Wushan Dengjiabao gao shuitu baochi de huiyi," 152–53; "Dengjiabao shuitu baochi dianxing diaocha baogao," 2–3.

17. Interview, May 2018.

18. Yan, "Wushi niandai Wushan Dengjiabao gao shuitu baochi de huiyi," 152–53; "Dengjiabao shuitu baochi dianxing diaocha baogao," 2–3; "Wushan xian shuitu baochi gongzuo kaizhan qingkuang."

19. Yan, "Wushan xian Dongshun xiang shuitu baochi gongzuo shi zenyang kaizhan de," 76. See also Wushan xian renmin weiyuanhui, "Wushan xian Dengjiabao san nian lai shuitu baochi gongzuo jiben zongjie."

20. Yan, "Wushan xian Dongshun xiang shuitu baochi gongzuo shi zenyang kaizhan de," 76. See also "Wushan xian Dengjiabao san nian lai shuitu baochi gongzuo jiben zongjie."

21. "Tianshui diqu titian zongjie," April 1961, 61, YRCC.

22. "Tianshui diqu titian zongjie," 61.

23. Wushan xian renmin weiyuanhui, "Wushan xian Dengjiabao san nian lai shuitu baochi gongzuo jiben zongjie."

24. "Wushan xian shuitu baochi gongzuo kaizhan qingkuang."

25. Yan, "Wushan xian Dongshun xiang shuitu baochi gongzuo shi zenyang kaizhan de," 76.

26. "Tianshui diqu titian zongjie," 61.

27. Yan, "Wushan xian Dongshun xiang shuitu baochi gongzuo shi zenyang kaizhan de," 76. See also Yan, "Wushi niandai Wushan Dengjiabao gao shuitu baochi de huiyi," 153; Wushan xian renmin weiyuanhui, "Wushan xian Dengjiabao san nian lai shuitu baochi gongzuo jiben zongjie."

28. Yan, "Wushan xian Dongshun xiang shuitu baochi gongzuo shi zenyang kaizhan de," 76. See also Yan, "Wushi niandai Wushan Dengjiabao gao shuitu baochi de huiyi," 153.

29. "Wushan xian shuitu baochi gongzuo kaizhan qingkuang."

30. Yan, "Wushi niandai Wushan Dengjiabao gao shuitu baochi de huiyi," 152–53; "Dengjiabao shuitu baochi dianxing diaocha baogao," 2–3.

31. "Wushan xian shuitu baochi gongzuo kaizhan qingkuang."

32. "Jianshe shanqu de bangyang: ji Dengjiabao zonghe kaifa, quanmian zhili shanqu de jingguo," *Gansu ribao*, December 19, 1957.

33. Interview, May 2018.

34. "Wushan xian shuitu baochi zhong de ji dian tihui," September 21, 1955, WCA.

35. Wushan xianzhi bianzuan weiyuanhui, *Wushan xianzhi*, 154–55, 261–62. For an overview of land reform, see Demare, *Land Wars*.

36. Interview, May 2018. See also Yan, "Wushi niandai Wushan Dengjiabao gao shuitu baochi de huiyi," 153; "Dengjiabao shuitu baochi dianxing diaocha baogao," 3; Wushan xianzhi bianzuan weiyuanhui, *Wushan xianzhi*, 328; Tianshui shi difangzhi bianweihui, *Tianshui shizhi*, 1114; "Wushan xian xia ban nian shuitu baochi gongzuo buzhi," July 16, 1954, WCA. According to the gazetteer of Wushan County, 64 percent of households in Wushan were members of mutual-aid teams by the end of 1953 and 82 percent were members by the end of 1954. Wushan xianzhi bianzuan weiyuanhui, *Wushan xianzhi*, 262. It is difficult to gauge the validity of these membership figures, since local cadres and officials were known to inflate reports about popular participation in mutual-aid teams and to exaggerate their achievements. See Hou, *Negotiating Socialism*, 156–57, 173, 192.

37. Shue, *Peasant China in Transition*; Madsen, "Countryside under Communism," 630–32; Li, *Village China*, 24–26; Hou, *Negotiating Socialism*.

38. Wushan xian renmin weiyuanhui, "Wushan xian Dengjiabao san nian lai shuitu baochi gongzuo jiben zongjie."

39. "Wushan xian xia ban nian shuitu baochi gongzuo buzhi."

40. Wushan xian renmin weiyuanhui, "Wushan xian Dengjiabao san nian lai shuitu baochi gongzuo jiben zongjie."

41. "Wushan xian shuitu baochi gongzuo kaizhan qingkuang."

42. Interview, September 2019; "Wushan xian shuitu baochi mofan Deng Haihai shiji," February 22, 1955, WCA.

43. Wushan xian renmin weiyuanhui, "Wushan xian Dengjiabao san nian lai shuitu baochi gongzuo jiben zongjie."

44. "Jianshe shanqu de bangyang." See also Wushan xian renmin weiyuanhui, "Wushan xian Dengjiabao san nian lai shuitu baochi gongzuo jiben zongjie."

45. Wushan xian renmin weiyuanhui, "Wushan xian Dengjiabao san nian lai shuitu baochi gongzuo jiben zongjie."
46. "Wushan xian shuitu baochi mofan Deng Haihai shiji."
47. "Wushan xian shuitu baochi mofan Deng Haihai shiji." See also "Jianshe shanqu de bangyang."
48. "Nonglinmu zhongdian gongzuozu de jianbao," April 24, 1954, WCA.
49. Wushan xian zhengfu, "Woxian yuan zhi wu yue shuitu baochi gongzuo jianjie baogao," June 8, 1954, WCA.
50. "Wushan xian tuiguang caomuxi gongzuo baogao," April 26, 1954, WCA. See also "Wushan xian yijiuwusi nian xia ban niandu caomuxi tuiguang gongzuo jihua," August 28, 1954, WCA; Wushan xian zhengfu, "Woxian yuan zhi wu yue shuitu baochi gongzuo jianjie baogao."
51. "Wushan xian tuiguang caomuxi gongzuo baogao."
52. "Women de jiaxiang yi jibenshang zhizhile shuitu liushi," 1956, GPA.
53. Wushan xian renmin weiyuanhui, "Wushan xian Dengjiabao san nian lai shuitu baochi gongzuo jiben zongjie."
54. Yan, "Wushan xian Dongshun xiang shuitu baochi gongzuo shi zenyang kaizhan de," 78.
55. Wushan xianzhi bianzuan weiyuanhui, *Wushan xianzhi*, 261–62.
56. "Wushan Dengjiabao zhongdian gongzuozu guanyu wuwu nian shang ban nian gongzuo qingkuang zongjie baogao," July 20, 1955, WCA.
57. "Wushan Dengjiabao zhongdian gongzuozu guanyu wuwu nian shang ban nian gongzuo qingkuang zongjie baogao."
58. "Wushan Dengjiabao zhongdian gongzuozu guanyu wuwu nian shang ban nian gongzuo qingkuang zongjie baogao."
59. Wushan xian renmin weiyuanhui, "Wushan xian Dengjiabao san nian lai shuitu baochi gongzuo jiben zongjie."
60. Yan, "Wushan xian Dongshun xiang shuitu baochi gongzuo shi zenyang kaizhan de," 76–77. See also Yan, "Wushi niandai Wushan Dengjiabao gao shuitu baochi de huiyi," 153; "Wushan xian shuitu baochi gongzuo kaizhan qingkuang"; Wushan xian renmin weiyuanhui, "Wushan xian Dengjiabao san nian lai shuitu baochi gongzuo jiben zongjie."
61. "Wushan xian xia ban nian shuitu baochi gongzuo buzhi"; "Wushan xian shuitu baochi gongzuo kaizhan qingkuang."
62. Yan, "Wushan xian Dongshun xiang shuitu baochi gongzuo shi zenyang kaizhan de," 76–77. See also Yan, "Wushi niandai Wushan Dengjiabao gao shuitu baochi de huiyi," 153; "Wushan xian shuitu baochi gongzuo kaizhan qingkuang"; Wushan xian renmin weiyuanhui, "Wushan xian Dengjiabao san nian lai shuitu baochi gongzuo jiben zongjie."

63. "Wushan xian xia ban nian shuitu baochi gongzuo buzhi"; "Dengjiabao shuitu baochi dianxing diaocha baogao," 6–7.
64. "Dengjiabao shuitu baochi dianxing diaocha baogao," 6–7.
65. Yan, "Wushan xian Dongshun xiang shuitu baochi gongzuo shi zenyang kaizhan de," 76–77. See also Yan, "Wushi niandai Wushan Dengjiabao gao shuitu baochi de huiyi," 153; "Dengjiabao shuitu baochi dianxing diaocha baogao," 6–7.
66. Yan, "Wushan xian Dongshun xiang shuitu baochi gongzuo shi zenyang kaizhan de," 77. See also Yan, "Wushi niandai Wushan Dengjiabao gao shuitu baochi de huiyi," 154; "Tianshui diqu titian zongjie," 62; Tianshui shi difangzhi bianweihui, *Tianshui shizhi*, 1115.
67. Yan, "Wushan xian Dongshun xiang shuitu baochi gongzuo shi zenyang kaizhan de," 76–77; Yan, "Wushi niandai Wushan Dengjiabao gao shuitu baochi de huiyi," 153.
68. Yan, "Wushan xian Dongshun xiang shuitu baochi gongzuo shi zenyang kaizhan de," 77; Yan, "Wushi niandai Wushan Dengjiabao gao shuitu baochi de huiyi," 154; "Tianshui diqu titian zongjie," 62; Tianshui shi difangzhi bianweihui, *Tianshui shizhi*, 1115; Wushan xian renmin weiyuanhui, "Wushan xian Dengjiabao san nian lai shuitu baochi gongzuo jiben zongjie."
69. Yan, "Wushi niandai Wushan Dengjiabao gao shuitu baochi de huiyi," 154.
70. "Wushan xian renmin zhengfu tongzhi," May 31, 1954, WCA; Wushan xian zhengfu, "Woxian yuan zhi wu yue shuitu baochi jianjie baogao."
71. Wushan xian zhengfu, "Woxian yuan zhi wu yue shuitu baochi gongzuo zongjie baogao."
72. "Wushan xian shuitu baochi gongzuo zhuanye huiyi zongjie baogao," September 7, 1955, WCA.
73. Wushan xian renmin weiyuanhui, "Wushan xian Dengjiabao san nian lai shuitu baochi gongzuo jiben zongjie."
74. "Wushan xian nongye laodong mofan ji huzhuzuzhang daibiao huiyi zongjie," March 1954, WCA.
75. Brown, *Laws of the Land*, 7–8. See also Anderson, *Ecologies of the Heart*, 15–17; Bruun, *Fengshui in China*, 4, 148.
76. "Wushan xian shuitu baochi gongzuo kaizhan qingkuang."
77. Wushan xian renmin weiyuanhui, "Wushan xian Dengjiabao san nian lai shuitu baochi gongzuo jiben zongjie."
78. "Dengjiabao shuitu baochi dianxing diaocha baogao," 22.
79. "Dengjiabao shuitu baochi dianxing diaocha baogao," 17.
80. Studies of Mao-era China usually define rural food "self-sufficiency" as 275–300 kg of raw grain or other staple carbohydrates per capita per year, and food availability in Dengjiabao fell well below that level. See Walker, *Food Procurement*, 3; Ash, "Squeezing the Peasants," 968.

81. Wushan xian Dengjiabao nong (shui) lin mu zhongdian gongzuozu, "Wushan Dengjiabao xingzhengcun gouhe zhili zongjie baogao," June 8, 1954, WCA.
82. Wushan xian Dengjiabao nong (shui) lin mu zhongdian gongzuozu, "Wushan Dengjiabao xingzhengcun gouhe zhili zongjie baogao."
83. Wushan xian Dengjiabao nong (shui) lin mu zhongdian gongzuozu, "Wushan Dengjiabao xingzhengcun gouhe zhili zongjie baogao."
84. "Wushan xian nongye laodong mofan ji huzhuzuzhang daibiao huiyi zongjie."
85. Wushan xian Dengjiabao nong (shui) lin mu zhongdian gongzuozu, "Wushan Dengjiabao xingzhengcun gouhe zhili zongjie baogao." See also "Wushan xian Dengjiabao nong (shui) lin mu zhongdian gongzuozu yijiuwusi niandu gongzuo jihua," March 29, 1954, WCA.
86. Wushan xian Dengjiabao nong (shui) lin mu zhongdian gongzuozu, "Wushan Dengjiabao xingzhengcun gouhe zhili zongjie baogao."
87. Wushan xian Dengjiabao nong (shui) lin mu zhongdian gongzuozu, "Wushan Dengjiabao xingzhengcun gouhe zhili zongjie baogao." The plan called for planting black locusts and other trees in the gullies. In addition to planting seaberry plants during the rainy season, the work team planned to build two hundred small earth dams and plant willow trees on them. Planting sweet clover and alfalfa on poor soils in the upper section of Kangjia Gully, on eroded slopes, and beside gullies, the plan asserted, would improve the soil, increase fertility, and provide fertilizer and fodder. See "Wushan xian Dengjiabao nong (shui) lin mu zhongdian gongzuozu yijiuwusi niandu gongzuo jihua."
88. Wushan xian Dengjiabao nong (shui) lin mu zhongdian gongzuozu, "Wushan Dengjiabao xingzhengcun gouhe zhili zongjie baogao." See also "Wushan xian nongye laodong mofan ji huzhuzuzhang daibiao huiyi zongjie."
89. Wushan xian Dengjiabao nong (shui) lin mu zhongdian gongzuozu, "Wushan Dengjiabao xingzhengcun gouhe zhili zongjie baogao."
90. Wushan xian Dengjiabao nong (shui) lin mu zhongdian gongzuozu, "Wushan Dengjiabao xingzhengcun gouhe zhili zongjie baogao." See also "Wushan xian Dengjiabao nong (shui) lin mu zhongdian gongzuozu yijiuwusi niandu gongzuo jihua."
91. Wushan xian Dengjiabao nong (shui) lin mu zhongdian gongzuozu, "Wushan Dengjiabao xingzhengcun gouhe zhili zongjie baogao."
92. Wushan xian Dengjiabao nong (shui) lin mu zhongdian gongzuozu, "Wushan Dengjiabao xingzhengcun gouhe zhili zongjie baogao." See also "Wushan xian Dengjiabao nong (shui) lin mu zhongdian gongzuozu yijiuwusi niandu gongzuo jihua."
93. "Wushan xian Dengjiabao nong (shui) lin mu zhongdian gongzuozu yijiuwusi niandu gongzuo jihua."

94. "Wushan xian nongye laodong mofan ji huzhuzuzhang daibiao huiyi zongjie." Reports from a village in Tan'ge district stated that when mutual-aid teams employed "dead points, living appraisal," members' enthusiasm for conservation increased. The "dead points, dead appraisal" method, by contrast, assigned a fixed number of points per day to each team member and did not add or deduct points based on work quality. "Wushan xian shuitu baochi gongzuo zhuanye huiyi zongjie baogao." For an explanation of these methods, see Li, *Village China*, 35.

95. Wushan xian Dengjiabao nong (shui) lin mu zhongdian gongzuozu, "Wushan Dengjiabao xingzhengcun gouhe zhili zongjie baogao."

96. Wushan xian Dengjiabao nong (shui) lin mu zhongdian gongzuozu, "Wushan Dengjiabao xingzhengcun gouhe zhili zongjie baogao." See also "Wushan xian Dengjiabao nong (shui) lin mu zhongdian gongzuozu yijiuwusi niandu gongzuo jihua."

97. "Wushan xian Dengjiabao nong (shui) lin mu zhongdian gongzuozu yijiuwusi niandu gongzuo jihua."

98. Wushan xian Dengjiabao nong (shui) lin mu zhongdian gongzuozu, "Wushan Dengjiabao xingzhengcun gouhe zhili zongjie baogao."

99. Wushan xian Dengjiabao nong (shui) lin mu zhongdian gongzuozu, "Wushan Dengjiabao xingzhengcun gouhe zhili zongjie baogao." See also "Wushan xian Dengjiabao nong (shui) lin mu zhongdian gongzuozu yijiuwusi niandu gongzuo jihua."

100. "Women de jiaxiang yi jibenshang zhizhile shuitu liushi."

101. Quotations in this and the following three paragraphs are drawn from Wushan xian Dengjiabao nong (shui) lin mu zhongdian gongzuozu, "Wushan Dengjiabao xingzhengcun gouhe zhili zongjie baogao."

102. Wushan xian renmin weiyuanhui, "Wushan xian Dengjiabao san nian lai shuitu baochi gongzuo jiben zongjie." See also "Wushan xian shuitu baochi gongzuo kaizhan qingkuang"; "Wushan Dengjiabao baoyu hou tuba sunhui qingkuang ji jinhou yijian," 24.

103. Wushan xian renmin weiyuanhui, "Wushan xian Dengjiabao san nian lai shuitu baochi gongzuo jiben zongjie."

104. "Women de jiaxiang yi jibenshang zhizhile shuitu liushi."

105. Wushan xian renmin weiyuanhui, "Wushan xian Dengjiabao san nian lai shuitu baochi gongzuo jiben zongjie."

106. "Wushan xian shuitu baochi gongzuo kaizhan qingkuang."

107. Wushan xian renmin weiyuanhui, "Wushan xian Dengjiabao san nian lai shuitu baochi gongzuo jiben zongjie." See also "Wushan xian shuitu baochi gongzuo kaizhan qingkuang"; "Wushan Dengjiabao baoyu hou tuba sunhui qingkuang ji jinhou yijian," 24.

108. Wushan xian renmin weiyuanhui, "Wushan xian Dengjiabao san nian lai shuitu baochi gongzuo jiben zongjie."

109. Wushan xian renmin weiyuanhui, "Wushan xian Dengjiabao san nian lai shuitu baochi gongzuo jiben zongjie." See also "Wushan xian shuitu baochi gongzuo kaizhan qingkuang"; "Wushan Dengjiabao baoyu hou tuba sunhui qingkuang ji jinhou yijian," 24.

110. Wushan xian renmin weiyuanhui, "Wushan xian Dengjiabao san nian lai shuitu baochi gongzuo jiben zongjie." See also "Wushan xian shuitu baochi gongzuo kaizhan qingkuang."

111. "Women de jiaxiang yi jibenshang tingzhile shuitu liushi."

112. On militarization and the environment in modern China, see Muscolino, *Ecology of War*, 245–46.

113. "Women de jiaxiang yi jibenshang tingzhile shuitu liushi."

114. By spring 1955, Dengjiabao residents had built 312 dams in the four gullies near the village. Wushan xian renmin weiyuanhui, "Wushan xian Dengjiabao san nian lai shuitu baochi gongzuo jiben zongjie." See also "Wushan xian shuitu baochi gongzuo kaizhan qingkuang."

115. "Wushan xian jiehe xiashou kaizhan shuitu baochi gongzuo qingkuang jianbao," July 16, 1955, WCA. See also "Wushan xian wuwu nian shuitu baochi gongzuo zongjie baogao," January 18, 1956, WCA.

116. "Wushan xian shuitu baochi gongzuo zhuanye huiyi zongjie baogao."

117. "Wushan xian shuitu baochi gongzuo di yi ci daibiao zhuanye huiyi zongjie baogao."

118. "Wushan xian shuitu baochi gongzuo di yi ci daibiao zhuanye huiyi zongjie baogao."

119. "Wushan xian shuitu baochi gongzuo di yi ci daibiao zhuanye huiyi zongjie baogao."

120. "Wushan xian shuitu baochi gongzuo zhuanye huiyi zongjie baogao."

121. "Wushan xian shuitu baochi gongzuo zhuanye huiyi zongjie baogao."

THREE "Getting Organized Is Powerful"

1. Ma, "Kongzhi zhu shuitu liushi de Dengjiabao cun," 2.

2. Ma, "Kongzhi zhu shuitu liushi de Dengjiabao cun," 2.

3. Ma, "Kongzhi zhu shuitu liushi de Dengjiabao cun," 2.

4. Pietz, *Yellow River*, 161. See also Greer, *Water Management*, 89–90.

5. Li, *Village China*, 31, 33, 34; Madsen, "Countryside under Communism," 634–37.

6. Tianshui zhuanyuan gongshu, "Wushan xian Dengjiabao nongye shengchan

hezuoshe shuitu baochi gongzuo shiji," 1955, GPA; "Dengjiabao gongzuozu dui xiashou hou shuitu baochi gongzuo jihua zhixing caoan," July 2, 1955, WCA; Wushan xian renmin weiyuanhui, "Wushan xian Dengjiabao san nian lai shuitu baochi gongzuo jiben zongjie."

7. "Wushan xian yijiuwuwu nian shuitu baochi gongzuo zongjie," December 30, 1955, WCA; Zhonggong Wushan xianwei, "Wushan xian guanyu xiaji shuitu baochi gongzuo anpai yijian," July 18, 1955, WCA.

8. Wushan xian renmin weiyuanhui, "Wushan xian Dengjiabao san nian lai shuitu baochi gongzuo jiben zongjie."

9. "Wushan xian shuitu baochi jishu xunlian gongzuo zongjie baogao," July 15, 1955, WCA.

10. "Wushan xian yijiuwuwu nian shuitu baochi gongzuo zongjie"; Zhonggong Wushan xianwei, "Wushan xian guanyu xiaji shuitu baochi gongzuo anpai yijian"; "Wushan xian shuitu baochi zhuanye huiyi zongjie baogao."

11. "Wushan xian renmin weiyuanhui baogao," July 31, 1955, WCA.

12. Wushan xian renmin weiyuanhui, "Wushan xian Dengjiabao san nian lai shuitu baochi gongzuo jiben zongjie"; "Wushan xian wuwu nian yuan zhi jiu yue fen shuitu baochi jianjie baogao," October 8, 1955, WCA.

13. Wushan xian renmin weiyuanhui, "Wushan xian Dengjiabao san nian lai shuitu baochi gongzuo jiben zongjie." See also "Wushan xian wuwu nian yuan zhi jiu yue fen shuitu baochi jianjie baogao."

14. Wushan xian renmin weiyuanhui, "Wushan xian Dengjiabao san nian lai shuitu baochi gongzuo jiben zongjie." See also "Wushan xian wuwu nian yuan zhi jiu yue fen shuitu baochi jianjie baogao."

15. "Wushan xian jiehe xiashou kaizhan shuitu baochi gongzuo qingkuang jianbao." See also "Wushan xian renmin weiyuanhui baogao."

16. "Wushan xian wuwu nian yuan zhi jiu yue fen shuitu baochi jianjie baogao."

17. "Wushan Dengjiabao zhongdian gongzuozu guanyu wuwu nian shang ban nian gongzuo qingkuang zongjie baogao."

18. Wushan xian renmin weiyuanhui, "Guohuai xiang quanmian kaizhan shuitu baochi gongzuo zongjie baogao," September 18, 1955, WCA.

19. "Wushan xian jiehe xiashou kaizhan shuitu baochi gongzuo qingkuang jianbao." See also "Wushan xian shuitu baochi gongzuo zhuanye huiyi zongjie baogao."

20. Wushan xian renmin weiyuanhui, "Wushan xian Dengjiabao san nian lai shuitu baochi gongzuo jiben zongjie."

21. Wushan xian renmin weiyuanhui, "Wushan xian Dengjiabao san nian lai shuitu baochi gongzuo jiben zongjie." See also "Wushan xian wuwu nian yuan zhi jiu yue fen shuitu baochi jianjie baogao."

22. "Wushan xian wuwu nian yuan zhi jiu yue fen shuitu baochi jianjie

baogao." Compensating members over several years for their investments in conservation projects closely resembled payments that cooperatives made to owners of irrigation works and other assets. See Shue, *Peasant China in Transition*, 289, 292.

23. "Wushan xian wuwu nian yuan zhi jiu yue fen shuitu baochi jianjie baogao." On the piece-rate method, see Shue, *Peasant China in Transition*, 302–3; Li, *Village China*, 36.

24. Zhonggong Wushan xianwei, "Wushan xian guanyu xiaji shuitu baochi gongzuo anpai yijian."

25. Wushan xian renmin weiyuanhui, "Wushan xian Dengjiabao san nian lai shuitu baochi gongzuo jiben zongjie."

26. Wushan xian renmin weiyuanhui, "Wushan xian Dengjiabao san nian lai shuitu baochi gongzuo jiben zongjie."

27. "Wushan xian yijiuwuwu nian shuitu baochi gongzuo zongjie"; Zhonggong Wushan xianwei, "Wushan xian guanyu xiaji shuitu baochi gongzuo anpai yijian."

28. "Wushan xian jiehe xiashou kaizhan shuitu baochi gongzuo qingkuang jianbao."

29. "Wushan xian wuwu nian yuan zhi jiu yue fen shuitu baochi jianjie baogao."

30. "Wushan xian yijiuwuwu nian shuitu baochi gongzuo zongjie"; Zhonggong Wushan xianwei, "Wushan xian guanyu xiaji shuitu baochi gongzuo anpai yijian"; "Wushan xian san nian lai shuitu baochi gongzuo jiben zongjie"; "Wushan xian shuitu baochi zhuanye huiyi zongjie baogao."

31. Wushan xian renmin weiyuanhui, "Wushan xian Dengjiabao san nian lai shuitu baochi gongzuo jiben zongjie."

32. Wushan xian renmin weiyuanhui, "Wushan xian Dengjiabao san nian lai shuitu baochi gongzuo jiben zongjie."

33. "Wushan xian yijiuwuwu nian shuitu baochi zongjie"; Zhonggong Wushan xianwei, "Wushan xian guanyu xiaji shuitu baochi gongzuo anpai yijian." On the "guaranteed work and guaranteed production" system, see Shue, *Peasant China in Transition*, 303.

34. "Wushan xian yijiuwuwu nian shuitu baochi zongjie"; Zhonggong Wushan xianwei, "Wushan xian guanyu xiaji shuitu baochi gongzuo anpai yijian."

35. "Wushan xian wuwu nian yuan zhi jiu yue fen shuitu baochi jianjie baogao."

36. "Wushan xian shuitu baochi gongzuo zhuanye huiyi zongjie baogao."

37. "Wushan xian renmin weiyuanhui baogao."

38. "Wushan xian shuitu baochi jishu xunlian gongzuo zongjie baogao."

39. "Wushan xian renmin weiyuanhui baogao."

40. "Wushan xian shuitu baochi gongzuo zhuanye huiyi zongjie baogao."

41. "Wushan xian renmin weiyuanhui baogao."

42. "Wushan xian renmin weiyuanhui baogao."
43. "Wushan xian shuitu baochi zhuanye huiyi zongjie baogao"; "Wushan xian shuitu baochi zhong de ji dian tihui."
44. "Wushan xian shuitu baochi jishu xunlian gongzuo zongjie baogao." See also "Wushan xian shuitu baochi zhuanye huiyi zongjie baogao."
45. "Wushan xian shuitu baochi gongzuo di yi ci daibiao zhuanye huiyi zongjie baogao," September 7, 1955, WCA.
46. "Wushan xian shuitu baochi zhuanye huiyi zongjie baogao."
47. Oi, *State and Peasant*, 44.
48. Oi, *State and Peasant*. See also Madsen, "Countryside under Communism," 632; Naughton, *Chinese Economy*, 233, 239; Li, *Village China*, ch. 3; Wemheuer, *Famine Politics*, 87–93.
49. "Wushan xian renmin weiyuanhui baogao."
50. Zhongguo gongchandang Wushan xian weiyuanhui, "Luomen qu shuitu baochi gongzuo kaizhan qingkuang," August 30, 1955, WCA.
51. "Wushan xian yijiuwuwu nian shuitu baochi gongzuo zongjie." See also "Wushan xian shuitu baochi zhong de ji dian tihui"; "Wushan xian yijiuwuwu nian shuitu baochi gongzuo zongjie (caogao)," WCA.
52. Grain production in Wushan County in 1949 was 29,490,000 kg in total and a meager 49 kg per *mu*. By 1956 output in the county had increased to 57,120,000 kg overall and 80.5 kg per *mu*. Wushan xianzhi bianzuan weiyuanhui, *Wushan xianzhi*, 267.
53. In 1952, Dengjiabao had 300 *mu* (20 hectares) of bunds and only 50 *mu* (3.33 hectares) of level terraces (accounting for 12.5 percent and 2 percent of total cultivated area, respectively); by 1955 it had 2,077 *mu* (138.46 hectares) of bunds and 340 *mu* (24.66 hectares) of terraces (85.4 percent and 13.8 percent of cultivated area). "Dengjiabao shuitu baochi dianxing diaocha baogao," 15, 22.
54. Data on per capita output in Dengjiabao come from the investigation conducted in 1961 by the Tianshui Water and Soil Conservation Experiment Station ("Dengjiabao shuitu baochi dianxing diaocha baogao," 17). Because the investigation sought to cut through false reporting that occurred during the Great Leap Forward and acquire accurate information on local conditions, I consider the data relatively reliable. Dengjiabao sold 6,300 *jin* of "surplus grain" to the state in 1954 (2.3 percent of total output) and 9,632 *jin* (3.25 percent of output) in 1955 ("Wushan xian Dengjiabao san nian lai shuitu baochi gongzuo jiben zongjie"; Liu, "Lü shui qing shan gaoyu tian"). Surplus grain sales increased to 24,141 *jin* (5.9 percent of output) in 1956 ("Qianmo zongheng hua guo manmu"). I have not found data on grain taxes in Dengjiabao for 1953–55, so my estimates assume a tax rate of 9 percent of output based on the tax rates for Gansu Province given

in Walker, *Food Procurement*, 50. Estimates for per capita grain availability after procurements from 1956–60 assume a total net extraction rate of 19.5 percent based on the 152,690 *jin* of grain tax payments and 185,750 *jin* of compulsory sales made by Dengjiabao during those years ("Dengjiabao shuitu baochi dianxing diaocha baogao," 5). If grain taxes are added, this rate roughly aligns with the reported 46,000 *jin* of surplus grain (11 percent of output) that Dengjiabao sold in 1957 ("Jianshe shanqu de bangyang") and is only marginally lower than the average total net procurement rates (taxes plus compulsory sales) in Gansu from 1953 to 1962 given by Ash, "Squeezing the Peasants," 979, 994. Food energy availability estimates rely on conversion ratios derived from Piazza, *Food Consumption*, 77. These estimates, it must be pointed out, are merely plausible calculations based on the simplest and most transparent assumptions. They may or may not reflect the actual annual figures and I have rounded them to avoid false precision. As a point of comparison, Walker (*Food Procurement*, 100, 152) estimates that per capita availability in Gansu after government transfers was 1,327 calories a day in 1953, 1,600 calories in 1954, 1,793 calories in 1955, 2,683 calories in 1956, 2,119 calories in 1957, and 1,552 calories in 1959.

55. "Wushan xian shuitu baochi jishu xunlian gongzuo zongjie baogao."
56. "Wushan xian shuitu baochi gongzuo zhuanye huiyi zongjie baogao."
57. "Wushan xian shuitu baochi gongzuo zhuanye huiyi zongjie baogao."
58. Wushan xian renmin weiyuanhui, "Guohuai xiang quanmian kaizhan shuitu baochi gongzuo zongjie baogao."
59. Quotations in this paragraph are from Wushan xian renmin weiyuanhui, "Guohuai xiang quanmian kaizhan shuitu baochi gongzuo zongjie baogao."
60. Wushan xian renmin weiyuanhui, "Guohuai xiang quanmian kaizhan shuitu baochi gongzuo zongjie baogao."
61. Wushan xian renmin weiyuanhui, "Guohuai xiang quanmian kaizhan shuitu baochi gongzuo zongjie baogao."
62. Wushan xian renmin weiyuanhui, "Guohuai xiang quanmian kaizhan shuitu baochi gongzuo zongjie baogao."
63. Wushan xian renmin weiyuanhui, "Guohuai xiang quanmian kaizhan shuitu baochi gongzuo zongjie baogao."
64. Wushan xian renmin weiyuanhui, "Guohuai xiang quanmian kaizhan shuitu baochi gongzuo zongjie baogao."
65. Wushan xian renmin weiyuanhui, "Guohuai xiang quanmian kaizhan shuitu baochi gongzuo zongjie baogao."
66. Wushan xian renmin weiyuanhui, "Guohuai xiang quanmian kaizhan shuitu baochi gongzuo zongjie baogao."
67. "Wushan xian shuitu baochi gongzuo zhuanye huiyi zongjie baogao."
68. Wushan xian renmin weiyuanhui, "Guohuai xiang quanmian kaizhan shuitu

baochi gongzuo zongjie baogao." See also "Wushan xian shuitu baochi gongzuo zhuanye huiyi zongjie baogao."

69. Wushan xian renmin weiyuanhui, "Guohuai xiang quanmian kaizhan shuitu baochi gongzuo zongjie baogao."

70. Wushan xian renmin weiyuanhui, "Guohuai xiang quanmian kaizhan shuitu baochi gongzuo zongjie baogao." See also "Wushan xian shuitu baochi gongzuo zhuanye huiyi zongjie baogao."

71. Wushan xian renmin weiyuanhui, "Guohuai xiang quanmian kaizhan shuitu baochi gongzuo zongjie baogao."

72. Wushan Dengjiabao gongzuozu, "Wushan Dengjiabao guanyu youlin fuyu qingkuang baogao," November 12, 1955, WCA.

73. Wushan Dengjiabao gongzuozu, "Wushan Dengjiabao guanyu youlin fuyu qingkuang baogao."

74. This total included 60.4 workdays contributed by Zhangjiabao from 1954 to summer 1955. Wushan Dengjiabao gongzuozu, "Wushan Dengjiabao guanyu youlin fuyu qingkuang baogao."

75. Wushan Dengjiabao gongzuozu, "Wushan Dengjiabao guanyu youlin fuyu qingkuang baogao."

76. Wushan Dengjiabao gongzuozu, "Wushan Dengjiabao guanyu youlin fuyu qingkuang baogao."

77. Wushan Dengjiabao gongzuozu, "Wushan Dengjiabao guanyu youlin fuyu qingkuang baogao."

78. On labor models, see Hershatter, *Gender of Memory*, ch. 8.

79. "Wushan xian Dengjiabao zhongdian gongzuozu yijiuwuwu nian gongzuo zongjie baogao," December 30, 1955, WCA.

80. Interview, May 2018.

81. "Wushan xian Dengjiabao zhongdian gongzuozu yijiuwuwu nian gongzuo zongjie baogao."

82. "Qingniantuan Wushan xianwei guanyu zhaokai qingnian shuitu baochi huodong fenzi hui jihua," August 1, 1955, WCA.

83. "Wushan xian yijiuwuwu nian shuitu baochi gongzuo zongjie."

84. "Wushan xian Dengjiabao zhongdian gongzuozu yijiuwuwu nian gongzuo zongjie baogao."

85. "Wushan xian shuitu baochi gongzuo xunlian gongzuo zongjie baogao."

86. Li, "Huiyi zai Yan'an zhaokai de wu sheng (qu) qingnian zaolin dahui," 30. For the text of Li's comments at the afforestation conference, see "Women de jiaxiang yi jibenshang zhizhi le shuitu liushi."

87. "Wushan xian Dengjiabao zhongdian gongzuozu yijiuwuwu nian gongzuo zongjie baogao."

88. "Wushan xian Dengjiabao zhongdian gongzuozu yijiuwuwu nian gongzuo zongjie baogao."

89. "Wushan xian renmin weiyuanhui tongbao," December 7, 1955, WCA.

90. Wushan Dengjiabao gongzuozu, "Dengjiabao liyong ba nei xu shui jiaoguan dong mai qingkuang baogao," December 7, 1955, WCA.

91. All quotes in this paragraph are from Wushan Dengjiabao gongzuozu, "Dengjiabao liyong ba nei xu shui jiaoguan dong mai qingkuang baogao."

92. Wushan Dengjiabao gongzuozu, "Dengjiabao liyong ba nei xu shui jiaoguan dong mai qingkuang baogao." For similar sentiments, see "Wushan xian Dengjiabao zhongdian gongzuozu yijiuwuwu nian gongzuo zongjie baogao."

93. Wushan Dengjiabao gongzuozu, "Dengjiabao liyong ba nei xu shui jiaoguan dong mai qingkuang baogao."

94. Wushan Dengjiabao gongzuozu, "Dengjiabao liyong ba nei xu shui jiaoguan dong mai qingkuang baogao."

95. "Wushan xian Dengjiabao zhongdian gongzuozu yijiuwuwu nian gongzuo zongjie baogao."

96. Wushan Dengjiabao gongzuozu, "Dengjiabao liyong ba nei xu shui jiaoguan dong mai qingkuang baogao."

97. Wushan Dengjiabao gongzuozu, "Dengjiabao liyong ba nei xu shui jiaoguan dong mai qingkuang baogao."

98. Wushan Dengjiabao gongzuozu, "Dengjiabao liyong ba nei xu shui jiaoguan dong mai qingkuang baogao." See also "Wushan xian Dengjiabao zhongdian gongzuozu yijiuwuwu nian gongzuo zongjie baogao."

99. Wushan Dengjiabao gongzuozu, "Dengjiabao liyong ba nei xu shui jiaoguan dong mai qingkuang baogao."

100. Wushan Dengjiabao gongzuozu, "Dengjiabao liyong ba nei xu shui jiaoguan dong mai qingkuang baogao."

101. Wushan Dengjiabao gongzuozu, "Dengjiabao liyong ba nei xu shui jiaoguan dong mai qingkuang baogao."

FOUR "Dams Have Really Worn Us Out"

1. Harrell, *Ecological History*, 98–103; Pietz, *Yellow River*, 175. The significance of chemical fertilizer shortages is discussed in Marks, *China*, 267–71.

2. On the nationwide water conservancy campaign, see Pietz, *Yellow River*, 174–82.

3. Harrell, *Ecological History*, 111.

4. Madsen, "Countryside under Communism," 637–39; Naughton, *Chinese Economy*, 234–36; Li, *Village China*, 39, 41; Shue, *Peasant China in Transition*, 292.

5. Harrell, *Ecological History*, 114; Pietz, *Yellow River*, 177.

6. Pietz, *Yellow River*, 181.

7. Wushan xianzhi bianzuan weiyuanhui, *Wushan xianzhi*, 262–63; Yu, "Wushan xian tuiguang 10 wan mu baogu he 20 wan jing tang ba jiao quan de lishi jiyi," 368.

8. Wushan xianzhi bianzuan weiyuanhui, *Wushan xianzhi*, 262–63. See also Wushan xian weihui, "Wushan xian bing she shengji de jingyan jieshao."

9. "Dengjiabao wuliu nian gongzuo kaizhan qingkuang," May 1956, WCA.

10. Yu, "Wushan xian tuiguang 10 wan mu baogu he 20 wan jing tang ba jiao quan de lishi jiyi," 368.

11. On "mass experience" in Mao-era scientific discourse, see Schmalzer, *Red Revolution, Green Revolution*; Rui and Matten, *Knowledge Production*; Fan, "Collective Monitoring, Collective Defense,"; Fan, "People's War."

12. The discursive significance of "old peasants" is analyzed in Schmalzer, *Red Revolution, Green Revolution*, 100–109.

13. Mostern, *Yellow River*, 25, 37.

14. Mostern, *Yellow River*, 44.

15. Mostern, *Yellow River*, 27.

16. Yu, "Wushan xian tuiguang 10 wan mu baogu he 20 wan jing tang ba jiao quan de lishi jiyi," 372.

17. Yu, "Wushan xian tuiguang 10 wan mu baogu he 20 wan jing tang ba jiao quan de lishi jiyi," 372.

18. "Wushan xian shuitu baochi gongzuo di er ci gongzuo qingkuang jianbao," February 23, 1956, WCA.

19. "Wushan xian shuitu baochi gongzuo di er ci gongzuo qingkuang jianbao."

20. "Wushan xian renmin weiyuanhui tongzhi," February 7, 1956, WCA.

21. "Wushan xian shuitu baochi gongzuo di er ci gongzuo qingkuang jianbao."

22. Heilmann, "Local Experiments." See also Schmalzer, *Red Revolution, Green Revolution*, 43–44.

23. Yu, "Wushan xian tuiguang 10 wan mu baogu he 20 wan jing tang ba jiao quan de lishi jiyi," 373.

24. Zhonggong Dongshun zhibu, "Wushan Dongshun xiang da jing wa quan qingkuang jianjie baogao," February 10, 1956, WCA; "Dongshun gaoji nongyeshe tao quan wa jing baogao," February 10, 1956, WCA.

25. "Dongshun xiang tao quan da jing qingkuang baogao," February 10, 1956, WCA.

26. Zhonggong Dongshun zhibu, "Wushan Dongshun xiang da jing wa quan qingkuang jianjie baogao." See also "Dongshun xiang tao quan da jing qingkuang baogao."

27. "Dongshun xiang tao quan da jing qingkuang baogao." See also "Dongshun xiang tao quan da jing qingkuang baogao."

28. Zhonggong Dongshun zhibu, "Wushan Dongshun xiang da jing wa quan qingkuang jianjie baogao." See also "Dongshun xiang tao quan da jing qingkuang baogao."

29. "Dongshun xiang tao quan da jing qingkuang baogao."

30. "Dongshun xiang tao quan da jing qingkuang baogao."

31. "Dongshun xiang tao quan da jing qingkuang baogao." Another report from Dongshun's higher-level cooperative did not mention one complaint or six misgivings, but instead spoke of "four resistances": "1) Work in the cooperative is busy and [we're] rushing to handle substantive problems, [so we] can't spare people to dig wells. 2) Digging wells and springs is not as important as hauling fertilizer. 3) Digging wells and springs cannot be done successfully in winter since there's no water; digging springs and wells can only be done in the springtime. 4) [We] don't have direction from technical cadres and have never dug wells; at the same time, if [we] dig them and they collapse, what will [we] do?" See "Dongshun gaoji nongyeshe tao quan wa jing baogao."

32. "Wushan Dengjiabao shanding shang zhaodao le shuiyuan," *Gansu ribao*, March 7, 1956.

33. Zhonggong Dongshun zhibu, "Wushan Dongshun xiang da jing wa quan qingkuang jianjie baogao."

34. Zhonggong Dongshun zhibu, "Wushan Dongshun xiang da jing wa quan qingkuang jianjie baogao." See also "Dongshun xiang tao quan da jing qingkuang baogao."

35. "Dongshun xiang tao quan da jing qingkuang baogao."

36. "Dongshun xiang tao quan da jing qingkuang baogao."

37. All quotations in this paragraph are from Zhonggong Dongshun zhibu, "Wushan Dongshun xiang da jing wa quan qingkuang jianjie baogao."

38. "Dongshun xiang tao quan da jing qingkuang baogao."

39. Zhonggong Dongshun zhibu, "Wushan Dongshun xiang da jing wa quan qingkuang jianjie baogao."

40. Zhonggong Dongshun zhibu, "Wushan Dongshun xiang da jing wa quan qingkuang jianjie baogao." A slightly different list appears in "Dongshun xiang tao quan wa jing qingkuang baogao."

41. Zhonggong Dongshun zhibu, "Wushan Dongshun xiang da jing wa quan qingkuang jianjie baogao"; "Dongshun xiang tao quan da jing qingkuang baogao."

42. Zhonggong Dongshun zhibu, "Wushan Dongshun xiang da jing wa quan qingkuang jianjie baogao."

43. Zhonggong Dongshun zhibu, "Wushan Dongshun xiang da jing wa quan qingkuang jianjie baogao"; "Dongshun xiang tao quan da jing qingkuang baogao."

44. "Dongshun xiang tao quan da jing qingkuang baogao"; "Wushan Dengjiabao shanding shang zhaodao le shuiyuan."

45. Zhonggong Dongshun zhibu, "Wushan Dongshun xiang da jing wa quan qingkuang jianjie baogao." See also "Wushan xian shuitu baochi gongzuo di er ci gongzuo qingkuang jianbao"; "Dongshun xiang tao quan da jing qingkuang baogao."

46. All quotations in this paragraph are from Zhonggong Dongshun zhibu, "Wushan Dongshun xiang da jing wa quan qingkuang jianjie baogao."

47. Zhonggong Dongshun zhibu, "Wushan Dongshun xiang da jing wa quan qingkuang jianjie baogao." See also "Wushan xian shuitu baochi gongzuo di er ci gongzuo qingkuang jianbao."

48. Zhonggong Dongshun zhibu, "Wushan Dongshun xiang da jing wa quan qingkuang jianjie baogao."

49. Zhonggong Dongshun zhibu, "Wushan Dongshun xiang da jing wa quan qingkuang jianjie baogao."

50. "Wushan xian shuitu baochi gongzuo di er ci gongzuo qingkuang jianbao."

51. Zhonggong Dongshun zhibu, "Wushan Dongshun xiang da jing wa quan qingkuang jianjie baogao."

52. Yu, "Wushan xian tuiguang 10 wan mu baogu he 20 wan jing tang ba jiao quan de lishi jiyi," 373.

53. Yu, "Wushan xian tuiguang 10 wan mu baogu he 20 wan jing tang ba jiao quan de lishi jiyi," 373.

54. Yu, "Wushan xian tuiguang 10 wan mu baogu he 20 wan jing tang ba jiao quan de lishi jiyi," 373.

55. Yu, "Wushan xian tuiguang 10 wan mu baogu he 20 wan jing tang ba jiao quan de lishi jiyi," 374.

56. All quotations in this paragraph are from Yu, "Wushan xian tuiguang 10 wan mu baogu he 20 wan jing tang ba jiao quan de lishi jiyi," 372–73.

57. Yu, "Wushan xian tuiguang 10 wan mu baogu he 20 wan jing tang ba jiao quan de lishi jiyi," 374.

58. "Wushan xian renmin weiyuanhui jinji tongzhi," February 28, 1956, WCA.

59. Yu, "Wushan xian tuiguang 10 wan mu baogu he 20 wan jing tang ba jiao quan de lishi jiyi," 374.

60. "Wushan xian yijiuwuliu nian shang ban nian shuitu baochi gongzuo qingkuang jianjie," June 29, 1956, WCA.

61. Wushan xian renmin weiyuanhui, "1956 nian shuitu baochi gongzuo kaizhan qingkuang zongjie baogao," January 15, 1957, WCA.

62. Wushan xian renmin weiyuanhui, "1956 nian shuitu baochi gongzuo kaizhan qingkuang zongjie baogao."

63. Wushan xian renmin weiyuanhui, "1956 nian shuitu baochi gongzuo kaizhan qingkuang zongjie baogao."

64. "Wushan xian yijiuwuliu nian shang ban nian shuitu baochi gongzuo qingkuang jianjie."
65. "Wushan xian yijiuwuliu nian shang ban nian shuitu baochi gongzuo qingkuang jianjie."
66. "Wushan xian shuitu baochi jishu xun gan huiyi zongjie," December 8, 1956, WCA.
67. Yu, "Wushan xian tuiguang 10 wan mu baogu he 20 wan jing tang ba jiao quan de lishi jiyi," 374.
68. Yu, "Wushan xian tuiguang 10 wan mu baogu he 20 wan jing tang ba jiao quan de lishi jiyi," 374.
69. Wushan xian renmin weiyuanhui, "1956 nian shuitu baochi gongzuo kaizhan qingkuang zongjie baogao."
70. Wushan xian renmin weiyuanhui, "1956 nian shuitu baochi gongzuo kaizhan qingkuang zongjie baogao."
71. "Wushan xian yijiuwuliu nian shang ban nian shuitu baochi gongzuo qingkuang jianjie."
72. "Wushan xian yijiuwuliu nian shang ban nian shuitu baochi gongzuo qingkuang jianjie."
73. "Wushan xian linye shuitu baochi zhuanye huiyi," September 26–30, 1956, WCA.
74. Lan Wenwei, "Xinguangshe weishenme hui jianshao shouru?" *Gansu ribao*, November 25, 1956.
75. Lan Wenwei, "Xinguangshe weishenme hui jianshao shouru?"
76. "Wushan xian shuitu baochi jishu xun gan huiyi zongjie."
77. "Zhonggong Wushan xianwei nongyeshe zhuren zuotanhui tingqu qunzhong yijian gaijin lingdao fangfa," *Gansu ribao*, December 19, 1956.
78. Wushan xian renmin weiyuanhui, "1956 nian shuitu baochi gongzuo kaizhan qingkuang zongjie baogao."
79. Wushan xian renmin weiyuanhui, "1956 nian shuitu baochi gongzuo kaizhan qingkuang zongjie baogao."
80. Yu, "Wushan xian tuiguang 10 wan mu baogu he 20 wan jing tang ba jiao quan de lishi jiyi," 375.
81. Yu, "Wushan xian tuiguang 10 wan mu baogu he 20 wan jing tang ba jiao quan de lishi jiyi," 374. Earlier archival documents give slightly different figures. According to a report on conservation work during the first half of 1956, when the irrigation campaign ended in late April, Wushan County claimed to have dug 3,986 wells, 5,157 ponds, 12,907 water cellars, 11,703 springs, and 5,946 ponds. The campaign supposedly also built 11,842 dams and constructed or repaired 500 channels. Irrigated land reportedly expanded by 119,500 *mu* (7,966.66 hectares)

and "point-irrigated" land reportedly increased by another 236,000 *mu* (15,733 hectares). But the report averred that 5,124 of these ponds, dams, and water cellars were "wasted goods," which amounted to 9.8 percent of the original total of 52,041. Subsequent investigations brought even more false reports to light. "Wushan xian yijiuwuliu nian shang ban nian shuitu baochi gongzuo qingkuang jianjie."

82. Yu, "Wushan xian tuiguang 10 wan mu baogu he 20 wan jing tang ba jiao quan de lishi jiyi," 374–75.

83. Yu, "Wushan xian tuiguang 10 wan mu baogu he 20 wan jing tang ba jiao quan de lishi jiyi," 375.

84. "Guanyu dangqian shuitu baochi gongzuo de chubu anpai yijian," November 6, 1956, WCA.

85. Yu, "Wushan xian tuiguang 10 wan mu baogu he 20 wan jing tang ba jiao quan de lishi jiyi," 375.

86. Wushan Xianghe tuba gongcheng weiyuanhui, "Wushan xian Xianghe gongcheng jieduan zongjie," July 15, 1956, YRCC; "Wushan xian yuan zhi san yue niansan ri fen shuitu baochi gongzuo di si ci wancheng qingkuang baogao," March 28, 1956, WCA.

87. Zhonggong Wushan xian weiyuanhui and Wushan xian renmin weiyuanhui, "Guanyu qingqiu Xianghegou tuba gongcheng fugong de baogao," October 10, 1956, YRCC; Wushan Xianghe tuba gongcheng weiyuanhui, "Wushan xian Xianghe gongcheng jieduan zongjie."

88. "Wushan xian yuan zhi san yue niansan ri fen shuitu baochi gongzuo di si ci wancheng qingkuang baogao"; Wushan Xianghe tuba gongcheng weiyuanhui, "Wushan xian Xianghe gongcheng jieduan zongjie."

89. Wushan Xianghe tuba gongcheng weiyuanhui, "Wushan xian Xianghe gongcheng jieduan zongjie."

90. Wushan Xianghe tuba gongcheng weiyuanhui, "Wushan xian Xianghe gongcheng jieduan zongjie." See also Zhonggong Wushan xian weiyuanhui and Wushan xian renmin weiyuanhui, "Guanyu qingqiu Xianghegou tuba gongcheng fugong de baogao."

91. Wushan Xianghe tuba gongcheng weiyuanhui, "Wushan xian Xianghe gongcheng jieduan zongjie."

92. Wushan Xianghe tuba gongcheng weiyuanhui, "Wushan xian Xianghe gongcheng jieduan zongjie."

93. Wushan Xianghe tuba gongcheng weiyuanhui, "Wushan xian Xianghe gongcheng jieduan zongjie."

94. Zhonggong Wushan xian weiyuanhui and Wushan xian renmin weiyuanhui, "Guanyu qingqiu Xianghegou tuba gongcheng fugong de baogao."

95. Wushan xian renmin weiyuanhui, "1956 nian shuitu baochi gongzuo kaizhan qingkuang zongjie baogao."

96. Zhonggong Wushan xian weiyuanhui and Wushan xian renmin weiyuanhui, "Guanyu qingqiu Xianghegou tuba gongcheng fugong de baogao."

97. Wushan Xianghe tuba gongcheng weiyuanhui, "Wushan xian Xianghe gongcheng jieduan zongjie."

98. Wushan Xianghe tuba gongcheng weiyuanhui, "Wushan xian Xianghe gongcheng jieduan zongjie."

99. Wushan Xianghe tuba gongcheng weiyuanhui, "Wushan xian Xianghe gongcheng jieduan zongjie."

100. "Wushan xian linye shuitu baochi zhuanye huiyi."

101. Wushan Xianghe tuba gongcheng weiyuanhui, "Wushan xian Xianghe gongcheng jieduan zongjie."

102. Wushan Xianghe tuba gongcheng weiyuanhui, "Wushan xian Xianghe gongcheng jieduan zongjie."

103. Zhonggong Wushan xian weiyuanhui and Wushan xian renmin weiyuanhui, "Guanyu qingqiu Xianghegou tuba gongcheng fugong de baogao."

104. Zhonggong Wushan xian weiyuanhui and Wushan xian renmin weiyuanhui, "Guanyu qingqiu Xianghegou tuba gongcheng fugong de baogao."

105. Zhonggong Wushan xian weiyuanhui and Wushan xian renmin weiyuanhui, "Guanyu qingqiu Xianghegou tuba gongcheng fugong de baogao."

106. Zhonggong Wushan xian weiyuanhui and Wushan xian renmin weiyuanhui, "Guanyu qingqiu Xianghegou tuba gongcheng fugong de baogao."

107. "Dui Wushan Xianghe tuba fugong de yijian," November 28, 1956, YRCC.

108. "Dui Wushan Xianghe tuba fugong de yijian." The experiment station estimated that building one dam (in addition to reinforcing and preparing its foundation) took 304,000 workdays. Mobilizing two thousand able-bodied laborers to construct one dam required around 150 days, not including workdays spent cleaning the dam's foundation and preparing materials. Building three dams at Xiang River gully required a total of 576,000 workdays, with three thousand able-bodied laborers devoting 192 days to the project.

109. "Dui Wushan Xianghe tuba fugong de yijian." Gansu's Agriculture and Forestry Department conveyed this decision to the Wushan county committee, the Tianshui experiment station, and other agencies on November 30. See "Gansu sheng nonglinting dui Wushan Xianghegou tuba fugong de yijian," November 30, 1956, YRCC.

110. Yu, "Wushan xian tuiguang 10 wan mu baogu he 20 wan jing tang ba jiao quan de lishi jiyi," 375.

111. Kong, "Dengjiabao huifu tuba ji liaojie dangqian shengchan qingkuang baogao," July 3, 1956, WCA.

112. Kong, "Dengjiabao huifu tuba ji liaojie dangqian shengchan qingkuang baogao."

113. Kong, "Dengjiabao huifu tuba ji liaojie dangqian shengchan qingkuang baogao."

114. Kong, "Dengjiabao huifu tuba ji liaojie dangqian shengchan qingkuang baogao."

115. "Tianshui shuibaozhan yijiuliuyi nian Wushan Dengjiabao shuitu baochi jiluben," 3.

116. Dengjiabao gongzuozu, "Dengjiabao Tiaozigou shanwan shuitang shigong qingkuang," December 10, 1956, WCA.

117. Dengjiabao gongzuozu, "Dengjiabao Tiaozigou shanwan shuitang shigong qingkuang."

118. In the first week, twenty workers dug 360 cubic meters of earth per day (22 percent of the estimated total of 1,627 cubic meters), so the work group expected to have the reservoir finished within twenty days. Dengjiabao gongzuozu, "Dengjiabao Tiaozigou shanwan shuitang shigong qingkuang."

119. Dengjiabao gongzuozu, "Dengjiabao Tiaozigou shanwan shuitang shigong qingkuang."

120. Dengjiabao gongzuozu, "Wushan xian Dongshun xiang Dengjiabao xieshui jianzhuwu muqian qingkuang baogao," December 10, 1956, WCA.

121. Dengjiabao gongzuozu, "Wushan xian Dongshun xiang Dengjiabao xieshui jianzhuwu muqian qingkuang baogao."

122. Dengjiabao gongzuozu, "Wushan xian Dongshun xiang Dengjiabao xieshui jianzhuwu muqian qingkuang baogao."

123. Wushan xian renmin weiyuanhui, "Guanyu Dengjiabao xieguan anzhuang jihua touzi baogao," December 13, 1956, WCA.

124. Wushan xian renmin weiyuanhui, "Guanyu Dengjiabao xieguan anzhuang jihua touzi baogao," note dated December 18, 1956.

125. Tianshui shuitu baochi gongzuo tuiguangzhan, "Guanyu Dengjiabao tuba anzhuang xieshuiguan bogei cailiao touzi 880 yuan de fuhan," December 24, 1956, WCA.

126. Seow, *Carbon Technocracy*, 282.

FIVE "Learn from Dengjiabao"

1. Muscolino, *Ecology of War*, 242–45.
2. Riskin, *China's Political Economy*, 122.
3. Ji, *Linguistic Engineering*, 89.
4. The costliest Great Leap hydraulic engineering project in Gansu was the Tao River diversion, which is masterfully explored in Liu, *Gongdi shehui*. See also Yang, *Tombstone*, 122–25.

5. On the importance of soil conservation for the Sanmenxia project, see Ding, "Yellow River."

6. Interview, May 2018.

7. All quotations in this paragraph are from Hu, "Yi ge lizheng shangyou de xianjin xian," *Renmin ribao*, October 8, 1958, 6.

8. All quotations in this paragraph are from Okie, "Beauty and Habitation," 260-61.

9. The classic treatment of how work connects people with nature is White, "Are You an Environmentalist." Coproduction of human experience and the environment through the labor of young people sent to Manchuria's Sanjiang Plain during the Mao era is discussed in Rogaski, *Knowing Manchuria*, ch. 8.

10. "Wushan xian shuitu baochi jishu xun gan huiyi zongjie."

11. "Dengjiabao dui quan xian ge she de shuitu baochi tiaozhanshu," November 25, 1956, WCA.

12. Dengjiabao gongzuozu, "Dongshun xiang Dengjiabao zai xian shuitu baochi huiyi hou shuitu baochi tuji qingkuang," November 30, 1956, WCA.

13. "Dengjiabao dui quan xian ge she de shuitu baochi tiaozhanshu"; "Dongshun xiang Dengjiabao zai xian shuitu baochi huiyi hou shuitu baochi tuji qingkuang."

14. "Dengjiabao dui quan xian ge she de shuitu baochi tiaozhanshu."

15. "Wushan xian renmin weiyuanhui zhuanfa Dongshun xiang Dengjiabao dongji shuitu baochi gongzuo jihua yi fen xi yingzhan," November 28, 1956, WCA.

16. "Wushan xian bai fen zhi liushi de tudi kongzhizhu shuitu liushi xianxiang," *Gansu ribao*, July 6, 1957.

17. "You yi ge Dengjiabao—Changjiawan," *Wushan bao*, August 4, 1957.

18. Ho, *Curating Revolution*.

19. "Qianmo zongheng hua guo manmu—Dengjiabao jiang daichu geng duo Dengjiabao (zhanlan manbu)," *Wushan bao*, October 16, 1957.

20. "Qianmo zongheng hua guo manmu."

21. "Qianmo zongheng hua guo manmu."

22. "Qianmo zongheng hua guo manmu."

23. Tianshui zhuanshu linshuiju, "Tianshui zhuanqu jinian lai shuili shuibao gongzuo fazhan qingkuang," 1958, 5–6, TMA.

24. Tianshui zhuanshu linshuiju, "Tianshui zhuanqu jinian lai shuili shuibao gongzuo fazhan qingkuang," 5–6. On Daquan Mountain, see Hao, "Construction of Terraced Fields," 109–10.

25. Tianshui zhuanshu linshuiju, "Tianshui zhuanqu jinian lai shuili shuibao gongzuo fazhan qingkuang," 5–6.

26. "Shangu xin cun—Dengjiabao," *Renmin ribao*, October 29, 1957, 4.

27. "Jianshe shanqu de bangyang."

28. Gu, "Lianghao de lingdao fangfa huihuang de jianshe chengjiu," 2.

29. "Quanguo shuitu baochi gongzuo huiyi shou jiang Dengjiabao Wushan xian Tianshui shuitu baochi shiyanzhan huo tedeng jiang," *Gansu ribao*, December 24, 1957. See also "Dengjiabao shuitu baochi gongzuo ronghuo quanguo yideng jiang," *Wushan bao*, November 16, 1957; "Jiangli baochi shuitu mofan," *Renmin ribao*, December 24, 1957, 2; Wushan xianzhi bianzuan weiyuanhui, *Wushan xianzhi*, 328–29; Tianshui shi difangzhi bianweihui, *Tianshui shizhi*, 1114–15.

30. "Quanguo shuitu baochi gongzuo huiyi zhongshi Wushan lingdao jingyan shuli le shanqu shuitu baochi gongzuo de huihuang bangyang," *Gansu ribao*, December 25, 1957.

31. "Quanguo shuitu baochi gongzuo huiyi zhongshi Wushan lingdao jingyan shuli le shanqu shuitu baochi gongzuo de huihuang bangyang."

32. "Quanguo shuitu baochi gongzuo huiyi zhongshi Wushan lingdao jingyan shuli le shanqu shuitu baochi gongzuo de huihuang bangyang."

33. "Quanguo shuitu baochi gongzuo huiyi zhongshi Wushan lingdao jingyan shuli le shanqu shuitu baochi gongzuo de huihuang bangyang."

34. Zhonggong Wushan xianwei, "Juda de bianhua."

35. "Ben sheng chaoe wancheng yuanding mingnian shuili jihua," *Gansu ribao*, December 31, 1957.

36. "Jinnian jiancheng sanqian ge 'Dengjiabao' jiang zai wu nian nei jiben kongzhi shuitu liushi," *Gansu ribao*, January 11, 1958; "Quansheng shuili shuitu baochi yundong jixu yuejin," *Gansu ribao*, January 24, 1958.

37. Tianshui zhuanshu linshuiju, "Tianshui zhuanqu jinian lai shuili shuibao gongzuo fazhan qingkuang," 11.

38. "Gansu zhengqu san nian nei jiben shixian shuilihua," *Gansu ribao*, February 22, 1958; "Xingxiu shuili baochi shuitu gaibian ganhan mianmao," *Renmin ribao*, February 18, 1958, 10. See also Yang, *Mian xiang qunzhong*, 215–16.

39. "Quansheng yi chuxian erqianwubai duo ge Dengjiabao," *Gansu ribao*, February 28, 1958.

40. "Quansheng yi chuxian erqianwubai duo ge Dengjiabao"; "Yiwanwuqian ge 'Dengjiabao,'" *Renmin ribao*, March 4, 1958, 4.

41. "Jixu qianjin zailai yi ge shengshi haoda de shuitu baochi tuji yundong," *Gansu ribao*, April 5, 1958. By mid-August, Gansu claimed to have exceeded its annual conservation target by controlling water and soil loss on 46,878 square kilometers of land and creating over 14,133 key points like Dengjiabao. "Shelun huanying quanguo di san ci shuitu baochi huiyi zai Gansu zhaokai" and "Quansheng chaoe wancheng shuitu baochi renwu," *Gansu ribao*, September 3, 1958.

42. "Zhou Enlai guanyu Huanghe guihua he Sanmenxia gongcheng wenti zhi Mao Zedong xin (yijiuwuba nian liu yue ershijiu ri)," 24.

43. Tianshui zhuanqu shuitu baochi weiyuanhui, "Yinfa Dengjiabao ge xiang shuitu baochi gongzuo de cuoshi he juti fangfa cankao you," May 15, 1958, QCA.

44. Tianshui zhuanyuan gongshu shuiliju, "Guanyu Tianshui xian Zhongliangqu zhaokai jishu geming cujinhui he Qingshui xian Hongfu xiang wu tian shixian liu ge Dengjiabao de tongbao," June 5, 1958, QCA.

45. All quotations in this paragraph are from Tianshui zhuanyuan gongshu shuiliju, "Guanyu Tianshui xian Zhongliangqu zhaokai jishu geming cujinhui he Qingshui xian Hongfu xiang wu tian shixian liu ge Dengjiabao de tongbao."

46. Tianshui zhuanyuan gongshu shuiliju, "Guanyu Tianshui xian Zhongliangqu zhaokai jishu geming cujinhui he Qingshui xian Hongfu xiang wu tian shixian liu ge Dengjiabao de tongbao."

47. "Qin'an xian chuxian Dengjiabao qingkuang baogao," May 19, 1958, QCA.

48. "Qin'an xian chuxian Dengjiabao qingkuang baogao."

49. "Jixu qianjin zai lai yi ge shengshi haoda de shuitu baochi tuji yundong."

50. Ji, *Linguistic Engineering*, 87–90; Muscolino, *Ecology of War*, 242–45.

51. Hu, "Yi ge lizheng shangyou de xianjin xian."

52. Tong, "Hongqi xian," 97.

53. Tong, "Hongqi xian," 97.

54. "Qianwan yingxiong da zhan Dengjiabao yao rang tuolaji rao shan feiben," *Gansu ribao*, July 10, 1958.

55. Interview, September 2019.

56. Interview, September 2019.

57. "Qianwan yingxiong da zhan Dengjiabao yao rang tuolaji rao shan feiben." See also Lan, "Rang Dengjiabao de guangrong qizhi zaidu piaoyang."

58. "Qianwan yingxiong da zhan Dengjiabao yao rang tuolaji rao shan feiben." On the Chenxiang tale, see Idema, "Precious Scroll"; Wilcox, *Revolutionary Bodies*, 99.

59. "Qianwan yingxiong da zhan Dengjiabao yao rang tuolaji rao shan feiben."

60. "Qianwan yingxiong da zhan Dengjiabao yao rang tuolaji rao shan feiben."

61. "Qianwan yingxiong da zhan Dengjiabao yao rang tuolaji rao shan feiben."

62. Gansu ribao, August 10, 1958.

63. "Jian shan bu jian gou cheng titian gengdi lian pian Dengjiabao shuitu baochi zhongdian gongcheng wangong," *Gansu ribao*, August 14, 1958. See also Hu, "Yi ge lizheng shangyou de xianjin xian"; Zhonggong Wushan xianwei, "Juda de bianhua"; Yao, "Wushan xian 'dayuejin' pianduan jishi," 111.

64. "Zhuoshui bian qingshui Xibei bian Jiangnan Wushan quanmian genzhi Weihe," *Gansu ribao*, July 24, 1958. See also "Yingjie quanguo di san ci shuitu baochi huiyi kaimu Wushan shiwan dajun zheng shan zhan shui," *Gansu ribao*, September 1, 1958.

65. Wushan xianzhi bianzuan weiyuanhui, *Wushan xianzhi*, 33. Wushan had a

population of 188,207 in 1954 and 189,380 in 1964. Wushan xianzhi bianzuan weiyuanhui, *Wushan xianzhi*, 111.

66. Tong, "Hongqi xian," 106.
67. Wushan xianzhi bianzuan weiyuanhui, *Wushan xianzhi*, 55. See also "Gaoju renmin gongshe hongqi Wushan Lintao shixian renmin gongshehua," *Gansu ribao*, September 9, 1958.
68. Li, *Village China*, 81–85; Madsen, "Countryside under Communism," 640–41.
69. "Gaoju renmin gongshe hongqi Wushan Lintao shixian renmin gongshehua."
70. Tianshui zhuanshu linshuiju, "Tianshui zhuanqu jinian lai shuili shuibao gongzuo fazhan qingkuang," 15–16.
71. Yao, "Wushan xian 'dayuejin' pianduan jishi," 111. Tianshui zhuanshu linshuiju, "Tianshui zhuanqu jinian lai shuili shuibao gongzuo fazhan qingkuang," 15–16. For songs inspired by the slogan, see Zhonggong Wushan xianwei xuanchuanbu and Wushan bao bianjibu, *Wushan min'ge*, 228, 230.
72. Yao, "Wushan xian 'dayuejin' pianduan jishi," 111.
73. The song appears in Lan and Zhu, "Wushan renmin xiu diqiu." See also Zhonggong Wushan xianwei xuanchuanbu and Wushan bao bianjibu, *Wushan min'ge*, 10–11.
74. Lan and Zhu, "Wushan renmin xiu diqiu."; Zhonggong Wushan xianwei xuanchuanbu and Wushan bao bianjibu, *Wushan min'ge*, 10–11.
75. "Jian shan bu jian gou cheng titian gengdi lian pian."
76. "Jian shan bu jian gou cheng titian gengdi lian pian." See also Zhonggong Wushan xianwei, "Juda de bianhua."
77. "Yingjie quanguo di san ci shuitu baochi huiyi kaimu."
78. "Jian shan bu jian gou cheng titian gengdi lian pian."
79. "Quanguo di san ci shuitu baochi huiyi kaimuci," *Gansu ribao*, September 3, 1958. Text of the speech also reprinted as Chen, "Quanguo di san ci shuitu baochi huiyi kaimuci," 3.
80. Hu, "Yi ge lizheng shangyou de xianjin xian."
81. "Canguan Dengjiabao yougan," *Renmin ribao*, September 20, 1958, 6. For a collection of big character posters and poems from the conference, see Gansu shuiliting, *Dazibao shige xuan*.
82. Yang, *Mian xiang qunzhong*, 216; Tianshui shi difangzhi bianweihui, *Tianshui shizhi*, 1114.
83. Interview, September 2019.
84. Interview, September 2019.
85. Zhonggong Wushan xianwei xuanchuanbu and Wushan bao bianjibu, *Wushan min'ge*, 231.
86. Interview, September 2019.
87. Interview with Deng Fenqin, September 2019.

88. Interview, September 2019.
89. Interview, September 2019.
90. Interview, September 2019.
91. Interview, September 2019.
92. "Tianshui shuibaozhan yijiuliuyi nian Wushan Dengjiabao shuitu baochi jiluben," 3.
93. Dengjiabao had 340 *mu* of level terraces in 1957 and 1,260 *mu* in 1958. Bunds decreased from 2,096 *mu* to 880 *mu* during the same period because the land on which they had been built was converted to level terraces. "Dengjiabao shuitu baochi dianxing diaocha baogao," 22.
94. The ratio of agricultural workdays to water and soil conservation workdays alone fell from 17.41:1 in 1957 to 4.9:1 in 1958. "Dengjiabao shuitu baochi dianxing diaocha baogao," 23.
95. Yang, *Tombstone*, 96. Sources on conservation campaigns in Tongwei can be found in Gansu sheng shuiliting, *Xue xianjin gan xianjin chao xianjin gaoju hongqi xiang qian jin!*; Gansu sheng shuiliting, *Zhengfu Huajialing*.
96. The term is drawn from Ross, *Ecology and Power*, 114.
97. Benson, "Aesthetic and Other Values," 222.
98. Scott, *Seeing Like a State*, 224–25.

SIX "Water Has Aroused the Girls' Hearts"

1. I adopt Joan Scott's definition of gender as "a constitutive element of social relationships based on perceived differences between the sexes" and "a primary way of signifying relationships of power," but admittedly pay more attention to the first part of the definition than the latter. Scott, *Gender*, 42.
2. Bray, *Technology and Gender*; Hershatter, *Gender of Memory*; Eyferth, "Women's Work"; Brown, "Dutiful Help"; Jacka, *Women's Work*, chs. 1–2.
3. On rural women in the Soviet Union, see Bridger, *Women in the Soviet Countryside*, 1987.
4. "Jianshe shanqu de yimian hongqi," 38.
5. "Dengjiabao shuitu baochi dianxing diaocha baogao," 2.
6. "Jianshe shanqu de yimian hongqi," 38.
7. "Jianshe shanqu de yimian hongqi," 38.
8. "Dengjiabao shuitu baochi dianxing diaocha baogao," 2; "Jianshe shanqu de yimian hongqi," 38. Oral history interviews also attest to the saying's prevalence. Dengjiabao is pronounced "Dengjiabu" in the local dialect, so the saying rhymes: *you nü bu jia Dengjiabu, xia shan tiao shui shizai ku.*
9. "Wushan xian de shuili he shuitu baochi zheng yi shi wu qianli de sudu, feiyue de fazhan zhe," 10.

10. Interview, May 2018.
11. Interview, May 2018.
12. "Jianshe shanqu de yimian hongqi," 48.
13. "Jianshe shanqu de yimian hongqi," 43–44. Local archives sometimes contain lists of five or six rarities. See Wushan xian renmin weiyuanhui, "1956 nian shuitu baochi gongzuo kaizhan qingkuang zongjie baogao"; "Wushan xian wuliu nian shuitu baochi chubu jianjie baogao," November 1956, WCA.
14. Liu, "Lü shui qing shan gaoyu tian," *Renmin ribao*, November 28, 1956.
15. Liu, "Lü shui qing shan gaoyu tian."
16. "Jianshe shanqu de yimian hongqi," 44.
17. "Wushan xian de shuili he shuitu baochi zheng yi shi wu qianli de sudu," 10.
18. On the New Marriage Law, see Diamant, *Revolutionizing the Family*; Hershatter, *Gender of Memory*, ch. 4.
19. Zhonggong Gansu sheng Wushan xianweihui bangongshi, *Qiongshan kujing bian le yang*, 50–53.
20. Chen and Ren, "Shui bu xia yuan, ni bu chu gou," 25.
21. Interview with Deng Fenqin, September 2019.
22. Chen and Ren, "Shui bu xia yuan," 22.
23. Interview with Deng Fenqin, May 2018.
24. Interview with Deng Fenqin, May 2018.
25. "Jianshe shanqu de yimian hongqi," 38. Dengjiabao's fuel resources met 73.7 percent of its residents' consumption needs in 1956, 58.2 percent in 1957, and 77.2 in 1958. Fertilizer supplies accounted for 98.2 percent of requirements in 1956, 97.6 in 1957, and 79.6 in 1958. Fodder resources were 92.8 percent of what was required in 1956, 97.9 percent in 1957, and 86.6 percent in 1958. "Dengjiabao shuitu baochi dianxing diaocha baogao," 21.
26. Wushan Dengjiabao gongzuozu, "Wushan Dengjiabao guanyu youlin fuyu qingkuang baogao."
27. Interview with Deng Fenqin, May 2018.
28. "Dengjiabao zai huang po zaizhi suanliu (suanci) de jingyan," 15.
29. Hershatter, *Women and China's Revolutions*, 233–34; Hershatter *Gender of Memory*, ch. 5.
30. "Zhonggong Wushan xianwei nongyeshe zhuren zuotanhui tingqu qunzhong yijian gaijin lingdao fangfa."
31. Dongshun zhibu shuji Gou Fengyi, "Dongshun xingkai san tiao qudao qingkuang baogao," March 27, 1956, WCA.
32. Dongshun zhibu shuji Gou Fengyi, "Dongshun xingkai san tiao qudao qingkuang baogao."
33. Kong, "Dengjiabao huifu tuba ji liaojie dangqian shengchan qingkuang baogao."

34. Wushan xian renmin weiyuanhui, "Gansu Wushan," 32–33.
35. "Wushan xian shuitu baochi gongzuo di er ci gongzuo qingkuang jianbao."
36. Weibei fangwentuan, "Wushan xian Guaner nongyeshe shuitu baochi gongzuo jingyan," 75. For another example of women building bunds, see "Wushan xian yijiuwuliu nian shang ban nian shuitu baochi gongzuo qingkuang jianjie."
37. Gansu sheng nonglinting shuiliju, "Dengjiabao kaizhan shuitu baochi gongzuo de jingyan," 78.
38. Interview with Deng Fenqin, May 2018.
39. Hershatter, *Gender of Memory*, 66–67, 104–5, 127–28.
40. "Wushan xian yijiuwuwu nian shuitu baochi gongzuo zongjie (caogao)."
41. "Wushan xian yijiuwuwu nian shuitu baochi gongzuo zongjie (caogao)."
42. "Dengjiabao shuitu baochi dianxing diaocha baogao," 23.
43. "Wushan Dengjiabao xingzhengcun gouhe zhili zongjie baogao."
44. *Zhonghua renmin gongheguo guowuyuan gongbao*, February 6, 1956, 92. See also Zhao and Woudstra, "Making Green the Motherland"; Li and Liu, "Selling Forestry Revolution."
45. "Lühua zuguo," *Renmin ribao*, February 17, 1956.
46. Dongshun xiang zhibu shuji Gou Fengyi, Long Fanyin, "Zhonggong Dongshun xiang zhibu wei er nian nei lühua quanxiang zhaokai xuanshi dahui," February 24, 1956, WCA. See also "Wei er nian nei lühua Dongshun quanxiang jiji kaizhan caiji shuzhong yundong," February 9, 1956, WCA.
47. Dongshun xiang zhibu shuji Gou Fengyi, Long Fanyin, "Wei er nian nei lühua Dongshun quanxiang jiji kaizhan caiji shuzhong yundong."
48. "Zhonggong Dongshun xiang zhibu wei er nian nei lühua quanxiang zhaokai xuanshi dahui."
49. Zhonggong Dongshun xiang zhibu, "Dongshun xiang kaizhan chunji zhishu zaolin qingkuang jianbao," March 18, 1956, WCA.
50. Zhonggong Dongshun xiang zhibu, "Dongshun xiang kaizhan chunji zhishu zaolin qingkuang jianbao."
51. Zhonggong Dongshun xiang zhibu, "Dongshun xiang kaizhan chunji zhishu zaolin qingkuang jianbao."
52. Zhonggong Dongshun xiang zhibu, "Dongshun xiang kaizhan chunji zhishu zaolin qingkuang jianbao."
53. "Wushan xian wuliu nian shang ban nian linye, shuitu baochi jianjie baogao," September 25, 1956, WCA.
54. Li and Liu, "Selling Forestry Revolution," 78.
55. "Wushan xian wuliu nian shang ban nian linye."
56. All quotations in this paragraph are from "Wushan xian wuliu nian shang ban nian linye."

57. "Wushan xian wuliu nian shang ban nian linye." See also "Wushan xian linye shuitu baochi zhuanye huiyi," September 26–30, 1956, WCA.

58. Dengjiabao gongzuozu, "Dengjiabao zhishu zaolin gongzuo baogao," October 8, 1956, WCA.

59. Tuan zhibu ji quanti funü, "Tiaozhanshu," November 27, 1956, WCA.

60. "Sheng fulian haozhao quansheng nongcun funü jiji xingxiu shuili zhansheng ganhan," *Gansu ribao*, October 18, 1957.

61. "Sheng fulian haozhao quansheng nongcun funü jiji xingxiu shuili zhansheng ganhan."

62. "Sheng fulian haozhao quansheng nongcun funü jiji xingxiu shuili zhansheng ganhan."

63. "Sheng fulian haozhao quansheng nongcun funü jiji xingxiu shuili zhansheng ganhan."

64. Tianshui zhuanshu linshuiju, "Tianshui zhuanqu jinian lai shuili shuibao gongzuo fazhan qingkuang," 5–6.

65. Miscarriages that resulted when pregnant women in Shaanxi had to perform hard labor are referred to in Hershatter, *Gender of Memory*, 173.

66. [Dengjiabao] gongzuozu, "Dengjiabao dangqian quanmian gongzuo anpai baogao," October 3, 1956, WCA.

67. Ma, *Geming fengge ji*, 219.

68. Ma, *Geming fengge ji*, 219.

69. On the "invisibility" of female domestic labor, including embroidery, in rural China during the 1950s, see Hershatter, *Gender of Memory*, ch. 7.

70. Interview with Deng Fenqin, September 2019.

71. Interview, September 2019.

72. Interviews with Deng Fenqin, May 2018 and September 2019.

73. Interview with Deng Fenqin, September 2019.

74. Interview with Deng Fenqin, September 2019.

75. Gansu sheng funü lianhe hui, "Yierling funü zai kuzhan shi tian ba ye shixian le sanba Dengjiabao," n.d. (1958), GPA.

76. Gansu sheng funü lianhe hui, "Yierling funü zai kuzhan shi tian ba ye shixian le sanba Dengjiabao."

77. Gansu sheng funü lianhe hui, "Yierling funü zai kuzhan shi tian ba ye shixian le sanba Dengjiabao."

78. Gansu sheng funü lianhe hui, "Yierling funü zai kuzhan shi tian ba ye shixian le sanba Dengjiabao."

79. Gansu sheng funü lianhe hui, "Yierling funü zai kuzhan shi tian ba ye shixian le sanba Dengjiabao."

80. Gansu sheng funü lianhe hui, "Yierling funü zai kuzhan shi tian ba ye shixian le sanba Dengjiabao."

81. Gansu sheng funü lianhe hui, "Yierling funü zai kuzhan shi tian ba ye shixian le sanba Dengjiabao."

82. Gansu sheng funü lianhe hui, "Yierling funü zai kuzhan shi tian ba ye shixian le sanba Dengjiabao."

83. Interview with Deng Fenqin, September 2019.

84. Hershatter, *Women in China's Revolutions*, 241; Hershatter, *Gender of Memory*, 196–98, 248–50.

85. Interview with Deng Fenqin, May 2018.

86. Interview with Deng Fenqin, May 2018.

87. Hershatter, *Gender of Memory*, 196, 249–50, 365.

88. "Zhongliangshe nü sheyuan haizi tuolei wenti jiejue de hao," *Wushan bao*, July 14, 1957.

89. "Zhongliangshe nü sheyuan haizi tuolei wenti jiejue de hao."

90. "Zhongliangshe nü sheyuan haizi tuolei wenti jiejue de hao."

91. "Zhongliangshe nü sheyuan haizi tuolei wenti jiejue de hao."

92. "Zhongliangshe nü sheyuan haizi tuolei wenti jiejue de hao."

93. Interview with Deng Fenqin, May 2018.

94. "Zhongliangshe nü sheyuan haizi tuolei wenti jiejue de hao."

95. "Dongshunshe de nongmang shitang," *Wushan bao*, July 21, 1957.

96. "Wushan caiqu wu xiang cuoshi jiejue laodongli buzu wenti," *Gansu ribao*, July 24, 1958.

97. "Wushan bianlun chu dapi laodongli," *Gansu ribao*, October 19, 1958.

98. Agarwal, *Gender and Green Governance*, ch. 2. Examples from Shaanxi can be found in Hershatter, *Gender of Memory*, 42–43, 150, 187.

99. Feierman, *Peasant Intellectuals*, 187–88; Mackenzie, *Land, Ecology and Resistance*, 160, 201.

SEVEN "Conservation Was Primary"

1. All quotations in this paragraph are from Deng, "Gansu shuitu baochi de xin jieduan," *Renmin ribao*, April 7, 1960.

2. "Dengjiabao shuitu baochi dianxing diaocha baogao," 17.

3. Riskin, *China's Political Economy*, 137.

4. Wemheuer, *Famine Politics*; Yang, *Tombstone*.

5. Interview, September 2019.

6. Tong, "Hongqi xian," 106.

7. Yao, "Wushan xian 'dayuejin' pianduan jishi," 111.

8. Interview with Deng Fenqin, September 2019. See also Wushan xianzhi bianzuan weiyuanhui, *Wushan xianzhi*, 106.

9. Yao, "Wushan xian 'dayuejin' pianduan jishi," 112; "Tianshui

shuibaozhan yijiuliuyi nian Wushan Dengjiabao shuitu baochi diaocha jiluben," 102–3.

10. All quotations in this paragraph are from Wang Haicheng, letter dated July 12, 1959.

11. Overall production in Wushan County was 29,485,000 kg (49 kg/*mu*) in 1949. Output reached approximately 57,120,000 kg (80.5 kg/*mu*) in 1956, but in 1961 it fell to 22,380,000 kg (35.5 kg/*mu*). Wushan xianzhi bianzuan weiyuanhui, *Wushan xianzhi*, 267.

12. Agricultural productivity in Dengjiabao plummeted from 176.5 *jin*/*mu* (88.25 kg/*mu*) in 1958 to 112 *jin*/*mu* (56 kg/*mu*) in 1960. "Dengjiabao shuitu baochi dianxing diaocha baogao," 17.

13. Tianshui shi tongjiju, *Tianshui sishi nian*, 38.

14. "Tianshui shuibaozhan yijiuliuyi nian Wushan Dengjiabao shuitu baochi diaocha jiluben," 109.

15. Yang, *Tombstone*, 130. According to another estimate, some 56,460 people in Wushan County perished during the famine. See Tong, "Wushan xian sannian kunnan shiqi," 195.

16. The Dengjiabao brigade's population decreased to 584 in 1959 and 569 in 1960. "Dengjiabao shuitu baochi dianxing diaocha baogao," 16.

17. "Tianshui shuibaozhan yijiuliuyi nian Wushan Dengjiabao shuitu baochi diaocha jiluben," 102. See also "Tianshui shuibaozhan yijiuliuyi nian Wushan Dengjiabao shuitu baochi diaocha jiluben," 60, 87, 90, 109.

18. "Tianshui shuibaozhan yijiuliuyi nian Wushan Dengjiabao shuitu baochi diaocha jiluben," 102.

19. "Tianshui shuibaozhan yijiuliuyi nian Wushan Dengjiabao shuitu baochi diaocha jiluben," 87.

20. "Tianshui shuibaozhan yijiuliuyi nian Wushan Dengjiabao shuitu baochi diaocha jiluben," 87, 88. See also "Tianshui shuibaozhan yijiuliuyi nian Wushan Dengjiabao shuitu baochi diaocha jiluben," 59, 60, 106–7, 109.

21. "Tianshui shuibaozhan yijiuliuyi nian Wushan Dengjiabao shuitu baochi diaocha jiluben," 87, 107, 119.

22. "Tianshui shuibaozhan yijiuliuyi nian Wushan Dengjiabao shuitu baochi diaocha jiluben," 87.

23. "Tianshui shuibaozhan yijiuliuyi nian Wushan Dengjiabao shuitu baochi diaocha jiluben," 108.

24. "Tianshui shuibaozhan yijiuliuyi nian Wushan Dengjiabao shuitu baochi diaocha jiluben," 87. For other negative assessments of dams and reservoirs, see "Tianshui shuibaozhan yijiuliuyi nian Wushan Dengjiabao shuitu baochi diaocha jiluben," 60, 61, 117.

25. "Tianshui shuibaozhan yijiuliuyi nian Wushan Dengjiabao shuitu baochi diaocha jiluben," 60, 87, 90.
26. "Tianshui shuibaozhan yijiuliuyi nian Wushan Dengjiabao shuitu baochi diaocha jiluben," 87.
27. "Tianshui shuibaozhan yijiuliuyi nian Wushan Dengjiabao shuitu baochi diaocha jiluben," 132.
28. "Tianshui shuibaozhan yijiuliuyi nian Wushan Dengjiabao shuitu baochi diaocha jiluben," 102.
29. "Tianshui shuibaozhan yijiuliuyi nian Wushan Dengjiabao shuitu baochi diaocha jiluben," 106.
30. "Tianshui shuibaozhan yijiuliuyi nian Wushan Dengjiabao shuitu baochi diaocha jiluben," 102.
31. "Tianshui shuibaozhan yijiuliuyi nian Wushan Dengjiabao shuitu baochi diaocha jiluben," 59.
32. "Tianshui shuibaozhan yijiuliuyi nian Wushan Dengjiabao shuitu baochi diaocha jiluben," 102.
33. "Tianshui shuibaozhan yijiuliuyi nian Wushan Dengjiabao shuitu baochi diaocha jiluben," 102–3.
34. "Tianshui shuibaozhan yijiuliuyi nian Wushan Dengjiabao shuitu baochi diaocha jiluben," 89.
35. "Tianshui shuibaozhan yijiuliuyi nian Wushan Dengjiabao shuitu baochi diaocha jiluben," 60–61.
36. "Tianshui shuibaozhan yijiuliuyi nian Wushan Dengjiabao shuitu baochi diaocha jiluben," 59.
37. "Tianshui shuibaozhan yijiuliuyi nian Wushan Dengjiabao shuitu baochi diaocha jiluben," 90.
38. "Tianshui shuibaozhan yijiuliuyi nian Wushan Dengjiabao shuitu baochi diaocha jiluben," 3.
39. Interview, September 2019.
40. Interview, May 2018.
41. Interview, May 2018.
42. "Tianshui shuibaozhan yijiuliuyi nian Wushan Dengjiabao shuitu baochi diaocha jiluben," 88.
43. "Tianshui shuibaozhan yijiuliuyi nian Wushan Dengjiabao shuitu baochi diaocha jiluben," 104. See also "Tianshui shuibaozhan yijiuliuyi nian Wushan Dengjiabao shuitu baochi diaocha jiluben," 88.
44. "Tianshui shuibaozhan yijiuliuyi nian Wushan Dengjiabao shuitu baochi diaocha jiluben," 108.
45. "Tianshui shuibaozhan yijiuliuyi nian Wushan Dengjiabao shuitu baochi diaocha jiluben," 108–9.

46. "Tianshui shuibaozhan yijiuliuyi nian Wushan Dengjiabao shuitu baochi diaocha jiluben," 88.
47. "Tianshui shuibaozhan yijiuliuyi nian Wushan Dengjiabao shuitu baochi diaocha jiluben," 88.
48. Interview, May 2018.
49. "Tianshui shuibaozhan yijiuliuyi nian Wushan Dengjiabao shuitu baochi diaocha jiluben," 103.
50. "Tianshui shuibaozhan yijiuliuyi nian Wushan Dengjiabao shuitu baochi diaocha jiluben," 104.
51. "Tianshui shuibaozhan yijiuliuyi nian Wushan Dengjiabao shuitu baochi diaocha jiluben," 45.
52. "Tianshui shuibaozhan yijiuliuyi nian Wushan Dengjiabao shuitu baochi diaocha jiluben," 103.
53. Interview, September 2019.
54. "Tianshui shuibaozhan yijiuliuyi nian Wushan Dengjiabao shuitu baochi diaocha jiluben," 120.
55. Thaxton, *Catastrophe and Contention*.
56. "Tianshui shuibaozhan yijiuliuyi nian Wushan Dengjiabao shuitu baochi diaocha jiluben," 107.
57. "Tianshui shuibaozhan yijiuliuyi nian Wushan Dengjiabao shuitu baochi diaocha jiluben," 108.
58. "Tianshui shuibaozhan yijiuliuyi nian Wushan Dengjiabao shuitu baochi diaocha jiluben," 109.
59. "Tianshui shuibaozhan yijiuliuyi nian Wushan Dengjiabao shuitu baochi diaocha jiluben," 91.
60. "Tianshui shuibaozhan yijiuliuyi nian Wushan Dengjiabao shuitu baochi diaocha jiluben," 92.
61. "Tianshui shuibaozhan yijiuliuyi nian Wushan Dengjiabao shuitu baochi diaocha jiluben," 103. Investigators found that Honggou brigade received ¥11,146 in compensation and Leijiashan's production teams each received ¥3,500. See "Tianshui shuibaozhan yijiuliuyi nian Wushan Dengjiabao shuitu baochi diaocha jiluben," 60.
62. "Tianshui shuibaozhan yijiuliuyi nian Wushan Dengjiabao shuitu baochi diaocha jiluben," 107.
63. "Tianshui shuibaozhan yijiuliuyi nian Wushan Dengjiabao shuitu baochi diaocha jiluben," 92.
64. Li, *Village China*, 97, 103.
65. Hershatter, *Gender of Memory*, 251–58.
66. Interview with Deng Fenqin, May 2018.
67. Zhang, "Wushan xian gongshehua chuqi de gonggong shitang," 184.

68. "Dengjiabao shuitu baochi dianxing diaocha baogao," 21.
69. Interview with Deng Fenqin, September 2019.
70. Interview with Deng Fenqin, September 2019.
71. Interview with Deng Fenqin, May 2018.
72. Lijiaping's population grew from 96 in 1957 to 102 in 1958, dipped slightly to 101 in 1959, but increased to 105 in 1960 and 107 in 1961. "Tianshui shuibaozhan yijiuliuyi nian Wushan Dengjiabao shuitu baochi diaocha jiluben," 93
73. Interview with Deng Fenqin, May 2018. On food shortages in dining halls, see Hershatter, *Gender of Memory*, 242.
74. "Tianshui shuibaozhan yijiuliuyi nian Wushan Dengjiabao shuitu baochi diaocha jiluben," 104.
75. Interview with Deng Fenqin, May 2018. On food gathering organized by dining hall personnel, see Zhang, "Wushan xian gongshehua chuqi de gonggong shitang," 184.
76. On the practice of "sitting the month," see Hershatter, *Gender of Memory*, 159–60; Gottschang, "Taking Patriarchy Out."
77. Interview with Deng Fenqin, May 2018.
78. Hershatter, *Women in China's Revolutions*, 240; Hershatter, *Gender of Memory*, 139, 247.
79. Interview with Deng Fenqin, May 2018.
80. The proportion of men in Wushan's population declined from 104.62 percent in 1958 to 99.92 percent in 1959, 98.38 percent in 1960, 98.10 percent in 1961, and 96.86 percent in 1962 before increasing again to 103.15 percent in 1963. Wushan xianzhi bianzuan weiyuanhui, *Wushan xianzhi*, 114–15. In Dengjiabao brigade, total female labor power outnumbered male labor power 147 to 132 in 1960. "Dengjiabao shuitu baochi dianxing diaocha baogao," 16. Lijiaping had a total of 30 female laborers (laodongli) and 29 male laborers in 1959. "Tianshui shuibaozhan yijiuliuyi nian Wushan Dengjiabao shuitu baochi diaocha jiluben," 93.
81. Macintyre, "Female Mortality Advantage"; Ó Gráda, *Famine*, 98–101; Speakman, "Mortality Profiles." On gendered differences in mortality during the Great Leap Forward famine, see Mu and Zhang, "Great Chinese Famine."
82. Yang, *Tombstone*, 131.
83. Sheng Wushan weisheng gongzuo zu, *Wushan xian xiaoer yingyang buliang zheng diaocha fangzhi baogao*, 1. Yanjing and Mulin are currently located in Zhang County and Yuchuan is in Gan'gu County, but during the Great Leap Forward they were all part of Wushan County. Wushan absorbed Zhang County in April 1958 and Gangu merged with Wushan in December 1958. The three counties eventually split in December 1961. Wushan xianzhi bianzuan weiyuanhui, *Wushan xianzhi*, 32–33, 35, 54–55.
84. Li, *Village China*, 97–99, 103–4.

85. Interviews with Deng Fenqin, May 2018 and September 2019.
86. All quotations in this paragraph are from "Tianshui shuibaozhan yijiuliuyi nian Wushan Dengjiabao shuitu baochi diaocha jiluben," 117.
87. "Tianshui shuibaozhan yijiuliuyi nian Wushan Dengjiabao shuitu baochi diaocha jiluben," 117.
88. "Tianshui shuibaozhan yijiuliuyi nian Wushan Dengjiabao shuitu baochi diaocha jiluben," 118.
89. All quotations in this paragraph are from "Tianshui shuibaozhan yijiuliuyi nian Wushan Dengjiabao shuitu baochi diaocha jiluben," 119–20.
90. "Huiyi wenjian zhi yi: Guanyu jin dong ming chun shuili gongzuo de anpai yijian," October 16, 1962, WCA.
91. "Huiyi wenjian zhi yi."
92. Interview, September 2019.
93. Interviews with Deng Fenqin, May 2018 and September 2019.
94. Zhongyang shuitu baochi jianchazu, "Gansu Wushan xian Dengjiabao, Baoziping, Laixing san ge shuitu baochi zhongdian diaocha baogao (caogao)," December 1960, QCA.
95. "Tianshui shuibaozhan yijiuliuyi nian Wushan Dengjiabao shuitu baochi diaocha jiluben," 118.
96. Zhongyang shuitu baochi jianchazu, "Gansu Wushan xian Dengjiabao, Baoziping, Laixing san ge shuitu baochi zhongdian diaocha baogao."
97. Zhongyang shuitu baochi jianchazu, "Gansu Wushan xian Dengjiabao, Baoziping, Laixing san ge shuitu baochi zhongdian diaocha baogao."
98. "Huiyi wenjian zhi er: Wushan xian linye gongzuo qingkuang ji jin dong ming chun linye gongzuo anpai yijian," October 16, 1962, WCA.
99. "Huiyi wenjian zhi er."
100. "Huiyi wenjian zhi er."
101. Bai, "Mianhuai Lei Yuanzhen laoshi," 93–94.
102. "Wu Guobin fuxianzhang zai Wushan xian, nongye, xumu, shuili, jiaotong huiyi shang de zongjie baogao," November 5, 1962, WCA.
103. "Wu Guobin fuxianzhang zai Wushan xian, nongye, xumu, shuili, jiaotong huiyi shang de zongjie baogao." See also Luo "Dengjiabao cun shengtai huanjing bianqian de lishi jiaoxun," 27; Tianshui shi difangzhi bianweihui, *Tianshui shizhi*, 1115. The county government installed an electric lift irrigation system in Dengjiabao in 1977, but after a few years it was no longer used due to the high cost of operation and was dismantled and sold for scrap in the early 1990s. Wushan xianzhi bianzuan weiyuanhui. *Wushan Xianzhi*, 316–17.
104. Output from the most productive terraced fields reportedly went from a peak of 350 *jin* (175 kg) per *mu* in the 1950s to 280 *jin* (140 kg) per *mu* in the 1970s

and 240 *jin* (120 kg) per *mu* in the 1990s. Luo, "Dengjiabao cun shengtai huanjing bianqian de lishi jiaoxun," 27–28.

105. Luo, "Dengjiabao cun shengtai huanjing bianqian de lishi jiaoxun," 27–28.

106. Calculated based on production agricultural data from China Data Online (https://www.china-data-online.com), accessed January 21, 2025, and census figures from Wushan xianzhi bianzuan weiyuanhui, *Wushan xianzhi*, 111.

107. The mean average for the seven years in which data are available is 254 kg per person and the median is 244 kg per person. See the chart "Nongye renkou ji liangshi fazhan zhuangkuang" in Tianshui shi tongjiju, *Tianshui sishi nian*, n.p.

108. Cited in Veg, *Minjian*, 96.

Epilogue

1. Interview, September 2019.
2. Several villagers that I interviewed spoke of this incident.
3. On Dazhai, see Shapiro, *Mao's War*, ch. 3; Schmalzer, *Red Revolution, Green Revolution*, 418–21.
4. Shapiro, *Mao's War*, 96.
5. Shapiro, *Mao's War*, 106–24.
6. Schmalzer, *Red Revolution, Green Revolution*, 43, 145–47.
7. Interview, May 2018.
8. Harrell, *Ecological History*, 184.
9. Xu and Tao, "Grain for Green," 262.
10. Xu and Tao, "Grain for Green," 245–46.
11. Xu and Tao, "Grain for Green," 232–33.
12. Zhou, "Wushan xian xin yi lun tui geng huan lin gongcheng jianshe kunjing ji celue," 97.
13. Zhou, "Wushan xian xin yi lun tui geng huan lin gongcheng jianshe kunjing ji celue," 97.
14. Wang, "Wushan xian tigao xin yi lun tui geng huan lin chengxiao de duice cuoshi," 69–70.
15. Xu and Tao, "Grain for Green," 248–49, 264.
16. Wang, "Wushan xian tigao xin yi lun tui geng huan lin chengxiao de duice cuoshi," 70.
17. Zhou, "Wushan xian xin yi lun tui geng huan lin gongcheng jianshe kunjing ji celue," 97
18. Ren et al., "Tianshui shi jin 30 nian lindi dongtai bianhua yaogan jiance yanjiu."
19. Xu and Tao, "Grain for Green."
20. Otsuki, "Vegetation Restoration," 235.

21. Xu and Tao, "Grain for Green," 262.
22. Xu and Tao, "Grain for Green," 262.
23. Xu and Tao, "Grain for Green," 263–64.
24. Harrell, *Ecological History*, 278–79.
25. Interview, May 2018.
26. Smith, *End of the Village*, 4.
27. Worster, *Dust Bowl*, 3.
28. Gramsci, *The Southern Question*, 70.
29. Harrell, *Ecological History*, 322.
30. Zhang, Zhang, and Yang, *Weiji*, 120.
31. Zhang, Zhang, and Yang, *Weiji*, 120–21.
32. Zhang, Zhang, and Yang, *Weiji*, 121.
33. Zhang, Zhang, and Yang, *Weiji*, 121.
34. Interview, May 2018.
35. Chi et al., "Spatial Patterns."
36. Shen et al., "Household Livelihood Vulnerability."

BIBLIOGRAPHY

Archival Documents

"Chao yuan cheng" [Copy of original petition]. Attached to notice from the Administrative Yuan, December 15, 1943, Institute of Modern History Archives, Academia Sinica, Taiwan, 20-59-003-05.

"Cheng Xingzhengyuan" [Petition to the Executive Yuan (from the Ministry of Agriculture and Forestry)], January 9, 1945, Institute of Modern History Archives, Academia Sinica, Taiwan, 20-59-011-08.

"Dengjiabao dui quan xian ge she de shuitu baochi tiaozhanshu" [Dengjiabao's water and soil conservation challenge to each cooperative in the entire county], November 25, 1956, Wushan County Archives, B9-yongjiu-370. Draft of document also found in B9-yongjiu-367.

[Dengjiabao] gongzuozu, "Dengjiabao dangqian quanmian gongzuo anpai baogao" [Report on Dengjiabao's current overall work arrangements], October 3, 1956, Wushan County Archives, B9-yongjiu-367.

Dengjiabao gongzuozu, "Dengjiabao Tiaozigou shanwan shuitang shigong qingkuang" [Dengjiabao Tiaozi Gully mountain bend reservoir work situation], December 10, 1956, Wushan County Archives, B9-yongjiu-367.

———. "Dengjiabao zhishu zaolin gongzuo baogao" [Dengjiabao afforestation work report], October 8, 1956, Wushan County Archives, B9-yongjiu-367.

———. "Dongshun xiang Dengjiabao zai xian shuitu baochi huiyi hou shuitu baochi tuji qingkuang" [Water and soil conservation assault situation in Dongshun township's Dengjiabao after the county water and soil conservation meeting], November 30, 1956, Wushan County Archives, B9-yongjiu-367.

———. "Wushan xian Dongshun xiang Dengjiabao shuitu baochi da fengshou qingkuang baogao" [Report on water and soil conservation and abundant harvest situation in Dongshun township's Dengjiabao, Wushan County], November 6, 1956, Wushan County Archives, B9-yongjiu-367.

———. "Wushan xian Dongshun xiang Dengjiabao xieshui jianzhuwu muqian qingkuang baogao" [Report on current situation of bypass structure in Dongshun township's Dengjiabao, Wushan County], December 10, 1956, Wushan County Archives, B9-yongjiu-367.

"Dengjiabao gongzuozu dui xiashou hou shuitu baochi gongzuo jihua zhixing caoan" [Executive draft of the Dengjiabao work team's plan for water and soil conservation work after the summer harvest], July 2, 1955, Wushan County Archives, B9-yongjiu-283.

"Dengjiabao shuitu baochi dianxing diaocha baogao (chugao)" [Dengjiabao water and soil conservation typical model investigation report (draft)], June 1961, Yellow River Conservancy Commission Archives, Zhengzhou, 21 2 T3-2-12.

"Dengjiabao wuliu nian gongzuo kaizhan qingkuang" [Dengjiabao 1956 work development situation], May 1956, Wushan County Archives, B9-yongjiu-367.

"Dongshun gaoji nongyeshe tao quan wa jing baogao" [Dongshun higher-level agricultural cooperative spring- and well-digging report], February 10, 1956, Wushan County Archives, 001-changqi-82.

"Dongshun xiang tao quan da jing qingkuang baogao" [Dongshun township spring- and well-digging situation report], February 10, 1956, Wushan County Archives, 001-changqi-82.

Dongshun xiang zhibu shuji Gou Fengyi, Long Fanyin, "Wei er nian nei lühua Dongshun quanxiang jiji kaizhan caiji shuzhong yundong" [To green the entire township of Dongshun in two years, actively develop a campaign to gather tree seeds], February 9, 1956, Wushan County Archives, 001-changqi-82.

Dongshun zhibu shuji Gou Fengyi, "Dongshun xingkai san tiao qudao qingkuang baogao" [Situation report on Dongshun opening three channels], March 27, 1956, Wushan County Archives, 001-changqi-82.

"Dui Wushan Xianghe tuba fugong de yijian" [Ideas on resuming work on Wushan's Xiang River earth dam], November 28, 1956, Yellow River Conservancy Commission Archives, Zhengzhou, 21 2 T3-3-5.

Gansu sheng funü lianhe hui, "Yierling funü zai kuzhan shi tian ba ye shixian le sanba Dengjiabao" [120 women have fought a bitter battle for ten days and eight nights to bring about a March 8 Dengjiabao], n.d. [1958], Gansu Provincial Archives, Lanzhou, 108-002-00038-0006.

"Gansu sheng nonglinting dui Wushan Xianghegou tuba fugong de yijian" [Gansu Province Agriculture and Forestry Department's ideas on resuming work on Wushan's Xiang River Gully earth dam project], November 30, 1956, Yellow River Conservancy Commission Archives, Zhengzhou, 21 2 T3-3-5.

"Guanyu dangqian shuitu baochi gongzuo de chubu anpai yijian" [Preliminary ideas on current water and soil conservation work arrangements], November 6, 1956, Wushan County Archives, B9-yongjiu-370.

"Huiyi wenjian zhi er: Wushan xian linye gongzuo qingkuang ji jin dong ming chun linye gongzuo anpai yijian" [Meeting document 2: Wushan County forestry work situation and work arrangement ideas for this winter and next spring], October 16, 1962, Wushan County Archives, B9-1.2-changqi-448.

"Huiyi wenjian zhi yi: Guanyu jin dong ming chun shuili gongzuo de anpai yijian" [Meeting document 1: Ideas on water conservancy work arrangements for this winter and next spring], October 16, 1962, Wushan County Archives, B9-1.2-changqi-448.

Kong Fengzhong, "Dengjiabao huifu tuba ji liaojie dangqian shengchan qingkuang baogao" [Report on Dengjiabao restoring earth dams and understanding the current production situation], July 3, 1956, Wushan County Archives, B9-yong-jiu-367.

Lowdermilk, W. C., Adviser to the Executive Yuan, "Preliminary Report on Findings of a Survey of a Portion of the Northwest for a Program of Soil, Water, and Forest Conservation," 1943, Yellow River Conservancy Commission Archives, Zhengzhou, MG 1.1–79.

Nonglinbu shuitu baochi shiyanqu, ed. *San nian lai zhi Tianshui shuitu baochi shiyanqu* [The Tianshui Water and Soil Conservation Experiment Area over the past three years], 1946, Institute of Modern History Archives, Academia Sinica, Taiwan, 20-59-013-03.

"Nonglinbu shuitu baochi shiyanqu sanshiliu niandu shang ban nian gongzuo jindu jiantao baogao biao" [Ministry of Agriculture and Forestry Water and Soil Conservation Experiment Area work progress examination report table for first half of 1947], July 1947, Gansu Provincial Archives, Lanzhou, 27-2-39.

"Nonglinbu shuitu baochi shiyanqu sanshiliu nian er yuefen gongzuo jianbao biao" [Ministry of Agriculture and Forestry Water and Soil Conservation Experiment Area February 1947 brief work report table], March 1947, Gansu Provincial Archives, Lanzhou, 27-2-25. Also found in Institute of Modern History Archives, Academia Sinica, Taiwan, 20-59-014-04.

"Nonglinbu shuitu baochi shiyanqu sanshiliu nian qi yuefen gongzuo jianbao biao" [Ministry of Agriculture and Forestry Water and Soil Conservation Experiment Area July 1947 monthly work report table], August 1947, Gansu Provincial Archives, Lanzhou, 27-2-39. Also found in Institute of Modern History Archives, Academia Sinica, Taiwan, 20-59-014-04.

"Nonglinbu shuitu baochi shiyanqu sanshiliu nian san yuefen gongzuo jianbao biao" [Ministry of Agriculture and Forestry Water and Soil Conservation Experiment Area March 1947 brief work report table], April 1947, Gansu Provincial Archives, Lanzhou, 27-2-25. Also found in Institute of Modern History Archives, Academia Sinica, Taiwan, 20-59-014-04.

"Nonglinbu shuitu baochi shiyanqu sanshiliu niandu yuan yuefen gongzuo jianbao biao" [Ministry of Agriculture and Forestry Water and Soil Conservation Experiment Area January 1947 brief work report table], February 1947, Gansu Provincial Archives, Lanzhou, 27-2-25. Also found in Institute of Modern History Archives, Academia Sinica, Taiwan, 20-59-014-04.

"Nonglinbu shuitu baochi shiyanqu sanshiqi niandu zhengji bijiao biao" [Ministry of Agriculture and Forestry Water and Soil Conservation Experiment Area 1948 achievement comparison table], January 1949, Gansu Provincial Archives, Lanzhou, 27-2-49.

"Nonglinbu shuitu baochi shiyanqu sanshiqi nian jiu yuefen gongzuo jianbao biao"

[Ministry of Agriculture and Forestry Water and Soil Conservation Experiment Area September 1948 brief work report table], October 1948, Institute of Modern History Archives, Academia Sinica, Taiwan, 20-59-015-04.

"Nonglinbu shuitu baochi shiyanqu sanshiqi niandu shang ban nian gongzuo jindu jiantao baogao biao" [Ministry of Agriculture and Forestry Water and Soil Conservation Experiment Area work progress examination report table for first half of 1948], August 1948, Gansu Provincial Archives, Lanzhou, 27-2-46.

"Nonglinbu shuitu baochi shiyanqu sanshiqi nian jiu yuefen gongzuo jianbao biao" [Ministry of Agriculture and Forestry Water and Soil Conservation Experiment Area September 1948 summary work report table], October 1948, Institute of Modern History Archives, Academia Sinica, Taiwan, 20-59-015-04.

"Nonglinbu shuitu baochi shiyanqu sanshisan niandu zhengji bijiao biao" [Ministry of Agriculture and Forestry Water and Soil Conservation Experiment Area 1944 achievement comparison table], January 1944, Gansu Provincial Archives, Lanzhou, 27-2-44.

"Nonglinbu shuitu baochi shiyanqu sanshisi niandu zhengji bijiao biao" [Ministry of Agriculture and Forestry Water and Soil Conservation Experiment Area 1945 achievement comparison table], January 1946, Gansu Provincial Archives, Lanzhou 27-2-44. Also found in Institute of Modern History Archives, Academia Sinica, Taiwan, 20-59-013-07.

"Nonglinbu shuitubaochi shiyanqu sanshiwu niandu zhengji bijiao biao" [Ministry of Agriculture and Forestry Water and Soil Conservation Experiment Area 1946 achievement comparison table], January 1947, Gansu Provincial Archives, Lanzhou, 27-2-63.

"Nonglinbu shuitu baochi shiyanqu Tianshui Nanshan shiyanchang dixingtu" [Topographical map of the Ministry of Agriculture and Forestry Water and Soil Conservation Experiment Area's Tianshui Nanshan experiment station], 1946, Institute of Modern History Archives, Academia Sinica, Taiwan, 20-59-013.

"Nonglinmu zhongdian gongzuozu de jianbao" [Brief report from Agriculture, Forestry, and Animal Husbandry Key Point Work Team], April 24, 1954, Wushan County Archives, B9-yongjiu-214.

"Qin'an xian chuxian Dengjiabao qingkuang baogao" [Qin'an County situation report on Dengjiabaos emerging], May 19, 1958, Qin'an County Archives, changqi-190-958.

"Qingniantuan Wushan xianwei guanyu zhaokai qingnian shuitu baochi huodong fenzi hui jihua" [Youth League Wushan County Committee plan for convening water and soil conservation activist meeting], August 1, 1955, Wushan County Archives, 1-yongjiu-12.

"San nian lai zhi Tianshui shuitu baochi shiyanqu" [The Tianshui Water and Soil Conservation Experiment Area over the past three years]. In *San nian lai zhi*

Tianshui shuitu baochi shiyanqu, edited by Nonglinbu shuitu baochi shiyanqu, 1946, Institute of Modern History Archives, Academia Sinica, Taiwan, 20-59-013-03.

"Tianshui diqu titian zongjie" [Summary of terraces in the Tianshui area], April 1961, Yellow River Conservancy Commission Archives, Zhengzhou, 21 2 T3-2-28-03.

"Tianshui shuibaozhan yijiuliuyi nian Wushan Dengjiabao shuitu baochi diaocha jiluben" [Tianshui Water and Soil Conservation Station 1961 Wushan Dengjiabao water and soil conservation investigation notebooks], Yellow River Conservancy Commission Archives, Zhengzhou, May 19, 1961, 21 2 T1-2-15.

Tianshui shuitu baochi gongzuo tuiguangzhan, "Guanyu Dengjiabao tuba anzhuang xieshuiguan bogei cailiao touzi 880 yuan de fuhan" [Reply letter on allocating material investment of ¥880 for Dengjiabao earth dam bypass pipe installation], December 24, 1956, Wushan County Archives, B9-yongjiu-367.

Tianshui zhuanqu shuitu baochi weiyuanhui, "Yinfa Dengjiabao ge xiang shuitu baochi gongzuo de cuoshi he juti fangfa cankao you" [Sending Dengjiabao's various water and soil conservation work measures and substantive methods for reference], May 15, 1958, Qin'an County Archives, changqi-190-958.

Tianshui zhuanshu linshuiju, "Tianshui zhuanqu jinian lai shuili shuibao gongzuo fazhan qingkuang" [Tianshui Prefecture's water conservancy and water and soil conservation work development situation over the past several years], 1958, Tianshui Municipal Archives, B34 141 056.

Tianshui zhuanyuan gongshu, "Wushan xian Dengjiabao nongye shengchan hezuoshe shuitu baochi gongzuo shiji" [Wushan County Dengjiabao Agricultural Producers Cooperative's water and soil conservation work achievements], 1955, Gansu Provincial Archives, Lanzhou, 216-001-0217-0004.

Tianshui zhuanyuan gongshu shuiliju, "Guanyu Tianshui xian Zhongliangqu zhaokai jishu geming cujinhui he Qingshui xian Hongfu xiang wu tian shixian liu ge Dengjiabao de tongbao" [Bulletin on Tianshui County's Zhongliang Canal holding technical revolution promotion meeting and Qingshui County's Hongfu township bringing about six Dengjiabaos], June 5, 1958, Qin'an County Archives, changqi-190-958.

Tuan zhibu ji quanti funü, "Tiaozhanshu" [Challenge letter], November 27, 1956, Wushan County Archives, B9-yongjiu-367.

Wei Zhanggen, "Titian gouxu zhi sheji yu shishi" [Design and implementation of terraces and channels]. In *San nian lai zhi Tianshui shuitu baochi shiyanqu*, edited by Nonglinbu shuitu baochi shiyanqu, 1946, Institute of Modern History Archives, Academia Sinica, Taiwan, 20-59-013-03.

"Women de jiaxiang yi jibenshang zhizhile shuitu liushi, Gansu sheng Wushan xian Dengjiabao tuan fenzhi shuji Li Xuding" [Our hometown has already fundamentally controlled water and soil loss: Gansu Province Wushan County Dengjiabao (Youth) League Branch Secretary Li Xuding], 1956, Gansu Provincial Archives, Lanzhou, 107-001-0333-0002.

"Wu Guobin fuxianzhang zai Wushan xian, nongye, xumu, shuili, jiaotong huiyi shang de zongjie baogao" [Assistant County Head Wu Guobin's summary report at Wushan County agriculture, animal husbandry, water conservancy, and transportation meeting], November 5, 1962, Wushan County Archives, B9-1.2-changqi-448.

Wushan Dengjiabao gongzuozu, "Dengjiabao liyong ba nei xu shui jiaoguan dong mai qingkuang baogao" [Report on Dengjiabao using water stored in dams to irrigate winter wheat], December 7, 1955, Wushan County Archives, B9-yongjiu-283.

———. "Wushan Dengjiabao guanyu youlin fuyu qingkuang baogao" [Report on tending young forests in Dengjiabao, Wushan], November 12, 1955, Wushan County Archives, B9-yongjiu-283.

Wushan xian Dengjiabao nong (shui) lin mu zhongdian gongzuozu, "Wushan Dengjiabao xingzhengcun gouhe zhili zongjie baogao" [Summary report on gully management in Wushan's Dengjiabao administrative village], June 8, 1954, Wushan County Archives, B9-yongjiu-214.

"Wushan xian Dengjiabao nong (shui) lin mu zhongdian gongzuozu yijiuwusi niandu gongzuo jihua" [Wushan County Dengjiabao Agriculture (Water Conservancy), Forestry, and Animal Husbandry Key Point Work Team 1954 work plan], March 29, 1954, Wushan County Archives, B9-yongjiu-214.

"Wushan Dengjiabao zhongdian gongzuozu guanyu wuwu nian shang ban nian gongzuo qingkuang zongjie baogao" [Wushan Dengjiabao Key Point Work Team summary report on work situation for first half of 1955], July 20, 1955, Wushan County Archives, B9-yongjiu-283.

"Wushan xian Dengjiabao zhongdian gongzuozu yijiuwuwu nian gongzuo zongjie baogao" [Wushan County Dengjiabao Key Point Work Team 1955 summary work report], December 30, 1955, Wushan County Archives, B9-yongjiu-283.

"Wushan xian jiehe xiashou kaizhan shuitu baochi gongzuo qingkuang jianbao" [Wushan County summary report on combining the summer harvest with the development of water and soil conservation work], July 16, 1955, Wushan County Archives, B9-yongjiu-280.

"Wushan xian linye shuitu baochi zhuanye huiyi" [Wushan County specialized meeting on forestry and water and soil conservation], September 26–30, 1956, Wushan County Archives, B9-yongjiu-371.

"Wushan xian nongye laodong mofan ji huzhuzuzhang daibiao huiyi zongjie" [Summary of Wushan County agricultural labor model and mutual-aid team leader representative meeting], March 1954, Wushan County Archives, B9-yongjiu-206.

Wushan xian renmin weiyuanhui, "Guohuai xiang quanmian kaizhan shuitu baochi gongzuo zongjie baogao" [Guohuai township summary report on full-scale development of water and soil conservation work], September 18, 1955, Wushan County Archives, B9-yongjiu-281.

———. "Guanyu Dengjiabao xieguan anzhuang jihua touzi baogao" [Report on investments for Dengjiabao's bypass pipe installation plan], December 13, 1956, Wushan County Archives, B9-yongjiu-367.

———. "1956 nian shuitu baochi gongzuo kaizhan qingkuang zongjie baogao" [1956 water and soil conservation work development situation summary report], January 15, 1957, Wushan County Archives, B9-yongjiu-369.

———. "Wushan xian Dengjiabao san nian lai shuitu baochi gongzuo jiben zongjie" [Basic summary of water and soil conservation work over the past three years in Dengjiabao, Wushan County], September 26, 1955, Wushan County Archives, B9-yongjiu-283.

———. "Wushan xian shuitu baochi zhong de ji dian tihui" [A few experiences with water and soil conservation in Wushan County], September 21, 1955, B9-yongjiu-280.

"Wushan xian renmin weiyuanhui baogao" [Wushan County People's Committee report], July 31, 1955, Wushan County Archives, B9-yongjiu-280.

"Wushan xian renmin weiyuanhui jinji tongzhi" [Urgent notice from Wushan County People's Committee], February 28, 1956, Wushan County Archives, B9-yongjiu-370.

"Wushan xian renmin weiyuanhui tongbao" [Wushan County People's Committee bulletin], December 7, 1955, Wushan County Archives, B9-yongjiu-283.

"Wushan xian renmin weiyuanhui tongzhi" [Wushan County People's Committee notice], February 7, 1956, Wushan County Archives, B9-yongjiu-370.

"Wushan xian renmin weiyuanhui zhuanfa Dongshun xiang Dengjiabao dongji shuitu baochi gongzuo jihua yi fen xi yingzhan" [Notice from Wushan County People's Committee forwarding copy of winter water and soil conservation work plan from Dongshun township's Dengjiabao in hopes that others will respond to the challenge], November 28, 1956, Wushan County Archives, B9-yongjiu-370. Earlier draft of this document also found in Wushan County Archives, B9-yongjiu-367.

"Wushan xian renmin zhengfu tongzhi" [Wushan County People's Government notice], May 31, 1954, Wushan County Archives, B9-1.2-changqi-172.

"Wushan xian shuitu baochi gongzuo di er ci gongzuo qingkuang jianbao" [Wushan County water and soil conservation work second work situation summary report], February 23, 1956, Wushan County Archives, B9-yongjiu-369.

"Wushan xian shuitu baochi gongzuo di yi ci daibiao zhuanye huiyi zongjie baogao" [Wushan County water and soil conservation work first representative specialized meeting summary report], draft document, September 7, 1955, Wushan County Archives, B9-yongjiu-281.

"Wushan xian shuitu baochi jishu xunlian gongzuo zongjie baogao" [Wushan County water and soil conservation technical training work summary report], July 15, 1955, Wushan County Archives, B9-yongjiu-281.

"Wushan xian shuitu baochi gongzuo kaizhan qingkuang" [Wushan County water and soil conservation work development situation], 1955, Wushan County Archives, B9-yongjiu-280.

"Wushan xian shuitu baochi gongzuo zhuanye huiyi zongjie baogao" [Wushan County water and soil conservation work specialized meeting summary report], September 7, 1955, Wushan County Archives, B9-yongjiu-281.

"Wushan xian shuitu baochi jishu xun gan huiyi zongjie" [Wushan County water and soil conservation technical cadre training meeting summary], December 8, 1956, Wushan County Archives, B9-yongjiu-371.

"Wushan xian shuitu baochi mofan Deng Haihai shiji" [The deeds of Wushan County's water and soil conservation model Deng Haihai], February 22, 1955, Wushan County Archives, B9-yongjiu-207.

"Wushan xian tuiguang caomuxi gongzuo baogao" [Wushan County sweet clover extension work report], April 26, 1954, Wushan County Archives, B9-1.2-changqi-172.

"Wushan xian wuliu nian shang ban nian linye, shuitu baochi gongzuo jianjie baogao" [Wushan County forestry and water and soil conservation work summary report for first half of 1956], September 25, 1956, Wushan County Archives, B9-yongjiu-369.

"Wushan xian wuliu nian shuitu baochi chubu jianjie baogao" [Wushan County 1956 water and soil conservation preliminary summary report], November 1956, Wushan County Archives, B9-yongjiu-369.

"Wushan xian wuwu nian shuitu baochi gongzuo zongjie baogao" [Wushan County 1955 water and soil conservation summary report], January 18, 1956, Wushan County Archives, B9-yongjiu-280.

"Wushan xian wuwu nian yuan zhi jiu yue fen shuitu baochi jianjie baogao" [Wushan County water and soil conservation summary report for January to September 1955], October 8, 1955, Wushan County Archives, B9-yongjiu-280.

"Wushan xian xia ban nian shuitu baochi gongzuo buzhi" [Wushan County water and soil conservation work arrangements for the second half of the year], July 16, 1954, Wushan County Archives, B9-1.2-changqi-172.

"Wushan xian yijiuwuliu nian shang ban nian shuitu baochi gongzuo qingkuang jianjie" [Wushan County water and soil conservation work situation summary for the first half of 1956], June 29, 1956, Wushan County Archives, B9-yongjiu-369.

"Wushan xian yijiuwusi nian xia ban niandu caomuxi tuiguang gongzuo jihua" [Wushan County sweet clover extension plan for the second half of 1954], August 28, 1954, Wushan County Archives, B9-1.2-changqi-172.

"Wushan xian yijiuwuwu nian shuitu baochi gongzuo zongjie" [Wushan County 1955 water and soil conservation work summary], December 30, 1955, Wushan County Archives, B9-yongjiu-280.

"Wushan xian yijiuwuwu nian shuitu baochi gongzuo zongjie (caogao)" [Wushan County 1955 water and soil conservation work summary (draft)], n.d., Wushan County Archives, B9-yongjiu-281.

"Wushan xian yuan zhi san yue niansan ri fen shuitu baochi gongzuo di si ci wancheng qingkuang baogao" [Fourth report on completion of water and soil conservation work in Wushan County from January to March 23], March 28, 1956, Wushan County Archives, B9-yongjiu-369.

Wushan xian zhengfu, "Woxian yuan zhi wu yue shuitu baochi gongzuo jianjie baogao" [Summary report on water and soil conservation work in our county from January to May], June 8, 1954, Wushan County Archives, B9-yongjiu-214.

Wushan Xianghe tuba gongcheng weiyuanhui, "Wushan xian Xianghe gongcheng jieduan zongjie" [Wushan County Xiang River project section summary], July 15, 1956, Yellow River Conservancy Commission Archives, Zhengzhou, 21 2 T3-3-5.

Ye Peizhong, "Xu" [Preface]. In *San nian lai zhi Tianshui shuitu baochi shiyanqu*, edited by Nonglinbu shuitu baochi shiyanqu, 1946, Institute of Modern History Archives, Academia Sinica, Taiwan, 20-59-013-03.

Zhonggong Dongshun zhibu, "Wushan Dongshun xiang da jing wa quan qingkuang jianjie baogao" [Summary report on well- and spring-digging situation in Wushan's Dongshun township], February 10, 1956, Wushan County Archives, 001-changqi-82.

Zhonggong Dongshun xiang zhibu, "Dongshun xiang kaizhan chunji zhishu zaolin qingkuang jianbao" [Dongshun township summary report on spring afforestation work development situation], March 18, 1956, Wushan County Archives, 001-changqi-82.

"Zhonggong Dongshun xiang zhibu wei er nian nei lühua quanxiang zhaokai xuanshi dahui" [CCP Dongshun township branch convenes oath meeting to green entire township in two years], February 24, 1956, Wushan County Archives, 001-changqi-82.

Zhonggong Wushan xianwei, "Wushan xian guanyu xiaji shuitu baochi gongzuo anpai yijian" [Wushan County summer water and soil conservation work arrangement ideas], Wushan County Archives, July 18, 1955, B9-yongjiu-280.

Zhonggong Wushan xian weiyuanhui, Wushan xian renmin weiyuanhui, "Guanyu qingqiu Xianghegou tuba gongcheng fugong de baogao" [Report on request to resume work on Xiang River Gully earth dam project], October 10, 1956, Yellow River Conservancy Commission Archives, Zhengzhou, 21 2 T3-3-5.

Zhongguo gongchandang Wushan xian weiyuanhui, "Luomen qu shuitu baochi gongzuo kaizhan qingkuang" [Luomen district water and soil conservation work development situation], August 30, 1955, Wushan County Archives, B9-yongjiu-281.

Zhongyang shuitu baochi jianchazu, "Gansu Wushan xian Dengjiabao, Baoziping, Laixing san ge shuitu baochi zhongdian diaocha baogao (caogao)" [Investigation report on Wushan County, Gansu's three water and soil conservation key points Dengjiabao, Baoziping, and Laixing (draft)], December 1960, Qin'an County Archives, changqi-116.

Published Sources

Agarwal, Bina. *Gender and Green Governance: The Political Economy of Women's Presence within and beyond Community Forestry*. Oxford: Oxford University Press, 2010.

An, Ping, Tomoe Inoue, Mingqing Zheng, A. Egrinya Eneji, and Shinobu Inanaga. "Agriculture on the Loess Plateau." In *Restoration and Development of the Degraded Loess Plateau*, edited by Atsushi Tsunekawa, Guobin Liu, Norikazu Yamanaka, and Sheng Du, 61–73. Tokyo: Springer Japan, 2014.

Anderson, David. "Depression, Dust Bowl, Demography, and Drought: The Colonial State and Soil Conservation in East Africa during the 1930s." *African Affairs* 83, no. 332 (July 1984): 321–43.

Anderson, E. N. *Ecologies of the Heart: Emotion, Belief, and the Environment*. New York: Oxford University Press, 2020.

Ash, Robert. "Squeezing the Peasants: Grain Extraction, Food Consumption, and Rural Living Standards in Mao's China." *China Quarterly* 188 (December 2006): 959–98.

Bai Zhixian. "Mianhuai Lei Yuanzhen laoshi" [Cherishing the memory of teacher Lei Yuanzhen]. *Wushan xian wenshi ziliao xuanji* 3 (1989): 88–99.

Baker, Mark. "Energy, Labor, and Soviet Aid: China's Northwest Highway, 1937–1941." *Modern China*. Published online November 17, 2023.

Beinart, William. "Introduction: The Politics of Colonial Conservation." *Journal of Southern African Studies* 15, no. 2 (January 1989): 143–62.

———. *The Rise of Conservation in South Africa: Settlers, Livestock, and the Environment 1770–1950*. Oxford: Oxford University Press, 2008.

———. "Soil Erosion, Conservationism and Ideas about Development: A Southern African Exploration, 1900–1960." *Journal of Southern African Studies* 11, no. 1 (October 1984): 52–83.

Beinart, William, and Lotte Hughes. 2007. *Environment and Empire*. Oxford: Oxford University Press, 2007.
"Ben sheng chaoe wancheng yuanding mingnian shuili jihua" [This province has exceeded its original water conservancy plans for next year], *Gansu ribao*, December 31, 1957.
Benson, John. "Aesthetic and Other Values in the Rural Landscape." *Environmental Values* 17, no. 2 (May 2008): 221–38.
Blackbourn, David. "Environmental History and Other Histories." In *The Future of Environmental History: Needs and Opportunities*, edited by Kimberly Coulter and Christof Mauch, 19–21. *RCC Perspectives* 3 (2011). Munich: Rachel Carson Center for Environment and Society.
Blaikie, Piers M. *The Political Economy of Soil Erosion in Developing Countries*. London: Longman, 1985.
Blaikie, Piers, and Harold Brookfield. *Land Degradation and Society*. London: Routledge, 1991.
Bray, Francesca. *Science and Civilisation in China*, Vol. 6, bk. 2, *Biology and Biological Technology: Agriculture*. New York: Cambridge University Press, 1984.
———. *Technology and Gender: Fabrics of Power in Late Imperial China*. Berkeley: University of California Press, 1997.
Bridger, Susan. *Women in the Soviet Countryside: Women's Role in Rural Development in the Soviet Union*. Cambridge: Cambridge University Press, 1987.
Brown, Jeremy. *City versus Countryside in Mao's China: Negotiating the Divide*. New York: Cambridge University Press, 2012.
———. "Spatial Profiling: Seeing Urban and Rural in Mao's China." In *Visualizing Modern China: Image, History, and Memory, 1750-present*, edited by James A. Cook, Joshua Goldstein, Matthew D. Johnson, and Sigrid Schmalzer, 1–18. Lanham, MD: Lexington Books, 2014.
Brown, Jeremy, and Matthew Johnson. *Maoism at the Grassroots: Everyday Life in China's Era of High Socialism*. Cambridge, MA: Harvard University Press, 2015.
Brown, Melissa J. "Dutiful Help: Masking Rural Women's Economic Contributions." In *Transforming Patriarchy: Chinese Families in the Twenty-First Century*, edited by Gonçalo Santos and Stevan Harrell, 39–58. Seattle: University of Washington Press, 2017.
Brown, Tristan G. *Laws of the Land: Fengshui and the State in Qing Dynasty China*. Princeton, NJ: Princeton University Press, 2023.
Bruun, Ole. *Fengshui in China: Geomantic Divination Between State Orthodoxy and Popular Religion*. Copenhagen: NIAS Press, 2003.
"Canguan Dengjiabao yougan" [Feelings on an observation visit to Dengjiabao], *Renmin ribao*, September 20, 1958.
Chen, Chao, Ding Huang, Yajun Zhang, Hao Zheng, and Kun Wang. "Invasion of

Farmland-Grassland Ecosystems by the Exotic Sweet Clovers, *Melilotus officinalis* and *M. albus*." *Journal of Food, Agriculture & Environment* 11, no. 1 (January 2013): 1012–16.

Chen Shoushan, and Ren Shiyin. "Shui bu xia yuan, ni bu chu gou" [Water does not go down the plateaus; silt does not go out of the gullies]. *Renmin huabao* 10 (1957): 23–25.

Chen Zhengren. "Quanguo di san ci shuitu baochi huiyi kaimuci" [Opening remarks at the Third Nationwide Water and Soil Conservation Conference]. *Renmin Huanghe* 10 (1958): 3–4.

Chi, Haojing, Yanhong Wu, Hongxing Zheng, Bing Zhang, Zhonghua Sun, Jiaheng Yan, Yongkang Ren, and Linan Guo. "Spatial Patterns of Climate Change and Associated Climate Hazards in Northwest China." *Scientific Reports* 13, no. 10418 (June 2023): 1–13.

Cohen, Myron L. "Cultural and Political Inventions in Modern China: The Case of the Chinese 'Peasant.'" *Daedalus* 122, no. 2 (Spring 1993): 151–70.

Day, Alexander F. *The Peasant in Postsocialist China: History, Politics, and Capitalism*. Cambridge: Cambridge University Press, 2013.

Demare, Brian. *Land Wars: The Story of China's Agrarian Revolution*. Stanford, CA: Stanford University Press, 2019.

Deng Baoshan. "Gansu shuitu baochi de xin jieduan" [A new stage of water and soil conservation in Gansu]. *Renmin ribao*, April 7, 1960.

"Dengjiabao shuitu baochi gongzuo ronghuo quanguo yideng jiang" [Dengjiabao's water and soil conservation work honored with highest nationwide prize]. *Wushan bao*, November 16, 1957.

"Dengjiabao zai huang po zaizhi suanliu (suanci) de jingyan" [Dengjiabao's experience planting seaberry (sea buckthorn) on barren slopes]. *Huanghe jianshe* 3 (1959): 15.

Diamant, Neil J. *Revolutionizing the Family: Politics, Love, and Divorce in Urban and Rural China, 1949–1968*. Berkeley: University of California Press, 2000.

Ding, Xiangli. "'The Yellow River Comes from Our Hands': Silt, Hydroelectricity, and the Sanmenxia Dam, 1929–1973." *Environment and History* 27, no. 4 (November 2021): 665–94.

Dodson, Belinda. "A Soil Conservation Safari: Hugh Bennett's 1944 Visit to South Africa." *Environment and History* 11, no. 1 (February 2005): 35–53.

Dong Xianghua. "Jiefang qianhou Tianshui shuitu baochi keyan shiyan gongzuo" [Scientific research and experiment work on water and soil conservation in Tianshui before and after liberation]. *Tianshui wenshi ziliao* 14 (2008): 376–84.

———. "Jiefang qian Tianshui de shuitu baochi gongzuo" [Water and soil conservation work in Tianshui before liberation]. *Tianshui wenshi ziliao* 2 (1988): 113–21.

"Dongshunshe de nongmang shitang" [Dongshun cooperative's busy-farming-season dining hall]. *Wushan bao*, July 21, 1957.

Eisenman, Joshua. *Red China's Green Revolution: Technological Innovation, Institutional Change, and Economic Development under the Commune*. New York: Columbia University Press, 2018.

Eyferth, Jacob. "One Country, Two Material Cultures." In *Material Contradictions in Mao's China*, edited by Jennifer Altehenger and Denise Y. Ho, 182–99. Seattle: University of Washington Press, 2022.

———. "State Socialism and the Rural Household: How Women's Handloom Weaving (and Pig-Raising, Firewood-Gathering, Food-Scavenging) Subsidized Chinese Accumulation." *International Review of Social History* 67, no. 2 (August 2022): 231–49.

———. "Women's Work and the Politics of Homespun in Socialist China, 1949–1980." *International Review of Social History* 57, no. 3 (December 2012): 365–91.

Fan, Fa-ti. "'Collective Monitoring, Collective Defense': Science, Earthquakes, and Politics in Communist China." *Science in Context* 25, no. 1 (March 2012): 127–54.

———. "The People's War against Earthquakes: Cultures of Mass Science in Mao's China." In *Cultures without Culturalism: The Making of Scientific Knowledge*, edited by Karine Chemla and Evelyn Fox Keller, 296–323. Durham, NC: Duke University Press, 2017.

Feierman, Steven. *Peasant Intellectuals: Anthropology and History in Tanzania*. Madison: University of Wisconsin Press, 1990.

Finnane, Antonia. "Water, Love, and Labor: Aspects of a Gendered Environment." In *Sediments of Time: Environment and Society in Chinese History*, edited by Mark Elvin and Liu Ts'ui-jung, 657–90. Cambridge: Cambridge University Press, 1998.

Fitzpatrick, Sheila. *Stalin's Peasants: Resistance and Survival in the Russian Village after Collectivization*. New York: Oxford University Press, 1994.

Food and Agriculture Organization of the United Nations. *Soil Conservation: An International Study*. Washington, DC: Food and Agriculture Organization of the United Nations, 1948.

———. *Training Rural Leaders: Shantan Bailie School, Kansu Province, China*. Washington, DC: Food and Agriculture Organization of the United Nations, 1949.

Friedman, Edward, Paul G. Pickowicz, Mark Selden, and Kay Ann Johnson. *Chinese Village, Socialist State*. New Haven, CT: Yale University Press, 1991.

Gansu sheng nonglinting shuiliju. "Dengjiabao kaizhan shuitu baochi gongzuo de jingyan" [Dengjiabao's experience developing water and soil conservation work]. *Huanghe jianshe* 1 (1958): 74–79.

Gansu sheng renmin weiyuanhui, ed. *Gansu sheng de shuili shuitu baochi* [Gansu Province's water conservancy and water and soil conservation]. Lanzhou: Gansu sheng renmin weiyuanhui, 1959.

Gansu sheng shuiliting. *Jianshe shanqu de bangyang—Dengjiabao* [A model for the construction of mountainous areas—Dengjiabao]. Lanzhou: Gansu sheng shuiliting, 1958.

———. *Xue xianjin gan xianjin chao xianjin gaoju hongqi xiang qian jin! Gansu sheng Dengjiabao Tongwei xianchang guanmo cujin dahui dazibao huiji* [Learn from the advanced, catch up with the advanced, surpass the advanced, raise high the red flag and go forward! Gansu Province Dengjiabao Tongwei on-site observation and promotion conference big character poster collection]. Lanzhou: Gansu sheng shuiliting, 1958.

———. *Zhengfu Huajialing* [Conquer Huajialing]. Lanzhou: Ganshu sheng shuiliting, 1958.

Gansu shuiliting, ed. *Dazibao shige xuan* [Big-character poster, poem, and song collection]. Lanzhou: Gansu sheng shuiliting, 1958.

"Gansu zhengqu san nian nei jiben shixian shuilihua" [Gansu strives to basically realize water conservancy-ization in three years]. *Gansu ribao*, February 22, 1958.

Gao Jishan. "Zhongguo shuitu baochi shihua" [Brief history of water and soil conservation in China]. In *Shuitu baochi zhi ziliao huibian, di yi ji*, edited by Huanghe shuitu baochi zhi bianweihui bianjishi and Shaanxi sheng shuitu baochi zhi bianweihui bangongshi, 54–67. Xi'an: Shaanxi shuitu baochi bianjibu, 1988.

"Gaoju renmin gongshe hongqi Wushan Lintao shixian renmin gongshehua" [Raising high the red flag of the people's communes, Wushan and Lintao realize people's communization]. *Gansu ribao*, September 9, 1958.

Goldman, Wendy Z. "Introduction: Primitive Accumulation and Socialism." *International Review of Social History* 67, no. 2 (August 2022): 195–209.

Goldstein, Joshua. *Remains of the Everyday: A Century of Recycling in Beijing*. Oakland: University of California Press, 2021.

Gottschang, Suzanne. "Taking Patriarchy Out of Postpartum Recovery?" In *Transforming Patriarchy: Chinese Families in the Twenty-First Century*, edited by Gonçalo Santos and Stevan Harrell, 201–18. Seattle: University of Washington Press, 2017.

Gouldner, Alvin W. "Stalinism: A Study of Internal Colonialism." *Télos* 34 (Winter 1977): 5–48.

Gramsci, Antonio. *The Southern Question* [1926], translated by Pasquale Verdicchio. Toronto: Guernica Editions, 2005.

Greene, J. Megan. *Building a Nation at War: Transnational Knowledge Networks and the Development of China during and after World War II*. Cambridge, MA: Harvard University Asia Center, 2022.

Greer, Charles. *Water Management in the Yellow River Basin of China*. Austin: University of Texas Press, 1979.

Gu Lei. "Lianghao de lingdao fangfa huihuang de jianshe chengjiu—jieshao Zhonggong Wushan xianwei lingdao shengchan de jiben jingyan (zhi yi)" [Excellent leadership methods, brilliant construction achievements—introducing the CCP Wushan County committee's basic experience leading production (part one)]. *Renmin ribao*, January 3, 1958), 2.

Hao, Ping. "A Study of the Construction of Terraced Fields in Liulin County, Shanxi Province in the Era of Collectivization." In *Agricultural Reform and Rural Transformation in China since 1949*, edited by Thomas DuBois and Huaiyin Li, 101–14. Leiden: Brill, 2016.

Harrell, Stevan A. *An Ecological History of Modern China*. Seattle: University of Washington Press, 2023.

He, Liang, James Cleverly, Chao Chen, Xiaoya Yang, Jun Li, Wenzhao Liu, and Qiang Yu. "Diverse Responses of Winter Wheat Yield and Water Use to Climate Change and Variability on the Semiarid Loess Plateau in China." *Climatology & Water Management* 106, no. 4 (July–August 2014): 1169–78.

Heilmann, Sebastian. "From Local Experiments to National Policy: The Origins of China's Distinctive Policy Process." *China Journal* 59 (January 2008): 1–30.

Hershatter, Gail. *The Gender of Memory: Rural Women and China's Collective Past*. Berkeley: University of California Press, 2011.

——— . *Women and China's Revolutions*. Lanham, MD: Rowman & Littlefield, 2019.

Ho, Denise Y. *Curating Revolution: Politics on Display in Mao's China*. New York: Cambridge University Press, 2018.

Hodge, Joseph Morgan. *Triumph of the Expert: Agrarian Doctrines of Development and the Legacies of British Colonialism*. Athens: Ohio University Press, 2007.

Hou, Xiaojia. *Negotiating Socialism in Rural China: Mao, Peasants, and Local Cadres in Shanxi, 1949–1953*. Ithaca, NY: Cornell East Asia Series, 2016.

Hu Jiwei. "Yi ge lizheng shangyou de xianjin xian—Wushan" [An advanced county vigorously striving to aim high—Wushan]. *Renmin ribao*, October 8, 1958.

Huanghe shuili weiyuanhui Huanghe zhongyou zhiliju, ed. *Huanghe shuitu baochi zhi* [Yellow River water and soil conservation gazetteer]. Zhengzhou: Henan renmin chubanshe, 1993.

Idema, Wilt. "The Precious Scroll of Chenxiang." In *The Columbia Anthology of Chinese Folk and Popular Literature*, edited by Victor Mair and Mark Bender, 380–405. New York: Columbia University Press, 2010.

Jacka, Tamara. *Women's Work in Rural China: Change and Continuity in an Era of Reform*. Cambridge: Cambridge University Press, 1997.

Ji, Fengyuan. *Linguistic Engineering: Language and Politics in Mao's China*. Honolulu: University of Hawai'i Press, 2004.

Jiang Shikui. "Yanghuai zaipei jingyan ji qi shuitu baochi xiaoyi de ceyan" [Black locust planting experience and an evaluation of its water and soil conservation effectiveness]. In *Shuitu baochi shiyan yanjiu chengguo huibian, 1942–1980 di er ji*, edited by Huanghe shuili weiyuanhui Tianshui shuitu baochi kexue shiyanzhan, 181–91. Zhengzhou: Huanghe shuili weiyuanhui, 1981.

Jiang Shikui and Zhang Bingzhong. "Weihe shangyou yanghuai shuitu baochi lin yanjiu baogao" [Research report on black locust water and soil conservation forests in the upper reaches of the Wei River]. In *Shuitu baochi shiyan yanjiu chengguo huibian, 1942–1980 di er ji*, edited by Huanghe shuili weiyuanhui Tianshui shuitu baochi kexue shiyanzhan, 124–39. Zhengzhou: Huanghe shuili weiyuanhui, 1981.

"Jiangli baochi shuitu mofan" [Rewarding water and soil conservation models]. *Renmin ribao*, December 24, 1957.

"Jian shan bu jian gou cheng titian gengdi lian pian Dengjiabao shuitu baochi zhongdian gongcheng wangong" [Sharp mountains have disappeared, gullies have become terraces, cultivated land is contiguous: work has been completed on the Dengjiabao water and soil conservation key-point project]. *Gansu ribao*, August 14, 1958.

"Jianshe shanqu de bangyang: ji Dengjiabao zonghe kaifa, quanmian zhili shanqu de jingguo" [A model for the construction of mountainous areas: a record of Dengjiabao's process of integrated development and comprehensive management of mountainous areas]. *Gansu ribao*, December 19, 1957.

"Jianshe shanqu de yimian hongqi—Dengjiabao" [A red flag in the construction of mountainous areas—Dengjiabao]. In *Wushan xian de shuitu baochi gongzuo dianxing jingyan*, edited by Zhonggong Gansu sheng Wushan xian weiyuanhui, 37–51. Beijing: Nongye chubanshe, 1959.

"Jinnian jiancheng sanqian ge 'Dengjiabao' jiang zai wu nian nei jiben kongzhi shuitu liushi" [This year three thousand "Dengjiabaos" will be established and within five years water and soil loss will be basically controlled]. *Gansu ribao*, January 11, 1958.

"Jixu qianjin zailai yi ge shengshi haoda de shuitu baochi tuji yundong" [Continue to advance in another water and soil conservation assault campaign with great momentum]. *Gansu ribao*, April 5, 1958.

Kimura, Reiji, and Naru Takayama. "Climate of the Loess Plateau." In *Restoration and Development of the Degraded Loess Plateau*, edited by Atsushi Tsunekawa,

Guobin Liu, Norikazu Yamanaka, and Sheng Du, 23–33. Tokyo: Springer Japan, 2014.

Kou, Meng, Patricio Garcia-Fayos, Shu Hu, and Juying Jiao. "The Effect of *Robinia pseudoacacia* Afforestation on Soil and Vegetation Properties in the Loess Plateau (China): A Chronosequence Approach." *Forest Ecology and Management* 375, no. 1 (September 2016): 146–58.

Laakkonen, Simo, Richard P. Tucker, and Timo Vuorisalo. "Hypotheses: World War II and Its Shadows." In *The Long Shadows: A Global Environmental History of the Second World War*, edited by Timo Vuorisalo, Richard Tucker, and Simo Laakkonen, 315–32. Corvallis: Oregon State University Press, 2017.

Lan Ping. "Rang Dengjiabao de guangrong qizhi zaidu piaoyang" [Make the glorious flag of Dengjiabao fly again]. *Gansu ribao*, July 10, 1958.

Lan Wenwei. "Xinguangshe weishenme hui jianshao shouru?" [Why did Xinguang cooperative's income decrease?], *Gansu ribao*, November 25, 1956.

Lan Wenwei and Zhu Quanfen. "Wushan renmin xiu diqiu" [Wushan's people remake the Earth]. *Gansu ribao*, July 24, 1958.

Leach, Melissa, and Cathy Green. "Gender and Environmental History: From Representation of Women and Nature to Gender Analysis of Ecology and Politics." *Environment and History* 3, no. 3 (October 1997): 343–70.

Li, Cheng, and Yanjun Liu. "Selling Forestry Revolution: The Rhetoric of Afforestation in Socialist China, 1949–61." *Environmental History* 25, no. 1 (January 2020): 62–84.

Li, Huaiyin. *Village China under Socialism and Reform: A Micro-History, 1948–2008*. Stanford, CA: Stanford University Press, 2009.

Li Ronghua. "Minguo Tianshui shuitu baochi shiyanqu mucao pinzhong de xuanyu" [The Tianshui Water and Soil Conservation Experiment Area's selection of pasturage grass varieties during the Republican period]. *Nongye kaogu* 4 (2017): 186–91.

Li, Xueling, Joshua Philp, Roger Cremades, Anna Roberts, Liang He, Longhui Li, and Qiang Yu. "Agricultural Vulnerability over the Chinese Loess Plateau in Response to Climate Change: Exposure, Sensitivity, and Adaptive Capacity." *Ambio* 45, no. 3 (2016): 350–60.

Li Yuming. "Huiyi zai Yan'an zhaokai de wu sheng (qu) qingnian zaolin dahui" [Remembering the Five Province (Area) Youth Afforestation Conference held in Yan'an]. *Shanxi linye* 1 (1995): 30–31.

Ling Daoyang and Ren Chengtong. "Xibei shuitu baochi shiye zhi sheji yu shishi" [Planning and implementation of water and soil conservation measures in the Northwest]. *Linxue* 9 (1943): 85–93.

Liu Bang. "Lü shui qing shan gaoyu tian" [Green water, blue mountains, and fertile fields]. *Renmin ribao*, November 28, 1956.

Liu Yanwen. *Gongdi shehui: Yin Tao shangshan shuili gongcheng de geming, jitizhuyi, yu xiandaihua* [Revolution, collectivism, and modernization in China: A case study of the Yintao water conservancy project in Gansu Province]. Beijing: Shehui kexue wenxian chubanshe, 2018.

Lowdermilk, Walter C. "Factors Influencing the Surface Run-Off of Rain Waters." In *Proceedings of the Third Pan-Pacific Science Congress, Tokyo, October 30th–November 11th, 1926*, 2122–47. Tokyo: National Research Council of Japan, 1929.

———. *Soil, Forest, and Water Conservation and Reclamation in China, Israel, Africa, and the United States*. Vol. 2. Berkeley: Regional Oral History Office, Bancroft Library, University of California, 1969.

"Lühua zuguo." [Make green the fatherland]. *Renmin ribao*, February 17, 1956.

Luo Hongyuan. "Dengjiabao cun shengtai huanjing bianqian de lishi jiaoxun" [Historical lessons from changes in the ecological environment of Dengjiabao village]. *Tianshui shizhuan xuebao (ziran kexue ban)* 18, no. 3 (1998): 27–28.

Ma Tieding. *Geming fengge ji* [Revolutionary style anthology]. Lanzhou: Dunhuang wenyi chubanshe, 1958.

Ma Yuping. "Kongzhi zhu shuitu liushi de Dengjiabao cun" [Dengjiabao village has controlled water and soil loss]. *Renmin ribao*, August 12, 1955.

Macintyre, Kate. "Famine and the Female Mortality Advantage." In *Famine Demography: Perspectives from the Past*, edited by Tim Dyson and Cormac Ó Gráda, 240–60. Oxford: Oxford University Press, 2002.

Mackenzie, A. Fiona D. *Land, Ecology and Resistance in Kenya, 1880–1952*. Edinburgh: Edinburgh University Press, 1998.

Madsen, Richard. "The Countryside under Communism." In *The Cambridge History of China*, Vol. 15, bk. 2, *The People's Republic of China*, edited by Roderick MacFarquhar and John K. Fairbank, 619–81. Cambridge: Cambridge University Press, 1991.

Manning, Kimberley Ens, and Felix Wemheuer, ed. *Eating Bitterness: New Perspectives on China's Great Leap Forward and Famine*. Vancouver: University of British Columbia Press, 2011.

Marks, Robert B. *China: Its Environment and History*. Lanham, MD: Rowman & Littlefield, 2012.

Merchant, Carolyn. *The Death of Nature: Women, Ecology, and the Scientific Revolution*. San Francisco: Harper & Row, 1990.

———. "Gender and Environmental History." *Journal of American History* 76, no. 4 (March 1990): 1117–21.

Mo Shiao. "Caomuxi shihua" [A brief history of sweet clover]. In *Shuitu baochi shiyan yanjiu chengguo huibian, 1942–1980 di er ji*, edited by Huanghe shuili weiyuanhui Tianshui shuitu baochi kexue shiyanzhan, 102. Zhengzhou: Huanghe shuili weiyuanhui, 1981.

———, ed. "Huanghe shuili weiyuanhui Tianshui shuitu baochi kexue shiyanzhan zhanzhi (songshen gao)" [Yellow River conservancy commission Tianshui Water and Soil Conservation Scientific Experiment Station Gazetteer (draft for review)]. Unpublished manuscript, 1992.

———. "Woguo caomuxi de yinzhong tuiguang jingguo" [The process of the introduction and extension of sweet clover in our nation]. *Caoye kexue* 8, no. 3 (1991): 66–67, 71.

———. "Zhongguo shuitu baochi de faxiangdi—Tianshui" [The birthplace of water and soil conservation in China—Tianshui]. In *Huanghe wangshi*, edited by Luo Xiangxin, 172–79. Zhengzhou: Huanghe shuili chubanshe, 2006.

Morgan, Ruth, and Margaret Cook. "Gender, Environment and History: New Methods and Approaches in Environmental History." *International Review of Environmental History* 7, no. 1 (2021): 5–19.

Mosley, Stephen. "Common Ground: Integrating Social and Environmental History." *Journal of Social History* 39, no. 3 (Spring 2006): 915–33.

Mostern, Ruth. "Loess Is More: The Spatial and Ecological History of Erosion on China's Northwest Frontier." *Journal of the Economic and Social History of the Orient* 62, no. 4 (May 2019): 560–98.

———. *The Yellow River: A Natural and Unnatural History*. New Haven, CT: Yale University Press, 2021.

Mu, Ren, and Xiaobo Zhang. "Why Does the Great Chinese Famine Affect the Male and Female Survivors Differently? Mortality Selection versus Son Preference." *Economics & Human Biology* 9, no. 1 (January 2011): 92–105.

Mulwafu, Wapulumuka Oliver. *Conservation Song: A History of Peasant-State Relations and the Environment in Malawi, 1860–2000*. Cambridge: White Horse, 2011.

Muscolino, Micah S. *The Ecology of War in China: Henan Province, the Yellow River, and Beyond, 1938–1950*. New York: Cambridge University Press, 2015.

———. *Fishing Wars and Environmental Change in Late Imperial and Modern China*. Cambridge, MA: Harvard University Asia Center, 2009.

———. "Refugees, Land Reclamation, and Militarized Landscapes in Wartime China: Huanglongshan, Shaanxi, 1937–45." *Journal of Asian Studies* 69, no. 2 (May 2010): 453–78.

———. "Wartime Water and Soil Conservation in Gansu." In *Living and Working in Wartime China*, edited by Brett Sheehan and Wen-hsin Yeh, 273–96. Honolulu: University of Hawai'i Press, 2022.

———. "'Water Has Aroused the Girls' Hearts': Gendering Water and Soil Conservation in 1950s China." *Past & Present* 255, no. 1 (May 2022): 351–87.

———. "Woodlands, Warlords, and Wasteful Nations: Transnational Networks and Conservation Science in 1920s China." *Comparative Studies in Society and History* 61, no. 3 (July 2019): 712–38.

Naughton, Barry. *The Chinese Economy: Transitions and Growth*. Cambridge: MIT Press, 2007.

Nygren, Joshua. "A 'Plow to Save the Plains': Conservation Tillage on the North American Grasslands, 1938–1978." In *The Great Plains: Rethinking a Region's Environmental Histories*, edited by Brian Frehner and Kathleen A. Brosnan, 202–29. Lincoln: University of Nebraska Press, 2021.

Ó Gráda, Cormac. *Famine: A Short History*. Princeton, NJ: Princeton University Press, 2009.

Oi, Jean C. *State and Peasant in Contemporary China: The Political Economy of Village Government*. Berkeley: University of California Press, 1989.

Okie, William Thomas. "Beauty and Habitation: Fredrika Bremer and the Aesthetic Imperative of Environmental History." *Environmental History* 24, no. 2 (April 2019): 258–81.

Otsuki, Kyoichi, Norikazu Yamanaka, and Sheng Du. "Vegetation Restoration on Loess Plateau." In *Restoration and Development of the Degraded Loess Plateau*, edited by Atsushi Tsunekawa, Guobin Liu, Norikazu Yamanaka, and Sheng Du, 233–51. Tokyo: Springer Japan, 2014.

Peet, Richard, and Michael Watts, ed. *Liberation Ecologies: Environment, Development and Social Movements*, 2nd ed. London: Routledge, 2004.

Perry, Elizabeth J. "Making Communism Work: Sinicizing a Soviet Governance Practice." *Comparative Studies in Society and History* 61, no. 3 (July 2019): 535–62.

Phillips, Sarah T. "Drylands, Dust Bowl, and Agro-Technical Internationalism in Southern Africa." In *Transatlantic Rebels: Agrarian Radicalism in Comparative Context*, edited by James Scott and Thomas Summerhill, 265–97. East Lansing: Michigan State University Press, 2004.

———. "Lessons from the Dust Bowl: Dryland Agriculture and Soil Erosion in the United States and South Africa, 1900–1950." *Environmental History* 4, no. 2 (April 1999): 245–66.

Piazza, Alan. *Food Consumption and Nutritional Status in the PRC*. Boulder, CO: Westview Press, 1986.

Pietz, David A. *Engineering the State: The Huai River and Reconstruction in Nationalist China, 1927–1937*. New York: Routledge, 2002.

———. *The Yellow River: The Problem of Water in Modern China*. Cambridge, MA: Harvard University Press, 2015.

"Qianmo zongheng hua guo manmu—Dengjiabao jiang daichu geng duo Dengjiabao (zhanlan manbu)" [Paths crisscrossing the fields, flowers and fruits as far as the eye can see—Dengjiabao will bring about even more Dengjiabaos (a stroll through an exhibition)]. *Wushan bao*, October 16, 1957.

"Qianwan yingxiong da zhan Dengjiabao yao rang tuolaji rao shan feiben" [Ten million heroes engage in a great war in Dengjiabao to let tractors speed round the mountain]. *Gansu ribao*, July 10, 1958.

"Quanguo di san ci shuitu baochi huiyi kaimuci" [Opening remarks at the Third Nationwide Water and Soil Conservation Conference]. *Gansu ribao*, September 3, 1958.

Quanguo mucao pinzhong shending weiyuanhui. *Zhongguo mucao dengji pinzhong ji* [Collection of registered Chinese pasturage grass varieties]. Beijing: Zhongguo nongye daxue chubanshe, 1999.

"Quanguo shuitu baochi gongzuo huiyi shou jiang Dengjiabao Wushan xian Tianshui shuitu baochi shiyanzhan huo tedeng jiang" [Nationwide Water and Soil Conservation Work Conference award winners: Dengjiabao, Wushan County, and the Tianshui Water and Soil Conservation Experiment Station receive special prizes]. *Gansu ribao*, December 24, 1957.

"Quanguo shuitu baochi gongzuo huiyi zhongshi Wushan lingdao jingyan shuli le shanqu shuitu baochi gongzuo de huihuang bangyang" [Nationwide Water and Soil Conservation Work Conference prioritizes Wushan's leadership experience in establishing a brilliant model for water and soil conservation work]. *Gansu ribao*, December 25, 1957.

"Quansheng chaoe wancheng shuitu baochi renwu" [Entire province exceeds its water and soil conservation mission]. *Gansu ribao*, September 3, 1958.

"Quansheng shuili shuitu baochi yundong jixu yuejin" [The entire province's water conservancy and water and soil conservation campaign continues to leap forward]. *Gansu ribao*, January 24, 1958.

"Quansheng yi chuxian erqianwubai duo ge Dengjiabao" [Over 2,500 Dengjiabaos have already emerged in the entire province]. *Gansu ribao*, February 28, 1958.

Ren Chengtong. "Gansu shuitu baochi shiyanqu zhi kancha" [Survey of the Gansu Water and Soil Conservation Experiment Area]. *Xibei yanjiu* 3, no. 6 (1941): 4–10.

———. "Jianshe Xibei yu shuitu baochi" [Constructing the Northwest and water and soil conservation] (1943). In *Kangzhan shiqi da houfang jingji kaifa wenxian ziliao xuanbian*, edited by Tang Runming, 470–72. Chongqing: Chongqing shi dang'anguan, 2005.

Ren Chong, Ju Hongbo, Zhang Huaiqing, and Huang Jianwen. "Tianshui shi jin 30 nian lindi dongtai bianhua yaogan jiance yanjiu" [Remote sensing research on dynamic changes in forest land in Tianshui over the last thirty years]. *Linye kexue yanjiu* 30, no. 1 (2017): 25–33.

Ren Chunguang. "Pingzhi shuitu zaofu renlei—Ji shuitu baochi zhuanjia Ren

Chengtong" [Controlling water and soil and benefiting humanity—remembering water and soil conservation expert Ren Chengtong]. In *Hou Ji chuanren: di yi ji*, edited by Zhongguo renmin zhengzhi xieshang huiyi Shaanxi sheng Xianyang shi weiyuanhui and Yangling qu weiyuanhui wenshi ziliao weiyuanhui, 237–55. Xi'an: Sanqin chubanshe, 1996.

Riskin, Carl. *China's Political Economy: The Quest for Development since 1949.* Oxford: Oxford University Press, 1987.

Robin, Libby. "Radical Ecology and Conservation Science: An Australian Perspective." *Environment and History* 4, no. 2 (June 1998): 191–208.

Rogaski, Ruth. *Knowing Manchuria: Environments, the Senses, and Natural Knowledge on an Asian Borderland.* Chicago: University of Chicago Press, 2022.

Ross, Corey. *Ecology and Power in the Age of Empire.* Oxford: Oxford University Press, 2017.

Rui Kunze and Marc Andre Matten. *Knowledge Production in Mao-Era China: Learning from the Masses.* Lanham, MD: Lexington Books, 2021.

Scharff, Virginia J., ed. *Seeing Nature through Gender.* Lawrence: University Press of Kansas, 2003.

Schmalzer, Sigrid. "Layer upon Layer: Mao-Era History and the Construction of China's Agricultural Heritage." *East Asian Science, Technology and Society: An International Journal* 13, no. 3 (September 2019): 413–41.

———. *Red Revolution, Green Revolution: Scientific Farming in Socialist China.* Chicago: University of Chicago Press, 2016.

Scott, James C. *Seeing Like a State: How Certain Schemes to Improve the Human Condition Have Failed.* New Haven, CT: Yale University Press, 1998.

Scott, Joan Wallach. *Gender and the Politics of History.* Rev. ed. New York: Columbia University Press, 1999.

Seow, Victor. *Carbon Technocracy: Energy Regimes in Modern East Asia.* Chicago: University of Chicago Press, 2022.

"Shangu xin cun—Dengjiabao" [Mountain valley new village—Dengjiabao]. *Renmin ribao*, October 29, 1957.

Shanguhyia, Martin S. *Population, Tradition, and Environmental Control in Colonial Kenya.* Rochester, NY: University of Rochester Press, 2015.

Shapiro, Judith. *Mao's War against Nature: Politics and the Environment in Revolutionary China.* New York: Cambridge University Press, 2001.

"Shelun huanying quanguo di san ci shuitu baochi huiyi zai Gansu zhaokai" [Editorial: Welcome the Third Nationwide Water and Soil Conservation Conference being held in Gansu]. *Gansu ribao*, September 3, 1958.

Shen, Jinyu, Wei Duan, Yuqi Wang, and Yijing Zhang. "Household Livelihood Vulnerability to Climate Change in West China." *International Journal of*

Environmental Research and Public Health 19, no. 551 (November 2022): 1–14.

"Sheng fulian haozhao quansheng nongcun funü jiji xingxiu shuili zhansheng ganhan" [Provincial Women's Federation calls on entire province's rural women to develop water conservancy and conquer aridity]. *Gansu ribao*, October 18, 1957.

Sheng Wushan weisheng gongzuo zu. *Wushan xian xiaoer yingyang buliang zheng diaocha fangzhi baogao* [Wushan County child malnutrition investigation and prevention report]. Lanzhou: Gansu sheng weishengting, Gansu sheng kexue jishu xiehui, Gansu sheng yiyao weisheng xiehui, 1961.

Shi Nianhai. "Lishi shiqi Huanghe zhongyou de senlin" [Forests in the Yellow River's middle reaches during the historical period]. In *Heshanji* Vol. 2, edited by Shi Nianhai, 232–314. Beijing: Shenghuo, dushu, xinzhi sanlian shudian, 1981.

Showers, Kate B. *Imperial Gullies: Soil Erosion and Conservation in Lesotho*. Athens: Ohio University Press, 2005.

———. "Soil Erosion and Conservation: An International History and a Cautionary Tale." In *Footprints in the Soil: People and Ideas in Soil History*, edited by Benno P. Warkentin, 369–406. Amsterdam: Elsevier, 2006.

Shue, Vivienne. *Peasant China in Transition: The Dynamics of Development toward Socialism, 1949–1956*. Berkeley: University of California Press, 1980.

Smil, Vaclav. *The Bad Earth: Environmental Degradation in China*. New York: M. E. Sharpe, 1984.

Smith, Nick R. *The End of the Village: Planning the Urbanization of Rural China*. Minneapolis: University of Minnesota Press, 2021.

Songster, E. Elena. *Panda Nation: The Construction and Conservation of China's Modern Icon*. New York: Oxford University Press, 2018.

Speakman, John R. "Sex- and Age-Related Mortality Profiles during Famine: Testing the 'Body Fat' Hypothesis." *Journal of Biological Science* 45, no. 6 (November 2013): 823–40.

Stross, Randall. *The Stubborn Earth: American Agriculturalists on Chinese Soil, 1898–1937*. Berkeley: University of California Press, 1986.

Syvitski, Jaia, Juan Restrepo Ángel, Yoshiki Saito, Irina Overeem, Charles J. Vörösmarty, Houjie Wang, and Daniel Olago. "Earth's Sediment Cycle during the Anthropocene." *Nature Reviews Earth & Environment* 3 (February 2022): 179–96.

Syvitski James P.M. and Albert Kettner. "Sediment Flux and the Anthropocene." *Philosophical Transactions of the Royal Society A* 369, no. 1938 (2011): 957–75.

Sze, Julie, ed. *Sustainability: Approaches to Environmental Justice and Social Power*. New York: New York University Press, 2018.

Thaxton, Ralph A., Jr. *Catastrophe and Contention in Rural China: Mao's Great*

Leap Forward Famine and the Origins of Righteous Resistance in Da Fo Village. New York: Cambridge University Press, 2008.

Tianshui shi difangzhi bianweihui, ed. *Tianshui shizhi, zhongjuan* [Tianshui municipal gazetteer, middle section]. Beijing: Fangzhi chubanshe, 2004.

Tianshui shi kexue jishu zhi bianjibu, ed. *Tianshui shi kexue jishu zhi* [Tianshui municipal science and technology gazetteer]. Lanzhou: Gansu wenhua chubanshe, 2004.

Tianshui shi tongjiju. *Tianshui sishi nian, 1949–1989* [Forty years of Tianshui, 1949–1989]. Beijing: Zhongguo tongji chubanshe, 1989.

Tianshui shuitu baochi kexue shiyanzhan. "Tianshui diqu de yanghuai gougu zaolin" [Tianshui area's black locust afforestation in gullies]. In *Huanghe zhongyou shuitu baochi kexue shiyan yanjiu gongzuo huiyi huikan*, edited by Shuilidianlibu Huanghe shuili weiyuanhui, 93–101. Zhengzhou: Shuilidianlibu Huanghe shuili weiyuanhui, 1958.

Tong Shubao. "Hongqi xian—Wushan" [Red flag county—Wushan]. *Tianshui wenshi ziliao* 16 (2010): 96–107.

———. "Wushan xian sannian kunnan shiqi" [Wushan County's three years of hardship] "Hongqi xian—Wushan" [Red flag County—Wushan]. *Tianshui wenshi ziliao* 16 (2010): 190–98.

Unger, Nancy C. *Beyond Nature's Housekeepers: American Women in Environmental History*. New York: Oxford University Press, 2012.

Veg, Sebastian. *Minjian: The Rise of China's Grassroots Intellectuals*. New York: Columbia University Press, 2019.

Voyles, Traci Brynne. *The Settler Sea: California's Salton Sea and the Consequences of Colonialism*. Lincoln: University of Nebraska Press, 2021.

Walker, Kenneth R. *Food Procurement and Consumption in China*. Cambridge: Cambridge University Press, 1984.

Wan Huiyu. "Jiefang qian de Tianshui linye" [Forestry in Tianshui before liberation]. *Tianshui wenshi ziliao* 4 (1990): 84–92.

Wang Chunying. "Wushan xian tigao xin yi lun tui geng huan lin chengxiao de duice cuoshi" [Wushan County's countermeasures to improve the effectiveness of the new round of returning farmland to forests]. *Xiandai nongye* 1 (2021): 69–70.

Wang Haicheng, letter dated July 12, 1959. From Zhonggong Gansu shengwei bangongting "renmin laixin" dang'an. In Zhongguo dangdai zhengzhi yundong shi shujuku, edited by Song Yongyi. http://ccrd.usc.cuhk.edu.hk/Title.aspx

Wang, Houjie, Naishuang Bi, Yoshiki Saito, Yan Wang, Xiaoxia Sun, Jia Zhang, and Zuosheng Yang. "Recent Changes in Sediment Delivery by the Huanghe (Yellow River) to the Sea: Causes and Environmental Implications in Its Estuary." *Journal of Hydrology* 391, no. 3–4 (September 2010): 302–13.

Wang, Houjie, Zuosheng Yang, Yoshiki Saito, J. Paul Liu, Xiaoxia Sun, and Yan

Wang. "Stepwise Decreases of the Huanghe (Yellow River) Sediment Load (1950–2005): Impacts of Climate Change and Human Activities." *Global and Planetary Change* 57, no. 3–4 (June 2007): 331–54.

Weibei fangwentuan, "Wushan xian Guaner nongyeshe shuitu baochi gongzuo jingyan" [Wushan County Guaner agricultural cooperative's water and soil conservation work experience]. In *Shuitu baochi cankao ziliao huiji (di yi ce)*, edited by Tianshui zhuanqu zhuan, xian, xiang sanji shuitu baochi zhongdian huiyi, 69–76. Tianshui: n.p., 1957.

Weisiger, Marsha L. *Dreaming of Sheep in Navajo Country.* Seattle: University of Washington Press, 2009.

Wemheuer, Felix. *Famine Politics in Maoist China and the Soviet Union.* New Haven, CT: Yale University Press, 2014.

Wen Si. "Gansu de jiupin gongzuo—shuili sheshi ji nongye gaijin" [Gansu's poverty-relief work—water conservancy measures and agricultural improvement]. *Dagong bao, Shanghai ban*, August 13, 1946.

White, Richard. "Are You an Environmentalist, or Do You Work for a Living?" In *Uncommon Ground: Rethinking the Human Place in Nature*, edited by William Cronon, 171–85. New York: W. W. Norton, 1996.

Who's Who in China. 6th ed. Shanghai: China Weekly Review, 1950.

Wilcox, Emily. *Revolutionary Bodies: Chinese Dance and the Socialist Legacy.* Oakland: University of California Press, 2019.

Worster, Donald. *Dust Bowl: The Southern Plains in the 1930s.* New York: Oxford University Press, 1979.

Wu, Xiao, Naishuang Bi, Jaia Syvitski, Yoshiki Saito, Jingping Xu, Jeffrey A. Nittrouer, Thomas S. Bianchi, Zuosheng Yang, and Houjie Wang. "Can Reservoir Regulation along the Yellow River Be a Sustainable Way to Save a Sinking Delta?" *Earth's Future* 8, no. 11 (November 2020): 1–9.

"Wushan bianlun chu dapi laodongli" [Debates in Wushan call forth large amounts of labor power]. *Gansu ribao*, October 19, 1958.

"Wushan caiqu wu xiang cuoshi jiejue laodongli buzu wenti" [Wushan adopts five measures to solve the problem of insufficient labor power]. *Gansu ribao*, July 24, 1958.

"Wushan Dengjiabao baoyu hou tuba sunhui qingkuang ji jinhou yijian" [Wushan Dengjiabao earth dam damage situation after heavy rainstorms and future ideas]. *Xin Huanghe* 10 (1954): 24.

"Wushan Dengjiabao shanding shang zhaodao le shuiyuan" [Wushan's Dengjiabao finds water on mountain top]. *Gansu ribao*, March 7, 1956.

"Wushan Dengjiabao shuitu baochi zongjie ji shinian guihua (1953–1962)" [Wushan Dengjiabao water and soil conservation summary and ten-year plan (1953–1962)]. *Xin Huanghe* 12 (1955): 52–61.

"Wushan xian bai fen zhi liushi de tudi kongzhizhu shuitu liushi xianxiang" [Wushan County has controlled the phenomenon of water and soil loss on 60 percent of its land]. *Gansu ribao*, July 6, 1957.

"Wushan xian de shuili he shuitu baochi zheng yi shi wu qianli de sudu, feiyue de fazhan zhe" [Wushan County's water conservancy and water and soil conservation is developing by leaps and bounds with unprecedented speed]. In *Wushan xian de shuitu baochi gongzuo dianxing jingyan*, edited by Zhonggong Gansu sheng Wushan xian weiyuanhui, 5–21. Beijing: Nongye chubanshe, 1959.

Wushan xian renmin weiyuanhui. "Gansu Wushan: shuili, shuitu baochi yundong yuejin zai yuejin ziran, shehui mianmao rixin yueyi" [Gansu Wushan: The water conservancy and water and soil conservation campaign is taking great leap after great leap, the face of nature and society changes with each day]. *Renmin Huanghe* 6 (1958): 30–33.

Wushan xian weihui. "Wushan xian bing she shengji de jingyan jieshao" [Introducing Wushan County's experience combining and upgrading cooperatives]. *Gansu ribao*, October 24, 1956.

Wushan xianzhi bianzuan weiyuanhui. *Wushan xianzhi* [Wushan County gazetteer]. Xi'an: Shaanxi renmin chubanshe, 2002.

Xiang Hua. "Gansu shuitu baochi gongzuo de jiwei kaichuangzhe" [Several inaugurators of water and soil conservation work in Gansu]. *Gansu wenshi ziliao xuanji* 39 (1994): 150–69.

Xin Shuzhi and Jiang Deqi. *Zhongguo shuitu baochi gailun* [An introduction to water and soil conservation in China]. Beijing: Nongye chubanshe, 1982.

"Xingxiu shuili baochi shuitu gaibian ganhan mianmao" [Undertake water conservancy, conserve water and soil, change the arid face (of the land)]. *Renmin ribao*, February 18, 1958, 10.

Xu Jintao and Ran Tao. "Grain for Green or Grain for Gain: An Empirical Investigation of Sloping Land Conversion Program in China." In *Discontented Miracle: Growth, Conflict, and Institutional Adaptations in China*, edited by Dali Yang, 223–65. Singapore: World Scientific Publishing, 2007.

Xu Wangsheng. "Zhongguo titian wenjian lu" [Record of information on China's terraces]. *Guoji shehui kexue zazhi* 39, no 2 (June 2022): 47–54.

Yan Wenguang. "Minguo shiqi shuitu baochi zhi zui" [The best of water and soil conservation during the Republican period]. In *Shuitu baochi zhi ziliao huibian, di er ji*, edited by Huanghe shuitu baochi zhi bianweihui bianjishi and Shaanxi sheng shuitu baochi zhi bianweihui bangongshi, 69–75. Xi'an: Shaanxi shuitu baochi bianjibu, 1988.

———. "Wushan xian Dongshun xiang shuitu baochi gongzuo shi zenyang kaizhan de" [How water and soil conservation work in Wushan County's Dongshun township developed]. In *Shuitu baochi zhi ziliao huibian, di er ji*, edited by

Huanghe shuitu baochi zhi bianweihui bianjishi and Shaanxi shuitu baochi zhi bianweihui bangongshi, 76–78. Xi'an: Shaanxi shuitu baochi bianjibu, 1988.

———. "Wushi niandai Wushan Dengjiabao gao shuitu baochi de huiyi" [Recollections of doing water and soil conservation in Wushan's Dengjiabao during the 1950s]. *Gansu wenshi ziliao xuanji* 34 (1992): 152–54.

Yang Hongwei. "1940 niandai de Tianshui shuitu baochi shiyanqu shulun" [Discussion of the Tianshui Water and Soil Conservation Experiment Area during the 1940s]. *Shuitu baochi yanjiu* 18, no. 6 (2011): 277–82.

Yang Jisheng. *Tombstone: The Great Chinese Famine, 1958–1962*. Edited by Edward Friedman, Guo Jian, and Stacy Mosher. Translated by Stacy Mosher and Guo Jian. New York: Farrar, Straus, and Giroux, 2012.

Yang Zhengfa. *Mian xiang qunzhong Li Peifu zhuan* [Face to the masses: Biography of Li Peifu]. Lanzhou: Gansu wenhua chubanshe, 2014.

Yao Zhicui. "Wushan xian 'dayuejin' pianduan jishi" [Fragmentary record of actual events in Wushan County during the Great Leap Forward]. *Tianshui wenshi ziliao* 16 (2010): 108–14.

"Yingjie quanguo di san ci shuitu baochi huiyi kaimu Wushan shiwan dajun zheng shan zhan shui" [Welcoming the opening of the Third Nationwide Water and Soil Conservation Conference, in Wushan an army of 100,000 advances against mountains and battles waters]. *Gansu ribao*, September 1, 1958.

"Yiwanwuqian ge 'Dengjiabao'" [15,000 "Dengjiabaos"]. *Renmin ribao*, March 4, 1958.

"You yi ge Dengjiabao—Changjiawan" [Another Dengjiabao—Changjiawan]. *Wushan bao*, August 4, 1957.

Yu Shenming. "Wushan xian tuiguang 10 wan mu baogu he 20 wan jing tang ba jiao quan de lishi jiyi" [Historical memories of Wushan County promoting 100,000 *mu* of maize and 200,000 wells, reservoirs, dams, water cellars, and springs]. *Tianshui wenshi ziliao* 14 (2008): 368–75.

Zhang Keren. "Wushan xian gongshehua chuqi de gonggong shitang" [Collective dining halls in Wushan County during the early period of communization]. *Tianshui wenshi ziliao* 16 (2010): 183–85.

Zhang Zhengxiu, Zhang Dongruo, and Yang Heng. *Weiji: Xibu huangmohua quanjing shilu* [Crisis: A panoramic veritable record of desertification in the west (of China)]. Lanzhou: Gansu renmin chubanshe, 2006.

Zhao, Jijun and Jan Woudstra. "'Making Green the Motherland': Greening the Chinese Socialist Undertaking (1949–1978)." *Studies in the History of Gardens and Designed Landscapes* 32, no. 4 (October 2012): 312–30.

Zhonggong Gansu sheng Wushan xianweihui bangongshi, ed. *Qiongshan kujing bian le yang* [Barren mountains and bitter circumstances have changed their appearance]. Beijing: Nongye chubanshe, 1958.

Zhonggong Wushan xianwei. "Juda de bianhua—Wushan xian shuili shuitu baochi jieshao" [A gigantic transformation—introducing Wushan County's water conservancy and water and soil conservation]. *Gansu ribao*, September 19, 1958.

"Zhonggong Wushan xianwei nongyeshe zhuren zuotanhui tingqu qunzhong yijian gaijin lingdao fangfa." [CCP Wushan County Committee agricultural cooperative directors meeting to listen to ideas of the masses and improve leadership methods]. *Gansu ribao*, December 19, 1956.

Zhonggong Wushan xianwei xuanchuanbu and Wushan bao bianjibu, ed. *Wushan min'ge* [Wushan folk songs]. Lanzhou: Dunhuang wenyi chubanshe, 1958.

Zhongguo kexue jishu xiehui, ed. *Zhongguo kexue jishu zhuanjia zhuanlue, nongxue bian: linye juan (yi)* [Brief biographies of Chinese scientific and technical experts, agronomy section: forestry (1)]. Beijing: Zhongguo nongye chubanshe, 1991.

Zhonghua renmin gongheguo guowuyuan gongbao [PRC National Affairs Council gazette], February 6, 1956.

"Zhongliangshe nü sheyuan haizi tuolei wenti jiejue de hao" [The problem of Zhongliang cooperative's female cooperative members being encumbered by children has been solved well]. *Wushan bao*, July 14, 1957.

"Zhongyang renmin zhengfu zhengwuyuan guanyu fadong qunzhong jixu kaizhan fang han, kang han yundong bing dali tuixing shuitu baochi gongzuo de zhishi (yijiuwuer nian shier yue shijiu ri zhengwuyuan di yibailiushisan ci huiyi tongguo)" [Directive from the Government Administrative Council of the Central People's Government on mobilizing the masses to continue to develop the campaign to defend against drought and resist drought, and vigorously carry out water and soil conservation work (passed by the 163rd meeting of the government administrative council on December 19, 1952)]. In *Jianguo yilai zhongyao wenxian xuanbian* Vol. 3, edited by Zhonggong Zhongyang wenxian yanjiushi, 395–97. Beijing: Zhongyang wenxian chubanshe, 1992.

"Zhou Enlai guanyu Huanghe guihua he Sanmenxia gongcheng wenti zhi Mao Zedong xin (yijiuwuba nian liu yue ershijiu ri)" [Letter from Zhou Enlai to Mao Zedong on the problems of Yellow River planning and the Sanmenxia project (June 29, 1958)]. *Dang de wenxian* 2 (1997): 22–30.

Zhou Yiping. "Wushan xian xin yi lun tui geng huan lin gongcheng jianshe kunjing ji celue" [Wushan County's project construction predicament and strategy for the new round of returning farmland to forests]. *Xin nongye* 3 (2021): 97.

"Zhuoshui bian qingshui Xibei bian Jiangnan Wushan quanmian genzhi Weihe" [Muddy water changes into clear water, the Northwest changes into Jiangnan, Wushan County completely controls the Wei River]. *Gansu ribao*, July 24, 1958.

INDEX

Page numbers in *italic* refer to illustrations.

aesthetics, 133–34, 152, 153–55, 156–57
afforestation: black locust trees, 36–39, 212, 237n87; vs. deforestation during Great Leap Forward, 203–4; in Dengjiabao, 91–95, 202–3; female labor and, 168–71; local views on, 188; post–Great Leap Forward, 205; "returning farmland to forest" campaign, 210–13. *See also* grass planting
Africa, 18, 19–20, 30
agriculture: in coordination with conservation, 56–58, 62, 65, 83, 126–27; disrupted by conservation, 154–56, 182–86, 188–92, 257n94, 262nn11–12; exaggerated production reports, 183, 186, 191, 192; famine (subsistence crisis), 183–84, 185–87, 193–95, 197–99, 207, 262n15; female labor, 164–67; in Gansu, 10; gender norms, 159–60; vs. irrigation campaign, 107, 119; "mutual aid between mountains and plains," 140–41. *See also* collectivization; grain; irrigation; water and soil conservation
alfalfa, 188, 237n87. *See also* sweet clover
Anti-Japanese War of Resistance (1937–45), 9, 19, 22–25, 34, 39–40
Australia, 19, 20

Baiquan township, 117
Bao Haizhen, 140–41
Bennett, Hugh Hammond, 20
birth rates, 183, 184, 199
black locust trees, 36–39, 212, 237n87

brigades, 199–200
Brown, Jeremy, 18
Brown, Tristan, 27, 229n34
bunds, earthen (contour banks): background, 19, 31–32; construction of, in coordination with farming, 57; demonstrations, 45–46, 48, 50, 52–53, 89; in Dengjiabao, 45–48, 50, 52–53, 58, 60, 242n53, 257n93; gully management and, 69; local views on, 188; photograph of, *46*; resistance to, 47–48, 87; in Wushan County, 58

Changjiawan village, 136
Chen Yonggui, 208
Chen Zhengren, 152
Chengguan township, 148
Chiang Kai-shek. *See* Nationalist government
childcare, 175, 177–79, 180
China. *See* Nationalist government; People's Republic of China
Chinese Communist Party (CCP), 8, 10, 40–41, 42, 71–72. *See also* People's Republic of China; water and soil conservation
climate change, 8, 217
Cohen, Myron, 8
collectivization: compensation for conservation and, 77–82, 90, 240n22; in Dengjiabao, 74–75, 76–77, 98–99, 104, 149, 182; grain procurement and, 84; higher-level cooperatives, 103–5, 131; lower-level cooperatives,

collectivization (*continued*)
74, 76–77, 104; militarization and, 132; in Wushan County, 104. *See also* communes; mutual-aid teams
colonialism, 18, 216
communes: introduction to, 14, 132, 149; compensation and, 195, 196, 264n61; conservation focus and agricultural neglect of, 182, 184–86, 188–95; post–Great Leap Forward, 199–200
compensation: for afforestation, 92–93; communes and, 195, 196, 264n61; cooperatives and, 77–82, 90, 240n22; "grain for green" program and, 210; for Kangjia Gully bypass channel, 129; mutual-aid teams and, 55–56, 62–63, 70–71, 238n94; piece-rate system, 79–80, 90, 99. *See also* work-point system
competition, 58, 133, 134–36, 170
conservation. *See* water and soil conservation
contour banks. *See* bunds, earthen
contour-channel system, 25, *26*, 28–31
cooperatives. *See* collectivization

Daliushu Gully (Daliushugou), 36, 37
dams (gully management), 61–69, *64*, 95–96, 125–26, 188, 237n87, 239n114, 251n108
Dangguan township (Kangle County), 175–76
Daquan Mountain (Daquanshan), 139
Dazhai brigade, 208–10
"dead points, living appraisal method" (*sifen huoping de banfa*), 63, 238n94
deforestation, 22, 203–4, 207. *See also* afforestation; fuel scarcity; grass planting

Deng Baoshan, 182
Deng Chenghai, 76
Deng Daisheng, 56, 93, 97
Deng Erjie, 80
Deng Fenqin: introduction to, 159; on childcare, 177, 179; on conservation labor, 167, 174, 176–77, 181; on contemporary quality of life, 213–14; on fuel scarcity, 164; on Great Leap Forward and subsequent famine, 196–98; health issues of, 208; and marriage and conservation, 162–64; photograph of, *158*; on recovery after famine, 200, 202
Deng Haihai: conservation mobilization and, 51–53, *54*, 60, 95; dam maintenance and, 125–26; death of, 208; Dengjiabao cooperative and, 76–77; in *Gansu Daily*, 139; irrigation campaign and, 108, 110; photograph of, *52*; on ponds, 96; winter irrigation and, 97
Deng Hanjie, 53, 60, 99–100, 108, 109, 111, 135
Deng Hanming, 100
Deng Hongshan, 76, 98
Deng Huangqing, 173
Deng Junfu, 52–53
Deng Junjie, 51, 66, 76–77
Deng Kejun, 100, 128, 135
Deng Madou, 45–46, 109
Deng Qingyi, 51
Deng Zicheng, 53, 108
Deng Zihui, 75
Dengjiabao Agriculture, Water Conservancy, Forestry, and Animal Husbandry Key Point Work Team, 62–63, 65
Dengjiabao village: aesthetics of conservation and, 133–34, 152–55;

afforestation and, 91–95, 168–71, 202–3, 205; agricultural decline, 182–83; agriculture coordinated with conservation, 126–27; background of, 44–45; bunds (contour banks), 45–48, 50, 52–53, 58, 60, 242n53, 257n93; childcare centers, 179; climate change and, 217; collectivization, 74–75, 76–77, 98–99, 104, 149, 182; conservation competitions and, 58, 134–36; as conservation model, 10, 12, 43, 94–95, 132–34, 136–39, 143–46, 152–53; contemporary quality of life, 213–14; Dazhai brigade and, 209–10; deforestation, 203–4; ducks in, 1; electric lift irrigation system, 266n103; fall from notoriety, 207, 208; famine recovery, 200–202, 204–5; fleeting conservation benefits, 1, *2*, *3*, 213, 216–17; "four rarities," 161, 258n13; fuel, fodder, and fertilizer scarcity, 91, 164, 258n25; gender ratio, 265n80; grain production and estimated consumption, 61, 85–86, 85, 101–2, 127, 155–56, 186, 205, 236n80, 262n12, 266n104; Great Leap Forward and famine, 183–84, 186–87, 197–99; "great war in Dengjiabao," 146–49, *147*, 153–55, 174, 182, 184–85, 188–93, 197; gully management (flood defense), 61–69, *64*, 95–96, 125–26, 237n87, 239n114; irrigation campaign and, 107–12; local views on conservation, 187–95, 195–96, 206–7; maps, *11*, *49*; marriage market, 160–63, 217, 257n8; mobilization efforts, 48, 50; *A Model for the Construction of Mountainous Areas—Dengjiabao* (booklet), *xii*, 1; mutual-aid teams, 51–53, 54–56, 58, 62–63; national recognition, 139–42; *People's Daily* on, 74–75, 101–2, 133, 139; pronunciation, 257n8; propaganda slogans, 100–101; resistance to conservation, 47–48, 72, 101; soil erosion, 45; terraces, 58, 257n93; Tiaozi Gully reservoir, 127–28; winter irrigation, 96–100. *See also* Wushan County

dining, communal, 179–80, 196–97, 200

Dongshun township: afforestation and, 168–69; communal dining, 179–80; communes and, 149; conservation competitions and, 58; female labor and, 165, 168–69; "great war in Dengjiabao" and, 148; irrigation campaign and, 107–12, 113, 130, 247n31; Wei River campaign and, 151

drought, 8, 44, 59, 60, 106–7, 217

Du Yinghua, 206

ducks, 1

Dust Bowl, 19–20, 215

earth dams. *See* dams

earthen bunds. *See* bunds, earthen

eating, communal. *See* dining, communal

environmental justice, 13

erosion. *See* soil erosion; water and soil conservation

Eyferth, Jacob, 18

famine. *See under* Great Leap Forward

Feng Qing, 91

Fengjiazhuang village, 87, 91

fengshui (geomancy), 27–28, 40, 44, 60, 72, 229n34

fertilizer, 22, 33, 34, 66, 164, 171–72, 237n87, 258n25

300   INDEX

First National People's Conference, 142
Five Province (Area) Youth Afforestation Conference, 95
flooding. *See* gully management
fodder, 33, 54, 66, 164, 202–3, 237n87, 258n25
forestation. *See* afforestation
fuel scarcity, 22, 34, 58, 91–93, 164, 181, 258n25

Gaikou cooperative, 123
Gangu county, 265n83
Gansu: agriculture, 10; climate change and, 8, 217; within Loess Plateau, 4; maps, *9*, *11*; rainfall at, 106; sweet clover and, 36; Tao River diversion in, 252n4; "ten thousand Dengjiabaos" campaign and, 132–33, 142, 175, 254n41; wartime significance of, 22–23. *See also* Dengjiabao village; Wushan County
Gansu Daily (newspaper), 117, 118, 136, 139–40, 148, 152, 165, 180
Ge Hong, 59–60
gender, 226n38, 257n1. *See also* men; women
geomancy (*fengshui*), 27–28, 40, 44, 60, 72, 229n34
Gouldner, Alvin, 227n42
grain: Dengjiabao production and estimated consumption of, 61, 85–86, 101–2, 127, 155–56, 186, 205, 236n80, 262n12, 266n104; state procurement of, 75–76, 84–86, 102, 183, 186, 206, 215, 242n54; Tianshui Prefecture production of, 186, 205, 267n107; Wushan County production of, 186, 205, 242n52, 262n11
"grain for green" program, 210–13
Gramsci, Antonio, 215

grass planting, 32, 93, 168, 188, 202–3. *See also* afforestation; sweet clover
grassroots cadres, 15–17, 43–44, 75–76, 105, 130, 208
Great Leap Forward (1958–61): aesthetics of conservation and, 133–34, 152–55, 156–57; agricultural disruptions of, 14–15, 182–84; communal dining and, 179–80, 196–97, 200; communes and, 196; deforestation during, 203–4, 207; exaggerated production reports, 183, 186, 191, 192; famine (subsistence crisis), 15, 183–84, 185–87, 193–95, 197–99, 207, 262n15; famine recovery, 199–202, 204–5; and "great war in Dengjiabao," 146–49, *147*, 153–55, 174, 182, 184–85, 188–93, 197; local views on conservation during, 187–95, 206–7; men and, 198–99; militarization and, 98, 132–33, 146, 149–52, 174, 184; Tao River diversion project and, 252n4; women and, 196–98, 199
Green, Cathy, 17
Greene, J. Megan, 24, 232n89
Guandi Gully, 92
Guaner cooperative, 123
Guangwu township, 84
Guanping village, 70
gully management (dams), 61–69, *64*, 95–96, 125–26, 188, 237n87, 239n114, 251n108
Guo Sishiwu, 87, 89
Guo Siyuesheng, 89
Guohuai township, 79, 86–91
Guojiazhuang village, 89, 90, 91

Harrell, Stevan, 103, 216
He Jili, 152
Heilmann, Sebastian, 43

hemp, 52, 87, 90, 161
Hershatter, Gail, 44, 167, 178
Ho, Denise, 136
"hollow villages," 213
Hongfu township, 143–45
Honggou brigade, 264n61
Hongxing (Red Star) People's Commune, 149
household registration (*hukou*) system, 8, 111, 215
Hualin commune, 199
Huo Weide, 142

irrigation: electric lift system, 266n103; winter campaign (1955–56), 96–100, 104
irrigation campaign (1956): introduction to, 103–5, 130–31; accidents, 119; burdens upon local workers, 116–18; conflicts with other agricultural and conservation campaigns, 114, 119; county-level reassessment, 124–25; Dongshun township and, 107–13, 130, 247n31; female labor, 165; Kangjia Gully bypass channel, 128–29; labor intensification, 105, 127, 131; limits of local mobilization, 129; local knowledge and, 105, 110–11, 113, 121, 130; mobilization strategies, 109–10; quantity over quality, 115–16, 118–19, 130–31; resistance to, 108–9, 113–14, 130, 138–39, 247n31; in Tianshui Prefecture, 138–39; Tiaozi Gully reservoir, 127–28, 252n118; in Wushan County, 104–7, 113–19, 249n81; Xiang River Gully project, 119–24, 251nn108–9

Kangjia Gully (Kangjiagou): afforestation and, 92, 171; bypass channel, 128–29; gully management and, 61, 62, 65, 69, 135, 237n87; map of, 49; winter irrigation campaign and, 99
Kangle County, 175–76
knowledge, local, 105, 110–11, 113, 121, 130
Kong Fengzhong, 125, 126, 127

Laakkonen, Simo, 39
labor intensification, 105, 107, 127, 131, 133, 136, 146, 190–91, 207. *See also* Great Leap Forward; gully management; irrigation campaign; women
land: reform campaigns, 42, 50, 55, 86, 193; tenure system, 31
Laojun Mountain (Laojunshan), 204
Leach, Melissa, 17
Leijiashan village, 188, 264n61
Lesotho, 18, 30
Li Baocai, 97
Li Baoxu, 56, 163
Li, Cheng, 169
Li Fusheng, 192, 194
Li Haiqing, 86
Li Jianyuan, 189, 194
Li Jincai, 56
Li Jinglin, 142, 145–46
Li Tongtong, 192, 194
Li Wanfu, 56, 65
Li Wanwan, 128–29, 135
Li Xiuyun, 135
Li Xuding: conservation views of, 187, 189, 191, 193, 195; death of, 208; Deng Fenqin and, 163; gully management and, 65, 67–69; irrigation campaign and, 111; as labor model, 94–95; photograph of, 94; sweet clover and, 54–55
Li Yongqing, 99
Li Zhichang, 201, 203

Li Zijun, 82
Lijiaping village: background of, 44; collectivization and, 77; conservation views of, 188, 195; famine (subsistence crisis) and, 197, 265n72; female labor and, 171; gender ratio of, 265n80; map, *49*; marriage market and, 163
Lin Gaisheng, 109
Lin Jinwa, 109
Lin Qiumei, 99
Lin Wanfu, 93
Ling Faxiang, 84
Liu, Yanjun, 169
Loess Plateau, 4–7, *5*, 8, 106. *See also* Dengjiabao village; Gansu; Tianshui Water and Soil Conservation Experiment Station; water and soil conservation; Wushan County
Longnan Water and Soil Conservation Experiment Area, 228n14
Longnan Water and Soil Conservation Extension Station, 232n1
Longquan district, 71
Longquan township, 151
Longtai township, 151, 153–54
Longwang Gully (Longwanggou), 36
Lowdermilk, Walter C.: conservation advice from, 10, 18, 19, 24, 40; photograph of, *26*; on terraces and contour channels, 25, 29, 31; Ye Peizhong and, 32
Luomen district, 84–85
Lushan Conference, 200, 206

Ma Jinlu, 97
Ma Shuangbao, 97
Ma Xingwu, 194–95
Mahe township, 80, 136
maize, 119

Majia Gully (Majiagou), *49*, 61, 62, 92
Majiashan village, 44–45, *49*, 92–93, 98, 111, 190–92
Mali district, 82–84
Mao Zedong, 8, 103, 132, 139, 185, 200, 209, 217
marriage market, 160–63, 217
Marx, Karl, 215
medicinal plants, 58
men, 198–99, 265n80
militarization, 98, 132–33, 146, 149–52, 174, 184
Model for the Construction of Mountainous Areas—Dengjiabao (booklet), xii, 1
models, promotion of, 43, 107, 139
Mosley, Stephen, 12
Mostern, Ruth, 6, 106
Mu Guiying, 176
Mulin commune, 199, 265n83
Multipurpose Plan for Permanently Controlling the Yellow River and Exploiting Its Water Resources, 75
mutual-aid teams: and comparison to communes, 193; compensation and, 55–56, 62–63, 70–71, 238n94; divisions within, 69–70; gully management and, 61–63, 65–69; and mobilization for conservation, 50–54, 57, 58, 60; transition to cooperatives, 74, 76–77; in Wushan County, 234n36

Nanyu township, 46, 48, 58
Nationalist government, 9–10, 19–21, 23–25, 40, 42, 71–72. *See also* People's Republic of China
National Program for Agricultural Development, 168
National Water and Soil Conservation Commission, 140

Nationwide Agricultural Socialist Construction Advanced Work Unit Representative Conference, 153
New Marriage Law, 162
New Socialist Countryside program, 213
Northern Song Dynasty, 6, 176
Northwest Agricultural Institute, 230n55
Nygren, Joshua, 40

Oi, Jean, 84
Okie, William Thomas, 134

Pan Xiangrui, 87
Panlong village, 117–18
People's Daily (newspaper): on afforestation, 168; on communes, 182; on Dazhai brigade, 209; on Dengjiabao conservation, 10, 74–75, 101–2, 133, 139, 153, 207; on marriage market, 162; on Wushan County, 140
People's Pictorial (journal), 159, 162–63
People's Republic of China (PRC), 7–8, 12–13, 214–16. *See also* Chinese Communist Party; collectivization; grain; Great Leap Forward; Nationalist government; water and soil conservation
Perry, Elizabeth, 42
Phillips, Sarah, 20
piece-rate system, 79–80, 90, 99
Pogen village, 82
political ecology, 13
ponds, 1, 68, 96, 115
propaganda: aesthetics of conservation, 133–34, 152–55, 156–57; for conservation mobilization, 13, 17, 48, 55, 60, 62, 86, 89, 100–101, 107, 175; on Dazhai brigade, 209; "hundred Dengjiabaos" campaign and, 136–37; on marriage market, 161–62; "speak bitterness to floods," 55

Qiaozi Gully (Qiaozigou), *49*, 61, 62, 92, 111
Qin'an County, 145–46
Qingshui County, 143

rainfall, 4, 6, 106. *See also* gully management; soil erosion
religion, popular, 59–60. *See also* geomancy (*fengshui*)
Ren Chengtong, 23, 24, 34, 37, 228n14
renumeration. *See* compensation
"returning farmland to forest" (*tuigeng huanlin*), 210–13
ridge tillage, 53
rural people: conservation and, 14–18, 43–44, 76, 82–83; local knowledge of, 105, 110–11, 113, 121, 130; and New Socialist Countryside program, 213; resistance from, 43–44, 47–48, 56–57, 59–60, 70–72, 82–83, 87, 101, 143; and rural-urban inequalities, 8, 214–16. *See also* collectivization; Dengjiabao village; grain; Great Leap Forward; women

Sanmenxia dam and reservoir, 132, 142
Schmalzer, Sigrid, 12, 15, 209
Scott, James, 156–57
Scott, Joan, 257n1
sea buckthorn, 164
Second Nationwide Water and Soil Conservation Conference, 140–42
self-reliance, 141, 209
Seow, Victor, 130
sewing groups, 180
Shapiro, Judith, 12, 209

Shen Manyuan, 43, 45, 48
Shi Bingzhi, 70
Showers, Kate, 30
Simen township, 117, 148
"six compares, six looks, and six changes," 88–89
Smith, Nick R., 214
soil erosion, 4, 6–7, 19–20, 22, 24–25, 45. *See also* gully management; water and soil conservation
Songshan township, 116
Soviet Union, 160, 227n42
sweet clover, 32–36; afforestation and, 92; experimentation with, 32–33, 35, 230n55; for fuel, fodder, and fertilizer, 33–34, 66; gendered division of labor and, 168; gully management and, 63, 65, 237n87; local views on, 188; mixed reactions and mobilization to, 48, 53–55; popularity of, 35–36, 231n70; unforeseen consequences of, 38
sweet potatoes, 45, 53, 127

Tang Dynasty, 6
Tan'ge district, 70, 169–70, 238n94
Tan'ge township, 115, 151
Tao, Ran, 210, 212
Tao River diversion, 252n4
technicians, local, 50, 90–91
technological optimism, 40
terraces, 6–7, 25, 28–31, 58, 114, 229n47, 257n93
Third Front campaign, 216
Third Nationwide Water and Soil Conservation Conference, 149, 152–53, 156, 193
Tianjiazhuang village, 19
Tianshui Prefecture: Dengjiabao valorized by, 138–39, 142; famine (subsistence crisis), 186; fuel scarcity, 34; grain production, 186, 205, 267n107; map of, *9*; photograph of, *27*; training for local technicians, 50
Tianshui Water and Soil Conservation Scientific Experiment Station (formerly Tianshui Water and Soil Conservation Experiment Area): background of, 9–10, 20–21, 24; black locust trees and, 36–39; continuation of, under PRC, 21, 40–42, 232n1; on Dengjiabao grain sales, 242n54; on famine recovery, 200–201; Kangjia Gully bypass channel and, 129; on labor needed for dam building, 251n108; on local conservation views, 187–96; map of, *21*; national recognition, 140; photograph of, *27*; sweet clover and, 32–36, 38; terraces, contour-channel system, and bunds at, 25–32, *26*, 229n47; and unforeseen consequences, 38–39; Xiang River Gully project and, 123–24
"Tianshui's three treasures" (*Tianshui san da bao*), 19
Tiaozi Gully, 127–29, 131, 135, 252n118
Tielong township, 77
Tongwei County, 156, 185
tree planting. *See* afforestation
Tucker, Richard, 39

"unified purchase and supply" (*tonggou tongxiao*) system, 75–76, 84–86, 102, 186, 206
urban-rural inequalities, 8, 214–16

Vuorisalo, Timo, 39

Walker, Kenneth R., 242n54
Wang Haicheng, 185

Wang Tingjun, 70, 89
Wang Zhiguo, 48, 50, 53, 95, 139
water: conservancy efforts, 106, 205, 207; female labor and, 160, 164, 181, 205, 217. *See also* irrigation
water and soil conservation (*shuitu baochi*): introduction to, 3–4, 8, 12–14, 18, 217–18; aesthetics of, 133–34, 152–57; agriculture disrupted by, 154–56, 182–86, 188–92, 257n94, 262nn11–12; Chinese Communist Party's adoption of, 10, 41, 43, 71–72; colonial parallels, 18; competition and, 58, 133–36, 170; in coordination with agriculture, 56–58, 62, 65, 83, 126–27; Dazhai brigade as model, 208–10; Dengjiabao as model, 10, 12, 43, 94–95, 132–34, 136–39, 143–46, 152–53; female labor, *166*, 167–68, 171–74, 176–77; fleeting benefits, 216–17; grassroots cadres and, 15–17, 43–44, 75–76, 105, 130, 208; health issues from, 208; land reform and, 50; local views on, 187–96, 206–7; Loess Plateau and, 4, 6–7; Mao-era environmental histories and, 12–13; militarization and, 98, 132–33, 146, 149–52, 174, 184; Nationalist government and, 19, 20–21, 23, 40; planetary impacts, 7; resistance to, 43–44, 47–48, 56–57, 59–60, 70–72, 82–83, 87, 101, 143; "returning farmland to forest" (*tuigeng huanlin*) program, 210–13; rural people and, 14–18, 43–44, 76, 82–83; technological optimism and, 40; transnational background, 19–20; wartime significance, 23–25, 39–40. *See also* afforestation; bunds, earthen; collectivization; compensation; Dengjiabao village; Great Leap Forward; gully management; irrigation; mutual-aid teams; propaganda; Tianshui Water and Soil Conservation Scientific Experiment Station; Wushan County
Water and Soil Conservation Committee (Tianshui), 143
Water Conservancy Bureau (Gansu), 124
Water Conservancy Bureau (Tianshui), 143
Wei River, 43, 74, 149–52, 169
Wei Zhanggen, 24–25, 29, 31
Wenjiasi village, 89
Wenquan township, 82
windmill, 161
women: introduction, 159–60, 180–81; afforestation and, 168–71; in agricultural labor, 164–67; childcare and, 175, 177–79, 180; communal dining and, 179–80, 196–97; in conservation campaigns, *166*, 167–68, 171–74, 176–77; double burden, 160, 181; famine (subsistence crisis) and, 184, 196–99, 207; gender ratio, 198–99, 265n80; health and fertility issues, 184, 198, 199; Kangle County's "three-eight Dengjiabao" campaign and, 175–76; marriage market and, 160–63, 217; miscarriages, 173, 260n65; quality of life improvements from conservation, 164, 181; sewing groups, 180; water scarcity and, 160, 164, 181, 205, 217
work-point system: about, 17, 63; afforestation and, 170; childcare and, 178–79; communes and, 196; factors affecting, 76, 77–82, 90, 104, 118; post–Great Leap Forward, 199–200
works teams, 42–43

World War II. *See* Anti-Japanese War of Resistance
Worster, Donald, 215
Wu Guobin, 201–2
Wushan County: afforestation campaign in, 168–71; campaign to cultivate maize, 119; collectivization in, 104; and conservation mobilization, 42–44, 48, 58, 101, 134–36, 138; drought in, 59, 60, 106; ethnic makeup of, 227n40; famine recovery in, 200–202, 204–5; fuel scarcity in, 58; gender ratio of, 198–99, 265n80; "grain for green" program and, 211; grain procurements in, 84–86; grain production in, 186, 205, 242n52, 262n11; Great Leap Forward famine and, 15, 185–86, 262n15; "hundred Dengjiabaos" campaign in, 132, 136–37; irrigation campaign in, 104–7, 113–19, 249n81; land reform in, 50; map of, *9*; media coverage of, 140; and mutual-aid teams, 50–53, 55–56, 234n36; population of, 42, 149, 232n2, 255n65; and resistance to conservation, 59–60, 82–83; sweet clover and, 53–54; Third Nationwide Water and Soil Conservation Conference and, 149, 152–53, 156, 193; Wei River campaign in, 149–52. *See also* Dengjiabao village
Wushan News (newspaper), 136, 137–38, 178, 179–80

Xi Gully (Xigou), *49*, 61, 92
Xiang River Gully, 119–24, 251nn108–9

Xinguang cooperative, 117
Xiyang County: Dazhai brigade, 208–10
Xu, Jintao, 210, 212

Yan Wenguang: about, 229n36; on black locust trees, 37; Dengjiabao conservation efforts and, 42–43, 45, 47–48; on earthen bunds, 31–32; on mobilization for conservation, 55, 58; on sweet clover, 34, 36; on terraces and contour channels, 28–31
Yanchi township, 46, 48, 58, 118
Yang Jisheng, 156, 186, 199
Yanjing district, 199, 265n83
Ye Peizhong, 24, 32, 33, 35–37
Yefu village, 89
Yellow River, 4, 6, 7, 10, 43, 75, 132
Yellow River Conservancy Commission, 24, 187, 228n14, 230n55
Youth Water and Soil Conservation Activist Meeting, 94–95
Yuanyang township, 115
Yuchuan commune, 199, 265n83

Zhang County, 189, 265n83
Zhang Kejun, 92, 97
Zhang Zixiang, 128, 135
Zhangjiabao village, 44–45, *49*, 92, 98, 244n74
Zhao Fansheng, 92, 98, 111
Zhaoping township, 59
Zhongliang cooperative, 178–79
Zhou Enlai, 43, 142, 153, 217